D1565619

Transforming
the Twentieth Century

Technical Innovations and Their Consequences

Vaclav Smil

OXFORD
UNIVERSITY PRESS

2006

OXFORD
UNIVERSITY PRESS

Oxford University Press, Inc., publishes works that further
Oxford University's objective of excellence
in research, scholarship, and education.

Oxford   New York
Auckland   Cape Town   Dar es Salaam   Hong Kong   Karachi
Kuala Lumpur   Madrid   Melbourne   Mexico City   Nairobi
New Delhi   Shanghai   Taipei   Toronto

With offices in
Argentina   Austria   Brazil   Chile   Czech Republic   France   Greece
Guatemala   Hungary   Italy   Japan   Poland   Portugal   Singapore
South Korea   Switzerland   Thailand   Turkey   Ukraine   Vietnam

Copyright © 2006 by Oxford University Press, Inc.

Published by Oxford University Press, Inc.
198 Madison Avenue, New York, New York 10016

www.oup.com

Library of Congress Cataloging-in-Publication Data

Smil, Vaclav.
   Transforming the twentieth century: technical innovations and their consequences /
Vaclav Smil.
      p.   cm.
ISBN 978-0-19-516875-4
1. Technological innovations—History—20th century.   I. Title.
T173.8.S6155 2006
303.48'3'0904—dc22   2005051836

9 8 7 6 5 4 3 2

Printed in the United States of America
on acid-free paper

Preface

This is the companion volume to *Creating the Twentieth Century: Technical Innovations of 1867–1914 and Their Lasting Impact* (published by the Oxford University Press in 2005; I use the acronym *CTTC* when I refer to it in this book). The books are stand-alone treatments of two unprecedented eras of technical advances, but reading them both, in either sequence, will deepen the understanding of those fascinating innovations that created and then transformed the modern world.

These brief prefatory remarks are a close replay of acknowledgments and comments that I offered in *CTTC*. Again, I wish I had more space to deal with the preconditions and repercussions of many innovations and to offer a wider range of reflections and criticisms. Again, my great intellectual debt is obvious: the book could not have been written without innovators, scientists, and engineers who transformed the modern world and later wrote or talked about their experiences, or without scholars and commentators (be they historians, economists, environmentalists, or philosophers) who tried to explain the changes and to set them in wider historical and social contexts. Images are, again, an integral part of this book, and Douglas Fast had once more an unusually challenging job of reproducing scores of photographs and designing many original illustrations.

Again, I offer no apologies for what some critics will see as too many numbers: extensive quantification is essential to convey the magnitude and the rapidity of the 20th century's technical transformations and their ubiquitous impacts. The metric system and scientific units and prefixes are used throughout (and are defined under Units and Abbreviations, pp. ix–x.) And, again, it is my strong personal preference to avoid (*pace* Ellul in the original French editions) the now so ingrained term "technology" (insensitively used in English translations of Ellul's work). Logically, technology refers to the scientific study of techniques and of their evolution; my concern is obviously with the techniques themselves—with the means (arts, crafts, knowledge) that we deploy to construct and manage civilizations—and with their innovative transformations.

And, lastly, a warning about what not to expect. This book is not a world history of the 20th century seen through a prism of technical innovations: as it traces the preconditions, genesis, and improvements of key modern techniques, it deals, as did *CTTC*, overwhelmingly with developments that originated in North America and Europe. Nor it is an economic history of the period written with an engineering slant: some thoughtful economists have already written a great deal from that useful perspective. This book is neither an elaborate argument in favor of technical determinism in modern history nor an uncritical homage to the era's achievements. As with *CTTC*, I prefer to leave its genre undefined. I see it simply as an incomplete and imperfect story of amazing technical transformations that is told from a variety of perspectives in order to understand better the complexities of the fascinating process, its stunning accomplishments, and its unforeseen (and often unforeseeable) failures.

Contents

Units and Abbreviations

Units

B	byte
°C	degree Celsius (unit of temperature)
dwt	deadweight tons
g	gram (unit of mass)
h	hour
hp	horsepower (traditional unit of power = 745.7 W)
Hz	hertz (unit of frequency)
J	joule (unit of energy)
K	degree Kelvin (unit of temperature)
kWh	kilowatt hour, unit of energy
lb	pound (unit of weight)
lm	lumen (unit of luminosity)
m	meter
oe	oil equivalent
Pa	pascal (unit of pressure)
rpm	revolutions per second
s	second
t	ton (metric ton = 1,000 kg)
V	volt (unit of voltage)
W	watt (unit of power)

Prefixes

n	nano	10^{-9}
μ	micro	10^{-6}
m	milli	10^{-3}
c	centi	10^{-2}

h	hecto	10^2
k	kilo	10^3
M	mega	10^6
G	giga	10^9
T	tera	10^{12}
P	peta	10^{15}
E	exa	10^{18}

Transforming the Twentieth Century

೧೨ I

Transforming the 20th Century:
Debts and Advances

> It is to quantity, scale and magnitude, and not to change in kind, that the deepest social impacts of science and technology during the 20th century are due.
>
> Philip Morrison

Complex societies that began to form after the retreat of the most recent Ice Age (completed about 10,000 years ago) have been possible only because of the Earth's biosphere. This thin envelope of life depends on solar radiation to energize the atmospheric and oceanic circulations, photosynthesis, and grand biogeochemical cycles, and it sustains the environment that has been suitable

FRONTISPIECE 1. Contrast of Mercedes models from years 1901 and 2000 exemplifies the process of technical transformations during the 20th century: the basics remain as they were invented and improved before WWI, but appearance and performance are radically different. In 1901, Wilhelm Maybach's Mercedes 35 was the most powerful and the best engineered car one could buy: its 5.9-liter four-cylinder engine developed 35 hp (26 kW) when running at 950 rpm, producing 4.4 W/cm^3 of the engine's volume. A century later, the eight-cylinder engine of a luxury Mercedes S500 displaced 5 liters, 15% less than the 1901_a model, but when running at 5,600 rpm it developed 302 hp or 45 W/cm^3, slightly more than 10 times the performance of the 1901_b model. External differences are obvious. Photographs courtesy of DaimlerChrysler Classic Konzernarchiv, Stuttgart.

for the evolution of higher organisms (Smil 2002a). In addition to these irreplaceable biophysical foundations, every society faces the risk of recurrent, and unpredictable, geophysical upheavals and the threats from space that can derail its development or end abruptly its existence.

The first category includes massive volcanic eruptions similar to those that created the giant calderas of Toba in Sumatra (73,500 years ago) and Yellowstone in the United States (630,000 ago). Similar eruptions would be catastrophic as billions to trillions tons of volcanic ash would bury everything within thousands of km downwind under layers of dust and as volcanic aerosols persisting in the stratosphere would drastically lower the atmospheric temperatures and greatly reduce the size of human populations (Rampino and Self 1992; Ambrose 1998). And even a smaller volcanic event could have enormous consequences. An eruption of Cumbre Vieja volcano at La Palma in the Canary Islands could cause a catastrophic failure of its western flank, and the resulting landslide of up to 500 km³ of rock would generate huge and rapidly moving (up to 350 km/h) tsunami that would cross the Atlantic and hit the eastern coast of North America with walls of water several tens of meters high (Ward and Day 2001; figure 1.1).

The most worrisome event in the second category is an asteroid impact. A smaller object (less than 100 m in diameter, larger than the famous 1908 Tunguska asteroid) arrives roughly once every millennium, and when it hits the open ocean it has a very limited effect on the biosphere. But a larger asteroid with a diameter of about 1,000 m and recurrence of once every million years has global consequences regardless of its point of impact (Smil 2002a).

There is nothing we can do to change the biophysical prerequisites of our existence or the recurrence of large natural catastrophes. In this sense our civilization is no different from the cuneiform or hieroglyphic realms of the Middle East of 5,000 years ago or from the early modern world of the 17th century. But in nearly all other respects our world differs fundamentally even from the situation that prevailed as recently as 1850—and the genesis of this change was the burst of technical innovations that took place during the two pre-WWI generations.

This astonishing concatenation of technical advances created the foundations of a new kind of civilization. These accomplishments were further refined and expanded by post-WWI advances and substantially augmented by new innovations, particularly those that were commercialized after WWII and that accelerated profound economic progress and sweeping social changes during the second half of the 20th century. As a result, by the late 1990s most of the world's six billion people lived in largely or overwhelmingly man-made rather than natural environments. Most of our daily interactions were with a still growing array of devices and machines rather than with soil, plants, and animals, and the energy that powered our productive activities and provided daily

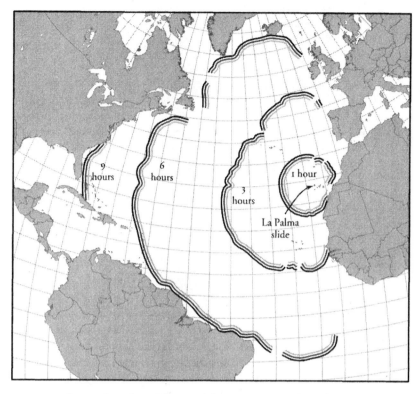

FIGURE I.I. Progression of possible trans-Atlantic tsunamis generated by a catastrophic failure of Cumbre Vieja volcano at La Palma in the Canary Islands (based on Ward and Day 2001) illustrates one of many inevitable natural events that cannot be controlled by any civilization.

comforts came overwhelmingly from fossil fuels or nuclear fission rather than from conversions of renewable (direct and indirect) solar flows.

Our food, our dwellings, our material possessions, our ways of travel, and our means of production and communication depend on incessant operation of countless devices, machines, and processes that created increasingly complex technical systems. In turn, these systems interact in complex ways, and none them could function without uninterrupted flows of fossil energies and electricity. Affluent societies—dominated by urban populations that derive most of their livelihood from services—became the clearest embodiments of this grand transformation. But low-income countries came to be in some respects even more existentially dependent on technical advances. China and India could not produce enough food for their nearly 2.5 billion people without massive applications of synthetic fertilizers and pesticides and without pumped irrigation, and they could not raise the living standard without producing for global markets that are accessed through telecommunication, computerization, and containerized shipping.

During the course of the 20th century, technical advances became the key determinants of the structure and the dynamics of astonishingly productive and increasingly interdependent economies, and they brought impressive levels of affluence and higher quality of life. At no other time did so many people (about two billion by the late 1990s) enjoy such a level of well-being, such an amount and selection of inexpensive food, such a choice of goods and services, such access to education and information, and such a high mobility and political freedoms. Comparisons for the Western world show that during the 20th century life expectancies rose from the mid-40s to the late 70s; cost of food as the share of disposable income fell by anywhere between 60% and 80%; virtually all households had electricity supply and were saturated with telephones, radios, TVs, refrigerators, clothes washers, and microwave ovens; shares of populations with completed postsecondary degrees increased (depending on the country) three- to fivefold; and leisure travel evolved from a rarity to the world's largest economic activity (figure 1.2).

No less important, these accomplishments contained a tangible promise of future improvements that should eventually spread this enviable way of life to the remainder of humanity. China's enormous post-1980 economic leap—aimed at emulating the previous advances in Japan, Taiwan, and South Korea—has been perhaps the best illustration of this promise. Most notably, as the country's average disposable income doubled and then quadrupled, a wave of incipient affluence swept the coastal regions where urban households became saturated with electric fans and color TVs: their ownership of clothes washers and refrigerators went from a negligible fraction in 1980 to more than 75% by the year 2000, and the rapidly advancing process of their *embourgeoisement* was perhaps best expressed by a considerable pent-up demand for signature machines of the century, passenger cars.

This book's goal is to trace the evolution of all important techniques that were behind these accomplishments, to explain their genesis and subsequent advances, to view the history of the 20th century through a prism of fascinating technical change. The intent is to use the prism's deliberate grinding in order to separate the stream of technical advances into its key constituents and to focus on every fundamental strand: this includes dwelling on some inexplicably neglected developments (and forgotten innovators) whose contributions shaped the course of modern history more profoundly than some well-known advances. A similarly systematic approach is impossible to use when dealing with pervasive synergies among these innovations: those links are so ubiquitous, and often so convoluted, that it would be tedious to point them out explicitly at every occasion.

For example, better-built yet cheaper cars needed stronger and less energy-intensive steels; new ways of steel production required cheaper electricity and

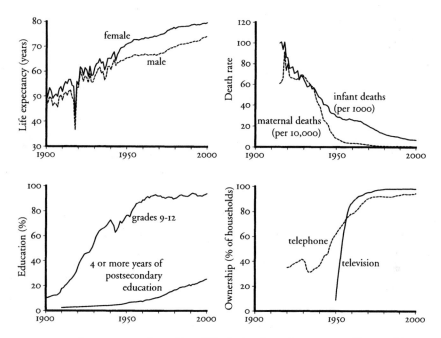

FIGURE I.2. Improvements in quality of life during the 20th century are illustrated here by U.S. statistics showing a gain of some three decades of average life expectancy at birth (top left), large declines of infant and maternal mortality (top right), a rise in high school enrollment and postsecondary education (bottom left), and virtually saturated household ownership of telephones and televisions (bottom right). Plotted from data in USCB (2004).

inexpensive large-volume supply of pure oxygen for steelmaking furnaces; more efficient electricity generation needed turbogenerators that could operate with higher pressures and temperatures and hence needed to be made of better steels; transmitting electricity with minimal losses led to the introduction of new conductors, including aluminum wires, but aluminum smelting required roughly an order of magnitude more energy than did steel production, and hence it needed additional electricity generation . . . And, as the following well-known car example illustrates, this pervasive interconnectedness also makes it impossible to spell out in detail economic, social, and environmental implications of every innovation.

Mass production of cars became, first, the largest and best-paying manufacturing industry of the 20th century and, then, a leader in automation and robotization that cut the labor force. Intensifying traffic necessitated large-scale construction of paved roads, and this was the main reason for hugely increased extraction of sand, rock, and limestone whose mass now dominates the world's mineral production and accounts for a large share of freight transport. Expanded road networks reordered the flows of people and goods and stimulated the growth of suburbs. Trimmed suburban, roadside, and golf-course grass became one of the largest (but purely ornamental) crops in North America, with lawns leaching fertilizer nitrogen and pesticide residues and replacing natural biodiversity. Suburban sprawl and inefficient vehicles also generated photochemical smog, and higher incidence of various health problems; this risk led eventually to emission controls, but catalysts used in this process . . .

Consequently, reading this book should be also a beginning of new inquiries. I detail many links, and spell out and quantify many consequences, but that will still leave many more synergies and impacts undefined and unmentioned. As you read about particular technical innovations, think first of their prerequisites and then begin to add many cascading links and spreading consequences. Of course, many such links and effects are obvious, perhaps even excessively researched and often in the category of worn-out clichés, while others had come as big and costly surprises, sometimes in just a matter of years, in other instances only after decades of established use. But while I strongly encourage the search for synergies, impacts, and causality, I do not interpret these links as proofs of technical determinism.

Limits of Causality

My position regarding the role of technical advances in history will disappoint those who believe in the autonomous development of new techniques that inevitably impose themselves on a society and dictate its fundamental features—as well as those who see them largely as social constructs whereby cultural and political peculiarities provide their decisive stamps on initially value-neutral innovations. But rejecting both of these positions does not mean that truth is somewhere in the middle, as shards of it can be found anywhere along the spectrum between the two extremes. As Heilbroner (1967:355) put it, "That machines make history in some sense . . . is of course obvious. That they do not make all of history, however that word be defined, is equally clear."

While I have no wish to promote simplistic technical determinism, this book will make it clear that many critical economic, social, and political features and trends of the 20th century are much more explicable—especially when seen in long-term, cumulative perspectives—through the synergy of science, technical advances, and high energy use than by the recourse to the traditionally dominant cultural, political, and ideological explanations. When seen through a slit of months and years, personalities and ideologies of the 20th century loom large, but the critical impress of technical advances becomes inescapable once the national and global fortunes are viewed with a multidecadal or a centennial perspective. Can there be any doubt that the Western affluence, clearly a key factor in promoting stable democratic societies and preventing violent conflicts, could not have been achieved with pre-1850 technical means? And as two very different examples—from two very different places and times but with a fascinating common denominator—illustrate, technical advances also have critical effect on the course of specific historical developments.

Historians have paid a great deal of attention to the expansionist spirit of the Wilhelmine Germany and the strategic prowess of the German General Staff (Görlitz 1953; Leach 1973). But the country's endurance during WWI owed ultimately more to a rapid commercialization of a brilliant scientific discovery than to the capabilities of military leadership (figure 1.3). In 1909 Fritz Haber finally succeeded where many other chemists failed and demonstrated the catalytic synthesis of ammonia from its elements, and in less than four years BASF, under the ingenious leadership of Carl Bosch, converted Haber's bench process into large-scale industrial synthesis in the Oppau plant (Smil 2001). When the war began, Germany's nitrate reserves, essential for explosives production, were good for only about six months, and the British

FIGURE 1.3. What was a greater determinant of Germany's endurance under a three-pronged military pressure and British naval blockade during WWI: the country's military leadership (left)—or Fritz Haber's (right) invention of ammonia synthesis from its elements? The central part of the portrait of the Kaiser Wilhem II and his top military leaders is reproduced from *The Times* (1915). Eric von Falkenhayn, the Chief of the German Army's General Staff, is the first man standing on the right. Fritz Haber's portrait by Emil Orlik is reproduced courtesy of the E.F. Smith Collection, Rare Book and Manuscript Library, University of Pennsylvania.

naval blockade prevented the mineral's imports from Chile (Stoltzenberg 2004). Only because of the first Haber-Bosch ammonia plant and the construction of a much larger Leuna plant could Germany synthesize the nitrates needed for munitions and explosives and thus to prolong its war-fighting capacity.

Three generations later, Deng Xiaoping's bold reform policies made China the world's fastest growing large economy and received an enormous amount of mass media coverage and analytical attention. But the reforms could not have succeeded without averting first the prospect of another famine. Between 1959 and 1961 the world's largest famine, caused largely by Mao's economic delusions, claimed the lives of 30 million people (Smil 1999a), and a generation later average per capita food supply stood merely at the pre-1959 level. Securing an adequate food supply was made possible only once China became the world's largest user of nitrogenous fertilizers, thanks to its import of the world's largest series of the most modern ammonia plants, which by the late 1990s were synthesizing enough of the key plant macronutrient to provide every citizen with average per capita food supply that rivaled the Japanese average (Smil 2001; FAO 2004).

But both of these examples also illustrate the critical interplay of human and technical factors. Only strong organizational capacities and the state's commitment made it possible to complete the first converter in Germany's second large ammonia plant by April 1917, after just 11 months of construction. And only Deng Xiaoping's radical break with the communal past and his *de facto* privatization of farming opened the way for a much more efficient use of new technical inputs in farming. Indeed, the pervasiveness of the modern state means that many technical developments were heavily promoted, or retarded, by massive government interventions, or by a state's benign or deliberate neglect. These realities apply across an entire range of modern techniques: I offer two examples of government-sponsored, or abetted, technical leadership, one regarding machines and the other one electronic codes.

Pan American Airways became a pioneer of advanced flying—with the first pre-WWII trans-Pacific flights, the first use of jet airplanes in the United States, and the key role in developing the world's first wide-bodied jet—largely because of the provisions of the U.S. Foreign Air Mail Act and of Juan Trippe's (Pan Am founder's) wooing of Latin American political leaders (Davies 1987; Allen 2000). The Act specified that only those corporations whose scale and manner of operation could project the dignity of the United States in Latin America could carry international mail, and do so only with the invitation of the serviced countries. By orchestrating a luxurious passenger service, making Charles Lindbergh a technical advisor, and gaining the confidence of the hemisphere's leaders, the company's assured monopoly in carrying the U.S. mail served as the foundation of its technical daring.

More than two generations later, after Microsoft attained a virtual monopoly in operating systems installed in personal computers, the U.S. government and the country's courts, so persistent in dismantling AT&T (a federal antitrust suit was filed in 1974, and the Bell System ceased to exist on January 1, 1984), were not as determined to seek and to impose a similar outcome. Eventual judgment to split the company into two independent entities would not have fundamentally changed its crushing dominance, and even this weak remedy was reversed on appeal, leaving the company's monopolistic and predatory practices intact and free in the position of a dubious technical leadership that it exercises by issuing new versions of its notoriously patched-up and highly vulnerable software. And in many other cases, governments have been actually principal paymasters behind new techniques.

For example, between 1947 and 1998 the U.S. nuclear industry received more than 96% of $(1998)145 billion that was disbursed by the Congress for all energy R&D (NIRS 1999), clearly an enormously skewed distribution considering the variety of possible conversion techniques that could have been promoted. In addition, the country's nuclear industries greatly benefited from experiences and innovations resulting from an even more generous, but much harder to quantify, federal support of military nuclear R&D. And in 1954 the Price-Anderson Act, section 170 of the Atomic Energy Act, guaranteed public compensation in the event of any catastrophic accident in commercial nuclear generation, a blanket protection not enjoyed by any other energy or industrial producer engaged in a risky enterprise.

Other notable U.S. examples of government-sponsored push with an initially dominant military component include the development of space flight and communication satellites, lasers, automated fabrication, robotization, composite materials, and integrated circuits. And the post-1973 U.S. move toward higher average fuel efficiencies of passenger cars did not come about because the country's major automakers were vying for technical leadership, but rather from direct government intervention that legislated a slowly improving performance and that raised the mean from the low of 13.5 miles per gallon (mpg) in 1973 to 27.5 mpg by 1985. Subsequent return to low oil prices sapped the government's resolve to continue along this highly desirable, and technically quite feasible, trajectory. By the century's end the mean stood still at 27.5 mpg while the continuation of the pre-1985 trend would have raised it to about 40 mpg, drastically cutting the need for crude oil imports! So much for autonomous technical advances!

Another important conclusion that weakens any simplistic claims in favor of universal technical determinism is that similar, or even superior, national accomplishments are no guarantee of specific outcomes. This point is perfectly illustrated with the Soviet achievements. Basic post-WWII Soviet research was essential in developing several key advanced technical concepts, including low-temperature physics (Nobels to Landau in 1962 and to Kapitsa in 1978) and masers and lasers (Nobels to Basov and Prokhorov in 1964 and to Alferov in

2000), while Piotr Ufimtsev's equations for predicting the reflections of electromagnetic waves from surfaces were eventually used by the U.S. designers to develop stealth aircraft.

Massive Soviet investment in military R&D produced not only huge arsenals but also many outstanding and pioneering designs. The country amassed the world's largest inventory of nuclear weapons that peaked at 45,000 warheads in 1986 and included the most powerful fusion devices ever tested. And although its fighter planes had less advanced electronics than did their U.S. counterparts, the expert judgment assessed several of them—most notably the MiG-29 and Su-25—as perhaps the world's best flying machines in their respective categories (Gunston 2002), and the same was clearly true about huge air transporters. More fundamentally, by the late 1980s the USSR was the world's largest producer of crude oil (ahead of Saudi Arabia) and natural gas (ahead of the United States) and the world's second largest producer of coal (behind the United States). All of these facts prove a considerable technical prowess—yet none of them could prevent the disintegration of the country's empire and soon afterward the collapse of its communist regime.

I revisit the limits of technical determinism in chapter 7. Here I reiterate my respect for complex, contradictory, and counterintuitive realities and my refusal to offer any simplistic conclusions regarding the role of technical advances in creating the modern world. The most comfortable summation I would offer would view this role in terms of *yin–yang* pairings: frequently dominant but most often only as *primus inter pares*; fundamental but not automatically paramount; increasingly universal but not immune to specific influences; undeniably autonomous in many respects but heavily manipulated in other ways; consequently a tempting subject for what might seem to be relatively low-risk forecasts yet what turns out to be repeatedly a matter of surprising and frustratingly elusive outcomes. In contrast, there is nothing uncertain about the genesis of this grand technical transformation.

The Unprecedented Saltation

Indisputable evidence demonstrates that evolution—be it of higher life forms or of humanity's technical capabilities—has been an overwhelmingly gradual and cumulative process. Yet the record also shows that the process is punctuated, recurrently and unpredictably, by periods of sudden gains. Fossils record the existence of these saltations, none of them more astonishing than the Cambrian eruption that began about 540 million years ago and that produced nearly all of today's animal lineages in about 50 million years, the time equal to a mere 1% of the evolutionary span. Similarly, history of technical advances, dominated by long periods of incremental gains or prolonged stasis, is interspersed with bursts of extraordinary creativity, but none of them even remotely approached the breadth, rapidity, and impact of the astonishing discontinuity that created the modern world during the two generations preceding WWI.

The period between 1867 and 1914, equal to less than 1% of the history of high (settled) civilizations, was distinguished by the most extraordinary concatenation of a large number of fundamental scientific and technical advances. Their synergy produced new prime movers, new materials, new means of transportation, communication, and information processing, and introduced generation, transmission, and conversion of electricity, the most versatile form of energy and the quintessential source of power in the modern world. No less remarkable, these bold and imaginative innovations were rapidly improved (often they were essentially mature within a single generation after their introduction), promptly commercialized, and widely diffused, creating the fundamental reordering of traditional societies and providing the lasting foundations of modernity: not only their basic operating modes but often many of their specific features are still with us.

Even a rudimentary list of these epoch-defining innovations must include telephones, sound recordings, permanent dynamos, light bulbs, practical typewriters, chemical pulp, and reinforced concrete for the pre-1880 years. The astonishing 1880s, the most inventive decade in history, brought reliable and affordable electric lights, electricity-generating plants, electric motors and trains, transformers, steam turbines, the gramophone, popular photography, practical gasoline-fueled internal combustion engines, motorcycles, automobiles, aluminum production, crude oil tankers, air-filled rubber tires, steel-skeleton skyscrapers, and prestressed concrete. The 1890s saw diesel engines, x-rays, movies, air liquefaction, and the first wireless signals. And the period between 1900 and 1914 witnessed mass-produced cars, the first airplanes, tractors, radio broadcasts, vacuum tubes (diodes and triodes), tungsten light bulbs, neon lights, common use of halftones in printing, stainless steel, hydrogenation of fats, air conditioning, and the Haber-Bosch synthesis of ammonia (without which some 40% of today's humanity would not be alive).

Genesis of these astonishing advances and their patenting, improvement, commercialization, and rapid diffusion were the subject of *Creating the 20th Century: Technical Innovations of 1867–1914 and Their Lasting Impact* (I use the acronym *CTTC* when I refer to it in this book). In that book I used a variety of primary American, British, German, and French sources (inventors' narratives, contemporary testimonials, patent applications) as well as a wide assortment of later assessments and topical histories in order to detail the origins and immediate elaborations of all fundamental innovations of that remarkable era. I also traced some of their subsequent long-term improvements and offered many assessments of their enormous socioeconomic impacts and their lasting indispensability for the functioning of modern societies.

Intensive research and incredibly rapid translation of pioneering designs into commercial realities of the first electric systems are the subject of *CTTC*'s first

FIGURE 1.4. Ranking the importance of technical advances is always arguable, but perhaps no other four innovators contributed to the creation of modern world, so utterly dependent on electricity (see chapter 2 of *CTTC*), more than did Thomas Edison, Charles Parsons, George Westinghouse, and Nikola Tesla (clockwise from top left). Edison's 1880 photograph is from the Library of Congress; Parsons's portrait is reproduced courtesy of the Tyne and Wear Museums, Newcastle upon Tyne; Westinghouse's portrait is reproduced courtesy of Westinghouse Electric; and Tesla's 1892 photograph is from the San Francisco Tesla Society.

topical chapter. The system of electricity generation, transmission, and industrial, commercial, and household use that was created completely *de novo* during the 1880s and 1890s is also a perfect illustration of *CTTC*'s key thesis about the truly revolutionary and lasting import of the era's innovations. Even the most accomplished engineers and scientists who were alive in 1800 would face, if translocated a century into the future, the electric system of the year 1900 with astonishment and near utter incomprehension. In 1900, less than two decades after the system's tentative beginnings, the world had a completely unprecedented and highly elaborate means of producing a new form of energy (by using larger steam turbogenerators), changing its voltage and transmitting it with minimized losses across longer distance (by using transformers and high-voltage conduits) and converting it with increasing efficiencies with new ingenious prime movers (electric motors), new sources of light (incandescent bulbs), and new industrial processes (electric arc furnaces).

In contrast, if the brilliant creators of this system, men including Thomas Edison, George Westinghouse, Nikola Tesla, and Charles Parsons (figure 1.4), could see the electric networks of the late 20th century, they would be very familiar with nearly all of their major components, as the fundamentals of their grand designs fashioned before 1900 remained unchanged. The same lack of shocked incomprehension would be experienced by the best pre-WWI engineers able to behold our automobile engines (still conceptually the same four-stroke Otto-cycle machines or inherently more efficient diesel engines), our skyscrapers (still built with structural steel and reinforced concrete), our wireless traffic (still carried by hertzian waves), or printed images (still produced by the halftone technique). These three classes of fundamental pre-WWI innovations—internal combustion engines, new materials, and advances in communication and information processing—are systematically examined in chapters 3–5 of *CTTC*.

Our quotidian debt to great innovators of the two pre-WWI generations thus remains immense, and even if you have no intent to find out the actual extent of this technical inheritance by reading *CTTC*, you can begin to realize it just by listing the devices, machines, and processes that you rely on every day and then trying to find their origins: the share that goes back to the 1867–1914 period is stunning. Some of these inventions—mostly such simple metallic items as paperclips, crimped caps on beer bottles, barbed wires, or spring mouse traps—remain exactly as they were at the time of their commercialization more than a century ago, but most of them were transformed into qualitatively superior products.

Transformations and New Departures

First, a brief semantic qualifier and an outstanding illustration of a modern technical transformation: the Latin *trānsformāre* means obviously changing the form, but in this book I use the term in its widest possible meaning that signifies *any substantial degree of alteration* and hence spans many different final outcomes. I am applying the term not only to individual objects (devices, tools, machines) but also to processes (casting of steel, machining of parts), networks (long-distance telephony), and systems (electricity generation). Consequently, high-speed railway transport that was pioneered in Japan during the late 1950s is a perfect example of such a transformative advance.

None of the system's key ingredients was a 20th-century invention. Steel wheels on steel rails—the arrangement that gives the advantage of firm contact, good guidance, low friction, and ability to move massive loads with low energy expenditures—was present at the very beginning of commercial railways during the 1830s. Electric motors, the most suitable prime movers for such trains, were powering trains already before the end of the 19th century: what took place after WWII was a critical shift from DC to AC, but by that time that, too, did not require any fundamental inventions. Pantographs to lead electricity from suspended copper wires, aerodynamically styled light aluminum car bodies, regenerative brakes to slow down the trains from speeds above 200 km/h— all of these key components had to be improved, but none of them had to be invented. And the first high-speed sets ran on ballasted track as did all previous trains.

But when these ingredients were integrated in a new system, railway travel was transformed. No wonder that when Japan National Railway sought the World Bank loan for its new trunk line (*shinkansen*), the bank's bureaucrats saw it as an experimental project and hence ineligible for funding. But Hideo Shima, Japan's leading railway engineer who traveled to Washington in 1960 to secure the loan, knew what he was talking about when he convinced them "that *shinkansen* techniques included no experimental factor but were an integration of proven advances achieved under the 'Safety First'" (Shima 1994: 48). This is the very essence of successful transformative engineering: a system assembled from proven ingredients whose synergies change a mundane experience to such an extent that it becomes not just new but highly desirable.

I had logged more rail travel by the time I was 25 than most people do in a lifetime, traveling in trains pulled by steam, diesel, and standard electric locomotives. I admired their mechanical ingenuity and knew many of their types and speeds. But when I stood for the first time at a platform of Tōkyō's central station and saw the sleek *shinkansen* trains (at that time still the first, o series trains with their bullet noses that now look old-fashioned) come and go at what seemed to be impossibly short intervals, it was a profoundly new experience. In subsequent decades I have traveled on *shinkansen* in the first-class Green cars as well as standing for hours in trains packed at the end of *obon* holidays. But always this is travel as an event because even when the rapidly receding scenery is hidden, even when standing in a crowded carriage, you know that on the same track and just a few minutes behind you is another centrally controlled sleek assembly of 16 cars with 64 asynchronous motors moving in the same direction at 300 km/h—and that when you arrive after a journey of hundreds of kilometers, you will be within a few seconds of the scheduled time!

The 20th century saw many other technical transformations of this kind as new developments changed the external appearance of a product, machine, or an entire assembly (and sometimes did so beyond an easy recognition) while retaining basic components and operating principles. As shown in this chapter's frontispiece, passenger cars are another prominent example of this transformation. The first automobiles of the late 1880s were open carriages with engines mounted under high-perched seats, with wooden wheels of unequal radius, dangerous cranks, and long steering columns. By 1901 Maybach's Mercedes set a new design trend, but outwardly even that pioneering vehicle had little in common with enclosed, low-profile aerodynamic bodies of modern cars with massive rubber tires, electric starters, and power-assisted steering. But their engines run according to the same four-stroke cycle that Nicolaus Otto patented in 1877 and that Gottlieb Daimler and Wilhelm Maybach adapted for high-speed gasoline-powered automobiles starting in 1886. As Otto would have said, *Ansaugen, Verdichten, Arbeiten, Ausschieben; Ansaugen, Verdichten . . .*

And cars also illustrate the realities of the second major category of technical transformations, when two objects made a century apart are outwardly very similar, even identical, while their operating mode had undergone a profound transformation. Shapes and sizes of basic components of Otto-cycle engines— cylinders, pistons, valves, cranks—are constrained by their function, and these precision-machined parts must be assembled with small tolerances and run at high speeds in reciprocating motion. But unlike their pre-WWI, or for that matter nearly all pre-1970, counterparts, car engines made during the 1990s were more than complex mechanical devices. Microprocessors of the engine control unit control and coordinate the timing of ignition, throttle position, the ratio of the fuel/air mixture, and its metering and use dozens of sensors to monitor the engine's performance. And since 1996 all U.S. passenger cars and light-duty trucks have been also equipped with diagnostic microcontrollers that detect possible problems and suggest appropriate action.

Other microprocessors (there were as many as 50 in a car of the late 1990s) control automatic transmission, cruise control, and antilock brakes; actuate seat belt pretensioners; deploy airbags; optimize the operation of anti-air pollution devices; and turn the entire vehicle into a mechatronic machine with more computing power than the Apollo 11 lunar landing module. As a result, the U.S. car industry became the country's largest purchaser of microprocessors, and in the year 2000 electronic components totaled about 8% of the average vehicle's value, or nearly $1,000 per car. Many other industries had seen the same kind of transformation during the century's last quarter as microprocessors were introduced into a steadily expanding range of products.

Analogical transformations affected the production of basic industrial materials as well as the delivery of common services. Haber-Bosch synthesis of ammonia remains the foundation of high yields in modern agriculture, but by the late 1990s its energy use per tonne of ammonia was only half of the total needed in 1920 (Smil 2001). And while the sequence of dialing, waiting for a connection, and listening to a distant voice was the same with a wired set in 1999 as it was in 1920, the obvious external differences between the two objects (square and bulky vs. sleek and trim shape, black vs. a rainbow choice of colors) were much less important than what was inside: all modern phones are fully electronic, while all pre-late-1970s devices were electromechanical.

Technical transformations of the 20th century made a great deal of qualitative difference as they brought increased power, speed, efficiency, durability, and flexibility. Even the most imaginative innovators of the pre-WWI era who invented and commercialized the basic techniques would be impressed by these gains. Many specific comparisons of these advances are cited in the topical chapters of this book, some relatively modest (because the gains were inherently constrained by mechanical, thermodynamic, or construction requirements), others beyond the range of normal imagination (most notably the gains in computing capabilities). And, regardless of the degree of their subsequent qualitative transformations, all innovations that were introduced during the two pre-WWI generations were changed because mechanized (and later automated or robotized) mass production supplanted their manual artisanal fabrication.

Again, the innovators of the pre-WWI era would be impressed by the extent of this mass production that made their inventions so much more affordable as the economies of scale helped to turn rare possessions into objects of common ownership and spread them around the world. The resulting affordability looks even more impressive when the costs are compared as shares of typical income rather than in absolute (even when inflation-adjusted) terms, and even then the costs undervalue the real gains because they ignore very different qualities of the compared products. A contrast of two machines in this chapter's frontispiece reminds us that in 1900 the car was an uncomfortable conveyance that required brute force to start by cranking, offered no protection against the elements, and guaranteed frequent breakdowns; in the year 2000 climatized interior, adjustable car seats, power-assisted steering and brakes, CD players, and multiple speakers offered comfortable rides, and engines ran with such a reliability that many new models required just a single annual checkup.

And the affordability, as well as quality, of services provided by complex technical assemblies and intricate engineering networks had improved to an even greater degree: American wages, electricity cost, and lighting efficiency offer perhaps the most stunning example of these gains (figure 1.5). In 1900, 1 kWh of electricity (enough to light a 100-W bulb for 10 hours) in a large eastern U.S. city cost about 15 cents (roughly $3.25 in year 2000 dollars) while a century later it sold for a mere 6 cents. With hourly wages in manufacturing (expressed in inflation-adjusted monies) rising from $4 in 1900 to $13.90 in the year 2000, electricity as a share of average income thus became almost 190 times more affordable. But in 1900 the average efficiency of an incandescent light bulb was only about 0.6%, while a century later fluorescent light could convert as much as 15% of electricity into light. Consequently, a lumen of electric light was roughly 4,700 times more affordable in the year 2000 than it was 100 years earlier.

But technical advances of the 20th century went beyond the elaboration and ingenious improvements of fundamental pre-WWI innovations. They in-

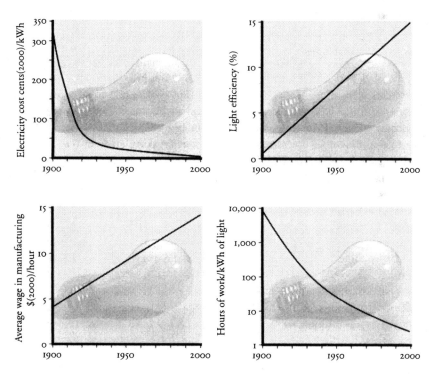

FIGURE 1.5. During the 20th century the cost of U.S. electricity (in constant monies) fell from about 325 cents to 6 cents per kWh (top left) while the efficiency of interior lighting rose roughly 25-fold (top right) and average hourly wages in manufacturing more than tripled (bottom left). The result: largely because of technical advances, a unit of light energy became roughly 4,700 times more affordable (bottom right). Plotted from data in Smil (2003) and USBC (1975).

cluded new products whose theoretical solutions and many key components predated 1914 (public radio, television, and gas turbines are the most prominent examples in this category) but whose practical application came only after WWI. And there were also entirely new achievements that sprang from laws that were understood by 1914 but whose realization had to wait not only for further accumulation of scientific and engineering progress but also for additional fundamental discoveries: nuclear fission and solid-state electronics exemplify these innovations, and both are dealt with in some detail in, respectively, chapters 2 and 5. Radio's pre-1914 progress is described in *CTTC* (chapter 5), and so just a few paragraphs concerning the genesis of television and gas turbines might be in order.

The entire phenomenon of television rests on the illusion of continuous movement that is created by rapidly changing sequence of images (minimum required frequency is 25–30 times per second). The key idea—serial transmission of individual pixel signals whose rapid sequence is reconstructed in a receiver by reversing the broadcasting process—was advanced by William Edward Sawyer in 1877. Proposals for mosaic receivers and scanning with revolving disks also go back to the late 19th century, as does the prototype of a cathode ray tube, demonstrated in 1878 by William Crookes, and its first practical design introduced by Karl Ferdinand Braun in 1897. The basic ingredients were thus in place before WWI, and by the mid-1920s a Mormon teenager, Philo Farnsworth, assembled them in his mind and soon also in a working model of the first television system (see chapter 5).

Gas turbine does not merely substitute one working medium (gas) for another (water vapor). Steam turbines are supplied from boilers by hot, pressurized fluid that is expanded in stages. Gas turbines subsume the induction of fuel, its compression, ignition, combustion, and exhaust in a single device—and unlike the internal combustion engines that do all of this in the same space (inside a cylinder) but intermittently in sequenced stages, gas turbines perform all those operations concurrently and continuously in different parts of the machine. This is why their design posed a much greater technical challenge.

Franz Stolze's designs embodied both the principle and key configurations of modern multistage machines, but his patented 1899 single-shaft turbine (driven by a primitive coal gasifier) barely produced any net power (New Steam Age 1942). Charles Curtis received his patent for a gas turbine engine (U.S. Patent 635,919) also in 1899, but the first small experimental machine with rotary compressors was designed in 1903 by Aegidius Elling in Norway. The Parisian *Société des Turbo-moteurs* built several machines between 1903 and 1906, and in 1908 Hans Holzwarth began his long career of gas turbine design. But all of these machines had efficiencies below 5%, too low for any commercial use, and breakthroughs in gas turbine engineering had to wait until after WWI.

Innovations and Inventions

Once more a brief definitional digression: I use the term "innovation" in the broadest sense of introducing anything new and "invention" as a more circumscribed category of devising an original device or machine or an entirely new synthetic, extractive, or fabrication process. All great inventors are innovators *par excellence*, but some of the 20th century's farthest-reaching innovations— such as the Toyota system of car production with its constant quality control and just-in-time deliveries of parts (chapter 4)—did not require any stunning inventions, merely ingenious applications or rearrangements of established practices. Given the enormous variety of post-1914 technical advances, this book cannot be their comprehensive survey: any attempt to do so would reduce it to a briefly annotated listing of items.

Instead, I adopt the same approach I follow in *CTTC* and pay reasonably detailed attention to the first-order innovations that remain critical for the functioning of the modern world. Chapter 2 thus assesses the energetic foundation of the 20th century civilization. I trace the evolution of its dependence on fossil fuel and electricity generation and follow the development of the three classes of new 20th-century energy converters: nuclear reactors, gas turbines and rockets. In chapter 3, I examine the material foundation of modern societies, paying particular attention to advances in making steel (as these alloys remain the most indispensable of all metals), and review the production of industrial gases (a class of fundamental innovations that is curiously neglected by most surveys of technical progress) and syntheses of plastics before ending with a brief history of silicon, the signature material of the electronic era.

Chapter 4 is devoted to sweeping transformations brought by mechanization, automation, and robotization, and I address these advances within three major categories: agricultural harvests and animal husbandry, extraction and processing of materials, and factory production. Chapter 5 addresses the sectors with a common denominator of mass and speed: transportation, information, and communication. Besides obvious segments on cars, trains, and airplanes, the transportation section also includes a lengthy review of advances in freight shipments. This is followed by brief histories of modern computing and electronics, with a particular stress on rapid advances in hardware, from transistors to microprocessors.

Consequently, my narratives dwell not only on the 20th century's iconic inventions—including nuclear reactors, jet engines, plastics, and computers— but also on innovations whose true importance is appreciated only by experts involved in their management and improvement but whose critical, and often hidden, contributions were no less essential for transforming the century's economic fortunes and social organization than the introductions of well-known advances. Materials are a major part of this surprisingly large category: how many people besides chemical engineers appreciate that no other compound is synthesized (in terms of moles) more abundantly than ammonia, how many know about the quest for continuous casting of sheet steel or what faujasite is good for? And the category of obscure fundamentals also includes machines (planetary grinders, three-cone drilling bits), massive assemblies (continuous casters, tension leg platforms, unit trains), and immaterial electronic codes (programming languages) and management procedures (*kaizen*).

The same dichotomy applies, naturally, to the innovators: their fame is hardly proportional to the fundamental importance of their contributions. While it is indefensible to survey the technical advances of the 20th century without writing about the famous men who created the nuclear era (Enrico Fermi, Robert Oppenheimer) or about the pioneers of the electronic age (Walter Brattain, John Bardeen, William Shockley, Jack Kilby, Robert Noyce), I also introduce the innovators whose names now either are almost entirely forgotten or are familiar only to small groups of experts. Here are six names of inventors whose brilliant ideas had their genesis during the first half of the 20th century: Joseph Patrick, Waldo Semon, Hans von Ohain, George Devol, Siegfried Junghans, George de Mestral. And here is another set from the second half, names of innovators whose ideas began transforming the world during your lifetime: Taiichi Ōno, Malcolm McLean, Douglas Engelbart, Nils Bohlin, John Backus, Dennis Ritchie.

If you scored 12 out of 12 you are a walking encyclopedia (and a particularly detailed one) of modern technical history. The two lists are actually carefully constructed. They include the names of people whose innovations were so fundamental that just about everything we touch and use in the modern world is (directly or indirectly) connected to them (Junghans, McLean), those whose ideas keep saving lives (Bohlin) or huge amounts of money (Ōno), and those whose very disparate contributions (made decades apart) helped to create the modern electronic society (Patrick, Ritchie). And they also include de Mestral and Engelbart, two men whose inventions made repetitive tasks easier and whose simple designs, after initially slow starts, came to be replicated in, respectively, many billions and hundreds of millions, of copies. Billions? Indeed!

In 1948 George de Mestral (1909–1990), a Swiss engineer, wondered how cockleburrs fastened to his pants and to his dog's coat: under his microscope he saw tiny hooks and spent the next eight years replicating the mechanism in plastic. His solution: a layer of soft loops pressed against a layer of stiffer hooks (made by cutting raised loops) to make *velours croché* that soon began its global conquest as Velcro (de Mestral 1961; figure 1.6). The plastic is now not only used every year in hundreds of millions pieces of clothing and shoes but also is sold in sheets, strips, rolls, and coins to make products ranging from display boards to ammunition packs.

Douglas Engelbart's invention did not become as ubiquitous as Velcro's characteristic unfastening sound, but it ranks among the most mass-produced electronic devices. He made the first prototype of an "x-y position indicator

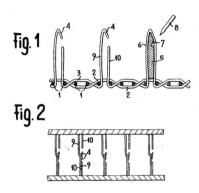

Sept. 13, 1955   G. DE MESTRAL   2,717,437
VELVET TYPE FABRIC AND METHOD OF PRODUCING SAME
Filed Oct. 15, 1952

Fig. 1

Fig. 2

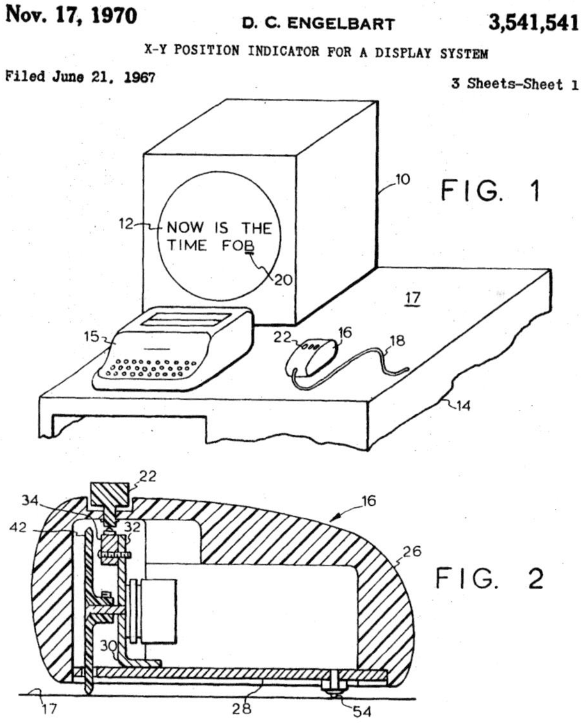

Nov. 17, 1970   D. C. ENGELBART   3,541,541
X-Y POSITION INDICATOR FOR A DISPLAY SYSTEM
Filed June 21, 1967   3 Sheets–Sheet 1

NOW IS THE
TIME FOR

FIG. 1

FIG. 2

FIGURE 1.6. Drawings that accompanied patent applications for two simple but ingenious inventions that have made life easier for hundreds of millions of people around the world: what George de Mestral originally called a "velvet type fabric" and later became universally known as Velcro, and what Douglas Engelbart described as "x-y position indicator for a display system" that later became affectionately called a computer mouse. Reproduced from de Mestral (1961) and Engelbart (1970).

23

for a display system" in 1964 at the Stanford Research Institute and filed the patent application in 1967 (Engelbart 1970; figure 1.6). The palm size of the device and its wire tail at the end made the nickname obvious: when sales of personal computers eventually took off (almost two decades after Engelbart's invention) computer mice were ready to dart around.

You will encounter many other unrecognized innovators as you read chapters 2–5, which survey technical advances that transformed the 20th century. These concise but fairly comprehensive surveys range from prime movers to programming codes and from versatile mass-produced materials to custom-made microchips. Once this task is done, I review key economic, social, and environmental impacts of these contributions in chapter 6. Because I have repeatedly demonstrated the futility of long-range forecasts (Smil 2003), I do not end the book with any specific predictions regarding the future of modern civilization in chapter 7, just with some musings on its durability.

ℰ✅ 2

Energy Conversions:
Growth and Innovation

> It is important to realize that in physics today, we have no
> knowledge of what energy *is*. We do not have a picture that
> energy comes in little blobs of a definite amount. It is not
> that way. However, there are formulas for calculating some
> numerical quantity . . . It is an abstract thing in that it does
> not tell us the mechanism or the *reasons* for the various
> formulas.
>
> Richard Feynman, *The Feynman Lectures on Physics* (1963)

Dominant prime movers are the key physical determinants of productive capacities and hence also of the quality and tempo of life in any society. The
20th century was energized mostly by two prime movers whose genesis during
the 1880s, and their subsequent evolution, are detailed in *CTTC*: internal combustion engines, whose large numbers dominate aggregate installed power ca-

FRONTISPIECE 2. High-flow swept fan blades with 3.2-m diameter and a conical spinner
of GE90-115B gas turbine aeroengine, the world's most powerful turbofan (top) whose
unprecedented size is obvious when mounted on GE's Boeing 747 during the first flight
test in the Mojave Desert (bottom). Fiber-and-resin blades are not just elegant and
efficient but also quite sturdy, as they can accidentally ingest a bird weighing 1.5 kg
and remain fully operational. Photographs courtesy of GE Aircraft Engines, Cincinnati,
Ohio.

pacity, and steam turbines, the most powerful energy converters in common use. But one new prime mover rose to great prominence: by the end of the 20th century, gas turbines were the world's most reliable, as well as highly durable, energy converters and hence the dominant prime movers in both military and commercial flight and the most convenient and highly flexible means of electricity generation.

The frontispiece illustration—an oblique view of General Electric's GE90-115B turbofan aeroengine—conveys something of the power and the beauty of these extraordinary machines. Their reliability is perhaps best attested by the fact that during the 1990s the two-engine Boeing 767 became the dominant trans-Atlantic plane (figure 2.1) and that it began to replace three- and four-engine aircraft on even longer trans-Pacific routes. During the 1990s aeroengines could operate, with the requisite maintenance, for up to 20,000 hours, that is, 2.2 years of nonstop flight, and stationary gas turbines could work for more than 100,000 hours: at 50% load, this equals more than 22 years of service. Reliability, convenience, and cleanliness made aeroderivative natural-gas–fueled gas turbines the fastest and the most economical way of meeting the demand for new electricity generation.

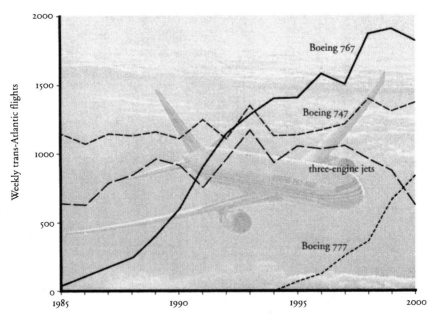

FIGURE 2.1. Reliability of modern gas turbines is impressively illustrated by the fact that just six years after its introduction, the two-engine Boeing 767 became the dominant airplane on trans-Atlantic routes. Based on a graph available from the Boeing corporation.

But this only increased our dependence on fossil fuels and intensified the most fundamental energy trend of the 20th century, the first period in history when fossil fuels were the globally dominant source of primary energy and when their use created new high-energy societies. Three interrelated trends governed these societies. The first one was rapid growth and maturation of basic extraction, transportation, conversion, and transmission techniques that resulted in the establishment of new performance plateaus after decades of impressive growth. The second trend was continuous change in the composition of primary energy supply that brought gradual decarbonization of the world's energy use, and the third was the growing importance of electricity.

Rising demand for electricity was satisfied primarily by the combustion of fossil fuels, but the worldwide construction of large dams and rapid post-1960 adoption of nuclear generation made important global, and some dominant national, contributions. History of nuclear generation deserves special attention because this revolutionary innovation is an excellent illustration of exaggerated hopes, unanticipated complications, and failed promises that often accompany technical advances. But the first practical conversion of nuclear energy was to deploy the chain reaction in weapons of unprecedented destructive power: this development, too, deserves closer attention.

Fossil-Fueled Societies

Sometime during the latter half of the 1890s (or, at the latest, before the end of the first decade of the 20th century) the aggregate energy content of biomass fuels (wood, charcoal, crop residues) consumed worldwide was surpassed by the energy content of fossil fuels, mostly coal burnt by industries, households, and in transport. Pinpointing the year of this transition is impossible because of the absence of reliable data concerning traditional biomass fuel consumption. The shift went entirely unnoticed at that time—its occurrence was reconstructed only decades later—and yet this was one of the most important milestones in human history, comparable only to the much more gradual emergence of sedentary farming.

This conclusion defies the common perception of the 19th century as the quintessential coal era, crediting coal with energizing the Industrial Revolution. That description is correct only as far as England and parts of continental Europe (Belgium, coal-mining regions of France, Germany, Bohemia, and Poland) are concerned, and it does not fit any of the three great economic powers of the 20th century: Russia, Japan and the United States. The first two countries became largely fossil-fueled societies only after 1900; the United States began to derive more than half of its primary energy from fossil fuels only during the early 1880s, and by 1900 it still got a fifth of it from wood (Schurr and Netschert 1960). The 20th century was the first period in history when our advances, exploits, and conflicts were energized mostly by carbonaceous fuels that had formed in the uppermost strata of the Earth's crust between 100 thousand and 100 million years ago. In contrast, every previous civilization relied on young (mostly decades-old) carbon in harvested trees and shrubs and, in deforested regions, on even younger (merely months old) carbon stored in crop stalks and straws. But the post-1900 global preponderance of fossil fuels had no simple correspondence with the share of the world's population whose daily lives directly depended on them.

By 1950 biomass use declined to 20% of the world's energy, and during the late 1990s it was just 10% (Smil 2003). But by the early 1970s about 90% of all energy in rural China were still derived from biomass (Smil 1988), and similar shares prevailed in the Indian countryside, Southeast Asia, sub-Saharan Africa, and parts of Latin America. In terms of overall energy use the global fossil fuel era thus basically coincides with the 20th century, but more than half of the world's population became dependent on fossil fuels for its everyday energy needs only during the 1970s. As already noted, the global adoption of fossil fuels was accompanied by three universal transformations: maturation of basic energy techniques, shifting composition of primary energy supply, and the rising importance of electricity that was helped by increasing reliance on two nonfossil sources: hydroenergy and nuclear fission. The latter technique was one of the 20th century's most remarkable innovations, and I look both at its enormous early promise and at its stagnation and impending decline.

Growth and Performance Plateaus

Extraction of fossil fuels is among the most reliably quantified human activities because—in contrast to biomass fuels that are mostly secured by hundreds of millions of individual families for their own consumption—coal and hydro-carbons have been always produced overwhelmingly by commercial enterprises for sale. Consequently, some inevitable errors in quantifying national and global use of fossil energies may come as much from conversions to common denominators as from inaccurate output statistics. During the 20th century consumption of fossil fuels rose almost 15-fold, from about 22 EJ/year to 320 EJ/year (UNO 1956; BP 2004). Primary electricity—generated by water, since 1956 from nuclear fission, and since 1960 from marginally important geother-mal, wind, and solar conversions—was negligible in 1900, but by the year 2000 it added an equivalent of nearly 40 EJ.

In this chapter I show that an unmistakable formation of S-shaped growth curves was a major recurrent theme in the history of the 20th-century energy techniques. Some of these curves became first apparent during the 1930s and 1940s, but nearly all of these rating and performance plateaus were only temporary, as the affected techniques resumed their rise after WWII, and new records were set in fast succession during the 1950s, 1960s, and 1970s. Fundamentally different plateaus then began to form as maximum specific ratings and conversion efficiencies displayed prolonged spells of minimal or no growth. Moreover, some techniques came rather close to the physical (thermodynamic, material) limits of their performance or their operation encountered environmental impediments or the lack of social acceptance that proved to be insurmountable at generally acceptable, or even at any, cost. As there are too many instances of this general maturation trend, I introduce just a few notable examples that involve transportation of crude oil and generation and transmission of electricity.

Crude oil tankers were indispensable for the 20th-century global energy trade (Ratcliffe 1985), but between 1884 (when the first vessel of this kind was launched) and 1921, their record capacities increased from slightly more than 2,000 to more than 20,000 dwt; they then stagnated for more than a generation. Precipitous growth resumed after WWII as the supertanker designation shifted from 50,000 dwt ships (before the mid-1950s) to 100,000 dwt vessels just a few years later (figure 2.2). In 1959 came *Universe Apollo*, the first 100,000 dwt ship; in 1966 Ishikawajima-Harima Heavy Industries completed record-sized 150,000 dwt *Tokyo Maru* and later in the same year the 210,000 dwt *Idemitsu Maru*. By 1973 there were 366 very large or ultralarge crude oil carriers, with the largest vessels in excess of 300,000 dwt (Kumar 2004).

Both the long-term trend and expert expectations pointed to ships of 1 Mdwt. Instead, the growth peaked with the launching of *Seawise Giant* in 1975 and its enlargement three years later. The ship was hit by missiles in 1988 during the Iran-Iraq war, but it was subsequently repaired, and the 564,650 dwt (nearly 459 m long) vessel continued its crude oil deliveries under its new name, *Jahre Viking*. Supertanker growth did not stop because of diminishing economies of scale or because of insurmountable technical problems, but rather because of operational considerations. Very large ships have to reckon with limited depths of many ports and with long distances needed to stop. Accidental oil spills affect marine life and pollute shores for years to come, and the penalties sought, as illustrated with the *Exxon Valdez* Alaska spill of March 24, 1989, can reach billions of dollars; insuring against such mishaps becomes prohibitively expensive. And the megaships on the order of 1 Mdwt could find only a handful of ports where to moor, losing the flexibility with which multinational oil companies use their tankers.

History of electricity generation offers many illustrations of temporary pre-WWII performance plateaus. Maximum size of steam turbogenerators rose from 1 MW in 1900 to 200 MW by the early 1930s, and after a period of stagnation the post-WWII ascent sent the maximum installed capacities to more than 1,000 MW by 1967 (figure 2.3; see also figure 2.15 in *CTTC* that

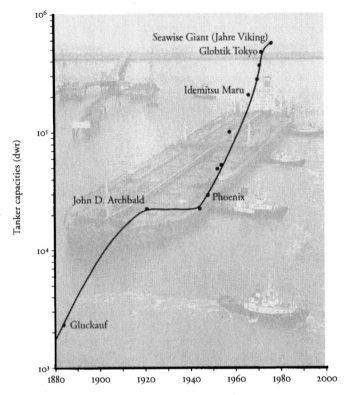

FIGURE 2.2. Maximum capacities of crude oil tankers, 1886–2000. In 1886 the *Gluckauf,* a sail-assisted Newcastle-built steamer, became the first bulk carrier with built-in tanks and a capacity of just 2,307 dwt. The *Jahre Viking,* launched as the *Seawise Giant* in 1976, displaces half a tonne. Based on figure 5.6 in Smil (1994).

shows the S-curves for steam temperature and pressure). At that time the industry anticipated machines in excess of 2 GW before the year 1980, but only a few units of about 1.5 GW went into operation before the year 2000.

Maxima in ratings of individual steam turbogenerators and thermal electricity-generating plants will be reflected in the highest transmission voltages. In North America these ratings rose rapidly until 1923, when they reached 230 kV. This remained the highest voltage until the mid-1950s (the Hoover Dam–Los Angeles 287.5 kV line was the only exception). The growth resumed with 345 kV in 1954 and stopped at 765 kV by 1965 when the world's first line of that voltage was installed by Hydro-Québec to bring electricity 1,100 km south from Churchill Falls in Labrador to Montréal. A new era of long-distance high-voltage DC transmission began on June 20, 1972, when Mani-

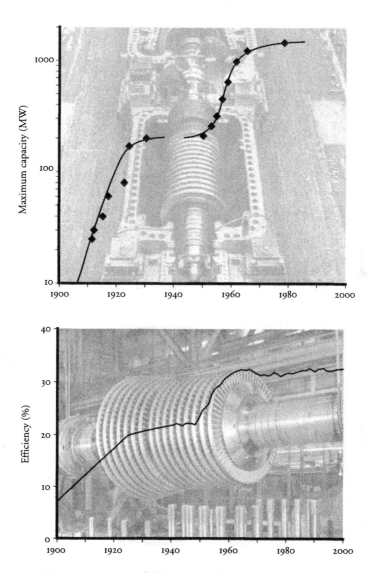

FIGURE 2.3. Maximum capacity of U.S. steam turbogenerators (top) and average efficiency of thermal generation of electricity (bottom), 1900–2000. The growth (top) shows two distinct S-curves, the first one with the saturation at 200 MW by the year 1930, the second one with the saturation at about 1.5 GW by the early 1980s (based on figure 1.9 in Smil 2003). Generation efficiency (bottom) reached its first plateau during the 1930s (slightly more than 20%) and the second one (surpassing 30%) by the early 1960s, and then it stagnated for the rest of the 20th century. Based on figure 1.17 in Smil (2003).

toba Hydro's 895 km long $\pm$ 450 kV DC line brought electricity from Kettle Rapids hydro station on the Nelson River to Winnipeg (Smil 1991).

The performance plateau that had caused the greatest concern in electricity-generating industry during the last quarter of the 20th century was the stagnation in the average heat rate of thermal stations. Reliable historical data for the United States show that after this rate rose to just over 30% during the early 1960s, it remained flat (figure 2.3). I should note that during the last quarter of the 20th century there were also some notable instances of actual declines in average ratings. The optimum size (the lowest cost per installed power) of new U.S. thermal electricity-generating stations rose steadily from less than 100 MW before WWII to more than 400 MW by the mid-1970s and to more than 1,000 MW by the 1980s. But then the rapid ascendance of gas turbines pushed it to the 50–150 MW range during the 1990s (Northeast-Midwest Institute 2000).

Energy Transitions and Decarbonization

Great supply transitions, whereby the dominant fuel is gradually replaced by a different source or by a mixture of new primary energies, are driven by combinations of environmental, economic, and technical imperatives. When the process is seen from an energetic perspective, there is one overriding explanation: principal driving force of energy transitions, and of the associated decarbonization of the primary supply, has been the rising power density of final energy use (Smil 1991; Ausubel 2003). Modern high-energy societies require high power densities in order to supply their cities (where most people now live), industries (where concentrated mass production is the norm), and transportation (only high-energy-density fuels are easily portable).

Moving from wood (commonly 18–20 GJ/t when absolutely dry) to coal (typically between 22 and 26 GJ/t) to refined oil products (40–44 GJ/t) to natural gas (53.6 GJ/t) taps fuels with progressively higher energy density. A home heating example illustrates how the use of these fuels affects storage and supervision requirements: wood requires space-consuming storage and time- and effort-intensive stoking of wood stoves; coal is a better choice on both counts; the same amount of energy in heating oil is easier to deliver, needs even less space to store, and can be fed automatically into a furnace; but natural gas is the best choice: "the strongly preferred configuration for very dense spatial consumption of energy is a grid that can be fed and bled continuously at variable rates" (Ausubel 2003:2). Natural gas pipelines take care of the feeding; a thermostat regulates the actual consumption rate by a furnace.

The first transition, from wood to coal, had its origins in extensive deforestation (not only because of fuel wood but also for wood needed for buildings and ships), rising costs of wood transported over greater distances to cities, and coal's fundamental advantages. Besides higher energy density, the fuel has also higher flame temperatures and is easier to transport. Origins of the British transition to coal actually predate the beginning of industrialization, while (as already noted) in other major Western economies, as well as in Japan, this shift began in earnest at different times during the 19th century (Smil 1994). This substitution began the still continuing decarbonization of the global energy supply.

Wood is made up largely of cellulose, a polymer of glucose, and lignin and contains about 50% carbon (C) and 6% hydrogen (H) by weight (Smil 1983). Taking 19 GJ/t as a representative mean, complete oxidation would release about 30 kg C/GJ (or 110 kg CO_2). Ultimate analyses of typical bituminous coals show that they contain between 65% and 70% C and about 5% H. Good bituminous coal will yield about 27 GJ/t, and its combustion will emit roughly 25 kg C/GJ (IPCC 1996; Hong and Slatick 1994). Moving from wood to coal will thus release typically 10–15% less carbon per unit of energy. Coal's primacy was eroded only slowly during the first three decades of the 20th century: it supplied about 93% of the word's primary commercial energy in 1910, 88% in 1920, and still almost 80% in 1930 (UNO 1956).

By 1950 the energy content of the global coal consumption was double that in 1900, but coal's share fell to slightly more than 60% as crude oil provided 27% and natural gas 10% of the word's total primary energy. And once post-WWII Europe and Japan began to put in place the foundation of modern consumer societies, coal's retreat and oil's ascent accelerated. By 1962 less than half of the world's primary energy was coming from coal, and even the two rounds of OPEC's large oil price rises of the 1970s could not open the way for coal's comeback. But they did slow down the rate of transition as coal's share declined from 34% of the total in 1970 to 30% by 1990 and 23% by the century's end (figure 2.4).

During the entire century, coal supplied about 5,500 EJ compared to about 5,300 EJ for crude oil. This difference is within the margin of conversion errors, so as a whole, the 20th century was an energetic draw between coal and oil—but during the century's second half crude oil's total energy surpassed that of coal roughly by a third. There were three major reasons for coal's relative retreat (in absolute energy terms, the fuel's output in the year 2000 was 4.5 times higher than in 1900). These conjoined factors were cost, environmental impact, and flexibility of use. Relatively high risks of coal production never limited the use of fuel. Early industrial societies tolerated high rates of fatal accidents and occupational diseases associated with underground coal mining no less than did the Ukraine and China of the 1990s, the two major coal producers with the highest rates of fatalities (in China more than 150 times higher than in the United States).

While modern techniques reduced the risk of mining accidents, they could not do anything about the progressively poorer quality of the fuel. In 1900 a

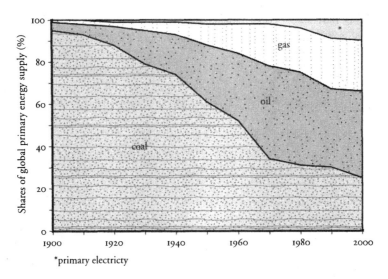

FIGURE 2.4. Shares of global primary energy supply, 1900–2000. Coal remained the single most important commercial fuel until 1966, but its subsequent retreat and the loss of major markets make any strong worldwide comeback highly unlikely. Calculated from data in UNO (1956, 2002) and BP (2004).

tonne of mined coal was equivalent to about 0.93 tonne of standard fuel (hard coal containing 29 GJ/t); by 1950 the global ratio was 0.83, and by the century's end it fell to just below 0.7 (UNO 1956, 2002). Declining quality means that larger masses of coal have to be extracted and transported and that, unless a greater investment goes into pollution controls, more emissions will be generated by the fuel's combustion. Mechanization of mining and improvements in bulk transportation were able to overcome the disadvantage of poorer quality, but major investments were needed to deal with coal's enormous air pollution potential. Beginning in the 1950s, electrostatic precipitators, rated to remove 99.9% of all fly ash, became a standard part of coal-fired stations, and various flue-gas desulfurization processes (which increase both the station's initial capital investment and its operation cost) have been commercialized since the late 1960s.

And even the best coal has 30% lower energy density than crude oil; it is much less convenient to store, transport, and distribute, and it cannot energize internal combustion engines, unless it is first expensively converted into liquids. Consequently, outside China and India, coal's market shrank to just one large and two secondary sectors (WCI 2001): electricity generation (in 2000 almost 40% of the world's electricity were generated in coal-fired plants) and production of metallurgical coke and cement. Even nations that pioneered coal mining turned away from it, although they still possess plentiful deposits. Most notably, in the year 2000 the United Kingdom, the world's second largest coal producer in 1900, extracted less than 20 Mt/year from 17 remaining private pits, and its peak labor force of 1.25 million miners (in 1920) was reduced to fewer than 10,000 men (Hicks and Allen 1999). And while in the year 2000 coal still provided nearly a quarter of the world's primary energy, the six largest producers (United States, China, Australia, India, Russia, and South Africa) accounted for slightly more than three-quarters of the world's total coal output, and most of the world's countries never used any of it.

But everybody is using crude oil. Refined oil products became the world's leading source of fossil fuels in 1966; during the 1970s their share peaked at about 44%, and in the year 2000 crude oil supplied about 40% of all commercial primary energy (BP 2004). Crude oil's role in modern societies is particularly critical in transportation, where its share is more than 90% of all energy. Land transport was also considerably facilitated by the availability of inexpensive paving materials derived from crude oil (and the fuel is also a valuable feedstock for chemical syntheses). Modern civilization is thus defined in many ways by its use of liquid fuels, and it will go to great lengths to assure their continued supply.

And using liquid fuels liberates much less carbon than does coal combustion. The ultimate analysis of crude oil shows carbon content of about 85%, and with 42 GJ/t, their typical emission factor will be about 20 kg C/GJ, 20–25% lower than for coals. Despite some significant differences in density, pour point, and sulfur content, crude oils have very similar energy content (42–44 GJ/t), about 50% higher than the standard hard coal (UNO 2002). And unlike coal, they are also conveniently (and relatively cheaply and safely) transported by pipelines and (very cheaply but with much higher risks) by tankers. Worldwide transition to oil was made possible by a combination of rapid technical progress and by discoveries of immense resources in the Middle East.

The fossil fuel with the lowest share of carbon is, of course, methane, the principal constituent of natural gases. During the first decade of the 20th century these gases contributed only about 1.5% of the world's commercial primary energy consumption, mostly due to the slowly expanding U.S. production. Expanded production was predicated on the availability of inexpensive large-diameter seamless pipes and efficient compressors. By 1950 the share of natural gas was still only about 10% of the world's energy, but then its cleanliness and convenience made it the preferred fuel for space heating, as well as for electricity generation. Despite this, natural gas did not become as important during the last quarter of the 20th century as the long-term trends appeared to suggest.

After the OPEC-driven oil price increases of the 1970s, coal's relative retreat proceeded at a slower pace, and crude oil, despite numerous predictions of imminent production decline, was also retreating more slowly. That is why by the year 2000 natural gas supplied no more than 25% of the world's commercial primary energy. With 75% of carbon in CH_4 and 35 MJ/m^3 (53.6 MJ/ kg), its combustion releases only 15.3 kg C/GJ, nearly 20% less than gasoline and 40% less than typical bituminous coal. Finally, global energy supply was further decarbonized by rising shares of primary electricity generation as the contributions of hydroenergy and nuclear fission rose from just 2% of the total in 1950 to about 10% by the year 2000. Overall carbon intensity of the world's energy supply thus declined from more than 24 kg C/GJ of commercial energy in 1900 to about 19 kg C/GJ in 2000, more than a 20% decrease.

Another way to look at decarbonization is to see it as the ascendancy of hydrogen and to trace the ratio of hydrogen and carbon in the dominant fuel. Ultimate analysis of wood shows that hydrogen and carbon make up, respectively, about 6% and 50% of its mass (Smil 1983), so the overall atomic ratio of the two combustible elements is about 1.4. But the actually applicable ratio is much lower because during the initial stages of wood combustion the hydroxyls (OH·) that are part of cellulose and hemicellulose escape to the atmosphere and hence a large part of the initially present hydrogen is unavailable to be oxidized. Complexity of wood's combustion processes makes generalizations suspect, but the effective H:C ratio of wood is almost certainly less than 0.5.

For bituminous coals containing 65% C and 5% C by weight, the atomic H:C ratio is almost exactly 1.0, while the analogical numbers for light oil distillates are 86% and 13% and 1.8; the H:C ratio of pure methane is 4.0. Ausubel (2003) assumed average atomic H:C ratios of 0.1 for wood (arguably too low), 1 for coal, 2 for crude oil and, obviously, 4 for methane when plotting the historic course of decarbonization. He found that it points to a global methane economy after 2030 and to a hydrogen-dominated economy (which would necessitate the production of large volumes of the gas without fossil energy) coming into existence during the closing decades of the 21st century.

Finally, the last major trend I must review before taking a closer look at new 20th-century prime movers also began before 1900 and also accelerated after 1950.

Electrification

The genesis and early achievements of electrification are covered in detail in *CTTC*. So were the multiple reasons for the superiority of electric lighting (its quality, cleanliness, efficiency, low cost), electric drive in industrial production (its flexibility, reliability, and accurate and convenient control), and transportation (all of the world's fastest trains are electric). Electricity's conversion also delivers high-quality thermal energy for markets ranging from the smelting of aluminum to household space heating. All of these advantages were appreciated from the very beginning of the electric era, but technical, economic, and infrastructural imperatives dictated gradual advances of electrification.

Early electricity generation was very inefficient and hence expensive. In 1900 the waste of fuel was astonishingly high, as the average U.S. heat rate of 91.25 MJ/kWh converted less than 4% of coal's chemical energy to electricity. The rate more than tripled by 1925 to nearly 14% and then almost doubled by 1950 to roughly 24% (Schurr and Netschert 1960). The nationwide mean surpassed 30% by 1960, and the best new stations reached, or even slightly surpassed, the 40% mark. Burning of pulverized coal (for the first time in 1919 at London's Hamersmith power station) and larger turbogenerators (see figure 2.3) operating at higher pressures and temperatures (rising, respectively, from less than 1 MPa to more than 20 MPa, and from less than 200°C to more than 600°C) were the principal reasons for the improved performance.

But, as already noted, all of these techniques matured by the late 1960s, and average generation efficiency remained stagnant for the remainder of the 20th century (see figure 2.3). Continuation of this poor performance was, together with the wastefulness of internal combustion engines in cars, one of the two greatest weaknesses of the modern energy system. After all, during the late 1990s energy wasted annually in U.S. thermal electricity generation surpassed Japan's total energy consumption! Even so, between 1900 and 2000 the average performance of thermal power plants rose by an order of magnitude, and the costs of generation, and electricity prices, declined impressively. Inherently capital-intensive and time-consuming process of building transmission and distribution networks meant that even in the United States fewer than 5% of farms had electric service right after WWI, compared to nearly 50% of all urban dwellings, and the country's rural electrification was rapidly completed only during the early 1950s (USBC 1975).

Electricity's numerous advantages and declining generation and transmission costs resulted in exponential growth of its generation and in constant rise of the share of the total fossil fuel supply needed to generate it (figure 2.5). The U.S. share rose from less than 2% in 1900 to slightly more than 10% by 1950 and to 34% in the year 2000 (EIA 2004). And this universal trend proceeded even more rapidly in many low-income modernizing countries. Most notably, China converted only about 10% of its coal to electricity in 1950; by 1980 the share surpassed 20%, and by the year 2000 it was about 30%, surprisingly similar to the U.S. share (Smil 1976; Fridley 2001). Global share of fossil fuels converted to electricity rose from slightly more than 1% in 1900 to 10% by 1950 and to slightly more than 30% by the century's end. And this supply was also augmented by greatly expanded hydrogeneration (now providing nearly 20% of the global electricity supply) and by the invention and commercialization of nuclear generation.

Increasing availability of affordable electricity brought a changing pattern

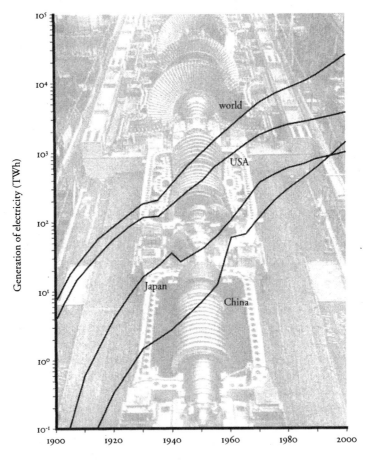

FIGURE 2.5. Electricity generation (worldwide and for the three largest producers), 1900–2000. Based on a graph in Smil (1999a) and data in EIA (2004).

of its use. During the first stage of electrification, which lasted in North America until the early 1930s, there were only two large markets, mechanical drive and lighting, and per capita consumption of electricity remained below 1 MWh/year. The only major appliances that were widely owned in the United States before WWII were vacuum cleaners and refrigerators (by 1940 nearly half of all U.S. households had them) and clothes washers (Burwell and Swezey 1990). In Europe and Japan these appliances became common only during the 1950s, and successive diffusion waves included frost-free refrigerators and dishwashers; in North America also came freezers, dryers, and first room and then central air conditioning.

During the same time, markets in affluent countries became saturated with smaller heating appliances ranging from toasters and coffee makers to (beginning in the mid-1970s) microwave ovens. Variety of these devices meant that no single appliance dominated the household use of electricity but that during the late 1990s U.S. households spent more on electricity than on any other source of energy (EIA 1999). Diffusion of labor-saving appliances was accompanied by the acquisition of new entertainment devices and personal computers, their attachments (printers, scanners), and other kinds of office equipment such as copiers and fax machines. These devices clearly increased the demand for electricity, but for many years it was unclear by how much.

Eventually it was demonstrated that during the late 1990s their demand amounted to only about 2% of the total U.S. electricity use (Kawamoto et al. 2000), but in absolute terms this was about 74 TWh, the total roughly equal to Indonesia's electricity generation! At the same time, electronic devices and the profusion of remote-ready equipment (TVs, VCRs, and audio) also became the major reason why the average U.S. household leaked constantly about 50 W, or 5% of all residential use (Meier and Huber 1997). All of these demands pushed the U.S. annual household electricity consumption above 4 MWh per capita, and the overall average rate surpassed 12 MWh per capita. In Europe these rates remained well below 10 MWh, in China still below 1 MWh.

Refrigerators are perhaps the best example of the universal diffusion of appliance ownership. A recent U.S. poll showed them to be the appliances that would the hardest to live without: 57% of respondents said so, compared to just 12% who chose air conditioning first (Shell Poll 1998). Commercial refrigeration made great advances during the 50 years before 1930, but household refrigeration was slow to take off (Nagengast 2000). Early models were too massive, too expensive, and too unreliable, and they used such flammable or toxic refrigerants as ammonia, isobutane, methyl chloride, or sulfur dioxide. During the 1920s better electric motors, compressors, and sealants made the machines mechanically adequate, but it was only in 1928 when Thomas Midgley introduced chlorofluorocarbons (CFCs) that the ownership of refrigerators took off (figure 2.6).

Before WWII nearly half of the U.S. households owned a refrigerator; during the 1950s the ownership began to spread in Europe and later to richer segments of urban populations in low-income countries, with some markets accomplishing saturation in little more than a single generation. CFCs were readily adopted as ideal refrigerants: they were stable, noncorrosive, nonflammable, nontoxic, and relatively inexpensive (Cagin and Dray 1993). After WWII their use spread to aerosol propellants, foam blowing, plastics production, cleaning of electronic circuits, extraction of edible and aromatic oils, and of course, air conditioners, the machines designed to refrigerate entire rooms

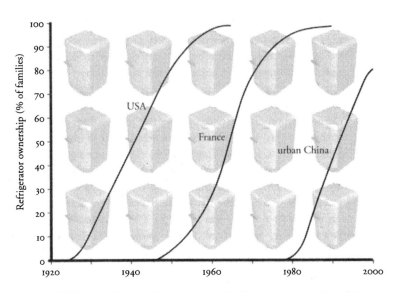

FIGURE 2.6. Diffusion of household ownership of refrigerators in the United States and France and in China's urban areas, 1920–2000. Based on graphs in Burwell and Swezey (1990) and Smil (1993, 2003).

(see chapter 2 of *CTTC*). By the 1960s they became common in the United States; by the 1990s they spread among affluent segments of populations living in hot-weather countries.

As microprocessors began to run, monitor, and serve myriads of industrial, commercial, transportation, and communication operations, 99.9% reliability of electricity supply became unacceptably low, and during the 1990s electricity-generating industry aimed at six nines, 99.9999% reliability, which would limit outages to just a few seconds a year. Electricity's indispensability now extends to every segment of national economy and everyday life: automation, robotics, and the entire information age are as unthinkable without it as are mass manufacturing and household chores. These ubiquitous benefits preclude any clear ranking of electricity's most important applications, but there is little doubt that from the existential point of view its most transformative impact was to improve human health (Ausubel and Marchetti 1996).

Vaccines (requiring refrigeration) eliminated a number of previously widespread infectious diseases (smallpox, diphtheria, whooping cough); incubators (requiring electric heating and constant monitoring of vital functions) provided increased chances for the survival of premature babies; water treatment (requiring electric motors for pumps and mixing) drastically reduced the incidence of gastrointestinal illnesses, as did the refrigeration of food (at the point of production, during transportation, and at home); electric lights made homes (staircase falls are a leading cause of accidents) and streets safer; and a variety of diagnostic, treatment, and surgical equipment (from x-rays to lasers) helped to prolong lives of hundreds of millions of people.

Finally, there is perhaps no better demonstration of electricity's macroeconomic importance than contrasting the intensity of its use in economy (kWh consumed per unit of gross domestic product) with the long-term direction of overall energy intensity (figure 2.7). The latter rate tends to increase during the early stages of industrialization but then it generally declines. The U.S. peak was in the early 1920s; by 1950 the rate declined by a third, and during the next 50 years it was almost exactly halved. Similarly, the energy intensity of the world economic output was more than halved during the 20th century (Smil 2003). In contrast, electricity intensity continued to increase even after 1950: electricity intensity of the U.S. economy rose about 2.7 times between 1950 and 1980, then declined a bit, but by the year 2000 it was still more than twice as high as two generations earlier (figure 2.7).

Nuclear Energy

Beginnings of the theoretical foundations of nuclear fission predate WWI. In the spring of 1896 Henri Becquerel (1852–1908) discovered uranium's radioactivity, and not long after the publication of his famous 1905 relativity paper, Albert Einstein (1879–1955) began to develop what he called an "amusing and attractive thought": in 1907 he concluded that "an inertial mass is equivalent with an energy content μc^2" (Einstein 1907:442). Demonstrating this equivalence with chemical reactions was entirely impractical, but Einstein knew that "for radioactive decay the quantity of free energy becomes enormous." In 1911 Ernest Rutherford's (1871–1937) studies of the penetration of thin layers of gold by α particles led him to propose a model of atomic nuclei (Rutherford 1911), and two years later Niels Bohr (1885–1962) revealed his simple model of the atomic structure with the nucleus surrounded by electrons in nonradiating orbits (Bohr 1913).

The two essential advances that opened the road to fission were made only at the beginning of the 1930s, both in Rutherford's famous Cavendish Laboratory in Cambridge. In 1931 John Douglas Cockroft (1897–1967) and Ernest T.S. Walton (1903–1995) achieved the first fissioning of an element by using high-voltage electricity to accelerate hydrogen protons in order to disrupt the nucleus of lithium (^{7}Li) and convert it to two α (^{4}He) particles. And in February 1932 James Chadwick (1891–1974; figure 2.8) provided the correct explanation of some of the earlier experimental results coming from Germany and France that produced "a radiation of great penetrating power."

Chadwick (1932:312) concluded:

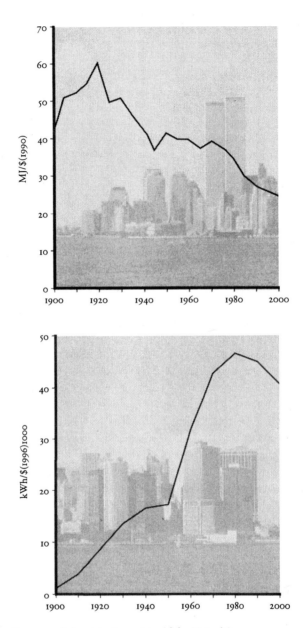

FIGURE 2.7. Energy and electricity intensities of the United States economy, 1900–2000. Based on graphs in Smil (1994, 2003) and data in EIA (2004).

These results . . . are very difficult to explain on the assumption that the radiation from beryllium is a quantum radiation . . . These difficulties disappear, however, if it be assumed that the radiation consists of particles of mass 1 and charge 0, or neutrons. The capture of the α-particle by the Be^9 nucleus may be supposed to result in the formation of a C^{12} nucleus and the emission of the neutron. From the energy relations of this process the velocity of the neutron emitted in the forward direction may well be about 3×10^9 cm. per sec.

FIGURE 2.8. In 1932 James Chadwick was the first physicist to posit the existence of the neutron. Photograph ©The Nobel Foundation.

Neutrons—the uncharged elementary particles that are actually just slightly more massive (about 1.0008 times) than protons and whose fast variety has velocity of about 1.4×10^9 cm/sec—do the splitting of nuclei of the heaviest natural elements in chain reactions.

In a lecture on September 11, 1933, Rutherford concluded that "anyone who looked for a source of power in the transformation of the atoms was talking moonshine" (Lanouette 1992:133). One man's irritation with this opinion had enormous consequences for the transformation of the 20th century. Leo Szilard (1898–1964)—a brilliant Hungarian physicist, Einstein's student in Berlin, and since April 1933 an exile in London—was an extraordinary intellectual adventurer whose original ideas swept a number of scientific disciplines, from designing with Einstein a refrigerator without any moving parts to probing several branches of modern biology.

But Szilard's innate inability to concentrate for long on a single research topic made him, in Lanouette's apt label, a genius in the shadows. After reading Rutherford's verdict, Szilard began to think, in his usual way while soaking in a bathtub or walking in a park, about the ways to prove that the *doyen* of nuclear physics was wrong. Szilard's *eureka* came as he stopped for a streetlight on Southampton Row:

> As I was waiting for the light to change and as the light changed to green and I crossed the street, it suddenly occurred to me that if we

could find an element which is split by neutrons and which would emit *two* neutrons when it absorbed *one* neutron, such an element, if assembled in sufficiently large mass, could sustain a nuclear reaction. I didn't see at the moment just how one would go about finding such an element or what experiments would be needed, but the idea never left me. (cited in Lanouette 1992:133)

And so it was that on September 12, 1932—little more than six months after Chadwick's publication of neutron discovery, and more than six years before the first neutron-driven fission took place in a German laboratory—Leo Szilard conceived the basic idea of nuclear chain reaction. This was a fundamental conceptual breakthrough, as Szilard's idea encompassed both the nuclear chain reaction and the critical mass of a fissionable element to initiate it and to sustain it. Unable to get any financial support to investigate the idea, Szilard applied for a British patent on March 12, 1934, identifying (using incorrect data) beryllium as the most likely element to be split by neutrons, but also naming uranium and thorium as other possible candidates.

During the subsequent years Szilard—preoccupied with the chain reaction idea but unwilling to concentrate on one task—was unable either to get a major research position to pursue the concept or to interest industrial leaders in researching its potential. His only success was that in 1936 the British authorities agreed to keep his patent secret in order to prevent its use in developing a nuclear weapon by a hostile power. That possibility appeared all too real as 1938 turned into 1939. In December 1938 Otto Hahn (1879–1968) and Fritz Strassman (1902–1980) irradiated uranium by slow neutrons and produced several new isotopes other than the transuranic elements whose formation was seen in previous experiments.

In their first report of these tests, they noted that this was "against all previous experience in nuclear physics" (Hahn and Strassman 1939b:15). Unable to explain this outcome, Hahn turned for help to Lise Meitner (1878–1969), Germany's first (Viennese-born) professor of physics with whom he collaborated in research on radioactivity since 1907 (figure 2.9). Their association ended with Meitner's forced exile to Sweden in July 1938 after her Austrian passport, which gave her protection against the Nazi anti-Jewish laws, became invalid with Hitler's annexation of Austria. Meitner, and her nephew Otto Frisch (1904–1979), at that time on a visit to Sweden from his exile in Copenhagen, interpreted the result correctly as nuclear fission: Frisch chose the term (*Kernspaltung* in German) after William Arnold, a visiting biologist, told him that was the proper way to describe dividing bacteria.

Hahn and Strassman conclusively stated that their experiments produced barium isotopes (atomic number 56) from uranium (atomic number 92) in a paper published on February 10, 1939, in *Naturwissenschaften* (Hahn and Strass-

FIGURE 2.9. Otto Hahn (left, in his office during the 1930s) and Lise Meitner (right, photograph from the late 1920s). Images courtesy of the Hahn-Meitner-Institut in Berlin.

man 1939a); a day later correct theoretical interpretation by Meitner and Frisch appeared in *Nature*:

> It seems therefore possible that the uranium nucleus has only small stability of form, and may, after neutron capture, divide itself into two nuclei of roughly equal size . . . These two nuclei will repel each other and should gain a total kinetic energy of c. 200 Mev, as calculated from nuclear radius and charge. (Meitner and Frisch 1939:239)

Five years later Hahn was honored for his discovery with a Nobel Prize in Chemistry; the award was revealed only in November 1945, and the award ceremony took place a year later (Hahn 1946). Meitner received neither the prize nor Hahn's generous recognition for her contributions: their long collaboration, in which she was often the intellectual leader, and the letters they exchanged between December 1938 and spring 1939 leave no doubt about Hahn's subsequent biased reinterpretation of actual events (Hahn 1968; Sime 1996; Rife 1999).

As pointed out by Meitner and Frisch, nuclear fission could liberate a stunning amount of energy, and physicists in Germany, the United Kingdom, France, the United States, and USSR immediately concluded that this reality could eventually lead to an entirely new weapon of an unprecedented destructive power. Philip Morrison, who was in 1939 Robert Oppenheimer's graduate student, recalls how he and his colleagues in Berkeley sketched "with a crudely correct vision . . . an arrangement we imagined efficacious for a bomb" and how their mentor in a letter on February 2, 1939, noted "that a ten centimeter cube of uranium deuteride . . . might very well blow itself to hell" (Morrison 1995:42–43). Soon afterward Szilard (together with Walter Zinn) and Enrico Fermi (1901–1954), together with Herbert Anderson, observed the release of fast neutrons. This new reality prompted Szilard to draft his famous letter to President Roosevelt that Albert Einstein signed and sent on August 2, 1939.

This intervention led eventually (during the summer of 1942) to the establishment of the Manhattan Engineer District (known simply as the Manhattan Project) and to the world's first fission bombs. The world's most expensive research project thus began in order to develop nuclear weapons before Germany did so. The fear was understandable: Germans had some of the world's leading nuclear physicists and access to uranium (from mines in the occupied Czechoslovakia), and they began their formal nuclear research program ahead of the United States. Manhattan Project's success opened up the intertwined path of nuclear arms race and fission-powered electricity generation, both being developments of immense complexity that have been portrayed too often in simplistic or biased terms. One retrospective judgment that cannot be challenged is that the extreme expectations were not—fortunately and regrettably, as the case may be—fulfilled. Nuclear weapons did not obliterate, as widely feared, the late 20th-century civilization, and nuclear fission did not furnish it, as was perhaps equally widely expected, with an unlimited source of inexpensive energy.

Nuclear Weapons

On September 17, 1942, Colonel Leslie Groves (figure 2.10)—an Army engineer who supervised the construction of the Pentagon and who was made Brigadier General on September 23, 1942—was named to head the Manhattan Project. Just two days after his appointment he secured the site of the first uranium isotope separation plant at Oak Ridge, Tennessee. Land for the bomb-making Los Alamos laboratory was purchased in November, and in December Robert Oppenheimer (1904–1967) was appointed the scientific director of the project (figure 2.10). This was done against the objections of the scientific leaders of the project, who thought Oppenheimer to be an administratively inexperienced theoretician, and even more so against the wishes of the Army Intelligence officers, who doubted his loyalty (Goldberg 1992). The project's challenges and achievements can be followed in fascinating personal reminiscences (Compton 1956; Hawkins, Truslow, and Smith, 1961; Groves 1962), historical accounts (Lamont 1965; Groueff 1967; Rhodes 1986), and extensive

FIGURE 2.10. The two men who were in charge of the Manhattan Project: General Leslie Groves (left) and physicist Robert Oppenheimer (right). Photographs are available from the Archival Research Catalog of the U.S. National Archives and Records Administration.

files on the World Wide Web (Manhattan Project Heritage Preservation Association 2004; Avalon Project 2003; NWA 1999).

The first sustained nuclear chain reaction was directed by Enrico Fermi at the University of Chicago on December 2, 1942. The first reactor was a large assembly of precisely machined long graphite bricks piled atop one another (hence Fermi's name for it, a pile) in a squash court underneath the (later demolished) football stadium bleachers at the University of Chicago (Allardice and Trapnell 1946; Wattenberg 1992). Thousands pseudospheres of metallic uranium and uranium oxide were emplaced in these bricks to form a precise three-dimensional lattice. Graphite acted as a moderator to slow down the released neutrons, and the control rods inserted into premachined slots to stop the reactor from working were strips of wood covered with neutron-absorbing cadmium foil. Fermi calculated that the pile would become critical after emplacing the 56th layer, and the 57th layer was laid on December 1, 1942.

The next day's experiments began at 9:45 A.M. with gradual withdrawal of control rods and proceeded through a series of small adjustments toward the criticality. After lunch and after a further series of adjustments, Fermi gave the order to George Weil to pull out the final control rod by another 30 cm. This was done at 3:25 P.M., and Fermi said to Arthur Compton, who stood at his side, "This is going to do it. Now it will become self-sustaining. The trace will climb and continue to climb, it will not level off" (Allardice and Trapnell

1946:21). And it did not, as the recording pen began to trace an exponential line and continued to do so for 28 min before the world's first nuclear reactor was shut down at 3:53 P.M. Szilard was on Fermi's team of 15 physicists who succeeded in using moderated neutrons to split uranium nuclei, and within days after this achievement he signed over his fission patents to the U.S. government.

Los Alamos scientists concentrated first on a weapon to be exploded by firing one part of a critical mass of ^{235}U into another, a design that did not need full-scale testing. Then they turned to a more complicated design of a plutonium bomb whose test became the first fission-powered explosion. Plutonium 239—produced by the irradiation of ^{238}U with neutrons in large water-cooled graphite-moderated reactors that were designed by Eugene Wigner (1902–1995) and built at Hanford, Washington—was used to make the first nuclear bomb. Its core was a 6-kg sphere of the metal that was designed to be imploded, compressed uniformly to supercriticality by explosive lenses. The test took place at Alamogordo, New Mexico, at 5:29:45 A.M. on July 16, 1945, and the explosion was equivalent to about 21 kt of TNT (figure 2.11).

Philip Morrison, who was a member of the Los Alamos group that measured the first bomb's critical mass, watched the explosion from the south bank of the base camp. He saw first

FIGURE 2.11. The first nuclear explosive device for the test code-named Trinity by Robert Oppenheimer being positioned at Alamogordo, New Mexico, in July 1945 (left). Mushroom cloud rises above Nagasaki on August 9, 1945 (right). Photographs are from the Archival Research Catalog of the U.S. National Archives and Records Administration.

a brilliant violet glow entering my eyes by reflection from the ground and from the surroundings generally . . . Immediately after this brilliant violet flash, which was somewhat blinding, I observed through the welding glass, centered at the direction of the tower an enormous and brilliant disk of white light . . . Beginning at $T = +2$ to 3 seconds, I observed the somewhat yellowed disk beginning to be eaten into from below by dark obscuring matter . . . In a matter of a few seconds more the disk had nearly stopped growing horizontally and was beginning to extend on a vertical direction . . . This turbulent red column rose straight up several thousand feet in a few seconds growing a mushroom-like head of the same kind. (Morrison 1945:1)

In retrospect it is clear that the uncharted theoretical and engineering road that led to the first nuclear weapon was traversed in a very short period of time (in less than 28 months after the project's formal start) thanks both to unprecedented concentrations of intellectual power and to enormous expenditures of energy. The project's participants included eight men who got received Nobel prizes before or during WWII (ranging from Niels Bohr in 1922 to Isidore Rabi in 1944) and 12 others who received them, in physics or chemistry, between 1951 (Glenn Seaborg) and 1989 (Norman Ramsey). Enormous energy needs were due to the separation of fissile isotope of uranium ^{235}U, which represents only 0.72% of the metal's natural mass that is dominated by ^{238}U. This was done electromagnetically by a process developed by Ernest O. Lawrence (1901–1958), and later also by thermal diffusion that was developed by Philip Abelson (1913–2004).

Oak Ridge's two uranium enrichment plants furnished the roughly 50 kg of uranium needed for the 12.5 kt bomb that destroyed Hiroshima at 8:15 A.M. on August 6, 1945. The bomb, delivered by a B-29 from Tinian, was dropped by a parachute, and it exploded about 580 m above the ground. Its blast wave (maximum speed of 440 m/s) carried about 50% of all energy liberated by the chain reaction and caused massive structural damage over a wide area, destroying all wooden structures within 2 km of the hypocenter and smashing reinforced concrete structures up to about 0.5 km away. The bomb's thermal energy was about a third of the total energy release, and the emitted infrared radiation caused severe burns (Committee 1981).

These two effects, the blast wave and the infrared radiation, were responsible for tens of thousands of virtually instant deaths, while the ionizing radiation caused both instant and delayed casualties. The best available casualty count is 118,661 civilian deaths up to August 10, 1946; military casualties and later deaths attributable to radiation exposure raise the total to about 140,000. A larger (22 kt) plutonium bomb that was dropped at 11:02 A.M. of August 9, 1945, on Nagasaki caused fewer than 70,000 casualties. For comparison, the firebombing of Tōkyō on March 9 and 10, 1945, killed 120,000 (Jansen 2000).

Bombs developed in order to preempt German nuclear supremacy were thus used for an entirely different, and initially quite unanticipated, purpose. Undoubtedly, they helped to speed up the end of the Pacific war. Arguably, they saved more lives than they took: this view is easily defensible particularly given the enormous casualties from the conquest of Iwo Jima and Okinawa and given the continuing calls for Japan's resistance by some of its military leaders (Jansen 2000).

And, regrettably, these nuclear bombings helped to launch two generations of dangerous superpower conflict. Arguments about the necessity and morality of using nuclear weapons preoccupied many physicists even before the first device was tested. These debates, and efforts to come up with effective international controls of nuclear weapons, have continued in the open ever since August 1945. Isidore Rabi (1898–1988), one of the key participants in the Manhattan Project, summed up the feeling of most of the bomb's creators on the 40th anniversary of Los Alamos founding when he entitled his speech "How Well We Meant" (Sherwin 1985).

Philip Morrison—who helped to assemble the bombs at Tinian in the Marianas before they were loaded on planes and who was in a small party of scientists who entered Japan on the first day of U.S. occupation—put the tragedy into a clear historical perspective by contrasting the effect of "old fires" (set by massive and repeated drops of jelly gasoline by huge fleets of high-flying B-29 bombers) with the new destruction:

> A single bomber was now able to destroy a good-size city, leaving hundreds of thousands dead. Yet there on the ground, among all those who cruelly suffered and died, there was not all that much difference between old fire and new. Both ways brought unimagined inferno . . . the difference between the all-out raids made on the cities of Japan and those two nuclear attacks remains less in the nature of the scale of the human tragedy than in the chilling fact that now it was much easier to destroy the populous cities of humankind. (Morrison 1995:45)

At least two facts are indisputable: until his death, Harry Truman, who gave the order to drop the bombs, firmly believed that he did so in order to destroy Japan's capacity to make war and to bring the earliest possible conclusion to the conflict (Messer 1985), and postwar examinations of the German nuclear research showed that Germany's physicists did not make any significant progress toward making a weapon. And we also know that this lack of progress was not because of any deliberate procrastination in order to prevent these weapons falling under Hitler's command: transcripts of conversations of German nuclear physicists that were secretly recorded during their internment in an English manor in 1945 show that even Werner Heisenberg, the leader of

German nuclear effort, had a very poor understanding how a fission bomb would work (Bernstein 1993; Bethe 1993).

The wartime USSR also had an active nuclear fission program, but its first atomic weapon, which was tested on August 29, 1949, was based on detailed information about the U.S. bomb that the Soviet secret service obtained during the second half of 1945 from Klaus Fuchs, a British physicist who participated in the Manhattan Project (Khariton and Smirnov 1993). The second bomb of Soviet design, smaller yet more powerful, was tested in 1951. The age of thermonuclear weapons began on November 1, 1952, with a 10.4 Mt blast at the Enewetak Atoll when the United States tested its first hydrogen device. Nine months later, on August 12, 1953, the USSR was the first country to test a hydrogen charge that could be used as a bomb (the first U.S. device was an immobile building-sized assembly weighing about 82 t). These events marked the opening rounds of four decades of superpower arms race that ended only with the collapse of the USSR in 1991.

The most powerful thermonuclear bomb that was tested by the USSR over the Novaya Zemlya archipelago on October 30, 1961, had an equivalent of 50 Mt of TNT. Its explosion, visible for thousands of kilometers, released 20 times as much energy as all the bombs dropped during WWII, its mushroom cloud stretching across 20 km and its shock wave circling the planet three times (Stone 1999). And less than 15 months later Nikita Khrushchev revealed that the country had an untested 100 Mt bomb. Between 1959 and 1961, during the three years of its peak nuclear weapon production, the United States made almost 19,500 new warheads at a rate of 75 a day (Norris and Arkin 1994). In total, the country produced some 70,000 nuclear weapons between 1945 and 1990; the USSR, about 55,000.

The maximum numbers of all kinds of nuclear weapons reached 32,500 in the United States in 1967 and 45,000 in the USSR in 1986; just over a third of this total (more than 13,000 in the United States and more than 11,000 in the USSR) were strategic weapons (mostly between 100 and 550 kt/warhead) that targeted major cities and military installations. These weapons could be delivered by the triad of launchers: bombers, submarine-based missiles, and land-based missiles (NRDC 2002). Long-range bombers were the first means of delivery (B-29s carried the bombs dropped on Japan), and by the end of the 20th century their most advanced varieties include the Soviet Tupolev 95 and the U.S. B-2 stealth planes.

The first nuclear submarine was commissioned on September 30, 1954, and by the end of the Cold War the submarine-launched missiles (SLBMs) were dominated by powerful Soviet-built SS-N-18 and American Tridents. And beginning in 1959 with the American Atlas 1, and then continuing with Titan 1 and 2 and Minuteman, and in the USSR with SS-24 and SS-25, hundreds of intercontinental ballistic missiles (ICBMs) were emplaced in fortified underground silos in bases largely in the Great Plains and mountain states in the United States and in both European and Asian parts of the USSR (NRDC 2002). Both ICBMs and SLBMs initially carried single warheads, but later they were tipped with multiple independently targeted reentry vehicles (MIRVs); for example, SS-18 carries 10 warheads of 550–750 kt, and the latest Peacekeeper (LGM-118A) launchers have ten 300 kt warheads.

Accuracy of ICBMs (measured in terms of circular error probability, CEP, the diameter of a circle within which half of the missiles would hit) improved thanks to better inertial guidance, midcourse correction, and eventually, terminal homing using missile-borne radar and satellite images: CEP of the U.S. ICBMs decreased from around 1,000 m to less than 100 m. Testing of the warheads was an exercise in risky global contamination. During the 1950s all of the Soviet and British weapon tests and nearly 90% of the U.S. tests were done in the atmosphere, introducing relatively large amounts of radionuclides that were, inevitably, diffused worldwide and contributed to higher rates of miscarriages, birth defects, and thyroid cancers.

This growing danger was eliminated (although not completely) in August 1963 when the United States and the USSR signed a Limited Test Ban Treaty that ended their atmospheric explosions of nuclear weapons (Cousins 1972). Andrei Sakharov (1921–1989), the leading creator of the Soviet hydrogen bomb, contributed greatly to Nikita Khrushchev's acceptance of the ban (Lourie 2002). However, France and China continued their atmospheric tests until, respectively, 1974 and 1980: by that time 528 weapons had been experimentally exploded in the atmosphere (NRDC 2004). The last underground tests in the United States and the USSR were done, respectively, in 1993 and 1990.

Proliferation of nuclear weapons beyond the two superpowers began with the United Kingdom (fission device in 1952, fusion bomb in 1957). France and China were added, respectively, in 1960 and 1964, and the beginnings of Israel's still unacknowledged arsenal date also to the 1960s. India's first test took place in 1974, South Africa acquired its first (and publicly unacknowledged) nuclear weapons by 1982, and Pakistan announced its first series of underground nuclear tests on May 28, 1998. Other nations, including Iraq, Iran, Libya, and North Korea, also tried (and some nearly succeeded) to build nuclear weapons during the last two decades of the 20th century. Four countries—South Africa and the three successor states of the USSR (Ukraine, Belarus, and Kazakhstan)—renounced their nuclear status, but at least three times as many have the intellectual, although not necessarily the technical, capacity to produce them.

The real purpose of the monstrous nuclear arsenal held by the two superpowers was to deter its use by the other side. There is no doubt that the possession of nuclear weapons (the MAD, mutually assured destruction, concept) was the main reason why the United States and the USSR did not fight a thermonuclear war. While the weapons were abominable but effective peace-keepers, the overall level of nuclear stockpiles—eventually nearly 25,000 strategic nuclear warheads with aggregate capacity over 5 Gt, equivalent to nearly half a million Hiroshima bombs—went far beyond any rational deterrent level. My very conservative estimate is that at least 5% of all U.S. and Soviet commercial energy consumed between 1950 and 1990 was claimed by developing and amassing these weapons and the means of their delivery.

And the burden of these activities continues with the safeguarding and cleanup of contaminated production sites. The U.S. nuclear weapons complex eventually encompassed about 5,000 facilities at 16 major and more than 100 smaller sites, and estimated costs of its cleanup, maintenance, and surveillance operations have been rising steadily (Crowley and Ahearne 2002). And a much greater investment would be needed to clean up and to safeguard the more severely contaminated nuclear weapons assembly and testing sites in Russia and Kazakhstan. The former USSR has at least 221 major military nuclear facilities that extensively contaminated surrounding areas (GAO 1995).

Even so, given the potentially horrific toll of a thermonuclear exchange between the United States and the USSR—Natural Resources Defence Council modeling shows that a major U.S. thermonuclear "counterforce" attack on Russian nuclear forces would kill 8–12 million people and a thermonuclear "countervalue" attack on Russian cities would cause 50 million deaths (McKinzie et al. 2001)—one could argue that the overall cost:benefit ratio of the nuclear arms race was acceptable. In contrast, there are no positive aspects of unchecked nuclear proliferation, particularly when there are possibilities of fissionable materials, weapon components, or complete weapons coming into the possession of terrorist groups or when a country such as North Korea chooses the threat of nuclear aggression as a tool of its foreign policy. Moreover, research performed during the last two decades of the 20th century demonstrated that effective defense against limited nuclear attacks will not be achieved in the near future: development of antimissile missiles did not produce any deployable system before the year 2000.

Nuclear weapons obviously transformed the great strategic relationships during the second half of the 20th century. At the same time, potential for their use by terrorists and blackmail-minded states appeared to be higher than at any time since 1945. And so at the century's end, we were as much in the need of an effective, and truly international, nuclear policy as we were half a century earlier at the very beginning of the nuclear era. Without any doubt, the best outcome would be if Philip Morrison's hope were to come true:

> The danger remains, and will remain until the powers (now almost a dozen of them) realize that practical arms control is the best way out of the dilemma of lawless in weapons in the time of modern science. Every

day I hope for a world move to end the danger by realized mutual control. I am an optimist still, against all my experience, but confirmed by all reason. (P. Morrison, personal communication, May 2004)

Electricity from Fission

Electricity generation powered by nuclear fission owes its genesis entirely to the advances achieved during the unprecedented dash to develop nuclear weapons, and the two endeavors remained closely related during the subsequent decades: countries that pioneered fission-based electricity generation—United States, United Kingdom, USSR, and France—were also the countries with nuclear arsenals. Concerns and fears surrounding the matters of nuclear armaments have thus cast their shadows over the peaceful development of fission for electricity generation. And by the time the demise of superpower confrontation finally weakened that link, commercial nuclear generation was experiencing many difficulties unrelated to its association with weapons—and the problems of nuclear weapon proliferation carried under the cover of commercial electricity generation became perhaps even more acute.

Conceptual foundations of fission reactors were laid out clearly by Enrico Fermi and Leo Szilard in their patent application for "neutronic reactor," which they filed on December 19, 1944, and which was granted and published only more than 10 years later (figure 2.12). The key physical prerequisite of the process was obvious:

> In order to attain such a self-sustaining chain reaction in a system of practical size, the ratio of the number of neutrons produced in one generation by the fissions, to the original number of neutrons initiating the fissions, must be known to be greater than unity after all neutron losses are deducted . . . We have discovered certain essential principles required for the successful construction and operation of self-sustaining neutron chain reacting systems (known as neutronic reactors) with the production of power in the form of heat. (Fermi and Szilard 1955:1)

The patent anticipated all principal types of future power reactors whose common major components include fissile fuel, moderator, control rods, blanket, and a reactor vessel to hold of these parts. The moderator is a material of low atomic weight used to slow down the neutrons in order to increase the probability of their encounters with fissile nuclei. The coolant is a fluid used to remove the heat generated by the chain reaction and to use for steam production for thermal electricity generation. Water makes both an excellent moderator and an efficient coolant, particularly when under pressure. The control rods are made of materials that capture neutrons, and their removal

May 17, 1955

E. FERMI ET AL

2,708,656

NEUTRONIC REACTOR

Filed Dec. 19, 1944

27 Sheets—Sheet 7

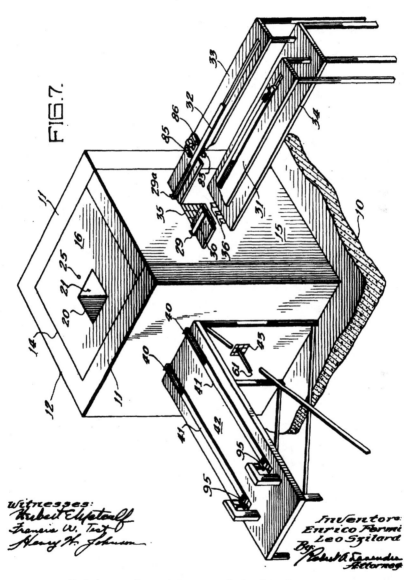

FIG.7.

FIGURE 2.12. Basic layout of neutronic reactor depicted in the U.S. Patent 2,708,656 filed by Fermi and Szilard in December 1944. The core (*14*) containing uranium and graphite stands on a concrete foundation (*10*) and is encased in concrete walls (*11*). Control rods (*32*) rest on rod platforms (*31*) ready to be inserted through apertures (*29*); in modern reactors, they are inserted from the top. Image is from the U.S. Patent Office.

and insertion start and terminate the chain reaction. The blanket is a reflector that scatters neutrons back into the reactor core, and reinforced vessels that hold the entire assemblies are designed to prevent the leakage of radioactive materials as well as to withstand considerable impacts from the outside.

Fermi and Szilard's patent envisaged a variety of reactors: those moderated by heavy water (D_2O) and using natural uranium (the combination chosen during the late 1950s for CANDU (CANada Deuterium Uranium) reactors of Canada's national nuclear program), those cooled by a gas (a method favored by the British national program), and those using enriched uranium with a light water moderator, the system that, starting during the late 1950s, became the principal choice of the U.S. nuclear industry. While nuclear fission was a new form of energy conversion, heat generated by the splitting of heavy nuclei had to produce steam to be used in the same way as in any thermal station, that is, expanded in turbines to drive large generators. Fermi and Szilard outlined the basic options of recovering the heat released by fission in both low- and high-pressure systems and by using exchangers for indirect steam generation as well producing steam directly in tubes passing through the reactor core in a boiling water reactor.

In 1944 Alvin Weinberg suggested using high-pressure water both as a coolant and moderator for a reactor fueled with slightly enriched in fissionable ^{235}U. This led to practical designs of pressurized water reactors (PWR) that were chosen first for submarine propulsion. A technique of unusual complexity was then transformed into a highly reliable means of providing steam for large-scale commercial thermal electricity generation in just two decades. Britain was the nuclear pioneer with its 10-year program of nuclear power plant construction announced in 1955 (Bertin 1957). Calder Hall (4 × 23 MW) in West Cumbria—using natural uranium metal fuel rods encased in finned magnesium alloy and pressurized carbon dioxide (CO_2) for cooling—began generating electricity on October 17, 1956 (Jay 1956). The station was shut down after more than 46 years of operation on March 31, 2003. Ten stations of the Magnox type (total capacity of about 4.8 GW) were commissioned between 1962 and 1971. The United Kingdom's second power program (totaling nearly 9 GW) was based on advanced gas-cooled reactors using slightly enriched UO_2 pellets contained in steel tubes.

The industry's American origins had their genesis in the U.S. Navy's nuclear submarine program. This development succeeded largely thanks to Hyman Rickover's (1900–1986) relentless effort to apply reactor drive to submarine propulsion (Rockwell 1992). The first nuclear-powered submarine, *Nautilus*, was put to sea in January 1955, but already 18 months before that the U.S. Atomic Energy Commission assigned the country's first civilian nuclear power project to Rickover, who used the same kind of GE's 1 in order to build the generating station in Shippingport, Pennsylvania. The reactor reached initial criticality on December 2, 1957, more than a year after Calder Hall. Real commercial breakthrough came only a decade later: American utilities ordered only 12 reactors before 1965, but 83 between 1965 and 1969, with PWRs as their dominant choice.

In these reactors water, pressurized to as much as 16 MPa, circulates through the core (packed with fuel in zirconium steel tubes) in a closed loop, where it is heated to between 300 and 320°C and transfers its energy content in a heat exchanger to a secondary circuit whose steam is used to generate electricity. PWRs use ordinary water both as a coolant and as a moderator. France also chose the design as the basis of its bold effort to produce most of its electricity from fission. In pressurized heavy water reactors of Canada's national program, D_2O is both a moderator and a coolant. By the time of OPEC's first round of sharp crude oil price increases during the fall of 1973, more than 400 reactors were in operation, under construction, or in various planning stages in 20 countries. OPEC's actions appeared to benefit the industry that would sever the link between fossil fuels and electricity, and during the 1970s nuclear enthusiasts expected that the world's electric supply will be soon dominated be increasingly more affordable nuclear energy.

There was also a worldwide consensus that water-cooled reactors are just a temporary choice to be replaced before the end of the century by liquid-metal fast breeder reactors (LMFBR). Their dominant design uses nonmoderated neutrons to convert the much more abundant but nonfissionable ^{238}U to fissile ^{239}Pu. The source of these neutrons is fuel that is enriched to a high degree with ^{235}U (15–30% compared to between 3% and 5% in water-cooled reactors) and is surrounded by a blanket of ^{238}U. Sodium was the liquid metal of choice due its cheapness, and excellent heat transfer and an LMFBR was eventually expected to produce at least 20% more fuel than it consumed. LMFBR represents one of the most costly and most spectacular technical failures of the 20th century. Other prominent examples are the quest for mass-produced electric cars and the development of synthetic fuels in the OPEC-squeezed United States of the early 1980s. What makes the breeder case so remarkable is an extraordinarily high degree of consensus regarding its desirability and its rapid impact.

The technique's origin coincides with the birth of the nuclear era: Szilard had anticipated breeders (and used the term) already in 1943; Alvin Weinberg and Harry Soodak published the first design of sodium-cooled breeder in 1945, and a small experimental breeder reactor near Arco, Idaho, was the world's first nuclear electricity generator: on December 21, 1951, it powered four 200-W lightbulbs, and the next day it lit the entire building in which it was located (Mitchell and Turner 1971). As the first (PWR) nuclear era was unfolding, Weinberg (1973:18) concluded that there is not "much doubt that a nuclear breeder will be successful" and that it is "rather likely that breeders will be man's ultimate energy source." During the 1970s LMFBR projects were under way in the United States, USSR, United Kingdom, France, Germany, Italy, and Japan. GE expected that breeders would account for half of all new large thermal generation plants in the United States by the year 2000 (Murphy 1974).

But in the United States these hopes lasted little more than 10 years. Declining cost of uranium and the rising costs of reprocessing facilities needed to separate plutonium from spent nuclear fuel made the option clearly uneconomical (von Hippel and Jones 1997). The U.S. breeder program was abandoned in 1983, but other countries continued to spend billions. France embarked on the construction of a full-scale breeder, the 1,200 MW *Superphénix* at Creys-Malville, its designers confident that its success will bring a virtually inexhaustible source of energy (Vendryes 1977). But the reactor, completed in 1986, had many accidents and operated at full power for only 287 days during the following 11 years; on February 2, 1998, the French Prime Minister confirmed its final shutdown after spending about US$10 billion and another US$2.5 billion for the decommissioning. Similarly, Japan's breeder (at Monju on the Tsuruga Peninsula) commissioned in 1994 was closed after 640 kg of liquid sodium leaked from its secondary coolant loop on December 8, 1995 (JNCDI 2000).

At the same time—and despite new proposals for inherently safe reactors—it became clear that the second nuclear era will not begin in the foreseeable future. During the 1990s nuclear generating capacities reached their peaks in all Western countries, and their gradual decline appeared inevitable. France was the only affluent economy with a large and successful program. The two keys to this achievement were public acceptance of the technique and the decision by Electricité de France (EdF) to base the entire program on standardized designs of PWRs and entire plants. The company eventually built 59 reactors sited at 20 coastal and riverine locations around the country. EdF also chose to reprocess the spent nuclear fuel in order to separate fissile ^{239}Pu formed by neutron capture from uranium and then to mix it with depleted uranium to produce mixed oxide fuel. This is more expensive than once-through use of uranium, but it reduces the volume of spent fuel.

During the late 1990s EdF's stations provided nearly 80% of the country's electricity and also generated steady export earnings. But even EdF placed its last order for a new nuclear station in 1991, and during the late 1990s the only two regions with new reactors under construction were East Asia (PWRs in Japan, China, and South Korea) and India (pressurized heavy water reactors). In Europe outside France and in North America, nuclear generation was in stagnation or retreat. In retrospect, it is obvious that the commercial development of nuclear generation should have been more deliberate and that far too little attention was paid to the public acceptance as well as to the long-term disposal of radioactive wastes (Cowan 1990; Smil 2003).

Conclusions about the economic benefits of fission-produced electricity were always questionable as they ignore enormous subsidies spent by many governments on nuclear R&D and a unique treatment of catastrophic risks. Between 1952 and 1998 the Atomic Energy of Canada received subsidies of CD$(1998)15.8 billion; at a 15% rate of return, this was equivalent to an opportunity cost of slightly more than CD$(1998)200 billion (Martin 1998). The U.S. nuclear industry received more than 96% of all monies, about $(1998)145 billion, that were appropriated by Congress between 1947 and 1998 for energy-related R&D (NIRS 1999). Opportunity cost of that investment would be on the order of $1 trillion.

And the U.S. nuclear industry could not have been launched without the Price-Anderson Act, section 170 of the Atomic Energy Act passed by the Congress in 1954, that reduced private liability by guaranteeing public compensation in the event of a catastrophic accident in commercial nuclear generation (USDOE 2001). No other energy supplier has benefited from such sweeping governmental guarantees. And we must also consider the eventual costs of decommissioning the plants (Farber and Weeks 2001) and, perhaps the greatest challenge for the nuclear industry, securing highly radioactive wastes for unprecedented spans of time, 100–1,000 years.

Alvin Weinberg, one of the architects of the nuclear era, asked a crucial question: "Is mankind prepared to exert the eternal vigilance needed to ensure proper and safe operation of its nuclear energy system?" (Weinberg 1972:34). In retrospect, Weinberg concluded that "had safety been the primary design criterion, rather than compactness and simplicity that guided the design of submarine PWR, I suspect we might have hit upon what we now call inherently safe reactors at the beginning of the first nuclear era . . ." (Weinberg 1994: 21). Even more important, promoters of nuclear electricity generation did not believe Enrico Fermi's warning that the public may not accept an energy source that produces large amounts of radioactivity as well as fissile materials that might come into the possession of terrorists. This warning seemed more relevant during the last decade of the 20th century than it was when Fermi made it before the end of WWII. The plutonium route that requires continuous transporting of the spent fuel to reprocessing plants and the return of mixed oxide fuel to generating stations is even more vulnerable to terrorist action.

Public perceptions of unacceptable risk were boosted by an accident at the Three Mile Island plant in Pennsylvania in 1979 (Denning 1985) and seven years later by an incomparably worse accidental core meltdown and the release of radioactivity during the Chernobyl disaster in Ukraine in May 1986 (Hohenemser 1988). This accident arose from the combination of a flawed reactor design and unacceptable operating procedures by inadequately trained personnel (WNA 2001). Steam explosion and fire released about 5% of the reactor's radioactive core into the atmosphere, and the drifting plume contaminated large areas of eastern and northern Europe. Actual health consequences were far less tragic than the exaggerated early fears, but the still continuing toll was considerable: 31 people were killed almost instantly or shortly after the accident,

134 were treated for the acute radiation syndrome, and 14 years after the accident there were 1,800 cases of additional thyroid cancer, mostly in children, and widespread feelings of stress and anxiety—but no evidence of higher overall cancer incidence or mortality (NEA 2002).

The fact that containment vessels and stricter operating procedures would make such an event extremely unlikely in any U.S. and Western European reactors made little difference: the event clearly reinforced the public perception of nuclear power being inherently unsafe. Neither the rising demand for electricity nor the growing concerns about CO_2 emissions were able to change nuclear power's fortunes: the expansive stage of the first nuclear era in the Western nations ended much sooner than the technique's proponents ever envisaged (Weinberg 1994). But as most of the era's stations were still in operation by the century's end, nuclear generation was making a substantial contribution to the world's electricity supply (Beck 1999; IAEA 2001).

By the end of 2000 the world had 438 nuclear power plants with a total net installed capacity of 351 GW, or about 11% of the global total. But because of their high operation reliability, reactors had availability rates significantly higher than fossil-fueled or hydro units, and hence they generated about 16% of the world's electricity in the year 2000 (IAEA 2001). This made them almost as important contributors as all of the world's hydro stations. But unlike coal-fired or hydro generation, nuclear generation was highly concentrated: just five countries—United States, France, Japan, Germany, and Russia—produced about 70% of the world total. Nuclear reactors made the greatest difference in France, where they generated 76% of all electricity. Lithuania inherited the largest Soviet-built station in Ingalina, and so it came second, with nearly 74%. Belgium placed third (57%) and Japan fourth (33%), the U.S. share was 20%, Russia's 15%, India's 3%, and China's slightly more than 1% (IAEA 2001).

In retrospect, nuclear generation could be seen as a significant technical success: after all, roughly 700 million people that now live in the world's largest affluent economies derive about 25% of their electricity from splitting uranium, and in 15 European countries the share is higher than 25%. Losing this capacity would have serious economic and social consequence, and even its gradual replacement will call for enormous investment in new generation infrastructure. Many nuclear reactors achieved impressive annual load factors of more than 95% (compared to fossil-fueled units whose load factors generally do not surpass 70%), lifetime records of the best-performing stations are more than 85%, and the best national lifetime averages are close to 80%. Nuclear generation in North America, Western Europe, and Japan has had an enviable safety record, and even an alarmist interpretation of low-level radiation's effects results in additional mortality far lower than that attributable to particulate emissions from coal-fired power plants (Levy, Hammitt, and Spengler 2000). And by the late 1990s fission generation helped to lower the global carbon emissions by nearly 10%.

A different interpretation sees the technique as an irresponsibly hurried, excessively costly, and unnecessarily risky experiment—with no radiation dose too low to avoid health effects (Fairlie and 1997)—that has left too many technical problems (above all, the permanent disposal of radioactive wastes) unsolved and that has engendered unacceptable security concerns ranging from terrorist attacks on nuclear stations to weapons proliferation (Chapin et al. 2002; Molander and Nichols 1985). That is why my best assessment of the technique combines an approbatory adjective with a condemnatory noun: the 20th century's use of fission for electricity generation was a successful failure.

New Prime Movers

The three kinds of machines that dominated the world's mechanical power capacity during the 20th century were the legacy of the 1880s, the most inventive decade in history. Their widespread and indispensable uses shaped both the economic possibilities of nations and the conduct of everyday lives (see chapters 2 and 3 of *CTTC* for details). These innovations—internal combustion engines suitable for mobile applications, electric motors, and steam turbines—were rapidly improved soon after their introduction, and all of them were widely commercialized within a single generation. In contrast, there was only one new prime mover whose practical design was introduced and impressively advanced during the 20th century: the gas turbine. In less than two decades after its introduction, this machine transformed many facets of modern societies: without it there would be neither affordable long-distance flights nor inexpensive long-distance deliveries of natural gas.

The gas turbine (GT) is an internal combustion engine that can burn both gaseous and liquid fuels but that differs from Otto and Diesel engines in three fundamental ways (Bathie 1996; Langston and Opdyke 1997; Saravanamuttoo, Rogers, and Cohen 2001): compression of gas precedes the addition of heat in a combustor, the combustion process is continuous rather than intermittent, and energy from the hot air flow is extracted by a turbine (figure 2.13). The simplest connection between the turbine and the compressor is through a single shaft. In twin spool GTs a longer shaft rotates inside a larger diameter shaft as they connect to respective low- and high-pressure segments of the turbine and the compressor; triple spools include yet another, intermediate, stage.

Compressors are either centrifugal flow, with air aspired near the center of an impeller, or axial with air flowing along the engine's axis. GT's power is used in two ways: to drive the compressor and to produce additional useful work. In aviation turbojets, the air is compressed 20–35 times the atmospheric level, and its temperature is raised by more than 500°C. Afterward this air is forced through the combustion chamber, and its temperature more than dou-

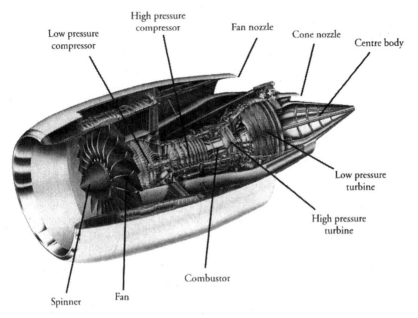

Low pressure
compressor

High pressure
compressor

Fan nozzle

Cone nozzle

Centre body

Low pressure
turbine

High pressure
turbine

Combustor

Spinner

Fan

FIGURE 2.13. Trimetric view of GE's GE90-115B aeroengine showing the principal components of modern gas turbines. Image courtesy of General Electric Aeroengines, Cincinnati, Ohio.

bles; some of the kinetic energy of this hot gas drives the turbine and the remainder leaves through the exhaust nozzle to generate a powerful forward thrust. In nonaviation GTs this energy is transmitted by a rotating shaft to drive electric generators, ship propellers, or compressors. Serious commercial development of these complex machines began in 1917 when Sanford Moss (1872–1946) set up a turbine research department at GE's steam turbine factory. Its first practical product was a turbo supercharger (using hot exhaust gases from a reciprocating engine to drive a centrifugal compressor) that boosted the power of Liberty piston engine from about 170 to 260 kW (GEAE 2002).

Supercharging was practiced more widely after WWI, but no fundamental progress in GT design took place until the 1930s, when the advances in aerodynamics and material science made it possible to come up with first commercially viable designs (Constant 1981; Islas 1999). Mass production of aeroturbines began during the 1950s with the advent of jet age, and machines for electricity generation began to find a growing market during the late 1960s with the need for more peaking power and for more flexible capacities. And during the 1980s the modification of jet engines for stationary applications and their use in land vehicles and ships began to blur the boundaries between the two turbine categories (Williams and Larson 1988).

The only prime movers with lower mass:power ratio than GTs are rocket engines. Their propulsion can develop enormous brief thrusts that can put payloads into terrestrial orbits or even let them escape the planet's gravity to follow the trajectories within the solar system. And at the beginning of August 2003, Voyager 1, launched in 1977, became the first spacecraft to approach, or perhaps already to exit, the region where the supersonic particle solar wind is slowed down by interstellar particles and that marks the outer limit of the solar system (Krimigis et al. 2003). Intensive engineering development of rockets capable of such achievements began only after WWI, and advances that were envisaged by the pioneers of rocket science—Konstantin Eduardovich Tsiolkovsky in Russia (1857–1935) and Hermann Oberth (1894–1989) in Germany—took place during the third quarter of the 20th century (von Braun and Ordway 1975; Neal, Lewis, and Winter 1995; Furniss 2001).

The most obvious indicator of advances in rocket propulsion is to compare Wernher von Braun's first and last rocket engines. In 1942 the ethanol-powered engine used to power the V-2 missile developed the sea-level thrust of about 250 kN. During its 68 s burn it imparted the maximum speed of 1.7 km/s to a 13.8-m-long missile whose explosive payload was less than 1 t. In contrast, during their 150 s burn, five bipropellant (kerosene and oxygen) F-1 engines of the first stage developed the sea-level thrust of about 35 MN (140 times that of V-2) that imparted to the nearly 109-m-tall Saturn V rocket velocity of 9.8 km/h as it sent Apollo 11 on its journey to the Moon (figure 2.14). Post-WWII

FIGURE 2.14. Kennedy Space Center, Cape Canaveral, Florida, July 16, 1969: fisheye lens view just after the ignition of Saturn V launching the Apollo 11 spacecraft on its journey to the Moon. NASA image 69PC-0421; available from Great Images in NASA.

development of rocket engines was driven primarily by military considerations: they propelled ICBMs and SLBMs, whose deployment transformed global strategy and great power politics. Manned space missions and unmanned exploration attracted a great deal of public attention but had little direct impact on ordinary lives.

In contrast, a long array of major socioeconomic transformations could not have taken place without rocket engines used as affordable prime movers in launching increasing numbers of communication and Earth observation satellites. The first crude weather satellites were launched in the early 1960s, and by the end of the 20th century there were hundreds of highly specialized assemblies circling the Earth, or matching the rate of its sidereal rotation 35,786 km above the equator and thus appearing to be parked in the geostationary mode. Perhaps the most rewarding use of images transmitted in real time by weather satellites was to minimize the U.S. hurricane casualties as early warnings give ample time for orderly evacuation of stricken areas. Telecommunication satellites drastically lowered the cost of long-distance telephone calls and mass data transfers, and global positioning systems made it possible to fix one's location on the Earth with a high degree of accuracy, a great advantage for tasks ranging from navigation to weapon targeting.

Turbines in Flight

The invention and early development of GTs for flight offers another remarkable example of parallel innovation (see chapters 4 and 5 of *CTTC* for the most famous pre-1900 examples involving Alexander Graham Bell and Elisha Gray, and Charles Hall and Paul Héroult). Interestingly, both leading inventors of jet engines—Frank Whittle in the United Kingdom and Hans Pabst von Ohain in Germany—started as outsiders and only after years of independent, and initially frustratingly slow, effort were their designs adopted and improved by major companies that developed them first for military applications. Frank Whittle (1907–1996) joined the U.K. Royal Air Force (RAF) as a boy apprentice in 1923 and became a pilot officer in 1928 (Golley and Whittle 1987). In the same year, during his last term at the RAF College, he began to think about radically new ways of propulsion, and in January 1930 he applied for his first gas engine patent (U.K. Patent 347,206) that outlined a very simple turbojet (figure 2.15).

There was no commercial interest in his invention, and when Whittle studied mechanical engineering at Cambridge University (1934–1936) the Air Ministry refused to pay the £5 renewal fee and the patent lapsed. While still at Cambridge, Whittle was approached by two colleagues who helped to arrange the financing for a new company, and Power Jets Ltd. was incorporated in March 1936. The company's first goal was to develop a single-shaft turbojet

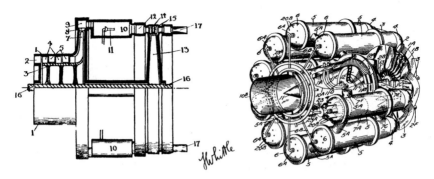

FIGURE 2.15. Cross section of a simple turbojet illustrated in Whittle's patent application (U.K. Patent 347,206) filed on January 16, 1930 (left), and a drawing of Whittle's first flight engine, W.1 (right), that accompanied the application for U.S. Patent 2,404,334 filed in February 1941 and granted on July 16, 1946. The engine's main components include the impeller with radial vanes (*1A*), 10 combustion chambers (*5*), turbine wheel (*12*), and the nozzle (*10B*). British patent drawing reproduced from Golley and Whittle (1987). The image is available from the U.S. Patent Office.

with single-stage centrifugal compressor. Much like Charles Parsons, the inventor of steam engine (chapter 2 of *CTTC*), Whittle approached his design from first principles. His mastery of thermodynamics and aerodynamics made it possible, in the words of Stanley Hooker at Rolls-Royce (RR), to lay down the engine's performance with the precision of Newton (Fulton 1996). Enormous challenges of this task included the achievement of several unprecedented ratings: combustion intensity, pressure ratio in a centrifugal blower, mass:power ratio, and material endurance.

British Thomson-Houston Company (BTH) was contracted to build the first experimental (4.4 kN) engine, and its bench tests began in April 1937. The engine's second reconstruction, with 10 separate combustion chambers, assumed the form that was depicted on Whittle's U.S. patent application and that was the basis of W.1, the first flight engine (figure 2.15). Its development was beset by many technical difficulties, lack of strong support from the Air Ministry and Ministry of Aircraft Production, and poor cooperation between Power Jets, BTH, and Rover Company, which was designated to produce an actual service engine.

Meanwhile, an entirely independent effort of Hans-Joachim Pabst von Ohain (1911–1998), who worked since March 1936 at Ernst Heinkel's company, had already produced the first experimental turbine-powered aircraft. Von Ohain began to think about a new mode of propulsion in 1933, when he was almost exactly the same age as Whittle, as a doctoral student in engineering at Göttingen (Conner 2001). He patented his design in 1935, and then in cooperation with Max Hahn and Ernst Heinkel's design team, he tested his first GT able to power an airplane—a centrifugal-flow engine developing nearly 5 kN—in March 1938 (Jones 1989). On August 27, 1939, its slightly more powerful version powered an experimental Heinkel-178 piloted by Erich Warsitz when it made the first test flight at the company airfield. Warsitz carried a hammer as his escape tool to break the cockpit if he got into trouble (Heinkel introduced the first ejection seats before the end of WWII; in the United States they appeared first on Lockheed's P-80C jet fighter in 1946). But this success did not result in any immediate large-scale commitment to further development of jet aircraft.

Whittle's engine finally took to the air in the experimental Gloster E.28/29 on May 15, 1941. Its smooth performance led to the decision to build W.2B engine developed by Power Jets for the Meteor fighter. After further delays RR finally replaced Rover as the engine's contractor in December 1942. Whittle recalls that when he stressed the great simplicity of the engine to the company's chairman, he was told that, "We'll bloody soon design the simplicity out of it" (Golley and Whittle 1987:179). And so they did—and RR remained in the forefront of jet design for the rest of the century (Rolls Royce 2004). In October 1941, a Whittle engine was also shipped to GE's factory in Massachusetts, and just 13 months later, on October 2, 1942, the first U.S. jet, XP-59A Airacomet (still inferior to the best propeller-driven planes of the day) made its first flight.

Gloster Meteor's prototype finally flew on March 5, 1943, but the plane entered the service only in July 1944. Its top speed of nearly 770 km/h speed made it possible to fly alongside a German V-1 missile and to flip it on its back with the plane's wing (Walker 1983). As with Whittle's machine, an improved version of von Ohain's turbine was developed by somebody else: in 1942 Anselm Franz, chief engineer at Junkers, designed the axial-flow turbojet Jumo 004, the world's first mass-produced jet engine used to power Messerschmitt Me-262, the world's first operational jet fighter (Wagner 1998). The plane was tested in March 1942, but it was first encountered in combat only on July 25, 1944. Eventually more than 1,400 Me-262 (Schwalbe) were built before the end of WWII, but only about 300 were deployed, and those in operation had a high failure rate.

This failure was fortunate because the technical performance of Me-262 was superior to that of any Allied fighter even until 1947 (Meher-Homji 1997). A more successful deployment would not have changed the outcome of the war, but it could have made the Allied invasion of Europe, which rested on air supremacy, much more difficult. Jet propulsion entered the war too late to make any difference on either side, but its low weight:power ratio of GTs and its powerful thrust made it the unrivaled choice for post-WWII fighters and bombers. Germany's defeat spelled the end of turbojets based on von Ohain's design; in contrast, the three GT manufacturers whose aeroengines dominated the global market during the second half of the 20th century—GE, Pratt & Whitney (P&W), and RR—got their start by producing improved designs of Whittle's machine.

Whittle himself was not involved in this post-WWII effort: during the war he suggested that Power Jets should be nationalized (they were), and in 1948 he retired from the RAF on medical grounds, never to work again directly on new jet engine designs. In 1976 he moved to Maryland with his new American wife. By that time von Ohain had been living in the United States for nearly 30 years, working most of that time at Wright-Patterson Air Force Base Aerospace Research Laboratory in Dayton, Ohio. Both men were eventually much acclaimed and honored for their inventions, but neither had any decisive influence on the post-WWII innovations in aeroengines: those came mainly from the leading makers, GE, P&W, and RR.

Better GTs, together with better aluminum alloys and advances in aerodynamic design, combined first to produce military planes that proceeded to break all kinds of aviation records (Loftin 1985; Younossi et al. 2002). GE had a particular success with its J47 turbojet: with 35,000 units by the late 1950s it was the world's most numerous GT (GEAE 2002). Six J47-GE-11 engines (each rated at 23.1 kN) powered Boeing's B-47 Stratojet, America's first jet bomber (figure 2.16), which introduced two lasting design features of all large jet aircraft during the remainder of the 20th century (Tegler 2000). After WWII George Schairer, Boeing's aerodynamicist, discovered German wind-tunnel data on swept-wing jet airplanes and this work became the foundation of B-47's slender, 35° swept-back wings. The second distinct feature were pod engines hung on struts under wings.

In 1948 Boeing won the competition to build the B-52, which, powered by eight P&W J57 turbojets (each initially rated at 44.4 kN), flew for the first time in 1955. This design has remained in service into the 21st century, being the only warplane flown by three generations of crews. The conflicts of the 1990s saw the deployment of both the venerable B-52 and the B-2, a stealth aircraft powered by GE's F-118. Any list of great U.S. jet fighters must mention F-86 Sabre (using one J47); the F-4 Phantom II powered by J79, GE's first engine making it possible to fly at Mach 2 or faster; and the F-15 Eagle (Walker 1983; Lombardi 2003). Sabre broke the sound barrier (at 1,080 km/h) in September 1948. Phantom (first flown in 1958) set more than a dozen speed and altitude records and served simultaneously with the U.S. Air Force, Navy, and Marine Corps.

The Eagle, introduced in 1979, became the superiority fighter of the last generation of the 20th century. Its two P&W turbofans can increase their steady thrust for short periods of time by using afterburners, that is, by burning additional fuel in the engine exhaust. This boosts the Eagle's total thrust by 67%, making it possible to accelerate to supersonic speed during a straight-up

FIGURE 2.16. B-47 Stratojet taking off. Because its turbojet engines could not develop enough thrust, the plane had 18 small rocket units in the fuselage for jet-assisted takeoff. Without any thrust reversers and antiskid brakes, the plane had to rely on a ribbon-type drag parachute to reduce its landing distance. The first test flight of the B-47 took place on December 17, 1947. Image from Edwards Air Force Base.

climb and reach more than Mach 2.5. Remarkable Soviet fighter jets of the Cold War period came from the two main design bureaus, Mikoyan and Gurevich, and Sukhoi. The MiG-15, powered by an RR engine, resembled the Sabre, which it faced during the Korean War. The MiG-21 eventually became the world's most widely used fighter (Gunston 1995). The delta-wing Su-15 capable of Mach 2.5 was the USSR's leading interceptor, and the Su-27 was the Eagle's counterpart.

In a matter of years the lessons learned from the design and operation of military jets began to be transferred to commercial aviation (Loftin 1985; Gunston 1997). On May 5, 1952, the de Havilland Comet 1, powered by four de Havilland Ghost engines, became the first passenger jet to enter scheduled service with flights between London and Johannesburg (Cowell 1976). Later in 1952 came the routes to Ceylon and Singapore and in April 1953 to Tōkyō. The first Comets carried only 36 people, their cabins were pressurized just to the equivalent of about 2.5 km above the sea level, and their maximum range was just 2,800 km. Their engines had a very low thrust:weight ratio of 0.17, making the airplanes prone to overrotation and loss of acceleration during takeoff. The Comet's engines were placed too close to the cabin in the wing roots, right next to the fuselage, causing concerns about the consequences of their disintegration. But at 640 km/h the planes was twice as fast as the best commercial propeller airplanes.

The plane's first two accidents during take-offs were attributed to pilot mistakes, but exactly a year after its introduction one of the airplanes disintegrated in the air shortly after takeoff from Calcutta, and two more catastrophic failures took place above the Mediterranean in January and April 1954 (ASN 2003). More than 20 Comet planes had to be withdrawn, and investigations traced the failures to fatigue and subsequent rupture of the pressurized fuselage: the destructive process began with tiny stress cracks that began forming around the plane's square window frames. A completely redesigned Comet 4 began flying in October 1958, but by that time there were two other turbojets in scheduled operation. Soviet Tupolev Tu-104 entered regular service on the Moscow-Omsk-Irkutsk route in 1956. Its military pedigree (it shared most of its parts with the Tupolev Tu-16 strategic bomber, code-named Badger by NATO) extended even to two braking parachutes to slow down the plane on landing.

But neither the Tu-104 nor the redesigned Comet proved to be a lasting departure. That came when the Boeing 707—the first U.S. commercial jetliner whose development, based on B-47, began in 1952 and whose prototype flew in 1954—entered service on October 28, 1958, with New York–Paris flight (Mellberg 2003). Its four P&W turbojets had the combined thrust of 240 kN, and with it Boeing launched its still expanding series of commercial jetliners (figure 2.17). In order of their introduction they were the 727, 737 (the best-selling jetliner of the 20th century with more than 3,800 planes of different versions shipped between 1967 and 2000), 747, 757 and 767 (both introduced in 1982), and 777, the only entirely new Boeing of the 1990s (flown since 1995).

Post-1960 expansion of jet travel called for more powerful and, after OPEC's oil price, also for significantly more efficient engines. This demand was met by the development of large turbofans (Coalson 2003). These machines, anticipated in Whittle's 1940 patents for a thrust augmentor, eliminated the turbojet's low propulsion efficiency at normal cruising speeds (even at 500 km/h, it wasted nearly 80% of its power) by reducing the nozzle exit velocity of combustion gases (Bathie 1996). Turbofans extract more power in the turbine in order to compress more air by an additional set of large-diameter fans that are placed ahead of the compressor. These fans compress the incoming air to only about twice the inlet pressure, and this air then bypasses the combustion chamber, thereby obviating the need for more fuel and resulting in lower specific fuel consumption. These two streams of exhaust gases (the rapid one from the core and the much slower bypass flow) generate higher thrust.

And unlike in turbojets, whose peak thrust comes at very high speeds needed for fighter planes, the peak thrust of turbofans is during low speeds, which makes them particularly suitable for large planes that need the power

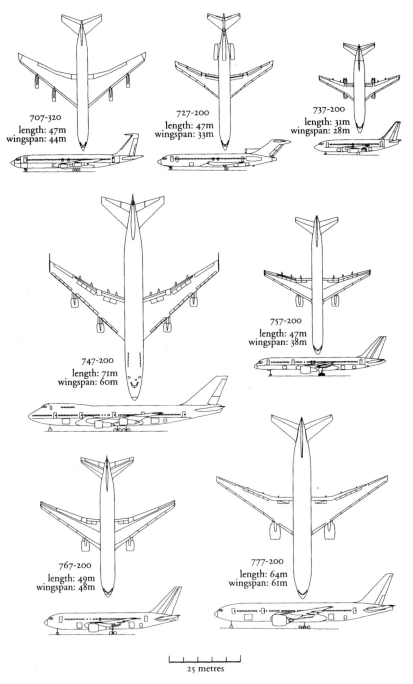

FIGURE 2.17. Nearly 70% of roughly 16,000 large commercial jets that were in service in the year 2000 were Boeings. This drawing shows scaled plans and frontal views of the company's 700 series planes. Adapted from the aerospace engineering department of California Polytechnic, San Luis Obispo, CA.

during takeoff (fully loaded Boeing 747 weighs nearly 400 t). As a result, take-offs became much less nerve-wracking: the turbojet Boeing 707 took up to 45 s to leave the runway, the first turbofans cut this to 25–30 s, and much more powerful engines of the 1990s can make commercial jets airborne in less than 20 s. Turbofans are also quieter as the high-speed, high-pitched exhaust from the engine's core is enveloped by slower and more voluminous bypass air.

In 1955 the Rolls-Royce JT3D Conway became the first commercial turbofan with a bypass ratio (core:bypass flow) of just 0.3; seven years later the Rolls-Royce Spey had a bypass ratio of 1.0, and in December 1966 P&W's famous JT9D engine, with the peak thrust of about 210 kN and bypass ratio of 4.8, was the first giant turbofan with double-shrouded (narrow and long) blades (Sample and Shank 1985; Pratt & Whitney 1999). This engine was chosen to power the wide-bodied Boeing 747, the plane that revolutionized intercontinental flight: Pan Am's founder and president Juan Trippe ordered it in 1966, and William Allen, Boeing's president, gambled the company's future by investing more than twice its worth in building the world's largest passenger jet (see figure 4.13 in *CTTC*).

The prototype 747 took off on February 9, 1969, and the first scheduled flight was on January 21, 1970 (Smil 2000b). A wide body (to allow for the placing of two standard ship containers side by side) and the bubble cockpit (for easy loading through an upturned nose) betray the original design intent: during the late 1960s, it was expected that supersonic jets will soon dominate all long routes and that 747s would become mainly cargo carriers. But supersonic travel remained limited to the expensive, noisy, and uneconomical Concorde—powered by four RR/Snecma turbojets totaling 677 kN with afterburner and capable of Mach 2.04—which operated on a few routes from London and Paris between 1976 and 2003. And the 747, rather than being just another compromise design, turned out to be, in Tennekes's (1997) memorable description, the only plane that obeys ruthless engineering logic.

During the 1990s Airbus gained a growing share of the large commercial jet market, but many flight experts still believe that the jumbo was the most revolutionary, if not the best, jetliner ever built. The 1,000th 747 was delivered on October 12, 1993, and by the end of the year 2000 the count approached 1,300 as different 747 versions had carried some two billion passengers, or one third of humanity. The Boeing 747 is an improbably graceful behemoth that combines symbolism and function, beauty and economy—a daring revolutionary design embodied in a machine that ushered the age of mass intercontinental travel and became a powerful symbol of global civilization (Smil 2000b).

Turbofans that entered service during the 1980s had bypass ratios between 4.8 and 6.0, and the most powerful engine introduced during the 1990s, GE's GE90, has the record high bypass ratio of 9.0. At the time of its introduction in November 1995, the engine was rated for the minimum of 330 kN; it was certified at 512 kN, and during tests one of its versions (GE90-115B) set the world record at 569 kN (GEAE 2003; figure 2.18). Its rated thrust is nearly 2.5 times that of the JT9D that was installed on the first Boeings 747. These powerful turbofans operate with temperatures around 1,500°C, hotter than the melting point of rotating blades, which must have elaborate internal air cooling. Diameters of their largest fans are slightly more than 3 m (equal to the diameter of the fuselage of Boeing 727); their weight:power ratios are less than 0.1 g/W, and their thrust:weight ratios have surpassed 6. Consequently, modern turbofans are not a limiting factor in building larger planes: in the year 2000 Airbus decided to power the world's biggest commercial jet (the A 380, for up to 840 people) with four GP7200 engines made jointly by GE and P&W project, each rated at 360 kN.

Unmatched reliability of the latest generation of turbofans is the principal reason for the extraordinary safety of modern commercial flying. In the late 1990s there were fewer than two accidents per million of departures compared to more than 50 in 1960—and of these infrequent mishaps fewer than 3% were attributable to engine failure during the 1990s (Boeing 2003b). And this reliability made it possible to use twin-engine jetliners on routes that take them

FIGURE 2.18. During the closing years of the 20th century, GE began developing the world's most powerful turbofan aeroengine, the GE90-115B, rated at 511 kN, shown here in the factory setting. Photograph courtesy of General Electric Aeroengines, Cincinnati, Ohio. See also this chapter's frontispiece for the engine's front view and its first test flight, and figure 2.13 for a trimetric illustration.

at some points more than one hour of flying time from the nearest airport. This old restriction, dating back to piston engines, was changed in 1985 when the ETOPS (extended range twin engine operations) authority for twin-engine commercial jets was extended to two hours. In 1988 it was raised to three hours, and in March 2000 some North Pacific flights were given permission to be as far away as 207 min of flying with one engine from the nearest airport (Reich 2003).

As already noted, this made Boeing 767 the dominant trans-Atlantic carrier (Boeing 2001). Because I experienced this shift personally, by boarding fewer 747s and DC-10s, I was not greatly surprised by its rapid progress—but I still vividly recall, after more than two decades of crossing the vastness of North Pacific on three- and four-engine planes, my first Asia-bound flight on a Boeing 767 (the trip made even more memorable by an extraordinarily strong jet stream on the return journey that pushed the plane for several hours above 0.9 Mach to make a record-time crossing). But it is the latest plane in the Boeing series, the 777 powered by GE90-115B engines, that now holds the record for flying on a single engine, 6 hours and 29 min set during its ETOPS tests (Boeing 2003a).

Industrial GTs

The world's first industrial GT was built by the Swiss Brown Boveri Corporation for the municipal electricity-generating station in Neuchâtel (ASME 1988). Its specifications show the modest beginnings of the technique, and their comparison with the best year 2000 ratings impressively shows enormous progress made in 60 years of technical development. Brown Boveri's first machine had an inlet temperature of just 550°C, rotated at 3,000 rpm, and it developed 15.4 MW, of which 11.4 MW was used by the compressor. Electricity generation thus amounted to just 4 MW, and its efficiency (without any heat recovery) was only 17.4%. The machinery—the compressor, turbine, and generator—was arranged in line, and it was, much like modern turbines, directly coupled (remarkably, the Neuchâtel turbine was still in operation by the year 2000). In contrast, the most advanced GT of the late 1990s, GE's MS9001H, rated 480 MW in 50 Hz combined cycle mode (i.e., with the recovery of exhaust heat) and had an inlet temperature of 1427°C, and its rate of 6 MJ/kWh resulted in the unprecedented efficiency of 60% (GEPS 2003).

These impressive advances, charted in figure 2.19, resulted in the world's most efficient combustion engines. They were made possible first by using the experience and innovations of jet engine industry and later by deploying new materials and scaling up the established designs. Mass production of GTs was stimulated by the November 1965 blackout that left 30 million people in the U.S. Northeast in darkness for up to 13 hours (USFPC 1965). Until that time

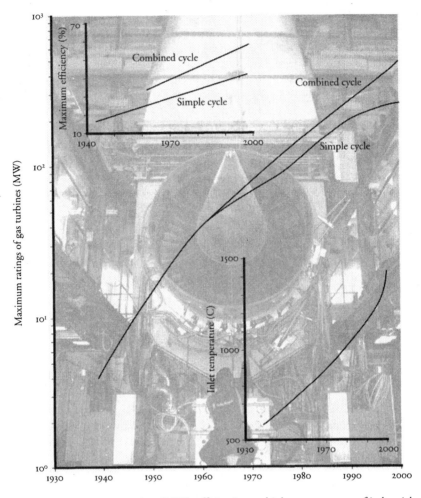

FIGURE 2.19. Maximum ratings (MW), efficiencies, and inlet temperatures of industrial gas turbines, 1938–2000. Based on figure 1.10 in Smil (2003) and data in Islas (1999).

the use of GTs in peaking plants was rare. The first American industrial GT (rated at just 1.35 MW) was made in 1948; by 1965 annual GT shipments reached 840 MW, but three years after the blackout they rose to 4 GW. Total U.S. GT capacity jumped from 1 GW in 1963 to 43.5 GW in 1975, but then the lower growth of electricity demand and large increases in the price of hydrocarbons ended any further capacity gains for a decade. But GT designs kept advancing, and after the world's hydrocarbon prices fell in 1985, stationary GTs became a common choice of utilities: by 1990 about half of the 15 GW of new capacity ordered in the United States employed GTs either in simple cycle or in combined cycle arrangements (Smock 1991).

The gas turbine's generating potential is best exploited when the machine is paired with a steam turbine (Horlock 2002). Exhaust gases leaving the turbine are hot enough to be used efficiently for downstream production of steam (in a heat recovery steam generator) for a steam turbine. In these combined cycle gas turbines (CCGT), two heat engines are thus coupled in series, and the cycle's efficiency is the sum of individual efficiencies minus their product. This explains why by the end of the 20th century the combination of two state-of-the-art machines (42% efficient gas and 31% efficient steam turbines) made it possible to reach 60% CCGT efficiency (0.42 + 0.31 − 0.13). Steam produced by the exhaust heat can be also used for industrial processing or to heat buildings in cogeneration (combined heat and electricity) plants.

GE, the leader in developing large stationary units, introduced its first 100 MW machine in 1976. Its firing temperature was 1,065°C, and thermal efficiency reached about 32%. By 1990 the worldwide capacity of new GT orders surpassed that of steam turbines (Valenti 1991); by the year 2000 GTs, and steam turbines for CCGT generation, represented 60% of all new capacity orders, and their installed capacity (12% of the total) was just ahead of all fission reactors (Holmes 2001). GTs were also used for mid-range and some base-load generation. By the 1990s even simple-cycle GTs were nearly as efficient as the best steam turbines (about 40%), and efficiencies of combined cycle generation were substantially ahead of any other commercially available choice. In 1990 GE's 150 MW turbine was the first machine to reach an efficiency of 50%. High-efficiency GTs offered, finally, an economic and flexible opportunity to break the long stagnation of average electricity-generation efficiency (see figure 2.3), and they were also the major reason for the already-noted decrease in the optimum power plant size.

The 1980s were the first decade when the orders for aeroderivative GTs (AGTs)—jet engines adapted for stationary application or for marine propulsion—began to rise as these machine matured (Williams and Larson 1988). GE began developing AGTs in 1959, and its LM6000 machine, introduced in 1992, was the first design to break the 40% efficiency mark (Valenti 1993). This GT was based on the engine used on Boeings 747 and 767 as well as on Airbuses, and its largest available versions can generate up to 50 MW (GE 2004). RR derived its largest stationary turbine, rated at 51.9 MW, from the Trent high bypass aeroengine that is in service on the Airbus A330 and Boeing 777. In 1986 P&W launched a program to base a new industrial GT on its JT8D series aircraft engine (Pratt & Whitney 2004). Its latest variants are streamlined SWIFTPAC units of 25 and 50 MW that come preassembled and configured as multitrailer modules able to generate electricity within one month after reaching their location.

On the other end of the ratings spectrum are microsize GTs in the 25–260 kW range that were originally developed for ground transportation and that provide inexpensive and reliable electricity in isolated locations or as emergency standby units (Scott 1997). And during the 1990s a cooperative effort between GE and the U.S. Department of Energy resulted in the development of the most efficient (and the most powerful) series of H System GTs. In contrast, the most advanced GT of the late 1990s, GE's MS9001H rates 480 MW in 50 Hz combined cycle mode (that is, with the recovery of exhaust heat), had an inlet temperature of 1427°C, and its rate of 6MJ/kWh resulted in the unprecedented efficiency of 60% (GEPS 2003). One of the greatest engineering challenges that had to be overcome in order to bring such machines to market included the development of single-crystal nickel-based superalloys for turbine blades. In addition, these large (up to 18.2 kg) single-crystal alloy blades need a ceramic coating in order to prevent their melting and provide resistance to oxidation and corrosion. A no less important challenge in developing large and efficient GTs was to control NO_x emissions.

In retrospect, the rise of GTs appears inevitable as the machines offer a number of highly valued advantages. From the basic structural point, simple rotational mechanics of GTs (as opposed to reciprocating motion of internal combustion engines) makes them relatively compact, extends their useful lifetime, makes them easier to maintain, and simplifies their sealing and lubrication. Their compactness implies relatively high power density and hence a limited footprint and a higher flexibility of location and, for smaller units, an easy transportability when mounted on barges and ships or loaded on trucks. GTs must be started externally, but they can reach full load in a matter of minutes (while steam turbines take hours to do so), making them a perfect choice for peaking electricity generation. GTs can use any kind of gas, light distillates, and heavier residual oils. And their unmatched efficiency, particularly in CCGT mode, makes for a highly economical operation.

This high efficiency also translates into a much reduced specific generation of CO_2: steam turbine generation fueled by coal produces more than 1 kg CO_2/kg, and by fuel oil, at least 0.8 kg, while CCGT will emit less than 0.4 kg/kWh (Islas 1999). Other environmental advantages include the fact that GTs do not require any external cooling and that new silencing systems can reduce their noise to below 60 dBA at the distance of 100 m. High reliability of GTs translates into relatively low maintenance costs, and high quality of exhaust heat (> 500°C) provides a valuable byproduct for many industrial processes. Their capital cost is lower than for coal-fired plants (this reduces the cost of electricity by about 10%), and, as already noted, even the largest units can be built much faster than steam turbines.

Finally, the wide range of GT sizes—from the smallest stationary microunits of just 25 kW to the largest industrial machines whose capacity approached 500 MW by the year 2000—offers a great deal of flexibility and modularity, and it means that they have been used in a still increasing range of applications. Not everything had gone well with the new powerful GTs. Despite some problems with extended commissioning periods, combustor accidents, rotor vibration, and unexpected downtime for repairs and replacements (Hansen and Smock 1996), there was a widespread agreement that GTs will continue to gain new market share and that they may eventually dominate thermal electricity generation.

Two other important segments of modern economies that were transformed after WII by GTs are natural gas transportation and marine propulsion. Modern, large-diameter (up to 142 cm) natural gas pipelines require the most economical yet highly reliable power for moving the gas. GTs placed at regular intervals along the pipeline route do this work by driving large centrifugal compressors (e.g., there are 41 compressor stations on the 4,451-km long pipeline carrying West Siberian natural gas to Europe). Most of these turbines are rated between 1 and 15 MW, but more powerful AGT units, rated in excess of 30 MW, entered the service during the 1990s. GTs also power pumps that move crude oil through pipelines, maintain pressure in oil wells, generate all required power on offshore hydrocarbon exploration and drilling platforms, compress gases blown into blast furnaces, and are used in refineries and chemical syntheses.

Naval propulsion is another large market where the initial skepticism was replaced with widespread acceptance. The earliest purchases were for naval vessels, hydrofoils, and hovercrafts. Orders for commercial marine AGTs became common during the 1990s: their compactness, low noise, and low emissions make them particularly suitable for passenger ships. During the late 1990s AGTs became the propulsion of choice for increasingly larger cruise ships, augmenting or replacing cheaper but much noisier and vibrating diesel engines. One area where GTs did not meet the initial expectation was wheeled transportation: trials in cars (particularly during the 1960s), trucks, buses, and trains did not result in any large-scale commercial deployment. One notable deployment in land vehicles was in heavy tanks: America's 60-t M1/A1 Abrams is powered by a 1.1 MW AGT-1500 Honeywell GT.

Rocket Engines

Rockets have a long and fascinating history that began in China soon after the formulation of gunpowder during the 11th century. Red glare of projectiles that William Congreve introduced in 1806 and that were used during the British attack on Maryland's Fort McHenry in 1814 found its way into the U.S. national anthem, but as the accuracy of the 19th-century artillery improved the interest in those inaccurate weapons ebbed and rocketry was prominently absent among the innovations of pre-WWI era. Rockets are quintessential Newtonian creatures. As they sit on their launch pads, they conform to the first law, and their repose can be altered only by the application of a thrust sufficient to lift them off. The second law, the force being the product of mass and acceleration, determines the thrust of their engines, and the third law (to every action there is an equal and opposite reaction) explains their flight. Imparting the requisite thrust to substantial payloads requires a great deal of power. Rocket engines are thus the world's most powerful but ephemeral prime movers (Sutton 1992; Sutton and Biblarz 2001).

Large steam turbines rotate for months before they are shut down for scheduled maintenance, GTs that cover peak demand are working for hours, and even fairly short car commutes mean that internal combustion engines (ICEs) work for at least 15–20 min at a time. In contrast, as already noted, Saturn V rocket engines worked for only 150 s in order to put Apollo 11 on its trajectory to the Moon, and the Space Shuttle's rocket engines were designed to fire for the maximum of 8 min. And while large steam turbines are as powerful as the rockets (and work continuously for thousands of hours), no energy converter can even remotely approach extraordinarily high thrust:weight (or very low weight:power) ratio of rocket engines.

Serious theoretical proposals for space travel and first rocket engine patents predate WWI. Robert H. Goddard (1882–1945) got his first patent for a two-stage rocket in 1914 (U.S. Patent 1,102,653); in 1915 he began testing rockets with De Laval nozzle (its convergent–divergent profile became eventually a standard feature of large rocket engines) and experimented with solid-propellant rockets in 1918 (Durant 1974). But systematic design and testing of rocket engines began only during the 1920s with toylike models. Goddard, whose work was supported since 1917 by the Smithsonian Institution, tested the world's first liquid-propelled rocket (liquid oxygen and gasoline) on March 16, 1926 (figure 2.20). In his report Goddard (1926:587) described how during this test of a small rocket

> weighing 5.75 lb empty and 10.25 lb loaded with liquids, the lower part of the nozzle burned through and dropped off, leaving, however, the upper part intact. After about 20 sec the rocket rose without perceptible jar, with no smoke and with no apparent increase in the rather small flame; it increased rapidly in speed and, after describing a semicircle, landed 184 feet from the starting point—the curved path being due to the fact that the nozzle had burned through unevenly, and one side was longer than the other.

And so—with a 2.6-kg projectile traveling at an average speed of a bit less than 100 km/h above a field near Auburn, Massachusetts—began the age of liquid rocket engines; just two generations later their advanced (and by the standards of the 1920s unimaginably more powerful) versions carried men to

FIGURE 2.20. Robert Goddard testing the world's first liquid-fuel rocket in 1926 (left) and lecturing on space flight (right). Photographs from Great Images in NASA.

the Moon. Goddard's first version of liquid-fueled rocket (shown in figure 2.20) had its small engine at the top, but that was soon changed to the standard configuration of engine surmounted by liquid oxygen and propellant tanks. Many other small models of similar engines were tested subsequently, with different degrees of success, in the Soviet Union, Germany, France, Italy, and Czechoslovakia (Durant and James 1974). As with turbojets, critical advances came only during WWII, but in this case they were limited to German development of cruise missiles led by Wernher von Braun (1912–1977).

Walter Dornberger recruited von Braun to work for the Wehrmacht's development of military rockets in 1932, and 10 years later they began testing the missile capable to reach England. Between September 8, 1944, and March 27, 1945, a total of 518 V-2 (*Vergeltungswaffe*) missiles hit London, killing about 2,500 people in London, destroying 20,000 houses, and creating a great deal of fear—yet all that with no effect on the war's outcome (Piszkiewicz 1995). Although the V-1, the first German V weapon, killed almost the same number of people, it did so with nearly five times as many hits as the V-2. And while the V-1 was a cheaply built, slow-flying (240 km/h) airplane (Fieseler Fi 103) powered by a pulse jet engine, the V-2 was a supersonic missile whose rocket engine was powered by a mixture of liquid oxygen and ethanol–water and whose high impact speed (about 750 m/s) caused considerably greater casualties and material damage. Rather inaccurate (CEP of 17 km), the V-2 carried an explosive payload of 730 kg.

In a well-known case of expertise transfer, virtually the entirety of von

FIGURE 2.21. Test firing of a V-2 rocket in the United States in 1946 (left; NASA photograph 66P-0631), and Wernher von Braun and Saturn IB (right; NASA photograph 6863092). Both images available from Great Images in NASA.

Braun's design team was brought to the United States in December 1945, where some its members were soon helping to launch V-2 rockets built from captured parts (figure 2.21). Eventually von Braun and his associates formed the core of NASA's Marshall Space Flight Center in Huntsville, Alabama. Their work proceeded slowly until the surprising launch of the Earth's first artificial satellite, the Soviet *Sputnik*, on October 4, 1957, launched by an R-7A rocket designed by a team led by Sergei Korolyov (1907–1966). Its engine, the RD-107 developed by the state Energomash company between 1954 and 1957, had four large main and two small steering combustion chambers, and it was also used to launch Yuri Gagarin's first manned orbital flight less than four years later (April 12, 1951). After some 15 upgradings, it was still in production during the 1990s (Energomash 2003).

Even before John Glenn orbited the Earth on February 20, 1962, John Kennedy announced the goal of landing men on Moon within a decade. Well-known milestones of the superpower space race followed (von Braun and Ordway 1975; Heppenheimer 1997). The United States rapidly gained the upper hand and then almost as rapidly pulled back to just low-orbital Skylab (1973–1980) and Shuttle flights (since April 1981). Gemini flights with their space-walks took place in 1965 and 1966; early Apollo Saturn launches prepared the ground for the first Moon landing in July 20, 1969; five more landings followed, the last one in 1972. Then, unmanned fly-bys and exploration of Mars (*Viking* landed on July 20, 1976) and Venus (by the Soviet *Venera*) informed us about the two nearest planets, and probes were sent to the outer planets of the solar system (*Voyager I* launched on September 5, 1977). The Soviet space program aimed at orbiting progressively more massive Soyuz, Salyut, and Mir space stations, and the construction of the International Space Station began November 1998.

First stages of Saturn rockets of the Apollo program were powered by Wernher von Braun's liquid propellant engines (Bilstein 1996). The single-start H-1 engine, used on the early missions, had 912 kN of thrust (figure 2.21). The restartable J-2, the first manned booster engine propelled by liquid hydrogen, developed 1.02 MN, and it was used on the second and third stages of Saturn V. And the F-1, the largest liquid rocket engine ever built (an order of magnitude more powerful than Saturn 1 engines) made the Moon landings possible: five of them (the four outboard ones gimbaled, the central one fixed) powered the first stage of Saturn V. The Rocketdyne division of Boeing got the contract to build F-1 in 1959, and none of them ever failed in flight. Each liquid oxygen–kerosene engine developed about 6.8 MN (27 GW) at sea level, and with the mass of 8.391 t its thrust:weight ratio was about 83 and mass: power ratio is just 0.0003 g/W (figure 2.22). Rocketdyne's Space Shuttle main

FIGURE 2.22. The F-1 was the largest-ever propulsion engine (sea-level thrust of 6.8 MN) developed for Saturn rockets of the Apollo program. The first image shows the oxidizer and fuel pumps, valves and ducts surmounting a conical thrust chamber, enveloped by a circular turbine exhaust manifold. The second image shows the nozzle extension that increased the overall length to 5.7 m and its maximum width to 3.7 m. These images are available from NASA.

engine, used in the Shuttle *Orbiter* between 1981 and 1998, was a much less powerful machine (2.28 MN), but it was reusable.

Engines powered by liquid propellants share four common basic features (Huzel and Huang 1992): separate storage tanks for the fuel and oxidizer; powerful turbopumps and requisite pipes and valves to deliver the liquids, and to control their flow, to a combustion chamber; a combustion chamber to generate high-pressure, high-temperature (2,500–4,000°C) gas; and a convergent–divergent nozzle (bell-shaped ones are most efficient) with a throat to expand the gas to supersonic speeds (2,000–4,000 m/s). Low-density propellants require larger tanks while cryogenic storage needs insulation; both options add to the mass of the launcher.

Although solid propellants generate less thrust per unit mass than do liquids, and engines that use them cannot be restarted, they have several obvious advantages: because they combine fuel and the oxidizer they do not need an external source of oxygen; they can be stored for long periods of time (even decades) without leaks or deterioration; engines are simpler as they do not need feed systems or valves; and rocket launches can be done within seconds. Solid propellants are thus an excellent choice for less powerful engines and for secondary boosters as well as for military missiles kept in place for long periods of time. In 1942 John W. Parsons, an explosives expert at California Institute of Technology, formulated the first castable composite solid propellant by combining asphalt (fuel and binder) with potassium perchlorate (an oxidizer).

Key improvements in the preparation of these propellants were made during the late 1940s and the early 1950s. In 1945 Caltech's Charles Bartley and his coworkers replaced asphalt with Thiokol (synthetic rubber). This polysulfide polymer was synthesized for the first time in 1926 by Joseph C. Patrick, and the eponymous corporation was formed in 1928 (Sutton 1999). In 1947 Thiokol Corporation began the systematic, and still continuing (now as Morton-Thiokol), development of solid propellant rockets. The second key innovation was the replacement of potassium perchlorate by ammonium perchlorate (AP) as an oxidizer (Hunley 1999). Another critical discovery was made at the Atlantic Research Corporation by Keith Rumbel and Charles B. Henderson, who found that adding large amounts of aluminum (Al) greatly increased the specific impulse of composite propellants: they used 21% Al, 59% AP, and 20% plasticized polyvinyl chloride (PVC).

Solid propellants, configured inside the casings mostly in five- to twelve-pointed stars, were used in America's first SLBMs (*Polaris* in 1960, with AP/Al/polyurethane propellant) and ICBMs. The three-stage Minuteman (introduced in 1962) had solid-propellant engines (powered by AP/polybutadiene acrylic acid and Al propellant), as did the first three stages of America's last ICBM deployed during the 20th century, the four-stage Peacekeeper. And in 1981 Thiokol introduced the world's largest solid rocket motor ever built for strap-on boosters to supply most of the thrust for the Space Shuttle's liftoff:

each booster carries 499 t of propellant and generates as much as 14.68 MN of thrust for around 120 s.

Until the mid-1960s the strategic and military importance of these new prime movers, deployed on a large variety of missiles, far surpassed their commercial use. Nonmilitary use of rocket propulsion began in the early 1960s with the first U.S. meteorological satellites, and in 1971 came LANDSAT, the first satellite dedicated to the monitoring of the Earth's land use. By the late 1990s there were several orbiting astronomical and a growing number of Earth-observation satellites providing information ranging from high-resolution ground surveillance (*IKONOS, SPOT*) to the changes in sea level (*TOPEX/ POSEIDON*). The first commercial satellites launched during the 1960s were one of the key ingredients of the still far from finished revolution in global communication (see chapter 5).

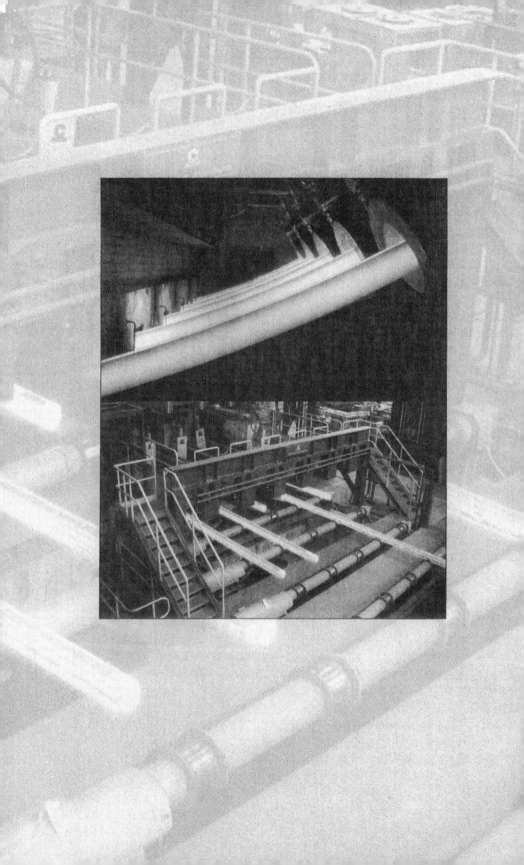

୯୬ 3

Materials:

Old Techniques and New Solutions

> More and more one comes to see that it is the everyday
> things which are interesting, important and intellectually
> difficult. Furthermore the materials which we use for every-
> day purposes influence our whole culture, economy and pol-
> itics far more deeply than we are inclined to admit . . .
>
> James E. Gordon, *The New Science of Strong Materials*
> (1976)

High material intensity of modern societies is inextricably linked through a
deviation-amplifying feedback with high use of energy. Rapid growth of aggregate material consumption would not have been possible without abundantly available energy in general, and without cheaper electricity in particular.
In turn, affordable materials of higher quality opened up new opportunities

FRONTISPIECE 3. Ferrous metallurgy of the second half of the 20th century was profoundly transformed by continuous casting of steel and the use of basic oxygen and
electric arc furnaces. These advances lowered the price and increased the quality of the
metal that continues to form the infrastructural foundations of modern civilization.
Curved strands of hot metal emerge from a continuous billet caster (top) on their way
toward the discharge roller table; in the cooling (spray) chamber area (bottom) the
strands exit toward the withdrawal unit. Photographs courtesy of CONCAST AG,
Zürich, Switzerland.

for energy industries thanks to advances ranging from fully mechanized coal-mining machines and massive offshore oil drilling rigs to improved efficiencies of energy converters. These gains were made possible not only by better alloys but also by new plastics, ceramics, and composite materials. In addition, new materials were developed to sustain the post-WWII electronic revolution as well as to advance new energy conversions, particularly the photovoltaic generation of electricity.

Dominant 20th-century trends in the use of materials thus closely resembled those in energy conversion: enormous increase in the overall volume, continued improvements of techniques that were introduced before WWI, and the emergence of entirely new processes and their rapid commercialization after WWII. There is, of course, a fundamental difference in variety. There are only three major classes of fossil fuels (coals, crude oils, and natural gases) and five major renewable energy flows (direct solar, wind, water, tides, biomass), and only a handful of prime movers (steam, water, wind, and gas turbines and internal combustion engines) are used to convert these energies into electricity, heat, and motion.

In contrast, modern civilizations now extract huge volumes of inexpensive and abundant basic construction materials (stone, gravel, sand, clay) and scores of metallic ores (from aluminum-yielding bauxite to zinc-yielding spharelite) and nonmetallic elements (from boron to silicon); produces thousands of alloys; separates huge volumes of industrial gases from the atmosphere; synthesizes increasing volumes of raw materials and plastics (overwhelmingly from nonrenewable hydrocarbon-based feedstocks); and creates an entirely new class of composite compounds. This chapter traces only the innovations in producing basic, high-volume materials that form the very structure of modern civilization. Steel must be necessarily first; then I look at inexplicably neglected advances in producing the most important industrial gases and at the syntheses of a still growing range of plastics. I close the chapter by describing the production of exceedingly pure silicon, the most important material of the late 20th-century electronics.

But before I begin these systematic accounts I must point out the two key material shifts—the overall increase of the annual throughput and a pronounced shift from renewable to nonrenewable resources—whose evidence emerged from a detailed U.S. record (Matos and Wagner 1998; Matos 2003). After excluding crushed stone and construction sand and gravel, the total materials used rose from about 100 Mt in 1900 to nearly 900 Mt in 2000, and while nearly two thirds of the 1900 total originated in wood, natural fibers, and agriculture products, a century later that share, including all recycled paper, dropped to less than 25% (figure 3.1). Matos and Wagner (1998) also estimated that in 1995 the global total of consumed materials, after growing nearly twice as fast as did U.S. use during the preceding generation, reached about 9.5 Gt. This means that the United States, with about 5% of the world's population,

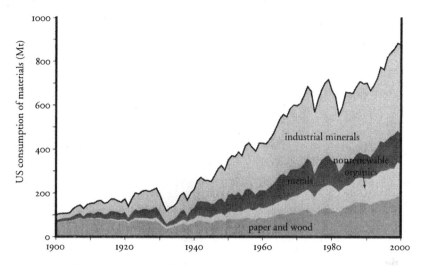

FIGURE 3.1. The two most notable conclusions that emerge from tracing the use of materials in the United States during the 20th century are the nearly ninefold increase in the total annual throughput and the drastic shift from renewable to nonrenewable substances. In 1900, about 65% of all materials (excluding stones, sand, and clay) originated in wood and agricultural products; a century later, that share dropped to slightly more than 20%. Plotted from data in Matos (2003).

claimed nearly 30% of all materials, a share even higher than its acquisition of fossil fuels (Smil 2003).

Still the Iron (Steel) Age

Despite new alloys, plastics, ceramics, and composite materials, the 20th century still belonged to the Iron Age, even though nearly all of the metal was used as steel. In the United States its absolute consumption peaked in 1973 (146 Mt, nearly 16 times greater than the 1900 level) and declined to as little as 80 Mt by 1982, and it ended the century almost 50% higher. Consequently, the metal's per capita consumption fell by more than a third from the high of about 680 kg in 1973 to just 435 kg by the year 2000—and the decline per unit of gross domestic product (GDP) was even steeper, from the peak of more than 50 kg/$1,000 in 1950 to just 13 kg by the year 2000 (figure 3.2). Similar shifts in absolute and relative consumption of steel also took place in Japan and in major European Union producers. In contrast, every one of these indicators rose in global terms.

By the year 2000 the global extraction of iron ore reached one billion tonnes a year, the mass that was surpassed only by the two leading fossil fuels (coal

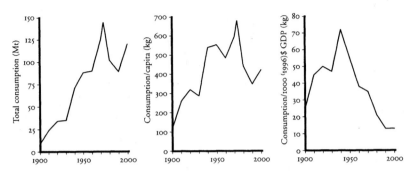

FIGURE 3.2. U.S. steel consumption during the 20th century: annual total and averages per capita and per unit of GDP. Plotted from data in Kelly and Fenton (2004) and IISI (2002).

and crude oil, each roughly at 3.5 Gt) and by the common building materials. Pig (cast) iron output was nearly 580 Mt, and virtually all of it was used to make steel. An additional 270 Mt of steel came from the recycled scrap, and hence the total steel output was almost 20 times as large as the combined total of five other leading metals: aluminum, copper, zinc, lead, and tin (IISI 2002). Steel output rising from less than 30 Mt in 1900 to about 850 Mt by 2000 t prorated to per capita rates of 18 and about 140 kg/year, and the intensity per $1,000 of the gross world product (GWP; in constant 1996 US$) nearly doubled from 14 to 26 kg. Steel's output reflected rather accurately the key economic trends: its expansion was checked by the economic downturn brought by crude oil price rises of the 1970s, and this resulted in the spell of 15 years of fluctuating output before the global steel production reached a new all-time high of 785 Mt in 1989.

Steel is produced by reducing the cast iron's high carbon content (> 4%) to mostly between 0.1% and 1% by alloying with other metals (most commonly with Cr, Mn, or Ni) and by physical treatment in order to achieve a variety of desired properties. The metal's qualitative importance is easy to see as we are surrounded by products and structures that either are unthinkable without it or could be built otherwise only at a much increased cost or with compromised performance. Steel's penetration of manufacturing and construction began before 1900 (see chapter 4 of *CTTC*), and it both accelerated and widened during the second half of the 20th century. This process was driven by expanding ownership of consumer items, by urban growth, and by widespread construction of major infrastructures.

Perhaps the best way to describe the importance of steel in modern society is to say that so much around us is made of it (purely, from scalpels to welded tanker hulls, or partially, from reinforced concrete to cars) and that just about everything around us is made with it (by tools, machines, and assemblies used in mining, processing, and manufacturing industries as well as in household tasks). Moreover, steel's qualities have improved as its uses have spread. High-strength steel, able to withstand stresses above 800 MPa, is used in car chassis and door guard bars. After a secondary hardening, steel with 10–12% chromium and small amounts of other rare metals withstands ultimate stress of more than 900 MPa and is used for gas turbines blades. Steel wires used for suspension cables of the world's longest bridges (Japan's Seto and Akashi) have tensile strength of, respectively, 1.6 and 1.8 GPa. High-chromium (17%) steel is suitable for parts subjected to high-temperature and high-pressure steam, while high-carbon (0.8% C, 16.5% Cr) steel is made into cutting tools and ball bearings (Bolton 1989).

An increasing share of the metal came from the recycled material, but by the year 2000 two thirds of the world's steel was still made from pig iron. This means that blast furnaces remain at the core of this vast metal-smelting enterprise. The largest pre-WWI units had internal volume of slightly more than 500 m³ and daily capacity of about 500 t. Hot metal from these furnaces was converted into steel predominantly in open hearth furnaces, cast into massive steel ingots, and only then, after reheating in soaking pits, shaped into semifinished products. All of this changed during the course of the 20th century. Blast furnaces grew enormously and so did the performance of open hearth furnaces, which were eventually displaced by basic oxygen furnaces as the process of ironmaking became integrated with steelmaking. The dominant trend toward increasing capacities had an innovative corollary in the emergence of small, specialized mills, and by the year 2000 the ironmaking techniques that dispensed with the blast furnace had captured about 7% of the world's iron production.

Blast Furnaces

The blast furnace (BF) is an excellent example of a centuries-old technique (its European origins predate 1400) that reached a relatively high level of structural and operational sophistication before 1900 but whose capabilities were transformed by impressive innovations during the 20th century. As old-fashioned, unwieldy, and unloved those massive assemblies may be, they are undoubtedly among the most remarkable artifacts of industrial civilization (Peacey and Davenport 1979; Walker 1985; Wakelin 1999). Their main sections, from the bottom up, are the circular hearth; the bosh, a rather short, truncated, outward-sloping cone within which are the furnace's highest temperatures (more than 1,600°C); the stack, the longest and slightly narrowing part where the countercurrent movement of downward-moving ore, coke, and limestone and upward-moving hot carbon monoxide (CO)-rich gases reduce oxides into iron; and the throat surmounted by an apparatus for charging raw materials (figures 3.3 and 3.4).

By 1914 the steady post-1800 growth of BF capacity increased the maximum output of largest units by roughly two orders of magnitude (see figure 4.1 in *CTTC*). The next, U.S.-led, period of accelerated expansion took place in order to support the unprecedented demand for steel during WWII (King 1948). Higher blast rates led to faster deterioration of brick linings—and to the introduction of water cooling. Large increases in the volume of ore, coke, and limestone inputs could not be supported by manual handling of inputs—and hence the mechanized skip hoists and automated dumping. The need for clean gas to run blowing engines led to better gas-cleaning equipment, including Frederick Cottrell's electrostatic precipitators whose installations began in 1919.

America's ironmaking continued its technical leadership into the 1950s. Between 1947 and 1948, Republic Steel introduced smelting under pressure (starting at 70–140 kPa), which led to considerable savings of coke. Use of highly beneficiated ores, enrichment of blast air by oxygen, injection of gaseous or liquid fuel injection through tuyeres, better refractories, carbon hearth lining, automated plug drill, and better operation controls were introduced and adopted during the 1950s (Gold et al. 1984). But before the end of that decade Japan emerged as the most innovative, and the most aggressive, ironmaking

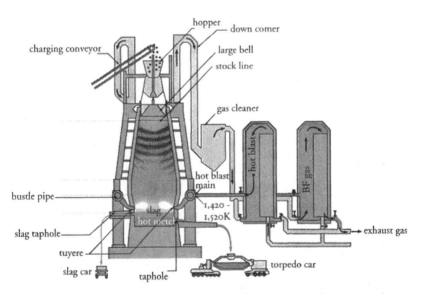

FIGURE 3.3. Principal components of a modern blast furnace and its associated equipment. Modified (with permission) from Morita and Emi (2003).

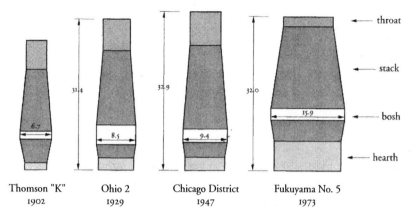

FIGURE 3.4. Record sizes of blast furnaces, 1902–1973. Based on Fig. 5-11 in Smil (1994)

power. After 1960 every one of the successive 16 furnaces holding the world record for internal volume was Japanese.

The Japanese perfected every important American ironmaking innovation and invested heavily into the requisite automated material handling, computerized controls, and operations research. During the 1960s Japan's pig iron production rose nearly six-fold from 11.9 to 68 Mt, and by 1974 it topped 90 Mt, a total surpassed only by the Soviet production that was coming also from large (2,000–3,000 m³) and highly automated (although not as efficient) BFs. And then, after centuries of gradual growth, BFs reached a clear growth plateau during the 1970s. By the year 2000, it appeared unlikely that we will see a significant number of larger units.

Maximum height of the largest units reached about 35 m (the overall height, including the charging, and gas-collecting superstructures, is about 80 m) and their internal volume is mostly between 2,000 and 4,000 m³, with maxima of about 5,200 m³ (figure 3.4). Hearths, with areas of 80–150 m², collect the liquid iron and slag (which removes such impurities as silicon, aluminum, and some sulfur) between tappings, and in their upper part they have between 15 and more than 40 tuyeres that admit pressurized hot (more than 1,200°C) air enriched with oxygen into the furnace. Hearths are lined with carbon brick; the remainder of the furnace with chamotte (burnt clay), and silicon-carbide bricks. Charged materials are delivered by a conveyor belt from the stockhouse, and pipes conduct waste gases (containing about 4 GJ/m³) to be cleaned and used to preheat the blast and also to generate electricity (figure 3.3).

These furnaces can operate under pressure of up to about 250 kPa, and they may produce hot (1,530°C) metal continuously for many years before their refractory brick interior and their carbon hearth are relined. Molten metal is released regularly through tapholes closed with a clay plug and opened up by a special drill, and the slag (often used by construction industry or as a mineral fertilizer) is removed through cinder notches. Maximum daily output of the largest furnaces is about 10,000 t of hot metal (figure 3.5). Mass and energy flows needed to operate large BFs are prodigious (Peacey and Davenport 1979; Sugawara et al. 1986). A furnace producing 10,000 t of metal a day will need more than 4.5 Mt of hot blast air a year, and it has to be supplied with about 1.6 t of pelletized ore, 400 kg of coke, 100 kg of injected coal (or 60 kg of fuel oil), and 200 kg of limestone for every tonne of iron. These charges add up to annual mass of 8 Mt of raw materials and an equivalent of nearly 2.5 Mt of good steam coal.

The three largest furnaces designed and built during the 1970s have been relined several times and are still working. Europe's largest BF, Schwelgern 1 of August-Thyssen Hütte in Duisburg-Schwelgern, was blown in during February 1973: 33 m tall, hearth diameter of 14 m, and capacity of 4,200 m³ allow daily output of 10,000 t of pig iron. By its 30th anniversary this BF had smelted 83 Mt of hot metal (Thyssen Krupp Stahl 2003). The world's largest BF—with the volume of 5,070 m³—was blown in at Kyūshū Oita Works in

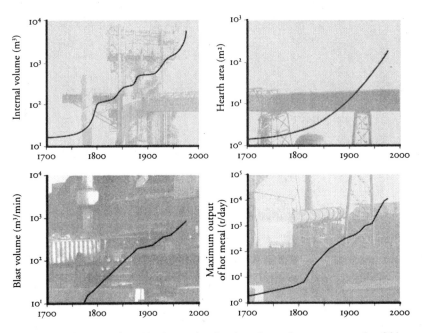

FIGURE 3.5. Four semilogarithmic graphs showing the 20th-century growth of blast furnaces in terms of the internal volume (top left), blast volume (bottom left), (top right) hearth area, and maximum daily output of hot metal (bottom left). Trends assembled from numerous metallurgical publications.

1976, and America's largest BF, Inland's No. 7 (3,600 m³ and about 9,000 t of hot metal per day) was blown in October of 1980 (McManus 1981).

By 1980 American ironmaking was in a steep decline as pig iron smelting fell to less than 40 Mt by 1982, from the peak of 91.9 Mt in 1973. European output also decreased and even the Japanese ironmaking had its first post-WWII setbacks. And so it appeared that, after almost exactly 250 years of growth, the smelting of iron with coke and limestone would be soon over. Yet by 1990—as the total number of BFs operating in the United States was down to just 60, from about 250 during the 1960s and 452 in 1920—it became clear that BFs will produce the bulk of the world's iron needs not only for the remainder of the century, but at least for the first two decades of the new one as well. Why this reprieve? Three reasons explain it: resilience of the basic smelting technique, its continuing improvements, and the relatively slow pace of the development and diffusion of alternatives.

BFs are reliable producers of large volumes of pig iron and are supported by elaborate supply systems of iron ore mines, limestone or dolomite quarries, pelletizing or sintering plants, coal mines, coking batteries, coal trains, ore and coal carriers, and harbors. Such proven, high-volume performers and such expensive infrastructures have considerable operational inertia, and the entire system is kept up with repairs and upgrades, especially at times of cyclical market upswings (McManus 1988). Better linings (including expensive graphitic refractories and cooling plates) allowed unprecedented extensions of typical BF campaigns. During the early 1980s campaigns were usually no longer than 3–5 years; by the late 1990s 8- to 10-year-long campaigns were not unusual, and the world record-holder, OneSteel's Whyalla BF in Australia that was relined in 1980, had the next planned overhaul in 2004, accomplishing a generation-long campaign (Bagsarian 2001). [OneSteel's Whyalla furnace was overhauled in August/September of 2004, only to suffer two cooling events that resulted in the loss of 140,000 tonnes of raw steel production (OneSteel 2005).] Better lining and better stoves made it possible to raise hot blast temperatures and to increase average daily output by 15–25%.

But the most effective way of improving the BF's longer term prospects was the reduction of coke consumption thanks to high coal injection rates. This option was neglected during the decades of low-cost hydrocarbons when increasing amounts of fuel oil and natural gas were used to replace coke. Only Kentucky's Armco ran against the trend, injecting pulverized coal through tuyeres at its Ashland plant since 1963. Rising oil prices led to a rapid Japanese adoption of the technique: Nippon Kokan Kabushiki (NKK) was Armco's first foreign licensee in 1981—and by 1985 oil-less operation was the leading BF technique in Japan. Coal injection was also spreading in Europe, and by the late 1980s its economies (replacing up to 40% of charged coke with coal costing only 35–45% as much per tonne) finally brought a growing U.S. interest (Hess 1989; McManus 1989).

By the end of the 1980s there were about 50 furnaces in Europe, Japan, and United States using at least 90 and as much as 175 kg of injected coal per tonne of hot metal, and by the late 1990s maxima were about 200 kg/t of hot metal, enough to reduce coke use by about 175 kg/t. In order to maintain high flame temperature, the practice of additional fuel injection requires oxygen enrichment of the hot blast air (AISI 1998). A minimum amount of coke is still needed to support the ore and limestone burden and to provide a permeable medium for the ascent of reducing gases and the descent of molten slag and metal. Besides considerable energy savings, the substitution also reduces the environmental impact of coking. And during the late 1990s the NKK pioneered partial coke replacement by used plastics, charging as much as 120,000 t of the pulverized material per BF in a year, saving coke (1.1 t/t of plastics, an equivalent of 1.5% of annual energy use) and reducing carbon dioxide (CO_2) emissions by about 3.5 kg C per tonne of hot metal (NKK 2001).

Despite the output stagnation and decline of the early 1980s and, again, in the early 1990s, the world's pig iron smelting grew by about 14% during the 20th century's last two decades when China emerged as the metal's leading producer. By the year 2000 its output of slightly more than 130 Mt accounted for more than 20% of the global output; it surpassed that of the European Union and was three times as large as the U.S. total (see figure 3.2 for U.S. figures). By that time East Asia—China, Japan, South Korea, and Taiwan—produced more than two fifths of the world's pig iron and a third of all crude steel; the latter share is lower because European and North American countries produce relatively more steel from scrap.

Steelmaking: Basic Oxygen Furnace and Electric Arc Furnace

In a 1992 paper, the president of research at Kawasaki Steel argued that the popular conception of steelmaking as the quintessential outmoded kind of industrial production was wrong because the process was transformed by a flood of innovations. He then concluded that "with little fanfare, it has become as impressive as that acme of modern manufacturing practice, integrated-circuit processing" (Ohashi 1992:540). Beginning during the 1950s, steelmaking underwent two largely concurrent waves of key technical substitutions: first, open hearth furnaces (OHFs) were replaced in all but a few countries by basic oxygen furnaces (BOFs) and second, BOFs were replaced by electric arc furnaces (EAFs). OHFs, dominant between the first decade of the 20th century and 1960s, eventually evolved into a much larger and more productive processing unit. The largest OHF used by U.S. Steel before 1910 had hearth area of about 40 m² and produced heats of 42 t, while the biggest furnace installed during WWII had hearth of about 85 m² and could accommodate heat of 200 t (King 1948). But the furnace was inherently inefficient, and once a better alternative became available it quickly prevailed (see figure 4.5 in *CTTC*).

By the year 2000 a mere 4% of the world's steel came from OHFs, as only the Ukraine and Russia produced major shares of the metal (50% and 27%) by using this quintessential 19th-century technique (IISI 2002). The OHF's demise was driven by BOF's rapid ascent, which was possible only once inexpensive large volumes of pure oxygen became available as already noted. The BOF process is basically an improved type of Bessemer's converter: Bessemer did actually take out a patent for oxygen blowing, rather than blowing plain air, to decarburize the metal (U.K. Patent 2,207 on October 5, 1858), but the gas was not available at reasonable cost and in large volumes until four generations later. The first adjective in the process's name refers to the use of basic magnesium oxide (MgO) refractory linings that are used to remove trace amounts of phosphorus and sulfur from the molten metal. The story of the BOF is notable for the fact that neither the technique's initial development nor its commercialization owes anything to the leading steel companies of the day and everything to the perseverance of one man and a vision of a few managers in a small company.

After his graduation in Aachen in 1915, Swiss metallurgist Robert Durrer (1890–1978) remained in Germany, and between 1928 and 1943 he was a professor of *Eisenhüttenkunde* at Berlin's Technische Hochschule, where he began years of experiments with oxygen in steel refining and smelting. After his return to Switzerland in 1943, he became a board member of von Roll AG, the country's largest steel company (Starratt 1960). In the same year C.V. Schwarz was issued a German patent (735,196) for a top-blown oxygen converter, and in 1946 a Belgian patent (468,316) by John Miles added some refinements to the basic concept (Adams and Dirlam 1966). But neither of these conceptual designs was actually tested while Durrer continued his experiments at von Roll's plant in Gerlafingen with the help of the German metallurgist Heinrich Hellbrügge.

In 1947 Durrer bought a small (2.5 t) converter in the United States, and with it, as he reported in the plant newspaper in May 1948:

> on the first day of spring, our "oxygen man" Dr. Heinrich Hellbrügge carried out the initial tests and thereby for the first time in Switzerland hot metal was converted into steel by blowing with pure oxygen . . . On Sunday the 3rd of April 1948 . . . results showed that more than half of the hot-metal weight could be added in the form of cold scrap . . . which is melted through the blast-produced heat. (Durrer 1948:73)

Hellbrügge found no major problems either with the durability of the oxygen nozzle or with the converter lining, and the ability to charge large amounts of scrap was particularly important as it reduced dependence on the primary

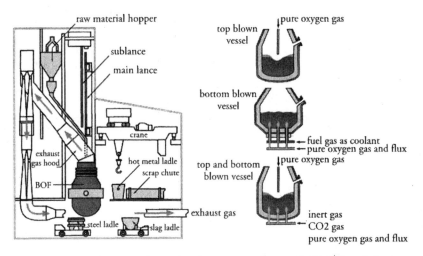

FIGURE 3.6. Typical setting of a modern basic oxygen furnace (BOF; left) and the three common ways it operates (right). Modified (with permission) from Morita and Emi (2003).

metal. And so we have, as in the case of Edison's incandescent light or Wrights' first engine-powered flight, the exact date of one of the key (albeit generally unappreciated) modern inventions.

Subsequent developments made the BOF commonly (but inaccurately) known as an Austrian invention. Soon after his success Hellbrügge told Herman Trenkler, the works manager at VÖEST (*Vereinigte Österreichische Eisen- und Stahlwerke AG*, the largest Austrian steelmaker), that the BOF process is ready for scaling up to commercial production. In a matter of weeks an agreement for a joint study of BOFs was concluded by von Roll, VÖEST, and Alpine Montan AG, another Austrian steelmaker. Theodor Eduard Suess of VÖEST's Linz plant and, simultaneously, managers at Alpine in Donawitz, organized the actual experiments. Problems such as the oxygen supply, position of the oxygen lance, and nozzle's cross section were resolved by June 1949; in December it was decided to proceed with the construction of two 30-t BOFs, and the first steel was produced on November 27, 1952 (Starratt 1960; VÖEST 2003). Alpine's BOF production began in May 1953.

VÖEST eventually acquired the rights to what became known as the Linz-Donawitz process (*LD Verfahren*)—although the Bessemer-Durrer process would be a more accurate identification of its intellectual and pilot-plant origins. None of the world's premier steelmakers in the United States showed any interest in the innovation that was perfected by a small Central European company whose total steelmaking capacity was less than one third of that of a single plant of U.S. Steel (Adams and Dirlam 1966). McLouth Steel in Trenton, Michigan, with less than 1% of the U.S. ingot capacity, pioneered the

American BOF steelmaking with three furnaces installed late in 1954 (Hogan 1971; ASME 1985). Although most steelmaking experts were convinced that the BOF is an innovation of far-reaching significance (Emerick 1954), U.S. Steel installed its first BOF only in 1964, as did Bethlehem Steel. But elsewhere the technique was diffusing rapidly: by 1970 half of the world's steel (and 80% of Japan's production) came from BOFs; 30 years later, as the use of EAFs increased, the U.S. and Japanese BOF shares were, respectively, slightly more than 50% and slightly more than 70%, and globally almost 60% of all steel was made by BOFs in the year 2000.

In a BOF, oxygen was initially blown in only as a supersonic jet from a water-cooled vertical lance onto molten pig iron, but starting in the late 1960s it was also introduced through the tuyeres at the furnace bottom, and combined systems are now common (Barker et al. 1998; figure 3.6). Bottom blowing is also used to introduce inert gas (argon) for stirring the charge and lime to remove excess phosphorus. Rapid oxidation lowers the metal's carbon content and other impurities, and hot gas leaving the furnace is 90% CO and 10% CO_2. The entire process is slightly exothermic, with the overall gain of about 200 MJ per tonne of crude steel. Typically about 50–60 m^3 of oxygen is needed per tonne of crude steel; the largest BOFs are 10 m high and up to 8 m in diameter, and the capacities range mostly from 150 to 300 t.

The substitution of OHFs by BOFs resulted in enormous productivity gains. BOFs require a much smaller volume of blown-in gas, no nitrogen gets dissolved in the hot metal, and the reaction's surplus heat can be used to melt added cold scrap. And the process is much faster because a BOF can decarburize a heat of up to 300 t of iron from 4.3% to 0.04% C in just 35–45 min compared to 9–10 hours in the best OHF. In labor terms this meant going from more than 3 worker-hours per tonne in 1920 to 0.003 worker-hours by 1999, a 1,000-fold gain (Berry, Ritt, and Greissel 1999). The only disadvantage of the BOF process has been the reduced flexibility of charges: while for OHFs, scrap can make up as much as 80% of the total, for BOFs it can be only up to 30%.

The EAF was yet another contribution of William Siemens, one of the greatest innovators of the 19th century (see figure 4.4 in *CTTC*), to ferrous metallurgy. But because of high cost and limited availability of electricity, his pioneering (1878–1879) experiments did not lead to any immediate commercial applications. Starting in 1888 EAFs made it possible to smelt aluminum and then to produce specialty steels, and the furnace remained in these roles, and with relatively limited unit capacities (first pre-1910 Héroult's EAFs rated just 3–5 t; those of the 1920s, mostly 25 t), until the 1930s. The EAF's use for large-scale steelmaking became attractive as electricity prices declined and once large amounts of scrap iron and steel became available.

The U.S. EAF output passed 1 Mt/year only in 1940, and by the end of WWII—during which the furnace capacities grew to 100 t/heat and the production of low-carbon steel was added to the traditional making of specialty alloys—the total was more than 3 Mt. By the early 1970s the largest capacities were more than 300 t and EAFs dominated the smelting of highly alloyed and stainless varieties. The scrap metal to feed EAFs comes from three major sources. The home (circulating) scrap that originates in ironmaking and during the conversion of ingots to finished products represented most of the recycled mass in integrated plants. Prompt industrial scrap comes from a multitude of processes, above all from metalworking and manufacturing. Composition of these two streams is well known, and their quality is acceptable. In contrast, obsolete metal, be it in the form of defunct machinery or old vehicles, ships and appliances, often contains undesirable ingredients either as added metals (e.g., tinned steel cans) or as contaminants.

The shift from BOFs to EAFs severed the link between steelmaking and blast furnaces and coking and made it possible to set up new, smaller mills whose location did not have to take into account the supplies of coal, ore, and limestone. This minimill option led to the development of the most dynamic, and the most competitive, segment of new steelmaking during the last third of the 20th century. These steelworks—with annual capacities ranging from less than 50,000 to as much as 600,000 t of metal—combine EAFs (charged with cold scrap) with continuous casting and rolling. Initially they made such low-grade products as bars, structural shapes, and wire rods, but during the 1980s they began to produce higher grades of steel (Barnett and Crandall 1986; Szekely 1987; Hall 1997).

Cost advantages drove this innovation: minimills, dispensing with blast furnaces, needed much lower capital investment (only 15–20% of the total needed for new BFs), and their operating costs were also considerably lower as continuous casting eliminated the equipment and energy needed for reheating and shaping the ingots (Jones, Bowman, and Lefrank 1998). By the mid-1970s there were more than 200 such enterprises worldwide, nearly half of them in Western Europe and 50 in the United States. By the year 2000 a third of the world's steel came from EAFs, and the United States, with 47% of its total output, had the highest share among major producers; China's EAF share was just 16%, Japan's 29%, and Russia less than 15% (IISI 2002). Steadily improving performance accompanied the EAF diffusion. In 1965 the best furnaces needed about 630 kWh/t of crude steel; 25 years later the best rate, with the help of oxygen blowing, was down to 350 kWh/t (De Beer, Worrell, and Blok 1998), and IISI (2002) reported that during the 1990s the global mean fell from 450 to about 390 kWh/t.

Concurrently, worldwide average tap-to-tap times declined from 105 to 70 min, while the tap weights rose from 86 to 110 Mt and productivity increased by more than 50% to 94 t/h. Increased consumption of oxygen, charging of hot and preheated metal, and higher power inputs were the principal reasons for these improvements. By the 1990s EAFs received commonly 30–40% of their total energy from oxyfuel burners and lances. With nearly 40 m³/t, a furnace at the Badische Stahlwerke in Kehl set the world record in April 1999 by producing 72 heats of nearly 80 t each, and the world's largest EAF (375 t) in Sterling, Illinois, consumed oxygen, delivered from eight fuel burners and two lances, at a nearly identical rate (Greissel 2000).

Scrap preheating, to as much as 800°C, also became fairly common, as did the charging of hot metal (up to 30–50% of the total). Ultrahigh-power more than 50 megavolt-ampere (MVA) transformers were first introduced in 1970, and the worldwide shift from AC to DC EAFs—resulting in lower specific consumption of electricity, electrodes (from as much as 7 kg/t of steel to as little as 1.75 kg/t), and refractories and in less noise—began in 1985 (Takahashi, Hongu, and Honda 1994; Jones 2003). There were also visible structural changes. Until the 1970s EAFs were commonly installed at grade level and needed pits for tapping and slag removal, while later furnaces were elevated above the plant floor, and efficient tapping without tilting became possible with the introduction of eccentric bottom taps (figure 3.7).

Continuous Casting

Diffusion of BOFs and EAFs was not the only key post-1950 transformation of steelmaking: the subsequent processing of the metal had also undergone a fundamental change. Traditional process involved first the production of steel

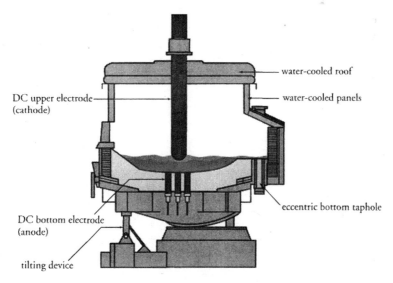

FIGURE 3.7. Cross section of a modern direct-current (DC) electric arc furnace with an eccentric taphole. Modified (with permission) from Morita and Emi (2003).

ingots, oblong pieces weighing 50–100 t that had to be reheated before further processing yielded standard semifinished products: slabs (from just 5 cm to as much as 25 cm thick and up to more than 3 m wide), billets (square profiles with sides of up to 25 cm used mainly to produce bars), and blooms (rectangular profiles wider than 20 cm used to roll I- and H-beams) that were then converted by hot or cold rolling into finished plates and coils (some as thin as 1 mm), structural pieces (bars, beams, rods), rails, and wire. This inefficient sequence, which often consumed as much energy as the steelmaking itself, was eventually replaced by continuous casting (CC) of steel (Morita and Emi 2003; Luiten 2001; Tanner 1998; Fruehan 1998; Schrewe 1991). The sequence BF–OHF–steel ingots, dominant until the 1950s, turned into the BF–BOF–CC and, as more steel scrap was used, increasingly into the EAF–CC process.

The idea of continuous casting had already been patented by Henry Bessemer in 1865 and was further elaborated by him nearly three decades later (Bessemer 1891). Various casting machines were tried and patented between the 1870s and 1920s, but the process was first successfully deployed only during the 1930s for casting nonferrous metals whose lower melting points made the operation easier. Siegfried Junghans, a German metallurgist, invented a vertically oscillating (reciprocating) mold. This invention eliminated the possibility of the solidifying molten metal sticking to the mold and causing shell tearing and costly breakouts of the liquid metal. Junghans designed the first working prototype in 1927 and applied for a patent in October 1933, and in 1935 he began a long period of independent development of steel casting.

Irving Rossi (1889–1991), an American engineer who had been involved in a number of business ventures in pre-WWII Germany, visited Junghans at his makeshift research workshop in 1936, and despite witnessing a less than perfect attempt at continuously casting a brass billet, he became convinced that the technique has an enormous potential (Tanner 1998). On November 15, 1936, Rossi received from Junghans exclusive rights to the basic patent and its followups for the United States and England as well as nonexclusive rights for other countries outside of Germany, and two years later also a commitment to share all information needed to build CC plants. In return he was to finance the commercialization of the process outside of Germany and by 1937 had the first U.S. orders for German-built brass casters. In 1947 Rossi convinced Alleghany Ludlum Steel to use the technique for casting steel in its Watervliet, New York, plant, where the first slabs were produced by an American-made (Koppers) machine in May 1949.

By 1949, Rossi's was not the only CC line, as steelmakers in United States, Germany, Japan, and Russia were experimenting with the technique—but it was the first, albeit very small, commercial CC success. Concurrently, Junghans's post-WWII work led to the first successful production runs at his workshop in Schorndorf in 1949, and in 1950 he set up an experimental plant in cooperation with Mannesmann AG at the company's works in Huckingen, which began casting in 1952. But Rossi remained the technique's leading pioneer, setting up first the Continuous Metalcast Corporation and then, in October 1954, establishing Concast AG in Zurich. The story of the company's success is detailed by Heinrich Tanner, a Swiss lawyer whom Rossi persuaded in 1954 to become its general manager (Tanner 1998).

Its great profitability rested on its ownership of key CC patents, which it shared with the licensees in return for receiving, without charge, any new knowledge and patents arising from the operation of CC plants. And the company made arrangements with CC machine builders to conclude sales contracts only with itself in return for marketing the technique worldwide and for bearing the responsibility for solving any metallurgical problems that might arise in their operation. The formula of comprehensive licensing, strengthened in 1970 by a patent interchange cooperation agreement with Mannesmann (the company's main competitor), proved so successful that Concast AG eventually controlled more than 60% of the world market for continuous casters, and in 1981 its increasingly monopolistic behavior led to its forced reorganization ordered by the antitrust authorities in the United States and Europe.

When measured by the frequency of U.S. patents, the years 1968–1977 were the peak of CC innovation, with more than 1,100 awards (Aylen 2002). Half of these were to the U.S. inventors, but as with the BOF, major U.S. companies largely ignored the technique while Japanese steelmakers embraced it (figure 3.8). Japan's first CC line was installed in 1955; two decades later Japan had more than 100 CC machines, and by the early 1980s more than 90% of Japanese steel came from CC machines, compared to slightly more than 40% in the United States, where the two-thirds mark was passed only by 1990 (Okumura 1994; Burwell 1990). But by the year 2000 more than 85% of the world's steel was cast continuously, with the shares (96–97%) basically identical in the European Union, United States, and Japan (figure 3.8). Even in China, now the world's largest steel producer, CC accounted for nearly 90%, and among the major steelmakers only Russia (50%) and the Ukraine (20%) were still far behind.

The casting process begins as the molten steel is poured first into a tundish (a large vessel holding enough metal to assure continuous flow), from which it flows steadily through a submerged entry nozzle into a water-cooled copper mold, where it begins to form a solid skin (Schrewe 1991). Vertically oscillating the mold prevents sticking, and as the metal descends drive rolls withdraw the strand at speeds of 1.5–2.8 m/min to match the flow of the incoming metal (figure 3.9). Support rolls carry and bend the strand, and water sprays cool it until the core becomes solid at the caster's end, 10–40 m from the inlet. At that point strands are cut with oxyacetylene torches. The earliest casters were of simple vertical type, and this design is used in a semicontinuous process to produce more than 90% of the world's commercial aluminum alloys.

Naturally, vertical casters required either tall buildings or excavations of

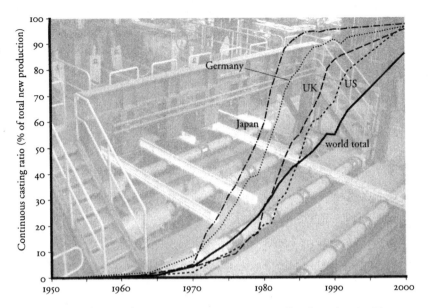

FIGURE 3.8. Diffusion of continuous casting, 1952–2000. Based on data in Okumura (1994) and data in IISI (2002).

deep pits; bending-type machines, introduced in 1956, reduced the height re-quirement by about 30%. Curved mold (bow-type) casters (figure 3.9)—de-signed independently by two Swiss engineers working at von Moos Steelworks and by Otto Schaaber, a metallurgist working for Mannesmann, during the late 1950s and introduced commercially in 1963—reduced the height require-ment yet again by at least 40%, and these remained the most popular machines until the early 1980s. They bend the metal strand into the horizontal plane as a progressively thicker solidified shell forms on its exterior. Post-1980 intro-ductions included vertical-bending, low-head, and horizontal designs (Oku-mura 1994). In all cases and with any metal, it is critical to prevent any de-formation and cracking of the forming metal strand.

The resulting semifinished products depend on the configuration of CC machines. During its earliest stages, the process could produce only billets (round or square) of limited cross section; larger blooms came next, and slabs were introduced during the late 1960s. The advantages of CC compared to ingot casting and subsequent primary rolling are numerous: much faster pro-duction (less than one hour vs. 1–2 days), higher yields of metal (up to 99% compared to less than 90% of steel to slab), energy savings on the order of 50–75%, and labor savings of the same magnitude. In addition, CC plants also need much less space. Going one step further is taking the hot slabs from CC directly to the rolling mill. This method yields the highest energy savings and

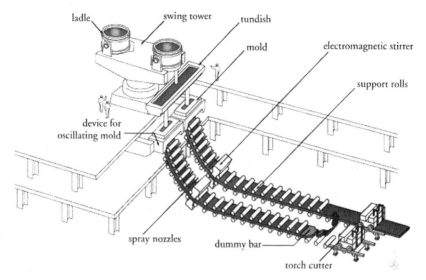

FIGURE 3.9. A typical layout of a two-stranded continuous steel slab caster. Modified (with permission) from Morita and Emi (2003).

reduces plant inventories of semifinished products, but high capital costs of retrofitting the operations delayed its wider adoption.

Development of thin slab casting began during the mid-1970s. Germany's Schloeman Siemag (SMS) first tested its Compact Strip Production in 1985, and America's Nucor deployed the world's first thin slab caster in Indiana in 1989. With this process, thin slabs, still retaining a liquid core, are reduced to 50 and 30 mm and are then directly hot-rolled into strips. Other thin slab casting systems include Italy's ISP and TSP, Germany's CPR, and Austria's Conroll commercialized by VÖEST-Alpine Stahl in Linz and in Avesta in Sweden (Ritt 2000). And during the 1980s some steelmakers began working on what was perhaps the industry's most coveted goal: producing hot strips (hot rolled coil steel) directly from a caster with no, or minimal, intermediary rolling. During the 1990s there were 13 different (and invariably very expensive and often very secretive) research and pilot projects in nine countries (Luiten 2001; Bagsarian 1998).

The first commercially successful strip caster designs came from Nippon Steel (in cooperation with Mitsubishi Heavy Industries) and from Australia's Broken Hill Proprietary (BHP) Corporation. Nippon Steel started its strip-casting operation at the Hikari plant secretly in October 1997 and made its success and its capacity (producing annually up to 500,000 t of 2–5 mm stainless strip up to 1.33 m wide) public in October 1998. During the same month BHP revealed its secret Port Kembla (New South Wales) operation: it began casting low-carbon steels from a 60-t ladle in strips of 1.5–2.5 mm, reduced by in-line rolling to 1.1 mm. Eurostrip, a joint undertaking of three major companies, cast its first strips, stainless steel 1.5–4.5 mm thick and 1.1–1.45 m wide (at speeds averaging 60–100 m/min), in Thyssen Krupp's Krefeld plant in December 1999 (Bagsarian 2000).

Strip casting does not use an oscillating mold, but rather replicates closely Bessemer's original twin-drum design (patented in 1857) that employed two rotating rolls (Bessemer 1891). Molten steel is poured between these water-cooled drums and cools rapidly, and the two solidifying shells are fused into a single strip as they are compressed between the drums (Takeuchi et al. 1994; figure 3.10). Cooling rates are 1,000 times faster than in conventional slab casting, and casting speeds can exceed 100 m/min. The major challenges are to

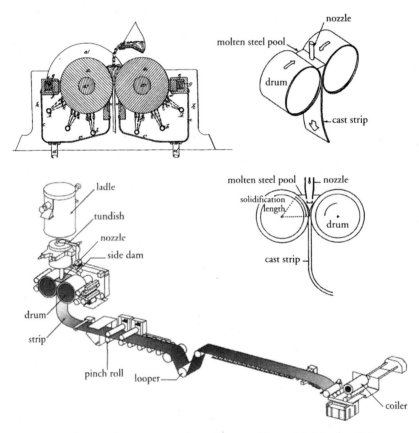

FIGURE 3.10. Bessemer's strip casting idea—illustrated here with his 1865 U.S. patent drawing—became commercially successful only during the 1990s (top left). Schematic drawings show a detail of the modern twin-drum caster (right) and of an entire strip casting line (bottom). Reproduced from Bessemer (1891) and modified (with permission) from Takeuchi et al. (1994) and Morita and Emi (2003).

maintain even feeding rate of liquid steel, to avoid premature solidification of edges, and to cope with extreme heat fluxes (up to 15 MW/m²) and temperature differences (up to 300°C/cm) in the forming strip. The greatest reward is, of course, the elimination of expensive rolling mills, which lowers the overall capital expenditure by 75–90% (Luiten 2001).

New Paths to Iron

The last two decades of the 20th century also saw the beginning of a radically new way of producing the civilization's dominant metal, the direct reduction of iron (DRI) that dispenses with coke and reduces iron ores in their solid state at temperatures well below the melting point of the metal (at only about 1,000°C). Fundamentally, this is an ancient process, as all pre-blast furnace (artisanal) iron was produced in this way: reducing ores in shallow hearths or small shaft furnaces with charcoal and then producing articles of wrought iron by repeating hammering of the spongy mass. Attempts to use DRI on industrial scale go back to the 19th century: most notably, between 1869 and 1877 William Siemens experimented with reducing a mixture of crushed high-quality ore and fuel in rotating cylindrical furnaces (Miller 1976). Two Swedish processes introduced during the 1920s remained limited to small-scale local production of iron powders (the Höganäs process is still used for metal powder), and the wider commercialization of DRI began only during the late 1960s.

By 1975 there were nearly 100 different designs (furnaces, kilns, retorts, fluidized bed reactors) using various reducing agents (coal, graphite, char, liquid and solid hydrocarbons, reformed gases), but only two categories of DRI production emerged as commercially important: processes using reducing gas that was prepared outside the reduction furnace, and techniques whose reducing gas is generated from hydrocarbons introduced into the furnace (Feinman 1999). Dominant natural-gas–based electrothermal shaft processes—the pioneering Mexican *Hojalata y Lamina*, whose latest version is marketed as HYL-III, and the U.S. MIDREX—reduce iron pellets or fines in an ascending flow of reducing gas and crushed limestone (Davis et al. 1982; Tennies et al. 1991; figure 3.11). The reducing gas is prepared by catalytic steam reforming of natural gas, which produces a mixture of CO and hydrogen ($CH_4 + H_2O \rightarrow CO + 3H_2$). Successful fluidized-bed processes of this type include Fior/FIN-MET, Iron Carbide, and Circored.

Coal-based processes use ore with fine fuel and slagging material either in rotary kilns (Krupp-CODIR, SL/RN, ACCAR) or in shafts and hearths (Kinglor-Metlor, Fastmet, INMETCO), and the reducing gas comes from hydrocarbons concurrently introduced into the furnace. The final product for all processes was initially just solid sponge iron, but its large specific area makes

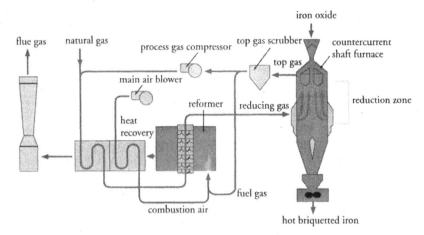

FIGURE 3.11. Schematic outline of the MIDREX process, the most successful way to produce iron by direct reduction. Modified (with permission) from Morita and Emi (2003).

it prone to reoxidation and unsuitable for transportation. In 1984 an additional step converted the sponge into hot briquetted iron (HBI) that is easily shipped and can replace scrap in EAFs or, because of its purity, makes high-quality steel. DRI's other advantages are the possibility to produce the metal in countries devoid of coking coal but rich in natural gas, flexible plant capacity, and lower energy cost and carbon use. The BF–BOF route requires an annual capacity of at least 2 Mt, but gas-based DRI is feasible with capacity of less than 0.5 Mt/year suitable for minimills. And while the most efficient BF–BOF route needs more than 13 GJ and emits about 285 kg C per tonne of liquid steel, natural-gas–based HBI–EAF combination needs less than 5.5 GJ and releases 166 kg C/t (Anderson et al. 2001).

There was a great deal of enthusiasm for these processes during the 1970s. Total output rose nearly tenfold during the 1970s to 7.1 Mt, and Miller (1976) forecast the annual production of sponge iron at 120 Mt by 1985—but the worldwide capacity of direct reduction plants in that year was slightly more than 20 Mt, and actual production was only about 11 Mt (MIDREX 2000). Worldwide output of DRI plants rose to 31 Mt by 1995 and to nearly 43 Mt (or about 7% of all iron) by the year 2000 (IISI 2002). More than 30 MIDREX plants produced two thirds of all DRI, and the three largest producers with annual output in excess of 5 Mt (Venezuela, Mexico, and India) accounted for more than two fifths of the total. But Japan did not have a single DRI plant, and both the European Union and the United States were negligible producers.

The ultimate goal of innovative ferrous metallurgy—direct ironmaking that produces liquid metal from raw materials and allows the use of any kind of coal and fine ores instead of coke and iron pellets, thereby cutting capital costs by eliminating both coke and agglomeration plants and significantly reducing CO_2 emissions—remained elusive (Luiten 2001). In 1988 a task force of the American Iron & Steel Institute estimated that it will take a decade to commercialize this new metal-making route, and five years later McManus (1993: 20) thought that "the race to find a coal-based replacement for the blast furnace is moving into the home stretch." But that was only wishful thinking as BFs remained the dominant producer of iron until the very end of the 20th century and will remain so for many years to come. Even if new DRI-based facilities, with annual capacities averaging 1 Mt per plant, were built at a net rate of 10 a year (aggregate additions during the 1990s were less than 3 Mt), it would take more than half a century to displace all BF iron.

Accomplishments and Consequences

Both the absolute and relative figures of 20th-century global steelmaking are impressive: a 30-fold increase of annual production (from 28 to 846 Mt), and an eightfold rise in per capita output (from less than 18 to nearly 140 kg/year). So is the cumulative aggregate: during the 20th century the world's steelmakers produced nearly 31 Gt of the metal, with half of this total made after 1980. What happened to this enormous mass? At least a 10th of all steel made since 1900 had been oxidized or was destroyed in wars, about a quarter had been recycled, and another 15% was embedded in above-ground structures and underground (or underwater) foundations and hence beyond easy recycling. The remainder represents the accumulated steel stock of about 15 Gt, or about 2.5 t per capita, that can be potentially made into new steel. A detailed Japanese account shows that the country's accumulated steel stock by the year 2000 was 1.3 Gt, or 10 t per capita (Morita and Emi 2003). Close to 10% of the world's accessible steel stock is in motorized vehicles, and currently about 2% of all accessible steel is reused annually as scrap.

Unfortunately, these impressive achievements were not matched by the perception of the industry's role in the modern world. I agree with Ohashi's (1992) previously cited assessment of the impressiveness of the advances in modern steelmaking, but I do not believe that this conclusion has any chance of widespread acceptance. During the closing decades of the 20th century, nearly all major steel producers were either losing money or surviving on assorted subsidies, and the industry with such a dismal record of devouring capital had little chance of being as glamorous as computer chip making, which produced some of the most spectacular investment returns in history. Steelmakers advanced their techniques in many impressive ways, and by the century's end they were delivering the highest-ever mass of the metal of unprecedented quality—but they were doing so within the confines of a mature, slow-growing industry that had largely lost its economic influence.

At the beginning of the 20th century it was steel that was the driver of America's stock markets (later in this chapter I describe U.S. Steel's impressive beginnings)—but by its end it was the computer industry in general, and integrated circuits in particular, that was seen as the leading driver of the New Economy. A simple what-if experiment allows us to see the relative importance of these sectors in a realistic perspective. An affluent, advanced, high-energy civilization is perfectly possible without integrated circuits: that is, indeed, what we were until the early 1970s. In contrast, no such society is possible without large-scale production and use of steel. The fact that by the year 2000 the combined market capitalization of the 10 largest U.S. steel companies was just a 10th of the value of Home Depot (which in that year became the latest addition to the Dow) says nothing about the relative importance of these two kinds of activities; it merely reveals the speculative bias of investors who, nevertheless, could not make it through a single day without steel.

Both iron- and steelmaking entered the 20th century as established, mature, mass-producing industries, but by its end they were profoundly transformed by technical advances that affected every aspect of smelting, casting, and finishing the metal. Steelmaking innovations followed in particularly close waves after 1950 as BOF, EAF, and CC techniques made the industry vastly more productive and less labor intensive, and because of steadily declining energy cost of pig iron and crude steel, also environmentally much more acceptable. At the beginning of the 20th century typical energy needs in ironmaking (virtually all of it as coke) were around 50 GJ/t of pig iron; by 1950 it was about 30 GJ/t, and during the late 1990s the net specific energy consumption of modern BFs was between 12.5 and 15 GJ/t (De Beer, Worrell, and Blok 1998), or at roughly twice the theoretically lowest amount of energy (6.6 GJ/t) needed to produce iron from hematite. These efficiency gains came mainly from reduced coke consumption, increased blast temperatures, and larger furnaces.

Decarburization of iron in OHFs and the subsequent shaping of steel could easily double the energy cost of traditionally finished products, and even the best integrated steel mills consumed typically more than 40 GJ/t in 1950. Typical gains that resulted from innovations in steelmaking and casting (with all figures per tonne of liquid metal) were, according to Leckie, Millar, and Medley (1982), more than 3 GJ for substituting BOFs (600 MJ for electricity needed to make oxygen: the smelting process itself is exothermic) for OHFs (4 GJ) and nearly 1 GJ to replace the rolling from ingots (1.2 GJ) by continuous casting (300 MJ). Combined effects of these innovations brought energy costs of steelmaking down to 25 GJ/t by 1975 and to below 20 GJ/t during the late 1990s, with nearly two thirds of that total used by BFs, just a few percent claimed by BOFs, and the rest needed for rolling and shaping (Leckie, Millar, and Medley 1982; De Beer, Worrell, and Blok 1998).

The U.S. average for the mid-1990s fell to about 19 GJ/t, and similarly, Japan's consumption averaged 19.4 GJ/t of crude steel in 2000 (JISF 2003). In contrast, the most efficient EAF-based producers of the late 1990s needed about 7 GJ/t. Continuing declines in energy intensity of ferrous metallurgy meant that in 2000 the production of roughly 850 Mt of the world's leading alloy needed about 20 EJ or slightly more than 6% of the world's total consumption of fossil fuels and primary electricity (Smil 2003). Had the energy intensity remained at the 1900 level, ferrous metallurgy would have claimed almost 20% of all the world's primary commercial energy in 2000. But despite these impressive efficiency gains, iron- and steelmaking remain the world's largest energy-consuming industries, claiming about 15% of all industrial energy use. In the United States, with its enormous energy use by households, transportation, and services, the share was much smaller, only about 8% of all energy used in manufacturing and just 2.5% of all primary commercial energy during the late 1990s (USDOE 2000).

At the beginning of the 20th century, rails were the single largest category of finished steel products; by its end sheets and strips, destined for automotive and household goods markets, were dominant: in the year 2000 they accounted for slightly more than half of U.S. steel output. Another key shift has been toward higher quality and higher performance steels: by the year 2000 the global production of stainless alloys (containing at least 13% Cr) approached 20 Mt/year (or more than 2% of the total output), and specialty steels are used in applications ranging from deep-water offshore drilling rigs to record-height skyscrapers.

Finally, a few paragraphs on the economic and social impacts of the changing pattern and cost of the global steel production. Western steelmaking became a mature industry within three generations after the beginning of its substantial expansion during the 1880s. Subsequently, Japan's innovation-driven quality-stressing ascent was much more important than the technically inferior Soviet expansion. Between 1946 and 1974 there were only three years (1954, 1958, and 1971) when the global steel output dipped; in contrast, the last quarter of the 20th century saw output declines in 10 years (figure 3.12). The slow rise of average price of finished steel that began after the end of the economic crisis of the 1930s changed into a steep ascent after OPEC's oil price hike of the early 1970s; once that rise was broken, steel prices began to fluctuate, sometimes by more than 10% a year. American steelmaking was especially affected by cheaper exports from Russia, Ukraine, and Asia, and compared to its global dominance that lasted until the early 1960s, it ended the century as a much weakened industry.

At the very beginning of the 20th century, U.S. Steel Corporation—formed by Charles M. Schwab, J. Pierpont Morgan, and Andrew Carnegie on April

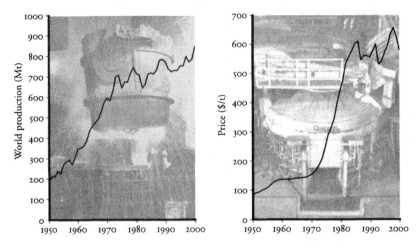

FIGURE 3.12. Global steel production and the average U.S. price per tón, 1950–2000.
Plotted from data in Kelly and Fenton (2004) and IISI (2002).

I, 1901—became the first company capitalized at $1.4 billion, and U.S. steel
mills contributed 36% of the global output (Apelt 2001). In 1945, with German
and Japanese industries in ruins, the United States produced nearly 80% of
the world's steel. Inevitably, that temporarily high share had to drop, but the
absolute output kept increasing (with inevitable fluctuations) until 1973. But
the post-1973 decline was unexpectedly harsh (Hall 1997). Between 1975 and
1995, 18 out of America's 21 integrated steelmakers merged, were bought, or
went bankrupt, and by the century's end the United States produced just 12%
of the world's steel. Yet the economic boom of the 1990s helped to lift the
country's annual steel output by about 13%, and the industry's productivity
rose to new highs and to a surprisingly competitive level, particularly in producing flat-rolled items.

But the stagnating and declining stock values of America's steel companies
accelerated the loss of prestige that was previously enjoyed by this key industry.
During the late 1970s three out of the world's top seven steelmaking companies
were still American (U.S. Steel, Bethlehem, and National Steel, ranking fourth,
fifth, and sixth, respectively), but by the year 2000 the largest U.S. company
(U.S. Steel) placed no higher than 14th as surging imports, low prices (they
actually declined between 1995 and 2000), and huge foreign excess capacity (at
250 Mt in 2000, almost twice the average U.S. consumption) caused more
than a dozen American steelmakers to file for bankruptcy between 1998 and
2000 (AISI 2002). Two other highly symbolic developments signaled U.S.
steel's decline: in 1991 USX, the parent company of U.S. Steel, was replaced
on the Dow 30 by Disney. Could there be a more incredible mark of decline

as the originally unmatched Schwab, Morgan, and Carnegie's creation of 1901 was ousted by a Mickey Mouse outfit of 1991? Six years later Bethlehem Steel was displaced by Johnson & Johnson (Bagsarian 2000).

Naturally, socioeconomic dislocations of this decline were substantial. In February 1943 the number of U.S. steelworkers represented by their union peaked at slightly more than 725,000 (Hogan 1971), and despite the subsequent rise in productivity, the industry still employed half a million workers by 1975 and 425,000 by 1980. But by 1991 the number dropped below 200,000, and the century ended with just 151,000 Americans making iron and steel, only about 20,000 more than were employed by the country's aluminum industry. Consequences of this unraveling of what was once the nation's leading industry can be easily seen by visiting such former strongholds of steelmaking as Pittsburgh, Pennsylvania, or Gary, Indiana. But even as America's iron and steel industry struggled, it did not stop innovating; one of the most notable proofs of this is the pioneering role of MIDREX Technologies of Charlotte, North Carolina, in developing and commercializing a new way for direct reduction of iron.

Industrial Gases

Jumping from the hardest mass-produced solid of modern civilization to the cryogenic distillation of atmospheric gases in air separation plants is not done here for the sake of contrast. Oxygen and nitrogen are the two elements that deserve to be ranked, together with steel, among a handful of man-made inputs whose incessant and inexpensive supply provided the material foundations of the 20th century. At the same time, production of these gases from the atmosphere is a nearly perfect example of those technical advances that, although indispensable for shaping the modern world, have been inexplicably neglected or, at best, treated much more cursorily than ferrous metallurgy in standard accounts of inventions and innovations. For example, Williams, in *The History of Invention* (1987), a treatment of exemplary breadth based on the multivolume Oxford set, does not devote even a single sentence to air liquefaction, cryogenics, or mass production of industrial gases.

This is inexcusable, as industrial gases—with hydrogen and carbon dioxide ranking in the overall importance behind oxygen and nitrogen—are now in demand by every major segment of modern economy. In the year 2000 the worldwide industrial gas market, growing by 7% a year, totaled about $34 billion, and according to some estimates industrial gases are used by producers and services that account for more than half of the global economic outputs (Freedonia Group 2002). And the industry is also a perfect example of technical innovations whose basic processes were developed, and to a considerable degree improved, during the two pre-WWI generations but whose true importance became clear only decades later as their more efficiently made products transformed the fortunes of many key modern industries.

During the first decade of the 20th century, none of the inventors of the separation of gases from liquefied air could have foreseen the decisive role that the two principal elements will have, respectively, in feeding billions of people and in producing the world's most important metal. As already noted, without inexpensive oxygen we would not be producing about three fifths of the world's steel in basic oxygen furnaces—and without equally inexpensive nitrogen we could not make cheap ammonia, now the precursor of all nearly inorganic nitrogenous fertilizers whose application made it possible to feed a world population of more than six billion people (Smil 2001; see also chapter 4 of *CTTC*).

And these are just two key uses of the two principal atmospheric gases. I already noted the use of oxygen to enrich air and to increase combustion temperatures in both blast furnaces and electric arc furnaces, and the gas is used for the same reasons in smelting color metals (copper, lead, zinc) and in production of glass, mineral wool, lime, and cement. Oxygen and oxygen–acetylene flames are indispensable in welding, particularly of large pieces that had to be previously cast as unwieldy units, and are also used for straightening, cutting, and hardening metals. Chemical syntheses, catalytic cracking of crude oil in refineries, coal gasification, wastewater treatment, paper bleaching (to replace chlorine dioxide), and oxygenation of aquacultural ponds (now the fastest expanding method of producing animal protein) are other major industrial users, dwarfing the element's well-known therapeutic applications.

Except for the mass flows for ammonia synthesis, nitrogen uses tend to be more low-volume affairs in a wide variety of tasks, most of them never thought of by even well-informed people. Shrink fitting—cooling such inner parts of metal assemblies as liners, pistons, pins or bushings by liquid nitrogen prior to their insertion in order to create a very tight fit—is an excellent example of such a specialized, but now very common, application. Unlike the traditional expansion fitting through the heating of the outer parts, this is a much faster method and one that causes no metallurgical damage (it can be used, naturally, also to disassemble tightly fitted parts). An altogether different class of nitrogen application is to use the gas as an inert blanketing agent to protect flammables and explosives or to prevent degradative reactions (you can now use it to protect your opened bottles of wine). Perhaps the best-known use of the gas is for freezing and cooling—be it of the ground (prior to drilling or tunneling) or blood, antiviral vaccines or bull semen, food or reaction vessels.

Hydrogen—another major industrial feedstock and the energy carrier of the new energy economy whose imminent coming has been prophesied by many ill-informed enthusiasts—cannot be, of course, taken economically from the air where it is present in a merest trace, about 0.00005% compared to

0.0036% for CO_2. Its first large-scale industrial production (for the Haber-Bosch synthesis of ammonia; see chapter 4 of *CTTC*) was done by the steam reforming of coal, but since the 1950s it has been made overwhelmingly by steam reforming of hydrocarbons, above all methane (CH_4), the dominant constituent of natural gases. Besides the mass flows for the synthesis of NH_3, hydrogen is also used in such diverse ways as making a multitude of compounds ranging from methanol, polymers, and solvents to vitamins and pharmaceuticals; to produce solid fats through the hydrogenation of unsaturated fatty acids; to cool large turbogenerators; and, as space enthusiasts know, as an excellent rocket fuel.

Oxygen and Nitrogen

Scientific foundations for extracting the two major constituent gases from the atmosphere were laid by the gradual advances of 19th-century physics and chemistry, with the single most important contribution made by Thomas Joule and William Thompson (Lord Kelvin) in 1852 (Almqvist 2003). They demonstrated that when highly compressed air flowing through a porous plug (a nozzle) expands to the pressure of the ambient air, it will cool slightly. The first experimental success in liquefying oxygen—yet another example of virtually simultaneous inventions whose frequency I note in *CTTC* as one of the markers of innovative intensity during the Age of Synergy—came just before the end of 1877 when Louis-Paul Cailletet, a metallurgist working in ironworks at Chatillon-sur-Seine, got an oxygen mist in his glass tube, and when Raoul Pictet's better apparatus in Geneva actually produced a limited but clearly visible flow of liquid oxygen.

Six years later in Kraków, Sigmund von Wroblewski and Carl Olszewski did a better job by liquefying oxygen at a pressure of less than 2 MPa and used the same apparatus to liquefy nitrogen. In 1879—a year after his lectures at Munich's *Technische Hochschule* inspired young Rudolf Diesel to devote himself to the design of a superior internal combustion engine (see chapter 3 of *CTTC*)—Carl von Linde (1842–1934) established *Gesselschaft für Linde's Eismaschinen* in Wiesbaden and began to work on improving the methods of refrigeration (figure 3.13). On June 5, 1895, he was granted German Patent 88,824 for his process for the liquefaction of atmospheric and other gases, which combined Thomson-Joule effect with what Linde termed countercurrent cooling (Linde 1916). Compressed air (at 20 MPa) was expanded through a nozzle at the bottom of an insulated chamber (achieving temperature drop of about 40°C), and it was used to precool the incoming compressed air in a countercurrent cooler; as the cycle is repeated, the temperature of the air expanded at the nozzle progressively declines, and the air eventually liquefies.

In 1902 Linde received German Patent 173,620 for the way to separate the

FIGURE 3.13. Carl von Linde (1842–1934), the inventor of artificial cooling systems and founder of Linde AG. Photograph from the Linde corporation.

principal gases from the liquefied air and set up the first commercial air separator at Höllriegelskreuth near Munich. The key feature of Linde's patent was rectification (i.e., purification by repeated distillation) through self-intensification: nearly pure oxygen vapor rising from the bottom of the rectification column was liquefied by encountering the cooler downward-flowing liquid mixture of oxygen and nitrogen. Georges Claude (1870–1960) introduced his new air liquefaction design also in 1902. Unlike Linde's liquefaction (with its simple nozzle expansion), his process used an external work (expansion engine) for refrigeration of the compressed air (the challenge of lubricating the piston at low temperatures had to be solved first), and his rectification method incorporated *retour en arrière* whereby the liquefied stream was first divided into oxygen-rich and oxygen-poor fractions, and the latter was used for a more efficient washing out of the oxygen from the ascending vapor.

By 1910 Linde perfected this approach by introducing a double rectification with the two streams first formed in the lower pressure column and then the final concentration of the lower boiling component (nitrogen) in the vapor and the higher boiling gas (oxygen) in the liquid done in the upper column. A century later these basic solutions devised by Linde and Claude are still the foundation of a large-scale production of oxygen, nitrogen, and argon (and Linde AG, headquartered in Wiesbaden, remains the leading supplier of cryogenic processes), but incremental improvements had resulted not only in much higher production volumes but also in lower capital and energy costs. A key innovation that dispensed with the need for any chemicals to remove H_2O and CO_2 from the air and allowed for operations at lower pressure (and hence with reduced energy inputs) was a regenerator designed by a German engineer Mathias Fränkl. This simple but highly effective device (initially patented in 1928) was incorporated into Linde-Fränkl process, whose patents date mostly from the first half of the 1930s and which became commercial in 1934.

Fränkl's regenerators (heat interchangers) were pairs of cylindrical vessels 4–5 m tall filled with wound corrugated thin metal bands in order to provide a very large contact surface that received intermittently (for periods of 1–4 min) the cold flow from one of the separated gases and warm flow from the incoming air. Obviously, when the plant separated both oxygen and nitrogen, two pairs of regenerators were needed. Water vapor and CO_2 in the incoming air are deposited as solids on the cooled regenerator packing, to be removed again as vapors by the outgoing gas as it is being warmed. These regenerators are very efficient, and the exchange takes place under less than 600 kPa of pressure. In 1950, Linde AG introduced the first Linde-Fränkl oxygen plant without high-pressure recycle and with stone-filled, rather than metal-filled, regenerators. The Linde-Fränkl process reduced the prices of gaseous oxygen by an order of magnitude, and another key innovation of the 1930s saw the expansion turbines replacing piston engines in refrigeration.

An operational innovation that was pioneered in the 1940s by Leonard Parker Pool of American Air Products brought production and sales of industrial gases to the places of their use. Instead of continuing the traditional production in central plants and then distributing the gases in cylinders, Air Products began to build on-site cryogenic units, and soon it was scaling them up. Without this combination of low-cost, high-purity oxygen made on site, or delivered inexpensively by a pipeline, there could have been no BOF revolution in steelmaking: a large BOF needs 20 t of pure oxygen for a single heat. Typical sizes of air separation plants were 50–100 t/day during the 1950s; plants above 200 t/day came during the 1960s, and by the end of the 1970s the ratings reached a plateau as Linde AG was building the world's largest air separation facilities with daily capacities of up to 2,300 t/day of pure O_2 and 800 t/day of N_2 (Linde AG 2003; Hansel 1996). The world's largest air compressors (built by Siemens) are used in some of these air separation plants: they have power up to 54 MW and handle volumes of up to 7200,000 m^3/h.

Cryogenic separation in these large units begins with the compression of ambient air (normally to about 600 kPa) and with the removal of moisture and carbon dioxide by cooling the gases. The reversing heat exchangers are still used, but most plants designed since the mid-1980s rely instead on molecular (zeolite) sieves (UIG 2003). Purified air is then refrigerated until it is partially liquefied by expansion through a turbine, and the main constituents of liquid air are then separated through distillation: nitrogen boils away at 77.4 K, argon at 87.3 K, and oxygen at 90.2 K. In oxygen plants, the gas from the high-pressure column undergoes additional purification in the low-pressure column. Cold gases and waste flow from the air separation columns are led back to heat exchangers, where they are warmed to near-ambient levels and emerge at low pressure (just more than 100 kPa) as they cool the incoming air: this arrangement minimizes the overall energy consumption and helps to raise the thermodynamic efficiency of cryogenic plants to around 35%.

Cryogenic distillation ceased to be the only method of producing oxygen and nitrogen with the introduction of adsorption techniques. Pressure swing adsorption for oxygen separation uses synthetic zeolite molecular sieves to adsorb selectively water, CO_2, and nitrogen and to yield 90–95% oxygen (Ruthven, Farooq, and Knaebel 1993). The technique's origins go back to the late 1930s when Richard M. Barrer began to create new zeolite structures from silicate alumina gels and to study their molecular sieving properties. In 1948 this line of research was taken up by the Linde Division of the Union Carbide Corporation, and by 1950 its chemists produced two new synthetic zeolites, Linde A and X, and filed a patent in 1953 (Breck 1974).

Final structures of these hydrated aluminosilicates were determined a year later (figure 3.14. Linde A, an environmentally friendly compound whose annual production surpassed 700,000 t by the late 1990s (global consumption of all synthetic zeolites reached nearly 1.4 Mt by 2000), proved to be an excellent medium to separate nitrogen and oxygen. Its many other uses range from adding it to detergents to remove calcium and magnesium from water, to binding radioactive cesium and strontium present in nuclear wastes. Acti-

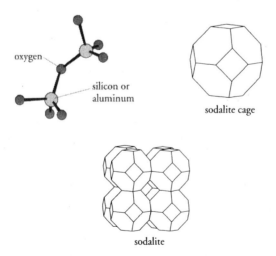

oxygen

silicon or aluminum

sodalite cage

sodalite

FIGURE 3.14. Tetrahedrons, composed of oxygen and aluminum or silicon, are the basic building blocks of zeolites (top left); 24 of them form sodalite cages (top right), which in turn combine to make larger structures such as sodalite (bottom) or synthetic zeolites (Linde A, X, Y). Straight lines in the framework images join the centers of two adjacent tetrahedrons. Based on illustrations in Kerr (1989).

vated carbon sieves are used to produce nitrogen with purities between 95%
and 99.5%. Vacuum swing absorption produces oxygen of similarly low purity
but with lower energy cost, and it has been the fastest growing segment of
oxygen production, particularly for plants rated at more than 20–30 t/day.

Pipelines (pressurized to about 3.5 MPa) are the cheapest way to distribute
oxygen, and their highest densities are along the U.S. coast of the Gulf of
Mexico, in the traditional steelmaking region south of the Lake Michigan, and
in Germany and Japan. Global production of oxygen was about 75 Gm^3 during
the late 1990s, with the European Union and the United States producing
each in excess of 15 Gm^3. As with most modern industries, there was a high
degree of concentration, with five companies—Linde (Germany), Air Liquide
(France), BOC (United Kingdom), and American Praxair and Air Products—
accounting for two thirds of the global output.

During the late 1990s steelmaking accounted for 40–60% of oxygen's use,
with the annual U.S. consumption of more than 8 Gm^3, nearly 20 times the
early 1950s rate (Hogan 1971; Drnevich, Messina, and Selines 1998). Oxygen
use in blast furnace enrichment and higher specific oxygen use in EAFs resulted
in relative decline of the gas blown into BOFs. In contrast, the market for
oxygen in cutting and burning, the first major innovation to use that industrial
gas, had been mature for some time. Controlled oxyacetylene flame of unprecedented temperature (3,480°C) that would, as Henri Louis Le Châtelier
(1850–1936) demonstrated in 1895, melt every common metal, was made possible by Linde's and Claude's invention and by the accidental discovery of the
quenching of calcium carbide in water that was made by James Morehead and
Thomas L. Wilson in 1892. Eleven years later, Thomas combined the two gases
to create an oxyacetylene torch whose use entails three flame settings: neutral
(with equal volumes of the two gases) used for welding, and carburizing (more
acetylene) and oxidizing (with higher oxygen flow) used for cutting with high
temperatures.

Hydrogen

BASF's first ammonia pilot plant in Ludwigshafen used hydrogen produced
from chlorine-alkali electrolysis, a process unsuitable for large-scale operation.
Other known methods to produce hydrogen were either too expensive or produced excessively contaminated flow. Given the company's (indeed, the country's) high dependence on coal, Carl Bosch concluded that the best solution
was to react the glowing coke with water vapor in order to produce water gas
(about 50% H_2, 40% CO, and 5% each of N_2 and CO_2) and then remove
CO cryogenically (Smil 2001). But in the summer of 1911 Wilhelm Wild (1872–
1951) began removing CO by a catalytic process during which the reaction of

the gas with water shifted CO to CO_2 and produced additional H_2. This *Wasserstoffkontaktverfahren*, patented in 1912 by Wild and Bosch, became the dominant technique of mass-producing hydrogen for the next four decades.

Of course, it was obvious to BASF engineers that a much better way of producing hydrogen gas would be the steam reforming of light hydrocarbons, and particularly pure methane (CH_4), the most economic feedstock for steam reforming because it has the highest H:C ratio of all hydrocarbons. Other gaseous alkanes (ethane, propane) are also excellent candidates for reforming, as is naphtha, a mixture of relatively light liquid hydrocarbons separated by fractional distillation of crude oil. Alvin Mittasch had begun the first BASF experiments with methane in 1912 using gas that was catalytically synthesized from CO and H_2, but it was only during the late 1920s when Georg Schiller found the way to reform CH_4 in an externally heated oven in the presence of nickel catalyst.

The interwar Germany had no ready access to any hydrocarbons, but Standard Oil of New Jersey licensed the process and began to use it in its Baton Rouge, Louisiana, refinery in 1931. The first ammonia plant based on steam reforming of methane was built by Hercules Powder Company in California in 1939. After WWII American industry converted rapidly to methane-based hydrogen, while in Europe and particularly in China, coal-based production continued for much longer. By the late 1990s roughly half of the world's hydrogen came from the steam reforming of natural gas. The source of carbon is different, but the two steps of this catalytic process are analogical to the pioneering Wild-Bosch method.

The first step involves the exothermic reaction of methane and steam (at 700–1,100°C and under pressures of 0.3–2.5 MPa) to produce H_2 and CO:

$$CH_4 + H_2O \rightarrow CO + 3H_2$$

The subsequent endothermic reaction of CO with water (at temperatures of 200°C or greater) shifts the monoxide to dioxide to form additional hydrogen:

$$CO + H_2O \rightarrow CO_2 + H_2$$

Finally, CO_2 (in steam reforming of natural gas: 7.05 kg of this gas is produced per kilogram of hydrogen) and traces of unreacted CO are removed by using standard adsorption processes. Pressure swing adsorption, introduced widely during the 1960s, can produce hydrogen that is 99.9999% pure (Ruthven, Farooq, and Knaebel 1993).

About 30% of the world's hydrogen is produced from liquid hydrocarbons (mainly from naphtha) in refineries, where nearly all of it is immediately consumed by two different processes: the gas is catalytically combined with intermediate refined products in order to convert heavy and unsaturated compounds to lighter and more stable liquids, and it is also used in the desulfurization of crude oil. Rising demand for cleaner burning, low-sulfur gasoline and diesel fuels and the greater use of heavier crudes has been the main reason for rapid increases of hydrogen in refining. Nearly 20% of hydrogen's global output still came from the steam reforming of coal, but less than 5% of the gas was derived by energy-intensive electrolysis of water that needs 4.8 kWh per cubic meter of hydrogen. In addition, methanol cracking units are used for low-volume and intermittent production of the gas.

By the end of the 20th century the global demand for hydrogen surpassed 50 Mt a year, with refineries being the second largest consumer after chemical syntheses. Anticipated evolution of hydrogen-based economy—with the gas used first in fuel cells as a carrier of clean energy in transportation—would make hydrogen a leading, and ultimately perhaps the dominant, fuel even for stationary uses (Smil 2003). The two best reasons for this transformation are the high energy density of the gas—at 120.7 MJ/kg, highest of any fuel, three times as high as that of liquid hydrocarbons and more than five times that of good steam coal—and its pollution-free combustion that generates only water. Well-known disadvantages are its low density and the high costs associated with its liquefaction and storage. Anticipations of hydrogen economy have already stimulated the research of alternative ways of hydrogen production, and the fate of hydrogen economy may be among the key indicators of technical changes of the early 21st century.

Remarkable New Materials

The second adjective in this section's title refers not only to entirely new compounds and combinations that were created, or at least commercially diffused, after WWI but also to many advanced variants of long-established materials whose widespread use helped to transform entire industries and consumption sectors. Steel and aluminum are the best examples of these continuing innovations: the hundreds of specialty steels and dozens of aluminum alloys that were used to build cars, appliances, airplanes, and myriads of components during the last decades of the 20th century did not even exist before WWII. Steelmaking was a decidedly mass-scale and mature, although constantly innovating, business even before WWI; in contrast, aluminum's use took off only after 1950 when its alloys became indispensable for the enormous expansion of commercial aviation and when they provided a key substitute for steel wherever the design required a combination of lightness and strength.

These uses have ranged from automobiles to railway hopper cars to space vehicles, and this substitution process is still far from finished. The rationale is always the same: in comparison with specialty steels, aluminum alloys cost more to produce and have a lower modulus of elasticity, but their lower specific density (typical alloys weigh 50% less than steel) and superior strength-to-weight ratio (nearly 50% better than steel) make for lighter yet durable structures. They also resist corrosion (thanks to a very thin layer of hard and transparent aluminum oxide) and can be repeatedly recycled (more than 70% of all automotive aluminum comes from old metal). As a result, these alloys— besides obviously dominating aircraft and spacecraft construction—have made inroads in sectors ranging from road transportation to offshore hydrocarbon production, and from electricity transmission to consumer packaging.

By the late 1990s an average new American passenger car contained about 120 kg of aluminum, an equivalent of about 7% of the vehicle's total mass, and twice the share during the late 1970s and four times the proportion during the early 1960s (AA 2003). The trend toward substantial replacement of iron and steel by aluminum began during the late 1970s with intake manifolds that were made traditionally of cast iron: by the mid-1980s nearly all of them were made of aluminum alloy 319 or 356 (Spada 2003). By that time the two next, and still continuing, waves of replacement had begun: cast aluminum wheels instead of fabricated steel rims, and cast aluminum engine cylinder heads and blocks. By the end of the 1990s about 60% of car and light truck wheels, 40% of engine blocks, and 90% of heads, pistons, and transmission cases were aluminum alloys.

In rail transport aluminum has been used increasingly since the 1970s for large-capacity (in excess of 50 t) hopper cars as well as for the world's fastest trains in Japan and France. Remarkably, studies show that even after 20 years of service the metal loss on floors and sidewalls of aluminum hopper cars used to carry different bulk loads (coal, ores, aggregates) was roughly 25% less than for steel cars (AA 2003). The first bridges with aluminum decks or superstructures date from the 1940s, and marine use of aluminum alloys has spread from small boats to structures cruise ships, yachts, and seawalls. On land the aluminum alloys are increasingly made into irrigation pipes, heat exchangers, and sheet piling.

But material substitution has been a constantly evolving process, and since the 1950s titanium has been replacing aluminum in high-temperature applications, above all in supersonic aircraft. Production of this metal is at least twice as energy intensive as that of aluminum (typically about 400 vs. 200 GJ/t), but it can withstand temperatures nearly three times as high (melting points are, respectively, 660 and 1,677°C). At the same time aluminum has been losing some of its old markets to a growing array of plastics. Global synthesis of all plastics rose from less than 50,000 t in 1930 to about 2 Mt in 1950 and to slightly more than 6 Mt by 1960. The subsequent exponential growth brought the total to nearly 150 Mt in the year 2000, a mass far surpassing that of aluminum and equal to about 18% of the world's steel production. By the late 1990s the U.S. plastics industry employed 10 times as many people (1.5 million) people as did steelmaking, another 850,000 were in upstream industries that supplied the raw materials, and 50,000 worked in recycling (APC 2003).

Global output of man-made polymers is dominated (nearly 80%) by the synthesis of thermoplastics, materials made up of linear or branched molecules (with no chemical bonds among them) that soften on heating but harden once again when cooled, have relatively high impact strength, and are easy to process. Polyethylene (PE) is the most important thermoplastic, accounting for nearly a third of the world's aggregate production of all polymers; polyvinyl chloride (PVC) accounts for nearly 20%, and polypropylene for roughly 15% (figure 3.15). The other major category, thermosets, are compounds whose bonds among molecules resist softening with heating (and hence have a greater dimensional stability than do thermoplastics) but decompose at higher temperatures (Goodman 1999). Production in this category is dominated by polyurethanes and epoxy resins, and other major categories include polyimides, melamines, and urea-formaldehyde (figure 3.15). Annual worldwide output of thermoset plastics during the late 1990s was roughly equal to the synthesis of polypropylene.

Steel, aluminum, and plastics were prominent because of their ubiquity, but the synergy of science, energy, and large-scale engineering helped to transform the 20th century with many other new materials whose contribution was due to their unique properties rather than to massive uses. In retrospect, the most important innovation in this category was the discovery of special conductive properties of certain elements: when extremely pure, they are insulators; when contaminated (doped) with minuscule quantities of other atoms (arsenic, boron, phosphorus), they conduct. This property has been brilliantly exploited in the design of semiconductors made of germanium and silicon. Silicon's physical properties make it a particularly good choice for transistors that are assembled in increasingly complex integrated circuits at the heart of all modern electronics. Finally, the closing decades of the 20th century saw the

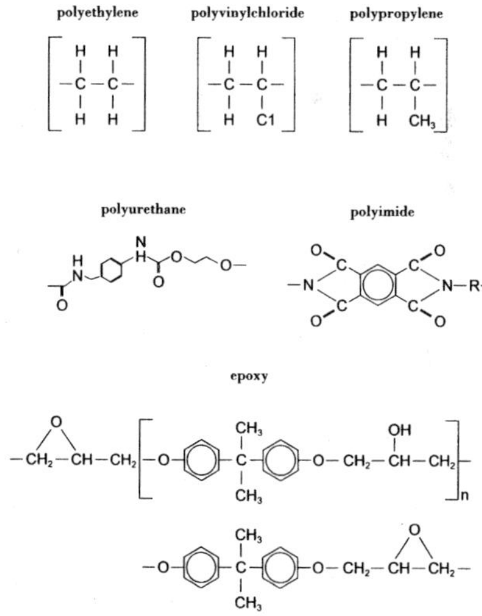

FIGURE 3.15. Structures of the three most important thermoplastics (polyethylene [PE], polyvinylchloride [PVC], and polypropylene) and three common thermoset plastics (polyurethane, polyimide, and epoxy).

rise of an entirely new kind of materials classed under a broad category of composites, as well as the discovery and a still uncertain but potentially enormous promise of nanostructures.

Multitude of Plastics

Plastics fit best the image of new 20th century materials. Their well-documented origins, seemingly endless introduction of new varieties during the first two thirds of the 20th century, their rapid conquest of many specialized markets, and their eventual substitution of metals, glass, and wood in countless industrial and household applications attracted a great deal of attention to their discoveries and their commercial success (APC 2003; PHS 2003; Vinylfacts 2003; Mossman 1997; Fenichell 1996; Marchelli 1996; Meikle 1995; Seymour 1989; Brydson 1975). Experimental foundations for the their synthesis were laid after 1860 during the pioneering decades of industrial organic chemistry, but several commercially successful compounds that were created during the closing decades of the 19th century were based on natural polymers. They did not form permanent shapes as they could be easily melted or attacked by chemicals. The most popular of these was celluloid, made from cellulose nitrate and camphor by the process patented by John Wesley Hyatt in 1870.

The age of durable plastics based on fully synthetic polymers was launched at the very beginning of the 20th century with the preparation of phenol-aldehyde resins. The basic reaction between phenol and formaldehyde had been studied since the 1870s, but until the late 1890s its only practical products were shellac substitutes (Berliner used shellac for his phonograph records: see chapter 5 of *CTTC*). In 1899 Arthur Smith was granted the first patent (U.K. Patent 16,274) for a phenol-formaldehyde resin that was cast in molds and set at low temperatures to be used for electrical insulation. Leo Hendrik Baekeland (1863–1944), a Belgian professor of chemistry who immigrated to New York in 1898, began to work on reactions between phenol and formaldehyde in his private laboratory (in Yonkers on the Hudson River) in 1902 (Bijker 1995). He could afford to become an independent researcher after he sold his patent of a photographic paper for instantaneous prints (Velox) to Kodak in 1899.

In June 1907 Baekeland succeeded in preparing the world's first thermoset plastic that was molded at temperatures between 150 and 160°C. The key to his discovery was to use the alkalies or bases "in such relatively small proportions that their presence does not interfere with the desirable qualities of the products . . . In fact in most cases the small amount of base persists in the final products and confers upon them new and desirable properties" (Baekeland 1909:1). Baekeland eventually obtained more than 100 patents on phenol-aldehyde plastics, and his General Bakelite Company, set up in 1910, was the first large-scale producer of a plastic compound. Bakelite could be set by heat into a hard substance that would retain its shape without fading or discoloration, would not burn, was impervious to boiling, would not dissolve in any common acid or solvent, and was also electrically resistant. Bakelite's brittleness was solved by the addition of short cellulose (or asbestos) fibers that made the plastic strong enough for many practical uses.

Bakelite enjoyed great popularity between the two world wars, initially as an electric insulator and in manufacturing small household objects, including classic black rotary dial telephones (figure 3.16), and it became a common material in light-weight weapons and military machines mass-produced in the United States during WWII. Bakelite was soon joined by a growing array of new synthetic materials, and any fairly comprehensive chronological treatment of these discoveries would be either too tedious (if fairly detailed) or it would amount to a confusing list of categories and substances (if limited to the merest recital of new compounds). By the end of the 20th century there were more than 50 kinds of plastics, and so the best approach to appreciating their rise, diffusion, and importance is to outline the highlights of their discoveries and then to concentrate in some detail on the two leading products whose widespread uses illustrate the extent and the intensity of our dependence on synthetic materials.

A notable commonality of post-Baekeland discoveries was the rising importance of institutionalized research as virtually all major plastic categories were discovered, and then commercially introduced, thanks to dedicated, and often fairly specifically targeted, research that was funded by major American (above all, DuPont) and European (IG Farben in Germany, Imperial Chemical Industries [ICI] in the United Kingdom) corporations. While skills of individual researchers remained a highly valued commodity and while accidents played role in several discoveries, the rise of modern plastics industry was one of the first instances where systematic corporate quests, rather than scattered efforts of brilliant or determined individuals, were decisive in creating new industries. This pattern was repeated with many technical advances after WWII.

The wave of new discoveries, powered by the progress of organic syntheses and directed by new corporate interests, began to form right after Baekeland's success. Cellophane, the first flexible plastic, was invented by Charles Frederick Cross in 1908, and it was water-

FIGURE 3.16. Classical rotary black telephone was the most commonly encountered Bakelite object for most of the 20th century. Photograph courtesy of Douglas Fast.

proofed by Jacques Edwin Brandenberger in 1912. Polymerization of vinyl chloride was patented in the same year, but the process suffered from a high rate of decomposition. Between 1911 and 1919 General Electric was granted many patents for the synthesis of alkyd resins, and in 1918 Hans John prepared the first resins that combined urea with formaldehyde. In 1920 Hermann Staudinger (1881–1965) replaced the long-reigning colloid theory of polymers, which saw the compounds as physical associations of small molecules, by the correct model of small molecular units linked in linear chains to form extremely large macromolecular masses, a paradigm shift that was rewarded in 1953 by a Nobel Prize in Chemistry.

The first post-WWI decade saw the spreading uses of Bakelite and cellophane (DuPont began to make it in the United States in 1924) and the introduction of styrene in 1925 (its polymer is now everywhere in insulation and packaging) and cellulose acetate (a nonflammable counterpart of celluloid) in 1927 (Brydson 1975); also in 1927 DuPont began a systematic program of fundamental research on polymerization. During the 1930s this work brought a still unsurpassed concatenation of discoveries that were rapidly converted into commercial processes for eagerly awaited products. In April 1930, a DuPont team led by Wallace Hume Carothers (1896–1937) discovered neoprene (synthetic rubber) and synthesized the first polyester superpolymer: an experiment with ethylene glycol and sebacic acid yielded a polyester that could be drawn out as a long fiber both in molten and cold form, but the substance was easily softened by hot water and hence it was of little practical use.

Only after Carothers turned to the polyamides did his systematic search find a number of substances that could produce permanent filaments, and among many candidates polymer 66, made by the reaction between hexamethylene diamide and adipic acid, was chosen for commercialization under the name Nylon (Hermes 1996). The U.S. patent for linear condensation of polymers was granted in 1937 (Carothers 1937), the pilot plant opened in 1938 (toothbrush bristles were the first application), large-scale synthesis began in December 1939, and stockings were the leading commercial product. DuPont's major rivals had their own successes. In 1930 IG Farben produced polystyrene, and in 1932 ICI began to investigate effects of very high pressure (up to 300 MPa) on organic reactions, an effort that eventually led to PE.

Three more fundamental discoveries complete the list of major synthetic advances of the 1930s. The first patent for soft and elastic methyl and ethyl acrylates dates back to 1912, and their production (for protective coatings and as interlayers in glass) began in Germany during the late 1920s. But during the winter of 1929–1930 William Chalmers, at McGill University in Canada, discovered that methacrylates form hard transparent polymers. ICI began to commercialize methyl methacrylate in 1933; by 1935 Röhm and Haas in Philadelphia was making sheets of Plexiglas, and a year later DuPont was producing Lucite. In 1933 Ralph Wiley at Dow Chemical accidentally discovered polyvinylidene chloride, now commonly known as Saran Wrap, a ubiquitous cling-packaging of food. In 1936 Pierre Castan (1899–1985) prepared an epoxide resin suitable for dental fixtures, and a year later Otto Bayer (1902–1982), at IG Farben's Leverkusen lab, discovered polyurethanes (first used for bristles).

Polytetrafluoroethylene (branded by DuPont as Teflon) was the last fundamental discovery of the 1930s. In 1938 Roy Plunkett at DuPont accidentally pumped chlorofluorocarbons (CFCs, Freon) into a cylinder that was left overnight in cold storage and found that the gas was converted into a white powder. Teflon's slipperiness, in addition to its resistance to cold, heat, and acids, is perfect for cooking surfaces and for such diverse uses as edges of windshield wipers, marine coatings, and aircraft toilets (DuPont 2003). New plastics discoveries of the 1940s included alkyd polyesters and polyethylene terephthalate (PET), the compound made from monoethylene glycol and purified terephthalic acid (figure 3.17).

PET was initially used as a fiber branded Terylene and Dacron, later as a film best known as DuPont's Mylar, and since 1973 as the preferred material for soft drink and water bottles as well as for fruit juice, peanut butter, salad dressing, and plant oil containers. Fortunately, this relatively expensive engineered resin is readily reusable, and half of all polyester carpet in the United States is now made from recycled PET bottles; other uses include fiberfill for sleeping bags and coats and such car parts as bumpers and door panels. As noted in chapter 1, during the late 1940s George de Mestral conceived a new plastic fastening system imitating cockleburs. The last year of the 1940s saw the introduction of perhaps the most frivolous plastic as James Wright at GE mixed silicone oil with boric acid and created *Silly Putty*. High-impact polyimide (for bearings and washers) came in 1955, and strong polycarbonate plastics—suited for optical lenses and windows, now so common in rigid transparent covers and, when metalized, as CDs— were introduced commercially in 1958.

But the decade's most significant breakthrough was the synthesis of PE at normal temperatures and low pressures by Karl Ziegler's team in Germany. Soon afterward Giulio Natta (1903–1979) began to use Ziegler's new organometallic catalysts to prepare polypropylene and

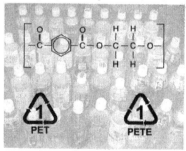

FIGURE 3.17. Polyethylene terephthalate (PET)—cheap, clear, lightweight, and shatter and heat resistant—is the dominant worldwide choice of material for water and soft drink bottles. Although the plastic is readily recyclable (identified with number 1 inside the recycling triangle and acronym PET or PETE underneath), tens of millions of such containers are discarded every day.

other stereoregular macromolecules (having spatially uniform structure, with all the side groups pointing in the same direction). These so-called isotactic polymers form helices (with side groups pointing outward) and combine lightness and strength, which are desirable in fabrics or ropes. For their discoveries Ziegler and Natta shared the Nobel Prize in Chemistry in 1963. During the 1960s came polyimide, polysulfone (electroplatable), and polybutylene; after 1970, thermoplastic polyester; and the 1980s saw the first liquid crystal polymers for high-performance electrical and surgical applications. DuPont's trademarked successes included Lycra, Kevlar, Nomex, and Tyvek.

Before taking closer looks at the two leading plastics—PE and PVC, whose uses illustrate best the extent to which these materials penetrated both the late 20th-century industrial production and everyday household chores—I must note the relatively small (but hard to replace) burden that plastics put on the nonrenewable resources of natural gas and crude oil: during the late 1990s the worldwide synthesis of all polymers claimed less than 4% of all hydrocarbons. Considering the reduced energy needs and environmental benefits of plastics that replaced wood and metals, this relatively small resource claim could be accommodated even in a considerably tightened hydrocarbon market. Crude oil and natural gas savings that would result from improvements in average fuel consumption in automobiles and from wider diffusion of high-efficiency natural gas furnaces should provide the needed feedstock.

PE and PVC

During the late 1990s PE and PVC accounted for nearly half of the world's synthesis of plastics, and their highly diverse uses still continue to expand. Although they are structurally very similar—PE's carbon chain carries only hydrogens, while in PVC every other carbon carries one chlorine atom—and share a number of commercial applications, they differ greatly where the perception of safe use and environmental impact are concerned. While PE is a generally acceptable material that can be effectively recycled, PVC has been seen by many critics as the most environmentally damaging of all common polymers: it requires hazardous chemicals for its production, it releases some of its additives while in use or after it gets landfilled, it emits toxic dioxin when burned, and it is not easily recycled. Consequently, the compound would seem to be a prime candidate for replacement by polymers that can be produced by new methods of green chemistry—and yet its applications, including those in the sensitive medical field, have been expanding (Brookman 1998).

The PE story began with ICI's already noted investigations of high-pressure syntheses in 1930. There were no immediate breakthroughs, but in March 1933 Eric W. Fawcett and Reginald O. Gibson found a white waxy solid after combining ethylene and benzaldehyde under 200 MPa. This discovery was not immediately followed up, and so it was two years later, after dismantling a defective apparatus because of a sudden pressure drop while retesting reactions with ethylene, that the white powder was again encountered and recognized as a new remarkable polymer whose synthesis required, as it happened by the accidental loss of pressure, the presence of oxygen (Mossman 1997). By 1936 the company patented a high-volume polymerization process and introduced large compressors for its first PE plant, which began working in September 1939, the day before the United Kingdom's declaration of war on Germany.

The compound's first important use came during WWII as an insulator for underwater cables and radars. The latter use reduced the weight of radar domes by hundreds of kilograms and allowed their placement onboard planes in order to detect German bombers under all weather conditions. ICI's original process required the unusual, and technically demanding, combination of high pressures (100–200 MPa) and temperature of 200°C. In 1953, while researching reactions promoted by various catalysts, Karl Ziegler (1898–1973; figure 3.18) and his colleagues at the Max Planck Institute for Coal Research in Mülheim discovered that ethylene gas could be polymerized very rapidly with some organometallic mixed catalysts that were very easy to prepare and that allowed the synthesis to proceed first at just 20 MPa and eventually at normal pressure (Ziegler 1963).

The catalyst used in the first series of successful experiments was a mixture of aluminum triethyl, or diethyl aluminum chloride, with titanium tetrachloride, and subsequently the team prepared many combinations of aluminum with such heavy metals as Co, Cr, Mo, Ti, V, and Zr, mixtures that became known as Ziegler catalysts.

Our experiment thus destroyed a dogma. It led, in addition, to a PE which differed markedly from the high-pressure product. Low-pressure PE not only has a better resistance to elevated temperatures and a higher density, but is also more rigid . . . The difference can be attributed to the fact that in

FIGURE 3.18. Karl Ziegler, whose work on mixed organometallic catalysts led to the discovery of high-density polyethylene (PE), was rewarded in 1963 by the Nobel Prize in Chemistry. Photograph © The Nobel Foundation.

our process molecules of ethylene are joined together linearly, without interruption, whereas in the high-pressure process chain growth is disturbed, so that a strongly branched molecule results. (Ziegler 1963:8–9)

While the branched low-density PE (LDPE) has specific gravity of 0.92–0.93 g/cm³, tensile strength as low as 9 MPa, and melting temperature as low as 98°C, the analogical maxima for high-density PE (HDPE) are 0.96 g/cm³, 32 MPa, and 137°C (EF 2003). Relevant patents for the production of HDPE were granted in 1954, and the first industrial production of HDPE began in 1956. But, as discovered by companies that rushed into its synthesis, the material had propensity to crack with time. The solution was found by making a compound with a small number of branches in the linear chain. The Phillips Petroleum process—developed during the 1950s by Robert L. Banks and J. Paul Hogan and commercialized in 1961—relies on a chromium catalyst, proceeds at a higher pressure than does Ziegler's synthesis, and produces HDPE with fewer branches (one ethyl branch for every 100 molecule chains, a third of the Ziegler's pattern) and hence with higher specific weight. Finally, by 1980 new catalysts made it possible to make linear LDPE.

PE industry thus offers a range of polymers of different weight, strength, and thermal resistance, but their production follows the same basic sequence: it starts with the thermal cracking of ethane ($C_2H_6 \rightarrow C_2H_4 + H_2$), which is followed by ethylene purification (a process that requires more than 100 separation stages and results in 99.9% purity), heating and compression, and catalytic conversion (with metallic catalyst suspended in the ethylene as the gas is introduced at the reactor's bottom) to PE. Conversion rate of about 97% is achieved by repeated recycling of unreacted ethylene in three to five hours. The reaction is highly exothermic, and the PE is removed as a granular powder that is melted and extruded.

Different PEs now constitute by far the largest category of global plastics, whose visible uses are only a small fraction of continuously expanding application. By far the most commonly encountered are thin but strong LDPE films that are made into ubiquitous bread, garbage, and grocery bags. Hidden uses range from insulation of electrical cables (with cross-linked PE to withstand heat) to artificial hip joints (with ultrahigh-density PE). The material is also spun into fibers and blow-molded into rigid containers (HDPE for milk jugs and detergent and motor oil bottles), gas tanks, pipes, toys, and a myriad of components ranging from delicate pieces to bulky parts. Given its dominance of the plastics market, it is fortunate that PE products could be successfully recycled: those made of HDPE are stamped with number 2 within the recycling triangle and are turned into trash cans, flower pots, and (again) detergent bottles. LDPE products are stamped with number 4 and reappear as new bags.

In contrast to PE, PVC—the world's second most important plastic (during the late 1990s its global consumption surpassed 20 Mt/year)—has a long history that had already begun in 1835 when Henri Victor Regnault produced the first vinyl chloride monomer. Eugen Baumann prepared its polymer in 1872, but a commercial polymerization that was patented in 1912 by Friedrich Heinrich Klatte produced a tough, horn-like material that was difficult to fashion into useful articles. In 1926 Waldo L. Semon (1898–1999), a researcher at the BF Goodrich Company in Akron, Ohio, began to experiment with PVC in order to create a new adhesive for bonding rubber to metal. Instead, he ended up with a new, plasticized vinyl: "This invention, in brief, consists in dissolving a polymerized vinyl halide, at an elevated temperature, in a substantially non-volatile organic solvent, and allowing the solution to cool, whereupon it sets to a stiff rubbery gel" (Semon 1933:1).

The discovery of PVC's mutability opened the way for large-scale production of different types of the plastic that, although trailing various PEs in the total global consumption, has acquired an unmatched variety of uses. A short fictional narrative in *CTTC* follows a modern office worker in a U.S. city through a part of his morning in order to highlight the continuing importance of technical inventions made during the 1880s, the most innovative decade of human history; a similar story can feature the ubiquity of today's PVC, be it in North America or East Asia. An alarm clock that wakes a sleeping woman and the lights and kitchen gadgets she uses to make breakfast are all powered by electricity that is delivered by PVC-insulated wires. Water for the shower, tooth brushing, and coffee is led through PVC pipes, as is the outgoing waste. Bathroom and kitchen floors may be made of PVC sheets or tiles, the lunch she packs could be in a PVC wrap, and it may be complemented by a drink in a PVC bottle. The car she will drive to work will have PVC undercoating to delay corrosion, and she will be surrounded by PVC in doors, instrument panel, and upholstery.

But even this level of saturation is modest compared to the degree of PVC dependence that the woman would encounter if a car accident were to land her in a hospital. There she would be enveloped by objects made of different kinds of PVC: disposable and surgical gloves, flexible tubing for feeding, breathing and pressure monitoring, catheters, blood bags, IV containers, sterile packaging, trays, basins, bed pans and rails, thermal blankets, labware. In aggregate, PVC is now the primary component in at least 25% of all medical products. Moreover, its uses, contrary to earlier expectations, have been actually rising as it keeps replacing more expensive polymers (Brookman 1998). And, risking the tedium of more detailed listings, I will mention just a few other key categories of PVC use: house siding, roofing membranes, window frames, Venetian blinds, shower curtains, blister packaging, hoses, garden furniture, greenhouse sheeting, electronic components, office supplies, toys, cable insulation, credit cards . . .

Besides its obvious versatility, PVC's two great advantages are its water and flame resistance. Its main drawbacks, in the eyes of some vocal critics, are the facts that its production, as well as its incineration, emits dioxins, that plasticizers used to soften the compound (above all, diethylhexyl phthalate [DEHP], a possible carcinogen) can evaporate into the indoor air and that the harmful additives can be leached from landfilled products. Consequently, Greenpeace (2003) has been campaigning for phasing out all PVC uses. In contrast, the polymer's defenders point to its low cost, its contributions to quality and safety of products (particularly of cars, where the undercoating extends vehicle life, carpets and coatings reduce noise, and the lowered weight saves fuel), minuscule volumes of released dioxins (of which not all are potentially dangerous), and biodegradability of leached plasticizers (Vinylfacts 2003).

Silicon

I have taken another jump in my survey of key materials that transformed the 20th century, and hence this section is not a continuation of the preceding look at polymers of which silicones (plural) are a smaller but important category. Scientific foundations for the production of these oxide polymers were laid between 1899 and 1944 by F.S. Kipping's research at Nottingham University; their commercial production began during the 1940s, and their relative constancy of properties across a large range of temperatures makes them the best possible lubricants and resins in environments with wide temperature variations as well as good insulators and excellent water repellents. My concern here is not with these silicon-oxygen polymers that have attached methyl or phenyl groups (i.e., silicones), but with the element itself, indeed, with its purest crystalline form without whose large-scale production there would have been no affordable microprocessors, and hence no modern inexpensive consumer electronics, as well as no photovoltaic cells and no optical fibers (Seitz and Einspruch 1998).

Silicon is, after oxygen, the second most abundant mineral in the Earth's crust. These two elements make up, respectively, nearly 28% and 49% of the crustal mass—but silicon never occurs in a free state, being always bound in silica (SiO_2, commonly encountered as quartz, sand, and sandstone) or in silicates (numerous compounds including feldspar and kaolinite). The quartz (or quartzite) form of silica is the best starting material for producing commercial silicon compounds as well as the pure element. Ferrosilicon's use began in 1902 as a deoxidant in steelmaking, and after WWI polycrystalline silicon became an important element in aluminum alloying.

Reduction of SiO_2 with carbon (coal or charcoal: $SiO_2 + 2C \rightarrow Si + 2CO$) uses graphite electrodes in large electric furnaces that operate at about

2,000°C, and it produces silicon with a purity (99%) that is quite unacceptable for electronic components. Nearly 60% of this metallurgical-grade silicon (whose output was just more than 1 Mt during the late 1990s) is still used for deoxidation and alloying, a third goes for the synthesis of silicones and other chemicals, and the small remainder (roughly 60,000 t) was the raw material for the production of semiconductors, solar cells, and optical fibers.

The difference between metallurgical and semiconductor silicon is truly astonishing: the latter is about one billion times purer (Föll 2000). The first step toward that goal is to react it catalytically with hydrochloric acid in order to produce trichlorosilane (Si + 3HCl → SiHCl$_3$ + H$_2$). This liquid is then further purified by distillation, and high-purity silicon is produced from it by the process of chemical vapor deposition. At this stage dopants, precisely calibrated amounts of impurities, are added in order to increase the conductivity. Pentavalent impurities (Sb, As, P) produce n-type semiconductors that conduct by additional free electrons; trivalent impurities (Al, B, Ga) produce p-type semiconductors, which conduct through electron deficiencies ("holes"). This production of doped polysilicon, pioneered by Siemens during the 1960s, must reckon with the extraordinary toxicity of the leading dopants (AsH$_3$ and PH$_3$), high combustibility of both H$_2$ and Si HCl$_3$, and extreme corrosivity of gaseous HCl. At the same time, extremely precise input controls are needed in order to produce homogeneous material at a slow (about 1 kg/hr) rate.

In the year 2000 about 20,000 t of semiconductor-grade polycrystalline silicon were produced by this exacting technique. At roughly $50/kg, this output was worth about $1 billion. Converting this extremely pure polycrystalline material into a single crystal is done overwhelmingly (about 99% of the element for electronic applications is produced this way) by a method that was discovered, accidentally, by a Polish metallurgist working in Berlin during WWI. When Jan Czochralski (1885–1953) dipped his pen into a crucible of molten tin rather than into the inkpot, he drew a thin thread of solidified metal that proved to be a single crystal. Once a small seed crystal replaced the nib, its slow pulling from the melt, accompanied by slow rotation and gradual lowering of the temperature, made it possible to produce crystals of metals (Sn, Pb, Zn) a few millimeters across and up to 150 mm long (Czochralski 1918). For 30 years this method was used just to study the growth and properties of metallic crystals.

Then came the invention of transistors (see chapter 4), and in 1948 Gordon K. Teal and J.B. Little, working at Bell Laboratories, used Czochralski's pulling technique to grow the first germanium crystals. The first silicon-based transistor followed in 1949, and in 1951 Teal and Ernest Buehler were growing the element's crystals and had patented improved crystal-pulling (as well as doping) designs (Buehler and Teal 1956; figure 3.19). By 1956 the largest crystal diameter doubled to 2.5 cm, and crystal weight increased eightfold compared to 1950.

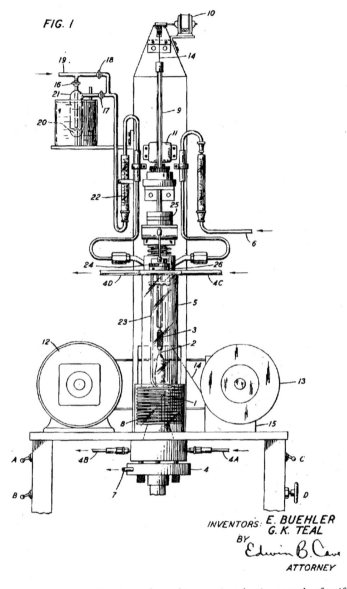

FIG. 1

INVENTORS: E. BUEHLER
                    G. K. TEAL
              BY
                    Edwin B. Cave
                                    ATTORNEY

FIGURE 3.19. Cross section of a device for making semiconductive crystals of uniform resistivity designed by Ernest Buehler and Gordon K. Teal in 1951. After the ingot (Ge in the original application) placed in the crucible (1) is completely molten, the spindle (9) with attached seed (20) is lowered to touch the melt. The vibrator (10) and rotator (11) are turned on, and then the motor (12) drives disks (13) so that the cable (14) draws up the spindle (9). Dopants are added from liquid (20) and gaseous (21) reservoirs. Illustration from Buehler and Teal (1956). Available from the U.S. Patent Office.

The subsequent performance growth was steady but slow until the mid-1970s (7.5 cm and 12 kg by 1973). The first 10-cm, 14-kg crystals came in 1980, and by the century's end the largest 200-kg crystals were 30 cm across (Zulehner 2003). While the amorphous silicon is a dark brown powder, the crystals have black to gray lustrous appearance, and no material made by modern civilization is as perfect as they are: their bulk microdefect density is below the detection limit of the best measuring tools we have, and impurities are present in concentrations below parts per billion, even parts per trillion.

Turning these perfect objects into wafers requires no less admirable fabrication techniques. As diamond-edged circular saws slice wafers (typically 0.1 mm thick, with ultrathin wafers of 25 μm), they also turn nearly half of the expensive crystals into dust, but the final polished product deviates no more than 1 μm from an ideally flat plane. This extraordinary accuracy had to be maintained for each of the roughly 100 million wafers that were produced in the year 2000 to serve as platforms for integrated circuits. The entire process of purifying silicon, growing its perfect crystals, and fabricating identical wafers became a key paragon of modern technical progress and a perfect example of a steeply rising value-added sequence. During the late 1990s pure quartz was sold for about $0.017/kg; metallurgical silicon cost $1.10/kg; trichlorosilane, $3/kg; purified polycrystalline silicon, $50–100/kg; monocrystalline rod, at least $500/kg; polished silicon slices, at least $1,500 (and as much as $4,000)/kg; and epitaxial slices, as much as $14,000/kg (Jackson 1996; Williams 2003).

Another critical use for crystalline silicon emerged during the 1950s almost concurrently with its electronic applications when the material was used to produce the first practical photovoltaic (PV) solar cells. A team at Bell Laboratories led the way in 1954, and by March 1958 *Vanguard I* became the first PV-powered satellite, drawing a mere 0.1 W from about 100 cm² of cells to power a 5 mW transmitter that worked for eight years. Just four years later Telstar, the first commercial telecommunications satellite, had 14 W of PV power (figure 3.20and in 1964 *Nimbus*, a weather satellite, rated 470 W. During the remainder of the 20th century the world had acquired entire fleets of satellites whose operation is predicated on silicon PV cells.

PV cells energize the increasingly complex geosynchronous assemblies that carry voice, now with such clarity that intercontinental conversations sound as if spoken in the same room, and data streams that include everything from billions of transactions that converge at the great bourses of the world every day to processed credit card records. Meteosats in high orbit improve weather forecasting and warn about incoming cyclones, and Earth observation satellites of many kinds that constantly monitor the oceans and the planet's surfaces allow us to follow the changing qualities of the biosphere. And, of course, there are also scores of low-orbiting spy satellites, some delivering images with resolution better than 15 cm.

FIGURE 3.20. *Telstar I*, designed and launched by Bell Laboratories in 1962, was the world's first active telecommunication satellite powered by photovoltaic (PV) cells. The spherical satellite was nearly 1 m in diameter and weighed 80 kg. Photograph used with permission of Lucent Technologies.

In contrast to rapidly diffusing space applications, land-based uses of PV cells remained rare even after David Carlson and Christopher Wronski fabricated the first amorphous silicon cells (cheaper than the crystalline ones) at RCA Laboratories in 1976. A quarter century later steady improvements pushed the efficiencies of new single-crystal modules to as much as 12–14%; thin-film cells convert 11–17% in laboratory settings, but their field performance is as low as 3–7% after a few months; multijunction amorphous silicon cells do better at 8–11%. Thin-film microcrystalline silicon is perhaps the best candidate for future mass applications (Shah et al. 1999). Global annual PV production for land-based electricity generation began advancing rapidly only during the 1990s, and it reached 200 MW_p (peak capacity) by the year 2000.

With about 85% of total PV production based on crystalline silicon (the rest using cheaper amorphous silicon) and with typical rates of 100 peak W/m², PV cell thickness of 300 μm, and silicon density of 2.33 g/cm³, this means that the annual requirement for crystalline PV cells amounted to almost 900 t in the year 2000, less than 5% of the total production (Föll 2000). This relatively small need was easy to satisfy by the material that failed to meet specifications for wafer production (10–12% of the total output) and is available at a considerable discount. The total installed PV capacity reached only about 1 GW (about half of it in the United States), still only a tiny fraction of more than 2.1 TW installed in fossil-fueled generators (Smil 2003). The largest PV cell producers were BP Solarex in the United States, Japan's Kyocera and Sharp, and Germany's Siemens (Maycock 1999).

And before leaving this remarkable element, I should note that its extraordinary purification also became essential for producing optical fibers, whose installation has revolutionized long-distance telecommunication and mass data transfer. Their principal raw material, as in all glass, is silica (about 75%); the remainder is a mixture of Na_2O, CaO, and Al_2O_3. The best lenses produced around 1900 were about 10,000 times more transparent than the first Egyptian glass made more than 5,000 years ago. After the 1960s production of pure silicon dioxide improved that performance another 10,000 times, and even greater transparencies are possible with new nonsilica glass.

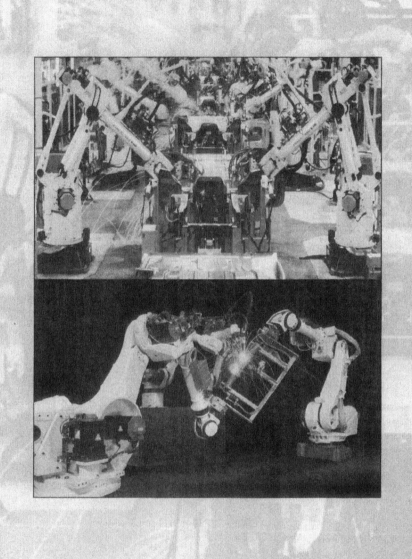

4

Rationalized Production:

Mechanization, Automation, Robotization

The world is nothing but raw material. The world is no more than unexploited matter . . . Gentlemen, the task of industry is to exploit the entire world . . . Everything must be speeded up. The worker's question is holding us back . . . The worker must become a machine, so that he can simply rotate like a wheel. Every thought is insubordination! . . . A worker's soul is not a machine, therefore it must be removed. This is my system.

> Factory owner John Andrew Ripraton revealing his vision for organizing mass production in "The System," a story by Karel and Josef Čapek published in 1908 (quoted in Klíma 2001:72–73)

FRONTISPIECE 4. Robots are the most advanced form of mechanization in industrial manufacturing. The top image shows one of the classic, and still very common, applications in automobile industry: not a single worker is in sight as an array of FANUC model S-400 robots spot weld car bodies in a large hall. The bottom photograph shows coordinated action of four FANUC robots: two large multipurpose R-2000iA models (with maximum load capacity of 165 kg at wrist) manipulate a part that is being welded by two small metal inert gas Arc Mate 100iB machines. Photographs courtesy of FANUC Ltd.

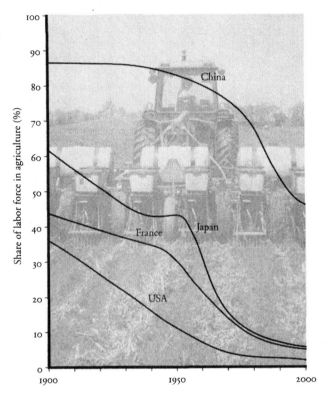

FIGURE 4.1. Declining shares of labor employed in U.S., Japanese, French, and Chinese agriculture, 1900–2000. Plotted from data in Ogura (1963), USBC (1975), Mitchell (2003), and FAO (2004).

One of the most remarkable attributes of modern civilization is that we are surrounded by an unprecedented variety of products whose abundance and variety, as well as their broad affordability, stem from their mass production by highly mechanized processes many of which were fully automated and robotized during the last two generations of the 20th century. These tasks are powered solely by inanimate prime movers, and the final products also embody variable amounts of energy that was expended previously on raw materials or feedstocks used to make the final products or to offer the desired services. Yet by the end of the 20th century the twin realities of complete mechanization of productive tasks and astounding economies of scale were taken so much for granted that most people would see them as unremarkable realities and would not single them out as key characteristics of modern life.

But it was only during the 20th century that the increasing availability of fossil fuels and electricity provided inexpensive means to energize *en masse* such affordable and highly versatile prime movers as internal combustion engines and electric motors whose power was used to mechanize just about every conceivable productive task and to take advantage of many obvious economies of scale. This trend was pervasive in both its categorical extent and its spatial reach: no kind of economic activity remained unaffected by it as ingenious machines had mechanized tasks that range (to give two mundane examples) from cutting and debarking of trees to filling and sealing drug containers or (to offer two more spectacular cases) from microslicing ultrapure silicon crystals to emplacing entire genome arrays on microchips.

One of the best-known images of this pervasive mechanization is shown as this chapter frontispiece: a view of a large hall in a car-making factory where robots move in precision-programmed steps to reach out and spot weld car bodies that move along on a belt. This is a mesmerizing choreography of metallic arms that have six degrees of freedom, of welding sparks and precise motion—with not a human in sight. This activity is a perfect example of the 20th century's productive transformations: energetic and material fundamentals (electric motors, high-quality steels) have their origins during the remarkable era of pre-WWI innovations, but the complexity of the entire assembly and its electronic controls are quintessential late-20th century advances.

And the absence of people in the hall is perfect illustration of the attendant labor shift from physical exertion and dexterity to intellectual effort of designing, maintaining, and improving the mechanized processes as we transformed ourselves from low-power, low-efficiency prime movers to highly versatile controllers of high-power flows. Perhaps the best-known illustration of this shift is the decline of agricultural employment. In all pre-industrial societies, this was the dominant category of occupation; in modern high-energy economies agricultural employment was reduced to the barest functional minimum. The United States was a leader in this process, with total farm employment falling below 50% already by 1880; by 1900 it was below 40%, by the mid-1950s it dropped below 10%, and during the late 1990s it was just 2% (USDA 2003).

And during the 20th century this trend was followed, and in the case of high-income countries also completed, in succeeding waves all around the world. Moreover, in some countries it progressed at an unusually rapid pace, a fact that becomes obvious when one compares, for example, the post-1900 rates of decline in the U.S. and French agricultural labor force with those in post-WWII Japan or post-1980 China (figure 4.1). But this universal trend was also due to extensive chemicalization of the entire food production process. In this chapter I concentrate on tracing these underlying technical advances in crop production, but I must stress that the same trend of rising dependence on fossil energy inputs affected also the three other major categories of biomass production: animal husbandry, fishing and aquaculture, and forestry.

Consequently, during the latter half of the 20th century, mechanization came to rule every aspect of biomass harvesting, from field crops to high-sea fishing, from giant cattle feedlots to intensive aquaculture ponds and cages holding shrimp and salmon, and from the destruction of tropical forests to short-rotation tree plantations. And, as with the crops, in most of these cases there were also major productive gains due to the inputs of chemicals (fertilizers, pesticides, herbicides, hormones, antibiotics) and modification of the genetic makeup of domesticated land animals, aquatic species, and planted trees. During the 20th century the extraction of sand, gravel, and stone, the inexpensive natural materials used in construction as well as in many kinds of industrial production, expanded much faster than the production of fossil fuels. But because of its inherently distributed nature, this extraction was not affected by the economies of scale to such a high degree as the mining of coal and the recovery of hydrocarbons that are reviewed in this chapter.

The chapter's last section deals with the diverse category of advances in industrial production, the activity that is still commonly called manufacturing despite the fact that fewer and fewer hands actually touch the products. This activity offers many spectacular examples of mechanization that range from brutally simple giant hydraulic presses that monotonically stamp out large steel parts for making cars or white goods to extremely complicated robotization of such rapidly evolving processes as the fabrication of microprocessors. And it is also in industrial manufacturing where mechanization led to perhaps the most dizzying economies of scale, to the most spectacular increase in the size of individual facilities and to the most impressive rise in the productivity of labor.

Agricultural Harvests

From the fundamental physical point of view, the great agricultural transformation of the 20th century can be best defined as the change of energy foundation (Smil 1991, 1994). All traditional agricultures, regardless of their outward features or the levels of their productivity, were powered solely by photosynthetic conversion of solar radiation, which produced food for people, feed for animals, recyclable organic wastes for the replenishment of soil fertility, and household fuel. Fuel needed for small-scale manufactures and for smelting of metals that were used to make simple farm tools was also derived from the photosynthetic conversion by cutting firewood and producing charcoal. Consequently, if properly practiced, traditional agricultures were energetically fully renewable as they did not require any depletion of accumulated energy stocks and did not use any nonsolar subsidies.

But this renewability did not guarantee either the sustainability of the traditional practices or reliable supply of food. Poor agronomic practices and overgrazing reduced soil fertility, and they also commonly resulted in excessive erosion (and desertification) and in the abandonment of arable or pasture lands. Low yields, often hardly changed over centuries, provided typically only marginal food surpluses in good years and resulted in recurrent food shortages, widespread malnutrition, and, during the times of natural catastrophes or wars, periodic famines. Intensification of traditional farming through fertilization with organic matter, irrigation, multicropping, plant rotations, and mechanization of some basic tasks that was also accompanied by more efficient use of draft animals could eventually support higher population densities, but it demanded higher inputs of human and animal labor.

Four universal measures that revolutionized traditional agriculture and turned it into a modern economic activity include the mechanization of field and crop processing tasks energized by engines and motors; use of inorganic fertilizers, and particularly of synthetic nitrogen compounds; applications of agrochemicals to combat pests and weeds; and development of new high-yielding cultivars. None of these advances could have happened without the inputs of fossil fuels and electricity or without the introduction of new prime movers. Consequently, modern farming is not just a skillful manipulation of solar energy flows but also has become an activity unthinkable without massive fossil fuel energy subsidies that are channeled directly through fuels and electricity used to power farm machinery and, more important, indirectly as energy embedded in numerous industrial products and used to support extensive agricultural research. Some of these innovations began during the 19th century, but most of them saw widespread adoption only after WWII.

Similarly, it was also only during the 1950s that mechanization and a variety of other energy subsidies began to transform both the scale of typical operations and the level of productivity in feed-grain–dependent animal husbandry in North America and Europe. A generation later this new mode of production began to diffuse in Asia. As a result, in some countries these new production methods resulted in animal concentrations up to five orders of magnitude larger than was usual in traditional peasant households. At the same time, wood harvesting and commercial fisheries also became highly mechanized and more productive, and hence also much more destructive.

Commercial logging was most often the activity that opened up previously untouched areas of tropical rain forest for human colonization. And by the late 1990s there were only three major fishing areas in the world ocean that had a history of increasing catches during the previous three decades. And it was the saturation and decline of ocean fish catches that stimulated the unprecedented post-1980 expansion of aquaculture, another intensive method of food production that is highly dependent on energy subsidies. Consequently, all biomass harvests, with the sole exception of grazing on unimproved pastures, were fundamentally transformed by the end of the 20th century as they became a part of the fossil-fuel–subsidized economy—with all of the attendant benefits (high productivity; low-cost food, fiber, and wood availability) and concerns (including, above all, many forms of environmental degradation).

But the transformation of cropping and animal husbandry was by far most important and most remarkable accomplishment because it made possible the near quadrupling of global population, and machines and chemicals were at its core. Resulting productivity gains were impressive, even stunning. Two examples make this clear. In 1900 U.S. wheat averaged about 40 hours of labor per hectare, but during the late 1990s it was no more than 100 min. And because of increased yields (from just 0.8 t/ha in 1900 to 2.8 t/ha in 2000) American farmers needed about three minutes to produce a kilogram of wheat in 1900, but only two seconds in the year 2000, and the best producers did it in one second! And the best broiler operations of the late 1990s could produce a marketable bird in less than 6 weeks with as little as 2 kg of feed per kilogram of live weight—compared to about three months and about 5 kg of feed in the early 1930s (Smil 2000a). But these achievements came at a considerable price.

Machines and Chemicals

At the beginning of the 20th century productivity of traditional agriculture in North America and in parts of Europe was already benefiting from innovations in materials and machinery design. Inexpensive steel brought curved moldboard plows into general use, mechanical grain harvesters became common, horse-drawn combines were used on some large U.S. farms—by 1915 they harvested more than 90% of California's small grains (Olmstead and Rhode 1988)—and threshing machines became widespread. But the traditional prime movers (human and animal muscles) remained unchanged, except for better feeding and breeding that produced heavier and more powerful horses. At the beginning of the 20th century a standard California combine with a cutting bar more than 6 m wide was pulled by a team of 25–35 horses.

But there were clear logistic limits in using more horses to pull a single machine, and when the total number of horses and mules working in the U.S. agriculture peaked during the second decade of the 20th century, their feeding required about a quarter of the country's extensive farmland. Consequently, this option of horse-drawn mechanization was available only to countries with large amounts of arable land. Substitution of these expensive animals by inanimate prime movers lagged far behind the analogical shift in industrial production mainly because early steam engines were simply too heavy for any fieldwork. Eventually, the machines became light enough to be used for stationary threshing, often directly in fields, and to pull gang plows.

But steam plows saw only limited use, particularly in the heavy clay soils of the Northern Plains, and the mechanization of field tasks began in the earnest only during the first decade of the 20th century once internal combustion engines had emerged, after a generation of slow improvements, as reliable and versatile prime movers. As explained in *CTTC*, diffusion of early tractors, machines of limited power and utility, was slow. The Dakotas and

California pioneered the trend, with about 20% of all farms reporting tractors by 1925, but it was only by the end of the 1920s that power capacity of gasoline tractors surpassed that of American horses and mules.

Basic configuration of modern tractors, including Harry Ferguson's hydraulic draft control system and low-pressure rubber tires, came together by the mid-1930s (Dieffenbach and Gray 1960). Afterward there were two trends that dominated the evolution of North American tractors: one toward lighter engines and frames, the other one toward more powerful machines. The latter trend included the shift to four-wheel drive and diesel engines that began during the 1950s. The mass:power ratio of early tractors was as high as 450–500 g/W, while modern tractors rated below 50 kW weigh 85–95 g/W and machines more than 100 kW as little as 70 g/W. The largest machines that worked on the U.S. Great Plains and Canadian prairies during the 1990s rated around 300 kW (figure 4.2). Rollover bars, first available in 1956, reduced the number of fatalities from tipping, and later they became incorporated into a closed cabin design that protects against noise and allows for air conditioning.

By 1950 the aggregate power capacity of tractors surpassed the power of all U.S. draft animals by nearly an order of magnitude, and by 1963 the U.S. Department of Agriculture stopped counting horses and mules that still worked on the farms, particularly in the Southeast. Stalinist USSR also produced more powerful tractors (including heavy caterpillar models), but in Europe, Asia, and Latin America the sizes remain much smaller, and the adoption

FIGURE 4.2. One of five models in the 2000 series four-wheel-drive tractors that were designed by Winnipeg's Bühler Versatile for large prairie fields. Their engines are rated between 216 and 317 kW (290–425 hp), and they can use implements that are up to 21 m wide. Photograph from the Buehler corporation.

of tractors proceeded much more slowly. Even in the richest European countries they did not displace horses until after 1950, and in the eastern part of the continent many working animals remained even after 1980. Post-WWII Asian mechanization relied on small hand-guided two-wheel tractors suited for garden-size rice fields: Japan pioneered the trend, and during the late 1980s some 40% of Chinese tractor power was in such two-wheel units rated at about 3.5 kW. By the 1990s sub-Saharan Africa remained the only major region largely untouched by widespread mechanization of fieldwork.

More powerful tractors made it much easier to introduce specialized implements: unit frame plows in 1915, power take-off–operated corn pickers in 1928, potato harvesters in 1940. These implements became much more diverse after WWII, and many of them were replaced by specialized self-propelled machines. These included grain combines, corn-silage harvesters (invented in 1915), self-tying hay and straw balers (since 1940), a mechanical spindle cotton picker that was developed by John and Mack Rust in 1949, and, in 1976, rotary and tine separator combines (Holbrook 1976; NAE 2000). Chemicals, seeds, and fuel were brought to fields and harvests taken away by trucks, ranging from light- and heavy-duty pickups to large grain haulers.

Internal combustion engines and electric motors also changed crop irrigation by tapping resources that could not be accessed easily with animate power and by greatly increasing the total volume of delivered water. Most field crops need mostly between 500 and 800 mm of water during their growing period. In arid and semiarid regions this was traditionally delivered by gravity through open ditches or lifted from wells, streams, and canals by a variety of simple irrigation machines powered by animals and also by people. The first step in modernizing irrigation was to substitute these low-flow devices with mechanical pumps driven by internal combustion engines that can, when well maintained, work for more than 20 years.

More efficient methods that did away with furrow-and-ridge irrigation spread only after 1950. The most efficient sprinkler technique, able to deliver at least 65% and even more than 90% of available water to plant roots in fields of 60–240 ha, is the center pivot patented by Frank Zybach (1894–1980) in 1952 (Splinter 1976). This technique distributes water (and also dissolved fertilizers or pesticides) from the central well through a long rotating arm carried by a series of wheeled supports. By the early 1970s this became the leading method of crop irrigation in the United States: groups of circles, seen from jets, dot the Great Plains and arid Western states. By the early 1990s the country had about 110,000 center pivots irrigating nearly 6 Mha. And after 1980 center pivots appeared in deserts of Libya, Egypt, and Saudi Arabia. The only rational use of water in such environments is drip irrigation that extends plastic pipes to individual plants or trees in order to deliver slowly the needed amounts of water to high-value vegetable, fruit, and flower crops.

Where deep wells had to be drilled to reach ancient or receding water tables, irrigation may be easily the most energy-intensive part of the cropping. Indirect energy costs are mainly due to the production of pumps, motors, and aluminum piping, while in some places extensive field grading is also necessary. Despite these costs irrigation expanded rapidly during the 20th century. In the United States it rose nearly fourfold, and globally it went from less than 50 Mha in 1900 to about 270 Mha by the year 2000 (or from about 5–19% of cultivated area), with half of the latter total irrigated by mechanical means (FAO 2004).

During the first decade of the 20th century crop cultivation in Western Europe and parts of the United States was also benefiting from increasing availability of inorganic fertilizers. Their production began already in 1841 when James Murray (1788–1871) began to sell liquid superphosphate made by dissolving bones in H_2SO_4. But only the extraction and treatment of phosphates gave rise to a new large-scale industry. Relatively small English phosphate production was surpassed, beginning in the late 1860s, by phosphate mining in North Carolina, and extraction of phosphate from Florida became dominant in 1888. The industry's principal product, the ordinary superphosphate, contained between 7% and 10% of the nutrient, an order of magnitude more than most recycled organic wastes. During the 1870s phosphorus-rich slag from smelting phosphatic iron ores further expanded the supply. Because potassium is mostly retained in crop residues, their recycling provides usually enough of the nutrient, but another new large-scale industry began in 1861 with the exploitation of the Stassfurt potash deposit in Saxony.

Securing enough nitrogen, usually the most important macronutrient to limit crop growth, was not that easy. During the latter half of the 19th century there were three possibilities: imports of guano and Chilean nitrates, and the recovery of ammonia from coke ovens. But by 1900 the combined worldwide extraction and capture of these fertilizers was equivalent to only about 340,000 t of assimilable nitrogen or no more than about 2% of all nitrogen that was removed by that year's global harvest. Western Europe was the main importer, while traditional agronomic management—recycling of crop residues and manures, and intercropping of cereals with legumes—remained virtually the only source of the nutrient not only in Asia, Africa, and Latin America but also in the United States and Canada. These practices relied on inherently limited amounts of relatively nitrogen-poor biomass, and while they could support good yields on a particular farm, they could not be the foundation of large-scale high-yielding cropping that was needed to feed increasingly urbanized populations that had higher disposable incomes and expectations of better nutrition.

The nitrogen barrier to higher yields was finally broken by Fritz Haber's invention of ammonia synthesis in 1909 and by Carl Bosch's leadership that turned a small bench demonstration into a new industrial process in less than four years. The genesis of this invention, its commercialization, and its truly revolutionary impact on agricultural productivity of the 20th century are described in *CTTC* (chapter 4) and in a greater detail in Smil (2001). The most notable post-WWI features of this process were the limited extent of intensive fertilization until the early 1950s, its subsequent expansion that peaked during the late 1980s at about 85 Mt N, and the stagnation during the 1990s (figure 4.3).

The post-1950 expansion was promoted both by major technical improvements of the Haber-Bosch synthesis of ammonia and by a sharp increase in demand that was brought by the introduction of new crop varieties whose high productivity rested on intensive fertilizer applications. Hybrid corn, introduced in the United States during the 1930s, was the first high-yielding cultivar: prehybrid average harvests were less than 2 t/ha while the 2000 har-

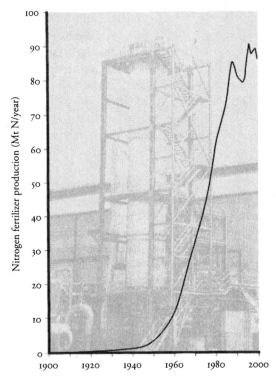

FIGURE 4.3. Global consumption of inorganic nitrogenous fertilizers rose from less than 400,000 t of nitrogen in 1900 to slightly more than 85 Mt in the year 2000. In 1900 most of this nutrient originated in Chilean $NaNO_3$ and in $(NH_4)_2SO_4$ recovered from coke ovens. Haber-Bosch synthesis of ammonia, first commercialized in 1913, became globally dominant by the early 1930s, and in the year 2000 more than 99% of nitrogenous fertilizers were compounds derived from improved versions of the process. Plotted from data in Smil (2001).

vest averaged 8.6 t/ha (USDA 2003). High-yielding cultivars of wheat and rice were introduced during the 1960s mainly through the work of CIMMYT in Mexico and IRRI in the Philippines. Their widespread adoption (only the sub-Saharan Africa did not benefit from their planting) was the main reason for the world's doubling of average rice yields and for a 2.5-fold increase of the wheat yield (FAO 2004).

Urea, a solid fertilizer with the highest nitrogen content, became the world's leading nitrogenous compound, and low-income economies, which used less than 5% of the world's inorganic nitrogen in the late 1940s, applied about 70% of it by the year 2000. At that time about half of the nutrient used annually by the world's crops and about 40% of the element available in the world's food proteins originated in the Haber-Bosch process (Smil 2001). In order to be effectively assimilated by growing crops, these applications had to be accompanied by rising use of the other two essential macronutrients, and by 1988 the world's crops received 16 Mt of phosphorus and about 23 Mt of potassium (IFA 2001). As with nitrogen, their subsequent use declined and stagnated during the 1990s: this shift was caused mainly by the demise of the Soviet bloc economies (where the overuse of nutrients was common) and by higher efficiencies of fertilizer use in the Western agriculture.

Post-1950 growth of fertilizer applications was accompanied by a widespread adoption of an entirely new agronomic tool, synthetic pesticides formulated to control invertebrates (mainly insects) and the spraying of herbicides to destroy weeds. Both insect and weed controls were commercially introduced during the 1940s. DDT (dichlorodiphenyl trichloroethane) was the first and for many years by far the most important insecticide (figure 4.4). Its first synthesis was made by Othmar Zeidler in 1874, but for more than half a century nobody recognized the compound's insecticidal properties (Mellanby 1992). In 1935 Swiss chemist Paul Hermann Müller (1899–1965) began his search for an ideal insecticide, that is, for a potent compound that would be

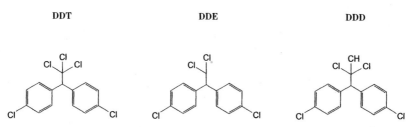

FIGURE 4.4. Structural formula of DDT (dichlorodiphenyl trichloroethane), the first commercial synthetic insecticide whose applications were eventually banned in affluent countries, and of its two breakdown products, DDE (dichlorodiphenyl dichloroethylene) and DDD (dichlorodiphenyl dichloroethane), which are among the most persistent environmental contaminants.

effective against many species while remaining stable for extended periods of time and having minimal impact on plants and higher animals. Four years later his tests singled out DDT. Post-WWII commercial sales, driven first by the insecticide's use against typhus-carrying lice and malarial mosquitoes, grew rapidly, and Müller was awarded a Nobel Prize in Physiology (Müller 1948).

Besides its use against disease vectors, the compound was applied to a variety of insect-infested crops, with potatoes and cotton receiving particularly large DDT applications. They were initially quite effective, and DDT proved to have a fairly low toxicity in mammals. But the compound is highly toxic in fish, and its persistence in the environment (half-life of about 8 years) led to its long-distance transport: it was found in Antarctic penguins and seals (Roberts 1981). Its bioaccumulation in body lipids eventually resulted in relatively high DDT levels in some human populations and dangerously high concentrations in wild species, particularly in raptors, where it caused thinning of egg shells and hence the failure to reproduce. In addition, many insect species gradually developed resistance against DDT. General use of the compound was banned in the United States as of December 31, 1972, after some 6,000 t were applied during the preceding three decades (USEPA 1972). Less toxic and more rapidly degradable insecticides took DDT's place.

Discovery of the first, and still very commonly used, hormone herbicides— 2,4-D, 2,4,5-T, and methylphenoxyacetic acid—has a remarkable history: it was made independently by not just two but by four groups of researchers— two in the United Kingdom and two in the United States during WWII between 1940 and 1943—and this caused a great deal of lasting confusion regarding both the timing and contributions of individual teams (Troyer 2001). The compounds are chlorophenoxyacetic acids, growth-regulating substances whose small quantities kill many broad-leaved weeds without any serious injury to crops (figure 4.5). Their first application as defoliants was by the British in Malaya between 1951 and 1963, and the much better known and massive American use of Agent Orange in Vietnam began in 1962 (Stellman et al. 2003). Agricultural uses started immediately after WWII: less than 500 kg were shipped in 1945, 30 times less than a decade later.

A great variety of both broad-spectrum and highly specific herbicides have been introduced since 1945, but 2,4-D remained the world's leading defense against field weeds for the rest of the century, and in the year 2000 it was still the third most widely used antiweed compound in North America. Other widely used compounds included atrazine, cyanazine, metolachlor, and trifluralin, but the most innovative addition was glyphosate, formulated by John E. Franz at Monsanto Company in 1971 (Franz 1974). This broad-spectrum post-emergence herbicide, the active ingredient of Monsanto's Roundup, shuts down plant metabolism as it inhibits the production of an essential growth enzyme and decomposes underground tissues (figure 4.5). Its greatest environmental advantage is that it acts only upon contact with green leaves and does

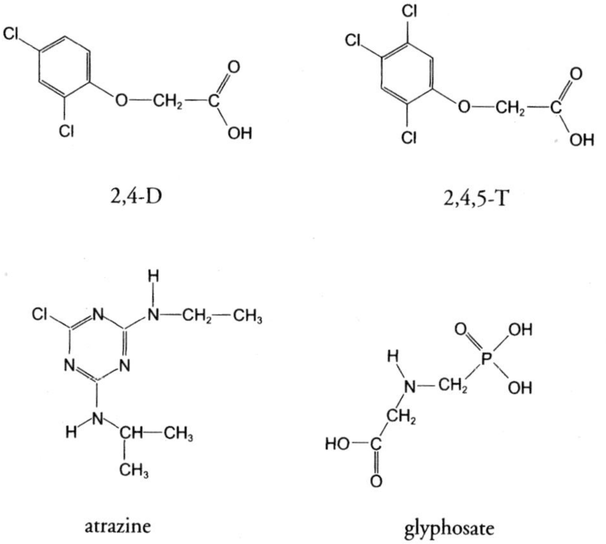

FIGURE 4.5. Structural formulas of four widely applied herbicides: 2,4-D and 2,4,5-T, two chlorophenoxyacetic acids that were first synthesized during WWII; atrazine, introduced in the early 1960s and a leading herbicide of the 1990s; and glyphosate (N-phosphonomethylglycine), patented by Monsanto in 1971.

not move through soil to affect other plants or to contaminate water. During the 1990s Monsanto developed transgenic varieties of glyphosate-resistant crops that were adopted rapidly in the United States and Canada but met with a great deal of resistance in Europe (Ruse and Castle 2002).

Animal Foods

Production of animal foods was transformed no less radically than the cultivation of crops. At the beginning of the 20th century only some pastoralist groups had large herds of cattle or sheep, but these were reared in a purely extensive manner by grazing on seasonally fluctuating amount of grassy phytomass, and their productivities were very low. In contrast, animal husbandry integrated with crop farming relied on small groups of animals whose ownership filled several important roles. They were the source of meat, eggs, and dairy foods; several large species were indispensable providers of draft in fieldwork and transportation, and of leather; and all species produced wastes whose recycling was essential for replenishing the fertility of nearby fields.

There were, naturally, major differences between such extremes as the U.S. and Chinese practices. In the first case, abundant land made it possible to practice both extensive grazing and feeding with concentrates, while the limited amount of China's farmland made grain feeding an exceptional practice, and most of the roughages did not come from high-quality cultivated hay but from poor grazing (on roadsides, stream banks) and feeding with food processing residues and wastes. Transformation of these traditional practices took place in North America and Western Europe between 1920 and 1960; in East Asia and parts of Latin America it began only after WWII.

Our species is naturally omnivorous, and eating of animal foods in general, and of meat in particular, is clearly a part of our evolutionary heritage (Smil 2002b). Cases of religious taboos aside, the limited meat consumption in traditional societies reflected inadequate means rather than dietary choices, and rising incomes created higher demand for meat. As internal combustion engines displaced horses and draft cattle, more land became available to produce high-quality feed for meat and dairy animals, and even more land could be planted to feed grains because of the rising yields of food grains and their declining direct consumption. Animal husbandry thus changed from the traditional pattern of small-scale diffuse operations integrated with cropping to increasingly concentrated large-scale animal factories that were often located far from major feed-producing regions, and even imported most of their feed from different continents (U.S. soybeans to Japan, Thai cassava to Europe).

These operations benefited from economies of scale in housing and breeding the animals, mixing their specific feeds, and processing their products. During the last quarter of the 20th century this shift toward larger units spread beyond North America and Europe, and two sets of examples—one using hogs and the other broilers—illustrate its magnitude. Around 1900 livestock farms in Illinois, on some of the world's richest farmland, had 100–200 hogs, which were fed grain but kept on pasture as much as possible (Spillman 1903). In 2000 all feeding in the United States was in confinement; operations with more than 2,000 animals accounted for two thirds of all hogs, and the piggeries with fewer than 100 animals had less than 2% of all animals in the inventory (USDA 2003).

In China, the world's largest pork producer, extensive rural surveys done between 1929 and 1933 showed that the usual number of livestock per farm included just two hogs and three chickens (Buck 1937). A 1996 survey found that half a million Chinese farms had more than 50 pigs, and there were more than 600 operations with 10,000–50,000 animals (Simpson et al. 1999). In the Netherlands during the late 1990s, broiler production was shifting from operations with flocks of up to 25,000 birds to farms with more than 50,000 birds (van Middelkoop 1996), and China had 250,000 farms with more than 1,000 laying hens and two with more than 10 million birds (Simpson et al. 1999). Such gigantic operations can be supplied only from another kind of large enterprise, from feed mills that process raw materials from a wide variety of sources into balanced mixtures designed to maximize productivity.

Animal foodstuffs are consumed above all for their high-quality protein, whose production entails inevitable metabolic losses. In order to produce 1 kg of protein, animals must consume anywhere between 2.5 kg (dairy cows) and more than 20 kg (cattle) of feed (Smil 2000a). Milk protein can be produced most efficiently, and aquacultured herbivorous fish (above all various carps) comes in a close second, followed by eggs and chicken meat. Pork production converts feed protein to lean meat only about half as efficiently as broilers do, and beef production is inherently the least efficient way of supplying dietary protein through animal feeding. Indeed, if one were to design animals whose feeding would maximize protein losses, one could not do much better than with cattle: their large bodies, long gestation and lactation periods (requiring large amount of feed for breeding females), and relatively high basal metabolic rates guarantee high feeding requirements.

These realities did not matter as long as the animals were totally grass fed, or fed only crop and food processing residues that are indigestible (or unpalatable) by nonruminant species. But with rising supplies of corn and soybeans, most U.S. beef was converted to a combination of grass and grain feeding, and during the late 1990s the average amount of concentrate feed needed to produce 1 kg of live weight for all beef cattle was 5.5 times higher than for broilers (USDA 2003). Since a larger share of a broiler's weight is edible, the multiple rises to about 7.5 times in terms of lean meat (Smil 2000a).

The scale of modern meat, egg, and dairy operations is unthinkable without widespread mechanization of feeding, watering, and waste removal, and a great deal of energy must be also spent on lighting and air conditioning of the structures that house often incredibly tightly packed animals. For example, high-density broiler houses pack 22–23 birds/m^2, leaving barely enough standing room. This crowding led to the use as prophylactic antibiotics to prevent bacterial diseases; other chemicals are used to control infestations, and growth hormones are given to stimulate meat and milk production. A similar set of disease-reducing and production-boosting chemicals is now used in aquaculture, with various species of carp and shrimp leading the production in Asia, and with salmon being by far the most important cultured fish species in Europe and North America (Lee and Newman 1997).

And the quest for feeding efficiency was carried clearly too far with the incorporation of treated high-protein animal wastes and tissues into commercial feeds. The latter practice had actually turned naturally herbivorous cattle into cannibalistic carnivores, and it was responsible for the spread of bovine spongiform encephalitis (BSE, or mad cow disease) in cattle and in the occurrence of variant Creutzfeldt-Jakob disease (vCJD) in humans. BSE was first detected in the United Kingdom in 1985, and before the end of the 1990s it was found in most European countries as well as in Japan (Wilesmith 1998). By the year 2000 there were 84 deaths from definite or probable vCJD (CJD Surveillance Unit 2004).

Potatoes Partly Made of Oil

This is how Howard Odum explained one of the fundamental misconceptions regarding the success of modern agriculture in his pioneering work on energy flows in society:

> The great conceit of industrial man imagined that his progress in agricultural yields was due to new know-how in the use of the sun . . . and that higher efficiencies in using the energy of the sun had arrived. This is a sad hoax, for industrial man no longer eats potatoes made from solar energy; now he eats potatoes partly made of oil. (Odum 1971:115–116)

This perfect summary of modern agricultural practices is also valid for all animal and aquacultured products, as we are now also eating meat, eggs, and salmon partly made of natural gas or nuclear electricity.

The overall magnitude of these energy subsidies is, of course, insignificant in comparison with the input of solar energy that powers photosynthesis, the water cycle, and atmospheric circulation, which there could be no biomass production. While an intensively cultivated cornfield in Iowa may receive annually 30 GJ/ha in direct and indirect energy subsidies, solar energy that will reach it during 150 days between planting and harvesting of the crop will amount to 30 TJ/ha, a 1,000-fold difference (Smil et al. 1983). But as correct as it is, this comparison is also misleading: solar energy is essential but free, but without fossil fuels and electricity—whose acquisition carries significant energy costs—the field's productivity would be a fraction of the subsidized harvest even if the maximum possible amount of human and animal labor were to be expended.

But quantifying how much oil, or electricity, is actually involved is not easy. Finding energy cost of individual crops is a task that is complicated not only by a number of problems that beset energy accounting in general but also by some specific challenges, and one that involves some unavoidably arbitrary decisions (Fluck 1992). Moreover, there are wide performance ranges in every category of major inputs. The most efficiently produced fertilizers—in terms of pure nutrients, representative means are 60 GJ/t nitrogen, 10 GJ/t phosphorus, and just 5 GJ/t potassium—may require 25% or even 50% less energy than those coming from aging enterprises or from less productive extraction. Synthesis of pesticides is generally a highly energy-intensive process that normally begins with petrochemical feedstocks, but some compounds require just around 100 MJ/kg while other need more than 200 MJ/kg of active ingredients (Helsel 1992). Packaging and handling may double these amounts.

Gravity irrigation may have negligible energy, cost while pumping water from deep aquifers and distributing it by center pivots may need more than 10 GJ/ha. Energy cost of producing field machinery may prorate to anywhere between 80 and 160 GJ/t, and fueling it has a similarly wide range of needs. Those rain-fed crops that receive only a limited amount of fertilizers and a minimum of cultivation—such as North American wheat—are grown with energy subsidies of no more than 350 kg of oil equivalent (kgoe) per hectare (about 15 GJ/ha), while intensive corn production gets easily more than 600 kgoe/ha, and irrigated high-yielding rice requires between 1,000 and 1,500 kgoe (40–60 GJ) per hectare. Comparisons per kilogram of the final product convert to around 5 MJ/kg of Manitoba spring wheat, 3 MJ/kg of Iowa corn, and up to 10 MJ/kg of Jiangsu rice. Vegetable fields, orchards, and vineyards need much higher energy subsidies per hectare (> 200 GJ/ha), but the rates per kilogram are similar to those for cereals. Large modern greenhouses are the highest energy consumers, with as much as 40 MJ/kg of peppers or tomatoes (Dutilh and Linnemann 2004).

Published nationwide evaluations based on the practices that prevailed during the last 30 years of the 20th century show means ranging from just 15 GJ/ha in U.S. agriculture to 78 GJ/ha in Israeli farming (Smil 1992). Typical Western European averages were 25–35 GJ/ha (but the Dutch mean was at least 60 GJ/ha), while the Chinese rate was above 30 GJ/ha. But the global mean of agricultural energy subsidies is greatly lowered by the fact that hundreds of millions of hectares of farmland in Africa and Latin America received no synthetic fertilizers and irrigation and were cultivated solely by animate labor. My conservative global account of all major direct and indirect inputs shows that during the late 1990s food production received at least 15 EJ of subsidies, an equivalent of about 360 Mt of crude oil, or just over 10 GJ/ha. Slightly more than 40% of it was used to produce inorganic fertilizers, and a similar share went to field machinery and its fuel. Giampietro (2002), whose global calculation also included the cost of preparing animal feeds and energy invested in the cultivation of forages, came up with a total of slightly more than 21 EJ (or 500 Mtoe) in 1997.

A complete account of energy costs of food supply should also include the expenditures in modern fishing, an activity that has become critically dependent on liquid fuels to propel ships and to refrigerate their catch and, indirectly, on steel, aluminum, and plastics used to make the ships. British skippers' rule of thumb of the 1980s was that it takes one tonne of fuel to get one tonne of fish (i.e., about 40 MJ/kg), and this ratio had only increased during the 1990s. Even when using a much less intensive mean that is more representative of fishing in Pacific and Indian Ocean, the total energy subsidies during the late 1990s added up to at least 50 Mtoe, a total that is less than the uncertainty in calculating the energy cost of global agriculture.

Annual subsidies equal to 400–500 Mtoe mean that during the late 1990s the world's agriculture was consuming about 5–6% of the world's primary commercial energy. In affluent countries, with high energy use in households and services, the rate may be as low as 3% while in some large populous nations it may be closer to 10% (Smil 1992; FAO 2000). Several detailed accounts of energy use in the U.S. agriculture ended up with very similar shares in 1970 (3%), 1974 (2.9%), and 1981 (3.4%) (Steinhart and Steinhart 1974; USDA 1980; Stout, Butler, and Garett 1984). Subsequent declines in the use of fertilizers and more widespread reliance on reduced tillage prevented any major change of the average rate per cultivated hectare, so by the late 1990s the U.S. share of agricultural energy use was almost certainly less than 3% of the nation's aggregate consumption of fuels and primary electricity.

Shares of 2.5–5% appear to be very modest amounts given the quantity and variety of the produced food—but they cover only a part of energy needed by the modern food system. Traditional growers produce either most or all of their own food, but a high degree of specialization means that now even farmers buy nearly all of their food. And because of a high degree of spatial concentration of this specialized production (both intra- and internationally), energy-intensive (cooling, refrigeration) food transport now spans increasing distances between growers and consumers. In North America fruits and vegetables commonly travel 2,500–4,000 km from fields to homes, and the global total of international food shipments surpassed 800 Mt in 2000, four times the mass in 1960 (Halweil 2002). To these high shipping costs must be added energies required for food processing, packaging, storing, retailing, cooking, washing dishes, shopping trips, and dumping the wastes.

None of these diverse activities can be quantified by a single mean, but rates of 50–100 MJ/kg of product are common in processing and packaging, 5–7 MJ/kg of food are usual for home cooking, and 2–4 MJ/kg are typically needed for a dishwashing event (Dutilh and Linnemann 2004). As a result, most food systems will easily claim at least twice as much energy as is used in food production. And in North America the combination of excessive processing and packaging, long distribution trucking to supermarkets, ubiquitous refrigeration, automatic dishwashing, and electricity-powered cooking appliances raises that multiple even higher. Even after excluding the energy cost of food-related car trips, Steinhart and Steinhart (1974) calculated that in 1970 energy use in the U.S. food system added up to almost 13% of the country's primary energy consumption, almost exactly four times the direct and indirect energy use in farm production. The processing industry, refrigeration, and home cooking each consumed more fuels and electricity than did the U.S. farms.

Mineral Extraction and Processing

During the course of the 20th century mineral extraction had become highly mechanized in all affluent countries, and so did the transportation and process of aggregates, ores, and fuels. Delivered costs of final products declined due to impressive economies of scale seen in terms of both costs of individual components and growing size of overall operations. Given the great variety of minerals, the progress and the scale of extractive mechanization, as well as the degree to which the production became concentrated, were far from uniform.

As already noted, these two trends—growing scales and concentrations—were the least pronounced in the case of bulky construction materials—clays, sand, gravel, and crushed stone (mostly from sedimentary formations as limestone and dolomite)—that make up the single largest category of extracted minerals. Their production remained highly decentralized in order to serve local markets for concrete, drywall, road, and building construction. The U.S. Geological Survey found that more than 90% of the U.S. counties produce one or more types of these minerals (USGS 1999). In all affluent countries their extraction became almost completely mechanized, but it rarely relies on machines of extraordinary size and capacity. There are not even any approximate global estimates to indicate long-term trends in the total production of these minerals, but fairly reliable U.S. historical statistics show that the consumption of construction materials, which accounted for more than a third of the 160 Mt of all materials used in 1900, expanded to constitute nearly 75% of 3.4 Gt of nonfuel minerals and biomass used by the country's economy by the year 2000 (Matos 2003).

This more than 40-fold increase in absolute terms was nearly a 12-fold rise in per capita terms (from less than 0.8 to slightly more than 9 t/year). Most of this expansion took place only after 1950, with more than half of the total mass consumed after 1975 (Matos and Wagner 1998; figure4.6). Although the extraction of billions of tonnes of natural aggregates receives little attention, these materials have an enormous variety of irreplaceable uses. To begin with, no other modern material is used as much as concrete in buildings and in industrial and transportation infrastructures (see also chapter 4 of *CTTC*). Crushed limestone, dolomite, and clay are used to make cement, and sand and gravel are mixed with it and make up about 80% of concrete. Similarly, more than 90% of asphalt pavements consist of aggregates, as do all bricks, wallboard, and glass and roofing tiles. And finely, ground aggregates go into products ranging from medicines to paints, from plastics to paper, and help to protect the environment as they purify water or remove sulfur dioxide from flue gases.

In contrast to the extraction of aggregates, new mining techniques were needed in order to exploit progressively poorer ore deposits at competitive cost. Iron ores provide a revealing example. Some of the best 19th-century iron-making was based on ores that contained more than 65% iron (pure magnetite, Fe_3O_4, has 72% Fe). During WWII the United States relied overwhelmingly on the Lake Superior's hematitic ores that averaged slightly more than 50% iron (Kakela 1981). By the early 1950s U.S. Steel had developed a process to crush and grind ultrahard, fine siliceous Mesabi Range taconite, a lean ore

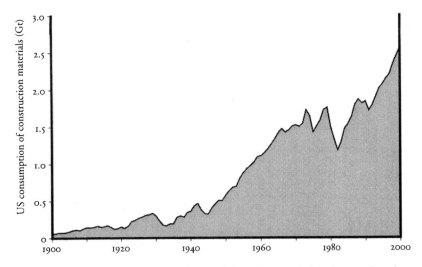

FIGURE 4.6. Natural aggregates are the uncelebrated material foundation of modern societies. No other minerals are extracted in such quantities as sand, gravel, and stone: by the end of 1990s the U.S. production surpassed 2.5 Gt, the total that amounted to more than a 40-fold increase since 1900. Plotted from data in Matos (2003).

whose content of hematite and magnetite is no more than 20–30% iron, and to concentrate the iron with magnetic separation to the range of 60–64%. In the case of many other ore deposits (above all, those of aluminum and copper), the main challenge was simply to reach them with the most economical open-cast mining techniques, and this quest resulted in larger and deeper surface mines.

Larger operations were also used to recover nonmetallic industrial minerals, whose consumption growth was led by increased mining of phosphates and potash for fertilizer. But the most conspicuous case of pervasive mechanization that relied increasingly on highly productive and often extraordinarily large machinery was the extraction of fossil fuels. During the first six decades of the 20th century this effort was dominated by coal production, with two concurrent trends of steadily advancing mechanization of underground extraction and rising contributions of surface mining. And soon after oil and gas production began to contribute more than half of the world's fossil fuels output, it was revolutionized by an ever bolder shift from land to offshore deposits that was made possible by larger exploratory drilling rigs and platforms able to work in greater depths.

As a result, extraction of fossil fuels now ranks among the least labor-intensive tasks in modern economies, and these activities were also only rarely seen by increasingly urban populations. Moreover, during the last generation of the 20th century the media focus on technical gigantism was displaced by the infatuation with the smallness—be it of microchips, genomic arrays, or putative nanomachines. And so even the images of extractive giants became relatively rare in mainstream media, and most people are entirely unaware of the existence of these remarkable machines and structures; the largest moving or fixed assemblies ever built on land or offshore do their work in obscurity.

Coal Mining Transformed

Traditional underground coal mining was one of the most taxing and most hazardous occupations entailing work in inherently risky conditions and killing the miners even long after they stopped working because of fatal lung diseases that resulted from long-term exposures to coal dust. Mechanization of underground mining began at the very outset of industrialization with steam-powered water pumping and hoisting, but actual extraction still used muscle power, with exceptionally high occupational risks, until the very end of the 19th century. Advances in mechanization of extraction and loading followed in successive waves, beginning in the United States, sweeping Europe after WWII, and finally spreading in China during the post-1979 era of economic reforms.

Pickaxes and shovels were replaced by hand-held pneumatic hammers and mechanized cutters and loaders. Joseph Francis Joy (1883–1957)—the inventor and manufacturer of efficient loading machines (the first U.S. patent obtained in 1919)—was perhaps the most important contributor to this shift. He eventually amassed 190 mining machinery patents, and during the 1930s he helped to design a saw loader, an early version of continuous miner (Joy Mining Machinery 2004).

Continuous miners, machines that grind coal from the face and dump it on an adjoining belt, spread rapidly, but they were eventually superseded by the most economical and the safest method of underground extraction, long-wall mining (Ward 1984; Barczak 1992). The technique uses large drum-shaped shearers that move down the length of a coal face, cutting out panels up to 2.5 m high, 80–200 m wide, and as much as 1.5 km long that are delimited by two side tunnels (figure4.7). Coal ground from the mine face is dumped onto a conveyor, but, unlike in continuous mining, the workers remain under a protective canopy of hydraulic steel supports that are, once a complete pass along the mining face is completed, lowered, moved forward, and reset, leaving the unsupported roof behind to cave in. This became possible only with new, very strong self-advancing steel supports that became available in the United Kingdom and Germany during the early 1960s. The technique can recover more than 90% of all coal, compared to just 50% in the traditional room-and-pillar operations.

But the largest coal production increases during the last third of the 20th

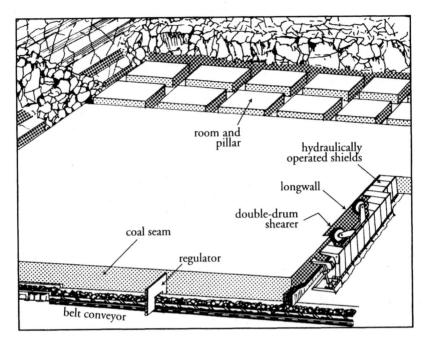

FIGURE 4.7. Longwall mining is the most efficient method of underground coal extraction, compared with room-and-pillar operations.

century came from new large-scale opencast operations in the United States, Russia, Australia, and China. During the late 1990s the largest of these mines produced annually more coal that did the entire formerly prominent coal-mining nations from their underground seams. With more than 60 Mt a year mined in the year 2000, the Powder River Coal Company's North Antelope/ Rochelle mine in Wyoming extracted twice as much as energy in solid fuel as did all of the United Kingdom's remaining deep mines—and even America's 10th largest surface mine (Belle Ayr, also in Wyoming) still outproduced, with about 15 Mt/year, about half of the world's 20 coal-mining nations (EIA 2003).

These operations witnessed one of the most remarkable instances of the economies of scale in mineral extraction through the deployment of ever larger excavation machines (shovels, and walking draglines) to remove thick over-burden layers (Hollingsworth 1966). In the United States, Bucyrus-Erie and Marion were the dominant makers of these machines (Anderson 1980). Capacities of the largest shovel dippers rose from 2 m^3 in 1904 to 138 m^3 in 1965; similarly, bucket volumes of the largest walking draglines increased from less than 3 m^3 before WWI to 168 m^3 before they stopped growing. These machines were obviously far too large to be moved and had to be erected on site from components shipped by several hundred railroad cars. Unlike their smaller versions, they were also too large to be powered by diesel engines and had to rely on dozens of electric motors.

Large stripping shovels had requirements equivalent to that of cities of 15,000–20,000 people, and the world's largest dragline used more electricity than a U.S. city of 100,000 people. But much like their smaller counterparts, these machines were controlled by a single operator, with only two hand levers and two foot pedals. The Marion 6360 shovel, built in 1965 for stripping work at Captain Mine in Illinois, was the world's heaviest excavating machine: it weighed 12,700 t (or as much as 32 fully loaded Boeing 747s) and was 21 stories tall, and its bucket was at the end of 65-m boom. At 12,247 t, the Bucyrus-Erie 4250W walking dragline that worked at the Ohio Power Company's Muskingum mine until 1991 was not far behind: it could dig more than 56 m deep, and with each pass it could remove 290 t of overburden.

Mechanization of underground extraction and introduction of larger machines in opencast mines resulted in consolidation of coal mining into a smaller number of larger operations, rising productivity of labor that lead to steadily falling labor force totals, and plummeting occupational deaths and injuries. In Germany's Ruhr region, one of Europe's oldest coal-mining areas, the share of mechanical coal extraction rose from less than 30% in the early 1950s to more than 95% by 1975, while the total number of operations fell by about 90% (Erasmus 1975). Average productivity of the U.S. underground mining rose from less than one tonne per worker per shift in 1900 to more than three tonnes per hour per worker by 2000, and in surface operations it surpassed 7.5 t/worker-hour (Darmstadter 1997). But productivities are as high as 6 t/miner-hour in longwalls and up to 300 t/worker-hour in the largest surface coal mines in Wyoming.

By the end of the 20th century, U.S. coal mining produced almost exactly four times more fuel than it did at its beginning, with less than 20% of labor force it had in 1900 (figure4.8). At the same time, accidental deaths declined

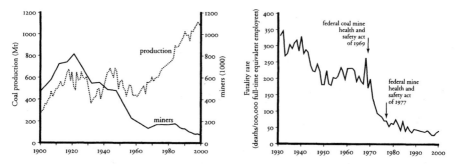

FIGURE 4.8. Production and work force in U.S. coal mines, 1900–2000 (left), and accidental death rate in coal mining, 1931–2000 (right). Plotted from data in Schurr and Netschert (1960), Darmstadter (1997), and MSHA (2004).

by 90% since the early 1930s (MSHA 2004). Among the world's remaining large coal producers, only China followed a peculiar path, as a much slower rate of mechanization in its large, state-owned enterprise was accompanied by two waves of indiscriminate openings of unmechanized small mines (Smil 2004). The first, short-lived pulse began in 1958, a part of Mao Zedong's delusionary Great Leap Forward that saw some 20 million peasants opening up more than 100,000 small mines to produce coal mostly for local smelting of inferior pig iron. The second major expansion was a part of Deng Xiaoping's post-1980 reforms, and by 1997 half of China's 1.3 Gt of raw coal originated in some 82,000 small mines that were distinguished by low productivity and dangerous working conditions. Their number was cut to 36,000 by the year 2000.

Except in China, where even during the 1990s most of coal was burned in the raw state, all major coal-mining countries treated the fuel for commercial sales by washing, sorting, and sizing in preparation plants, many of which were also equipped to remove inorganic (pyritic) sulfur from the fuel in order to lower sulfur dioxide emissions. Unit trains—permanently coupled assemblies of powerful diesel locomotives and about 100 light-weight (aluminum) cars each with a capacity of up to 90 t that continuously peddle between a mine and a plant (Glover et al. 1970)—were adopted in order to provide the least expensive means of taking the fuel from large mines to more distant markets.

Once arriving at its destination, a rotary car dumper turns the cars 140–160° to unload coal, or mechanical trippers open the hatches for bottom-dump unloading. Moving coal at the plant from storage bunkers, silos, or outdoor stockpiles to coal mills or directly to boilers is done by belt conveyors, stackers, reclaimers, in-ground hoppers, or plow feeders (McGraw 1982). All early electricity-generating plants burned coal very inefficiently in lumps on fire grates. The first tests with pulverized coal combustion—blowing the mixture of air and finely milled coal into a boiler and burning it in a swirling vortex—predate WWI, but the practice was widely commercialized only after 1920. Modern electricity-generating plants use mills to reduce the fuel to fine particles, with about 70% having a diameter less than 75μm, similar to the size of baking flour particles.

Oil and Gas Industries

Until the end of the 19th century, drilling for hydrocarbons relied solely on cable tool rigs. These machines were improved but fundamentally unchanged versions of Chinese percussion drilling that was first used during the early Han dynasty more than 2,000 years ago, which relied on men jumping on a lever in order to raise heavy iron bits attached by long bamboo cables to bamboo derricks (see figure 1.2 in *CTTC*). The deepest well completed by this process in China in 1835 was 1 km deep (Vogel 1993). The famous first U.S. percussion-drilled oil well, completed on August 27, 1859, at Oil Creek, Pennsylvania, struck oil at a depth of 21 m after penetrating 10 m of rock (Brantly 1971). Steam engines, rather than human muscles, powered new oil discoveries for the next 50 years, but the raising and dropping of a heavy metal bit hung from a manila rope or wire in order to fracture and pulverize the drilled substrate, and then bailing out the cuttings from the hole, remained laborious. Even so, the record depth reached with this technique, at a gas well in Pennsylvania in 1925, was more than 2,300 m.

The first rotary rig was introduced in the Corsicana field in Texas in 1895, but the technique began to spread only after WWI, and even in the U.S. cable tool rigs outnumbered rotaries until 1951 (Brantly 1971). Main components of a rotary rig are a heavy rotating circular table, drill pipes inserted in its middle, and the hole-bottom assembly at the drill string's end (Devereux 1999). Tables were driven by gearing, originally powered by steam engines, and later by diesels or diesel-powered electric motors. As the drilling progresses, sections of threaded drill pipes are added, but as a drilling bit wears out the pipes have to be withdrawn from the well, stacked, and reattached after a new bit is mounted (the process is called tripping). The weight of the drill string is increased by heavy drill collars placed just above the bit.

Drilling mud (water-, oil-, or synthetics-based fluid) pumped at high pressure down the drill string and through the bit cools the rotating bit, makes the removal of cuttings a continuous and easy operation, and exerts pressure on the well sides to help prevent the hole from caving in (Van Dyke 2000). Casings of varying diameters is then installed and cemented in place in order to stabilize the well. The performance of rotary drilling was much improved with the invention of a superior bit that replaced fishtails and circular-toothed drills used with the early rotaries, which were good only for penetrating soft formations. Howard Robard Hughes (1869–1924) invented the tool after he failed to drill through extremely hard rock while wildcatting in Texas in 1907.

Hughes's expertise consisted only of unfinished law studies and seven years of experience in oil drilling, but in November 1908, after he spent just two weeks on a new design (while visiting his parents in Iowa), he filed his application for a rotary cone drill

> provided with two cutting members 4 which preferably consist of frusto-conical-shaped rollers having longitudinally extending chisel teeth 5 that disintegrate or pulverize the material with which they come in contact . . . These cutting members 4 are arranged at an angle to each other . . . and are rotatably mounted on stationary spindles 6 . . . (Hughes 1909:1).

The numbers refer to the figures that accompanied the patent (figure 4.9), and this simple design made it possible to drill wells 10 times faster than with fishtail bits. In 1909 Hughes formed a partnership with Walter B. Sharp (1870–1912), and the Sharp-Hughes Tool Company (since 1918 just Hughes Tool) began to make the bits and to lease them at $30,000 per well (Brantly 1971). Hughes and his engineers developed many modifications and improvements of the basic conical drill design, including the tricone bit. For more than two decades it was considered impossible for the teeth on the cutters of a three-

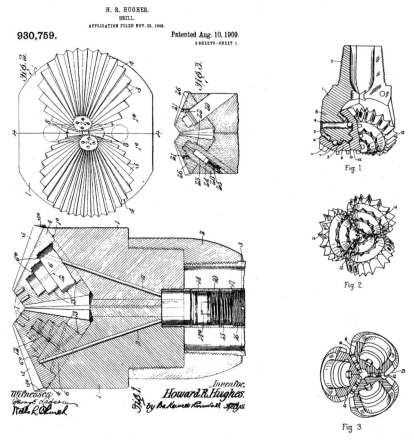

FIGURE 4.9. The first three figures that accompanied Howard Hughes's patent application for a conical drilling bit filed in November 1908 (U.S. Patent 930,759), and the figures from the patent application for a three-cone bit submitted by Floyd L. Scott and Lewis E. Garfield of the Hughes Tool Company in April 1933. Images from the U.S. Patent Office.

cone bit to interfit, but the problem was solved by Floyd L. Scott and Lewis E. Garfield by a design patented in 1934 (figure 4.9). Compared to standard two-cutter bits, this provided much better support on the well bottom, reduced vibration, and allowed for faster yet smoother drilling. A different set of improved bits, designed in 1913 by Granville A. Humason, used rolling cutters placed on the bit face in the shape of an X and it evolved from the first design of cross-roller bit.

A great deal of ancillary equipment and new operation practices had to evolve to make the rotary drilling less expensive and more predictable. Key advances included the first diamond drill (in 1919), heavy drill collars for added weight and rigidity, and various well control devices to cope with high pressures in the well and to prevent catastrophic blowouts. Modern compact bits are covered with a layer of fine-grained synthetic diamonds, and they may last long enough to complete a well 2 km deep. Efficient cementing of wells and automatic well logging were other key advances, and the companies that remained the world leaders in these two activities for the rest of the 20th century bear the names of the two individuals who pioneered the innovations.

In 1912 Conrad Schlumberger (1878–1936), a physics lecturer at École des Mines, proposed to use electrical measurements in order to map subsurface rock bodies, and in 1919 Erle P. Halliburton (1899–1957) started his oil well cementing company in Oklahoma (Allaud and Martin 1976; Haley 1959). Halliburton patented his cement jet mixer in 1922 (U.S. Patent 1,486,883) and Henri Doll, Schlumberger's son-in-law, produced the first electrical resistivity well log in Pechelbronn field in 1927. In 1931 the company introduced electrical well logging, simultaneous recording of resistivity and spontaneous potential produced between the drilling mud and water present in permeable beds. A multivalve stack to control well flow ("christmas tree") was introduced in 1922, and by the 1990s the best control-flow devices could resist up to 103 MPa. Procedures were developed to control well blowouts, extinguish fires, and cap the wells: Myron Kinley and Red Adair were the pioneers of these often risky operations (Singerman 1991).

Faster operation and increased drilling depths—records progressed from less than 2,000 m before WWI to 4,500 m by the late 1930s and 6,000 m a decade later—led to a spate of new discoveries. In the United States, 64 giant oilfields were discovered between 1900 and 1924, but 147 were added during the subsequent 25 years (Brantly 1971). The largest pre-1950 finds included the first giant oilfields in Iraq (Kirkuk in 1927), Saudi Arabia (Abqaiq in 1940; Ghawar, the world's largest oilfield, in 1948), Kuwait (Burgan, the second largest, in 1938), and Venezuela (Nehring 1978). By the 1970s production from wells deeper than 5,000 m became common in some hydrocarbon basins, particularly in Oklahoma's Anadarko Basin. With rapid post-WWII expansion of oil industry—from less than 500 Mt in 1950 to about 3.5 Gt by the year 2000, when there were almost one million wells in more than 100 countries—every one of its infrastructural elements had to get bigger in order to meet the rising demand.

These challenges were particularly demanding in offshore drilling. The first drilling from wharves was done in California as early as 1897, and the first platforms were extended into Venezuela's Lake Maracaibo in 1924. But the first well drilled out of the sight of land (nearly 70 km from Louisiana shore) was completed by the Kerr-McGee Corporation in the Gulf of Mexico in just 6 m of water only in 1947 (Brantly 1971). Offshore drilling then progressed from small jackup rigs for shallow near-shore waters—the first one, Offshore Rig 51, was built in 1954—to drill ships able to work in up to 3,000 m of water and semisubmersible rigs for year-round drilling even in such stormy waters as the Barents and North seas. The Offshore Company that launched the first jackup eventually combined with three other pioneers of marine drilling to form Transocean, Inc., whose long list of firsts includes self-propelled jackups, dynamically positioned semisubmersibles, and rigs capable of year-round drilling in extreme environments (Transocean 2003).

During the 1970s the company introduced the Discoverer-class drill ships that repeatedly set new drilling records: by the end of the 20th century their fifth generation was capable of working in waters up to 3,000 m deep. But Shell Oil was the first company to deploy a semisubmersible rig, the Bluewater I, in 1961 in the Gulf of Mexico. By the century's end industry's worldwide surveys listed nearly 380 jackups (mostly in waters between 30 and 90 m), about 170 semisubmersibles (for depths up to 300 m), and about 80 drill ships and barges for the total nearly 640 marine drilling rigs (*World Oil* 2000). The concurrent increase in the size of offshore production platforms eventually produced some of the most massive structures ever built (figure 4.10).

The world's tallest and heaviest drilling and production platform of the 1970s was Shell's Cognac in the Gulf Mexico, at 308 m just surpassing the height of the Empire State Building (Irving 1979). Three years later, in November 1982, the Statfjord B platform began its operation in the Norwegian sector of the North Sea: its four massive concrete columns and storage tanks at its base made it, with slightly more than 800,000 t, the heaviest object ever moved by man. By 1989 Shell's Bullwinkle, sited in 406 m of water and weighing about 70,000 t, became the world's tallest pile-supported fixed steel platform (SEPCo 2004). In 1983 the first tension-leg platform (TLP) in the Hutton field in the U.K. sector of the North Sea was anchored by slender steel tubes to the seafloor 146 m below the surface.

By the year 1999 the Ursa TLP, a joint project of a group of companies lead by the Shell Exploration and Production Company, was the largest structure of its kind (SEPCo 2004). Its total displacement of about 88,000 t surpasses that of a Nimitz-class nuclear aircraft carrier; it rises 146 m above water and is anchored with 16 steel tendons to massive (340 t) piles placed into the

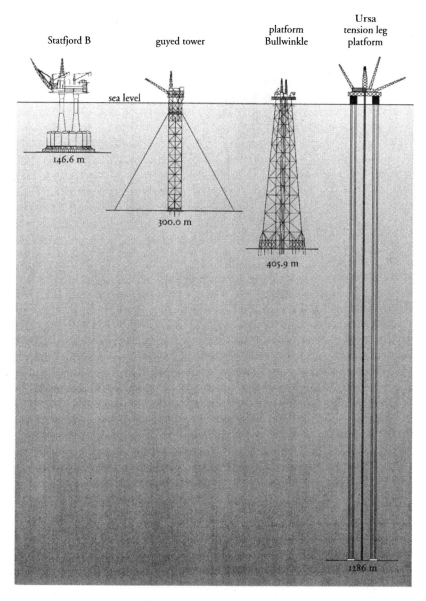

FIGURE 4.10. New designs of large hydrocarbon production platforms have resulted in more massive structures anchored in increasing depths of water. Simplified drawings based on a variety of graphs and photographs in trade publications.

seafloor 1,140 m below the surface (figure 4.11). SPAR, another innovative design, is also moored by steel lines, but its deck is supported by a single large-diameter cylinder. Drilling in deeper waters also required the development of new subsea production systems with wells connected to manifolds on the ocean floor and with highly reliable hydraulic and electrical umbilicals and pipelines to shallower waters. By the century's end the world record holder in this respect was the Mensa area in the Gulf of Mexico, with a depth of about 1.6 km and a 100-km pipeline (SEPCo 2004).

These innovations brought new oil and gas resources from further offshore in the Gulf of Mexico, from the North Sea, and from Southeast Asian, Australian, and West African waters. By the late 1990s nearly 30% of the world's crude oil was coming from underneath the sea. And although the volume and the pressure of hydrocarbon reservoirs remained the principal natural determinants of the rate of hydrocarbon extraction, two innovative trends changed the actual extent of fuel recovery. As exploratory and production drilling reached into deeper strata and as wells could deviate farther from the vertical, it became possible to tap more deposits through extended reach and horizontal drilling. In addition, improved methods of secondary oil recovery increased the share of liquids that could be extracted from parental rocks.

The problem of unintentional deviation from the vertical was recognized for the first time only during the mid-1920s in Oklahoma, and its eventual studies by Arthur Lubinski in the 1950s resulted in the development of directional drilling, which made it possible to complete several wells from a single location. This is now a common practice; for example, the initial plans for the just-mentioned record-depth Ursa TLP were for 14 producing wells. Even more complicated extended-reach drilling at more extreme angles and horizontal drilling began to be commercialized only during the 1980s (Society of Petroleum Engineers 1991; Cooper 1994). Directional drilling uses steerable down-hole motors that are powered by the pressurized mud flowing in cavities between a spiral-fluted steel rotor and a rubber-lined stator. A bend is used to point the bit away from the vertical axis when the drill string is not rotating and then a mud motor powers the drill in the pointed direction. This new course can be then maintained by rotating the entire drill string that includes the bent section.

Steerable down-hole motors are also used by a new drilling technique that was introduced during the late 1990s that uses narrow (5–7 cm in diameter) steel tubing wrapped on a large drum mounted on a heavy trailer (Williams et al. 2001). The tubing is unreeled into a well, where the bit is rotated by a down-hole motor powered by the mud pressure. This slim-hole drilling eliminates the tripping (removing or replacing the drilling pipe in order to change the bit or the drill string). Benefits of directional drilling are obvious; for example, if the oil-bearing strata are 3 km below the surface, then drilling at 70° rather than at 60° angle off the vertical will make it possible to develop

FIGURE 4.11. The Ursa tension leg platform (TLP) is operated by SEPCo about 210 km southeast of New Orleans. Its height from the seafloor to the top of the drilling rig is 1,286 m. Its fabrication began in July 1996; oil and gas production began in March 1999. The project cost $1.45 billion. Photograph courtesy of SEPCo, Houston, Texas.

an area 55% larger from a single site. As the costs of this technique declined, its performance matched and surpassed that of standard vertical drilling. The world's longest extended-reach well, BP's Wytch Farm M11 on the Dorset coast in southern England, was completed in 1998 after reaching 10,658 m to tap deposits under Poole Bay; its true vertical depth was 1,605 m, and it took only 173 days to complete (AGOC 1998).

Pressure that is naturally present in crude oil reservoirs rarely suffices to release more than 30% of the oil that is originally in place. Secondary recovery techniques use water flooding or gas injection in order to increase the pressure within a reservoir and to force more of the fuel from the parental rock. These interventions can increase the typical rate of recovery close to, or even above, 40% (Schumacher 1978). More costly tertiary recovery techniques aim to enhance crude oil's fluidity by introducing steam or solvents in order to reduce the fuel's viscosity, and this boosts the recovery to as much as 60%.

While modern coal preparation is basically a set of simple physical procedures (washing, sorting, sizing, milling), crude oils undergo a complex process of refining, a combination of physical and chemical treatments. Refining separates the complex mixture of hydrocarbons into more homogeneous categories and adds a great deal of value to final products. In terms of specific weight and progressively higher boiling points, these categories range from petroleum gases (short-chain alkanes, C_nH_{2n+2}, that boil away at temperatures lower than 40°C and are used as fuel and petrochemical feedstocks) and naphtha through gasoline (mixtures of alkanes and cycloalkanes, C_nH_{2n}, boiling at 40–200°C), kerosene (jet fuel), and diesel fuel to long-chained (more than 20 atoms) lubricating and heavy oils. Residual solids—coke, asphalt, tar, waxes—boil only at temperatures higher than 600°C.

Early refining relied strictly on heat (delivered as high-pressure steam at 600°C) to separate these complex mixtures into their constituent fractions. Consequently, if a particular crude oil contains only a small share of highly volatile hydrocarbons, its refining produces largely medium and heavy products. This was a highly unsatisfactory outcome once the growing car ownership began to increase the demand for gasoline. Most of the world's crude oils are not rich in light fractions: medium and heavy crudes that dominate Saudi exports contain 48–55% heavy gas oil and residual oil, some West Texas crudes had less than 15% of the lightest fractions, and some Louisiana oils even less. Without an effective technical solution the extent of driving and flying would have remained a direct function of crude oil quality. The first relief came in 1913 when William Burton (1865–1954) obtained his patent (U.S. Patent 1,049,667) for thermal cracking of crude oil that relied simply on the combination of heat and high pressure to break heavier hydrocarbons into lighter mixtures (Burton 1913).

A year after Burton was granted his patent, Almer M. McAfee patented the first catalytic cracking process (U.S. Patent 1,127,465): it relied on heating crude oil in the presence of aluminum chloride, a compound able to break long hydrocarbon molecules into shorter, more volatile chains. But because the relatively expensive catalyst could not be recovered, thermal cracking remained dominant until 1936 when Sun Oil's Pennsylvania refinery in Marcus Hook put on-line the first catalytic cracking unit designed by Eugène Houdry (1892–1962) to produce a larger share of high-octane gasoline. This French engineer began his quest for light fuel with research into conversion of France's large lignite reserves into gasoline, and subsequently changed the feedstock to heavy liquids. This is why his invention, developed after his move to the United States with the help of Socony Vacuum and Sun Oil, was based on the patent, originally filed in France in 1927, for converting purified hydrocarbons into lighter compounds and enriching them by hydrogen (Houdry 1931).

But Houdry's method required the operation to shut down while the aluminosilicate catalyst, covered by a coke layer, was regenerated. Warren K. Lewis and Edwin R. Gilliland of MIT replaced the fixed catalyst by a more efficient moving-bed arrangement, with the catalyst circulating between the reaction and the regeneration vessels. This innovation spread rapidly, and by 1942 90% of all aviation fuel produced in the United States was obtained through catalytic cracking, providing us with yet another instance of an invention that was ready at the time of the greatest need—in order to defeat the Axis in WWII (Houdry's second invention that made a key contribution to the war effort was his butane dehydrogenation process to make synthetic rubber).

And even greater yields of high-octane gasoline were achieved in 1942 with the commercialization of airborne powdered catalyst that behaves like a fluid in "a process and apparatus in which solid material in finely divided form is intermingled in a gaseous medium and the resulting mixture passed through a treating zone" (Campbell et al. 1948). This fluid catalytic cracking, invented by a group of four Standard Oil chemists in 1940, was further improved in 1960 with the addition of a synthetic zeolite, a crystalline aluminosilicate with a structure of uniform pores (see figure 3.14) that provided an exceptional active and stable catalyst composite to facilitate the cracking of heavy hydrocarbons (Plank and Rosinski 1964:1). Zeolite Y chosen for catalytic cracking improved the gasoline yield by as much as 15%.

For the remainder of the 20th century fluid catalytic cracking remained the leading process in all modern refineries that used a variety of crudes to produce large quantities of high-octane gasoline and other light fractions. During the 1950s Union Oil Company developed the process of hydrocracking (commonly referred to by the proprietary name Unicracking), which combines catalysis at temperatures higher than 350°C with hydrogenation at relatively high pressures, typically 10–17 MPa. Large-pore zeolites loaded with a heavy metal (Pt, W, or Ni) are used as dual-function (cracking and hydrogenation) catalysts, and the main advantage is that high yields of gasoline are accompanied by low yields of the lightest, and less desirable, alkanes (methane and ethane).

But gasoline would have been used inefficiently without solving a problem that is inherent in Otto's combustion cycle: violent engine knocking caused by spontaneous ignition of the fuel–air mixture that produces a pressure wave traveling in the direction opposite to that of the spreading flame. In order to minimize this destructive knocking, the compression ratios of early internal combustion engines were held below 4.3:1, limiting the engine efficiency and leading to concerns about the adequacy of crude oil supplies in America's expanding post-WWI gasoline market. GM's research, led by Charles F. Kettering (1876–1958), identified the addition of ethanol as an effective solution, but producing the alcohol from food crops was prohibitively expensive, and there was no commercial technique to make it from cellulosic biomass. As a result, GM began a systematic research program to explore beyond such known but expensive additives as bromine and iodine.

This search was led by Thomas Midgley (1889–1944; figure 4.12). After promising trials with tetraethyl tin, the group tried tetraethyl lead—$(C_2H_5)_4$Pb—on December 9, 1921, and found it highly effective even when added as a mere 1/1,000th of the fuel's volume (Wescott 1936). The first leaded gasoline was marketed in February 1923, and the compression ratio of engines eventually

FIGURE 4.12. In December 1921 Thomas Midgley, Jr., found that the troublesome knocking of Otto-cycle engines can be eliminated by the addition of small amounts of tetraethyl lead to gasoline. Midgley's photograph is reproduced here with the permission of Thomas Midgley IV.

rose to the range of 8:1—10.5:1. Besides saving energy in driving, leaded aviation fuel made it possible to develop more powerful, faster, and more reliable aeroengines, machines that reached the peak of their performance during WWII before they were eclipsed by gas turbines. Midgley's solution was inherently risky (already by 1924 12 workers had died of acute lead poisoning), but leaded gasoline became a prominent environmental concern only when deteriorating air quality forced the adoption of catalytic converters, Eugène Houdry's third fundamental invention patented in 1962. These devices drastically cut the emissions of carbon monoxide, nitrogen oxides, and unburned hydrocarbons, but in order to prevent the poisoning of the platinum catalyst, the vehicles must use unleaded gasoline.

Advances in Factory Production

The transformation label is particularly apposite for factory manufacturing because by 1900 its mechanization was well established and highly diversified. Many ingenious machines were designed even during the pre-industrial era, including such curiosities as intriguing anthropomorphic or zoomorphic automata (Wood 2002). Some relatively large factories were in place even before the commonly accepted beginning of the Industrial Revolution, and the rise of the factory, led by cotton spinning and other textile manufactures, was obviously one of the signature trends of Western industrialization. But Mokyr (2002:150) reminds us that the transition to large-scale production was "more gradual and nuanced than mass-production enthusiasts have allowed for," and that very small-scale business was still very much in place until the very beginning of the 20th century: he cites the French census of 1906 that showed a third of the country's manufacturing labor force working at home.

Some of these limits were the function of underdeveloped markets, but technical constraints were undeniable as early industrial mechanization was limited by low power ratings of available prime movers and by the variety and quality of materials used in machine building. The post-1800 diffusion of steam engines and post-1870 availability of inexpensive steel ushered in the era of increasingly large-scale mechanization—but the steam engine was far from being an ideal prime mover able to provide reliable and flexible drive needed for many productive tasks, early steels did not have qualities that were required by many industrial processes, and machine-tool makers could not meet many demands of the emerging high-performance market. Only the combination of electric motors, specialty steels, and better machine tools provided the energetic and material foundations for efficient and ubiquitous mechanization.

The history of new prime movers and better steels is traced in detail in *CTTC*, so just a few paragraphs on machine tools are in order here. Their complex history is surely among the most neglected topics in the study of modern technical advances, a reality that is particularly puzzling given their key position in the creation and transformation of modern societies. Pre-1900 advances left the machine makers with a wealth of carbon steel tools whose maximum hardness is obtained only after tempering (heating and quenching). Even then, their high carbon content (0.7–1.2%) makes them fairly brittle (Bolton 1989). Better tools were introduced at the very beginning of the 20th century thanks to the determination of Frederick Winslow Taylor (1856–1915), a rich Philadelphia Quaker whose career progressed from an apprentice patternmaker, engineer, and machinist to a manager and the world's first efficiency expert.

While working as a senior manager at Bethlehem Steel in 1898, Taylor decided to investigate the reasons for repeated failure of tempered cutting tools. Together with a metallurgist, J. Maunsel White, he set out to determine how heating affects the cutting speed. They found a marked improvement with temperatures higher than 1,010°C, and the greatest increase in performance after heating the tools to the maximum temperature to which it was possible to raise the carbon-tungsten steel without destroying it (Taylor 1907). When these tools were eventually used in the company's machine shop, the speed of main overhead shafts (in the pre-electric motor era) was increased 2.3–3.1 times. Bethlehem Steel's lathe using Taylor's tool was a surprising magnet for visitors at the Paris Exposition in the summer of 1900. As noted by Henri Le Châtelier (quoted in Copley 1923:116),

nobody quite believed at first in the prodigious result which was claimed by the Bethlehem Works, but we had to accept the evidence of our eyes when we saw enormous chips of steel cut off from a forging by a tool at such high speed that its nose was heated by the friction to a dull red color.

High-speed steel came along just in time to be incorporated into more productive machines to supply the growing automotive market. In 1903 Charles Norton (1851–1942) introduced a crankshaft-grinding machine whose wide wheel could reduce a steel journal to the desired diameter in a single cut in just 15 min—compared to the five hours previously needed for slow lathe turning, filing, and polishing. Just two years later James Heald (1864–1931) launched his planetary grinding machine, whose unprecedented accuracy turned out cylinders with deviations of less than 0.0062 mm. This outstanding design was retained by all similar machines during the 20th century.

Well-known designers of automobiles and airplanes could not have turned their ideas into mass-produced realities without Taylor's tools and Norton's and Heald's machines used in engine manufacture. But, as Rolt (1965:220) noted, "one may search the pages of popular motoring histories in vain for the names of Heald or Norton. Like all great toolmakers, their fame has never penetrated far beyond the four walls of the machine shop." Further development of original high-speed steels led to Stellite, a cobalt–chromium–tungsten alloy introduced in 1917 whose performance did not deteriorate even at red heat stage. The next qualitative jump took place in 1928 when Krupp unveiled at the Leipzig Fair its tungsten-carbide tools made by mixing pulverized tungsten carbide with cobalt, pressing the mixture into a required shape, and sintering it. These small cutting tips that could go through 120 m of cast iron in 1 min compared to 45 m for Stellite and 23 m for the Taylor-White high-speed alloy (Rolt 1965). Further speed was gained by the cam-type regulating wheel for precision grinding machines, an innovation developed by the Cincinnati Milling Machine Company between 1932 and 1935, and by internal centerless grinders introduced by the Heald Machine Company in 1933.

By the early 1930s a new combination of superior industrial prime movers and tools was thus in place: the transition from inefficient steam engines and directly harnessed water power to efficient and versatile electric motors was basically accomplished in all major North American and European industries, and new carbide tools brought rapid machining speeds. Soon the unprecedented requirements of war economies accelerated the diffusion of mass production and made a high degree of mechanization the standard practice not only in all industrial sectors but also in transport and in many kinds of services. And after 1950 this trend was enriched by two qualitatively superior ways of mechanization: automation and robotization.

Mass Production

As explained in *CTTC*, the traditional artisanal production could not be rapidly dislodged by the impressive technical innovations of the two pre-WWI generations. Mechanization of textile mills was a major exception, as it had been advancing for more than a century, but the first lightbulbs of the early 1880s had to be mouth-blown, the first electric motors of the late 1880s had to be hand-wound, and the first automobiles of the 1890s had to be built by skilled machinists and mechanics who transferred their know-how from steam engines, carriages, and bicycles to car chassis and Otto and Diesel engines. And the idea of assembly production also had a long gestation period. Its oldest obvious precursor (in reverse) goes back to Cincinnati's meat packers of the 1830s, who pioneered the stepwise butchering of hogs. By 1890 Chicago's famous Union stockyards fine-tuned these disassembly lines to process 14 million animals a year (Wade 1987). A more kindred experience came from large-scale bicycle assembly during 1890s, the decade of runaway demand for those simple machines.

Ford's system (see chapter 3 of *CTTC*) was fully deployed for the first time at the Highland Park factory in 1913 on a chassis assembly line that accommodated 140 workers along its 45 m length (Lewchuk 1989). The result was impressive: in 1913 Ford made nearly 203,000 cars, more than five times as many as the second-ranked Willys-Overland and about 40% of the U.S. production, and roughly 70 times the output of the largest British automakers. By 1915 Ford was also making, rather than buying, all major car components, and in 1917 he began to build a new River Rouge plant in Dearborn near Detroit, Michigan (figure 4.13). By 1928 the plant became the world's largest manufacturing complex and the paragon of vertical integration (HFMGV 2004). Within its "ore to assembly" confines, Ford not only made all car components (from engines to upholstery) but also produced electricity, coke, pig iron, rolled steel, and glass, with raw materials brought in by Ford's fleet of freighters and by his own railroad company.

At its peak operation during the 1930s the plant covered 800 ha, employed more than 100,000 people, and produced a car every 49 s. And Ford carried his pursuit of high-volume, low-cost production of one standardized item not only to kindred manufacturing of tractors and airplanes but also to soybean extraction (providing feedstock for plastics). Under Alfred Sloan's (1875–1966) leadership, GM, Ford's greatest rival, pursued a different strategy by operating separate car divisions and specialized component makers and by creating new groups of financial and marketing managers. The divisions offered an enduring range of choices—from affordable Chevrolets to luxurious Cadillacs—in order to capture all segments of the market, and the company's annual change of its cars' exterior appearance was hiding a high degree of standardized parts that were mass produced for long periods. And on the assembly floor GM followed the basic Fordist precept of dispensable labor performing repetitive tasks.

Ford's innovations in macroorganization of factory processes were complemented by Taylor's scientific management, with its attention to individual labor tasks. Taylor believed that human work is essentially a set of techniques that can, and should, be not just improved but possibly optimized in order to

FIGURE 4.13. Ford's mammoth River Rouge plant in 1952, during the peak years of its production. The complex, built between 1917 and 1928 at the confluence of the Rouge and Detroit rivers, was the ultimate embodiment of vertical integration: its facilities included wharves and marshaling yards; an electricity-generating plant; blast furnaces; steel, tire, glass, and paper production; large assembly halls; and a peak labor force of more than 100,000 people. Photograph courtesy of Ford Motor Company.

maximize productivity, lower prices, and bestow benefits on all (Taylor 1911). Taylor's quest arose from personal observations of ubiquitous inefficiency in America's pre-1900 factories, particularly from the disdain for what he called "systematic soldiering" of deliberately underperforming workers. His remedy was systematic management of labor based on scientific principles that he believed to be applicable to all social activities. He was not very successful in turning his precepts into reality: after three years of trying to introduce scientific management at Bethlehem Steel, he was fired by the company's president in May 1901.

But eventually both his grand ideas and specific methods of detailed task-timing studies attracted an enormous amount of attention that ranged from condemnation (from labor unions and many intellectuals), through enthusiastic but often misinformed acceptance, to careful implementation (Copley 1923; Kanigel 1997). As a quote from his 1911 treatise shows, Taylor could sound callous: "[T]he first requirement for a man who is fit to handle pig iron . . . is that he be so stupid and so phlegmatic that he more nearly resembles in his mental make-up the ox." But he also believed that the combined knowledge and skills of managers "fall far short of the combined knowledge and dexterity of workmen under them" and that using his method in order to set quotas to overtire a worker "is as far as possible from the object of scientific management."

He had also little use for the antagonistic postures of workers and management and argued for "the intimate, hearty cooperation" between the two "in doing every piece of work" (quoted in Copley 1923:159). He was an excellent researcher: a century later his exercise of evaluating 12 variables that affect the performance of metal cutting remains a *tour de force* of engineering and managerial inquiry. And any young worshippers of the great originality of modern Japanese factory management (more on this below) who may have never heard about the rich Philadelphia Quaker who worked for years as an ordinary machinist should read Taylor's brief 1911 *magnum opus*. They would find that the three great alliterative tenets of Toyota's famed production system—*muda, mura,* and *muri,* reductions of, respectively, non-value-adding activities, uneven pace of production, and excessive workload—are nothing but pure Taylor.

Ford's classical process of mass production was widely copied. Ford's factories in Dagenham in Essex (since 1931) and in Germany introduced the production model directly to pre-WWII Europe. Among the many future top car company executives who made the pilgrimage to pre-WWII Detroit were Giovanni Agnelli (who later became the CEO of Fiat) and Kiichiro Toyoda (of what was at that time the fledgling Toyota Motor Company), who came in 1937 and spent a year acquiring an intimate understanding of Ford's system. WWII provided a great stimulus for the diffusion of mass production patterned on Ford's great example. Sudden demands for unprecedented numbers of machines and weapons and for an enormous array of specialized components led to extensive copying of established mass production procedures. For example, during the last quarter of 1940 the U.S. military received just 514 aircraft; four years later the country's aircraft production capacity was 20 times larger, and actual deliveries in 1944 amounted to 96,000 airplanes (Holley 1964).

To meet this need, companies built plants of unprecedented size and capacity, including Ford's Willow Run bomber plant near Detroit, Douglas Aircraft's plant in Long Beach, California (figure4.14), Dodge's Chicago aircraft engine plant, and the Bell Bomber (B-29) plant in Marietta, Georgia. And after the war ended the methods of mass production were reapplied vigorously to the manufacturing of passenger cars and extended to the making of consumer items for the growing population. Some wartime advertisements explicitly promised this shift as they portrayed new conveniences and appliances filling the American dream (Albrecht 1995), and many of these promises became realities for the country's large middle class within the first two post-WWII decades. And so for some 60 years after its introduction, modified and

FIGURE 4.14. Mass production for war: women workers grooming lines of transparent noses for A-20 attack bombers. The original 1942 caption read, "Stars over Berlin and Tokyo will soon replace these factory lights reflected in the noses of planes at Douglas Aircraft's Long Beach, Calif., plant." National Archives photo 208-AA-352QQ-5 by Alfred Palmer.

improved versions of Ford-type assembly remained the dominant method of mass manufacturing as more and less complex machines and consumer products were made by the combination of repetitive, indeed numbing, tasks performed by expendable workers along moving assembly lines.

But the growing complexity of modern automobiles—Ford's Model T could be assembled in just 84 steps, while assembling the cars of the 1950s required commonly more than 5,000 parts—began to force the refinement of the traditional system, and then during the 1970s two different kinds of innovations began its dismantling. The first one was overwhelmingly nontechnical, relying on a superior form of manufacturing organization, fine-tuned coordination of supplies, and ongoing quality control. Its birthplace was not the giant assembly factories or the leading business schools in the United States but the floors of Japanese automobile plants whose managers were determined to produce the world's highest-quality cars (Womack, Jones, and Roos 1991; Fujimoto 1999). Genesis of this approach goes to the 1930s, and in 1970 this new way of mass production became formally known as the Toyota Production System (TPS).

TPS's common informal generic name is lean production, and its origins were laid by the efforts of Kiichiro Toyoda (1894–1952)—the son of Sakichi Toyoda (1867–1930), the inventor of an automatic loom (in 1924)—who established a new car company, Toyota Motor, in 1937 and adapted Ford's system for smaller production volume. Toyoda also tried to reduce the component inventories by developing a subcontractor network that was able to supply the parts in a more timely manner. Major management changes were under way only after Eiji Toyoda (1913–), Sakichi's nephew, became the company's managing director in 1950 and after the Japanese car industry surpassed its pre-WWII production peak (in 1953) and began its climb to global leadership. By 1960 Japan produced nearly half a million cars (more than 10 times the 1941 total), by 1970 the total surpassed five million, and in 1990 the annual output peaked at nearly 13.5 million units.

Toyota led this expansion thanks to its new-style manufacturing that combined elements of the Ford system and of several other American approaches with indigenous practices and original ideas (Fujimoto 1999). Ford Motor Company's training within the industry and William Deming's (1900–1993) stress on statistical quality control evolved into two key conjoined ingredients of TPS: *kaizen*, the process of continuous improvement; and the dedication to total quality control, whose key components are not just automatic detection of defects and shutdown of machines (*jidoka*) but also foolproof prevention of errors (*poka-yoke*). Traditional mass production facilities had a great deal of space devoted to postproduction quality control, and extensive reworking areas were required to fix numerous, often cumulative, problems. In contrast, TPS aims to prevent big problems by doing things right the first time, by building in quality (*tsukurikomi*).

This goal is achieved by constantly detecting and immediately fixing any defects. Any worker who notices a problem can pull the overhead line-stop cord, and the team leader is called in to resolve the matter; in addition, some lines are designed to stop automatically when a serious problem is encountered. The stress of *muda*, *mura*, and *muri*; quality circles, small groups of workers aiming to solve arising problems; workers' involvement in preventive maintenance; and general adherence to cleanliness and neatness of the workplace are among other key ingredients of the constant quest for quality. Taiichi Ōno (1912–1990), an engineer who joined the company in 1932 and who became an assembly shop manager at the Nagoya plant in 1950, was the chief proponent of some of these innovative solutions, which he began to put in place during the 1950s (Ōno 1988).

Early innovations that sought to overcome the company's precarious financial situation by raising productivity without much capital investment included multitask job assignment (*takotei-mochi*), a major departure from traditional Fordist practice of single repeated motions; and levelization of production pace (*heijunka*), which mixes the making of different kinds of products on the same line and which required detailed planning of the assembly sequence. But Ōno's main contribution was to perfect the just-in-time system of parts delivery organized by using the *kanban* (signboard) technique aimed at producing a smooth, continuous work flow. Printed cards attached to parts or assemblies carry the relevant information on these inputs, with the production *kanban* circulating within each assembly process and withdrawal *kanban* used to transfer parts from the preceding process to replace the used parts (Toyota Motor Company 2004). Fine-tuning of this practice cut inventories as subcontractors delivered the needed parts as close to the time of their actual use as was logistically possible.

Reduced inventories minimize the space needed inside factories and limit the amount of capital that is tied up in accumulated parts. These are significant considerations given the fact that the late-1990s car models were assembled from about 30,000 parts. During the study of management practices of the world's leading car companies done by MIT's International Vehicle Program in the early 1990s, the initial plant survey form asked how many days of inventory were in the plant. "A Toyota manager politely asked whether there was an error in translation. Surely we meant *minutes* of inventory" (Womack, Jones, and Roos 1991:80). In 1986 the inventory in Toyota's Takaoka plant averaged two hours, compared to 2 weeks in a GM plant in Massachusetts.

Most of the TPS features were embraced and further developed by other Japanese carmakers. Their diffusion was instrumental in flooding the world in general, and North America in particular, with high-quality exports. And once the Japanese carmakers set up operations in the United States, the transplanted production system proved as effective in Ohio and Tennessee as it did in Motomachi or Takaoka. By the century's end Japanese companies were making nearly 30% of all passenger cars made in the United States, while American and European automakers not only adopted many elements of the Japanese system but also purified some of them into even more extreme practices (Fujimoto 1999). And during the 1980s the just-in-time approach became perhaps the most widely accepted Japanese innovation to improve productivity in many other branches of manufacturing (Voss 1987).

What emerged before the end of the 20th century was yet another management hybrid. Taylor's pervasive concern about waste remains universally valid, but other assumptions that underpinned its operation proved to be counterproductive. While recognizing the value of workers' collective expertise, he failed to take advantage of it because he reduced their participation to the efficient execution of single tasks and relied on a one-way, downward flow of information in a factory. And post-1950 linear programming models demonstrated that the optimization of individual tasks does not necessarily optimize the performance of the entire process. Japanese innovations proved immensely influential as the quest for lean production was adopted by the Western manufacturing. Its benefits were also extended to multiproject management, also pioneered by Toyota Motor, which aims to introduce products that share key components (e.g., engines or chassis in cars) but that are developed by separate teams for particular market segments. Cusumano and Nobeoka (1999) called this "thinking beyond lean."

Automation and Robotization

Unlike the primarily organizational approach of the lean production, the second category of innovations that transformed the classical industrial factory combined innovative machine design with the increasing computing power. "Automatization" would be a more correctly derived noun—from the Greek term for statues that divine Hephaistos imbued with life, αὐτόματοι—but the shorter "automation" prevailed after John Diebold (1952) used it in the title of his pioneering book. In turn, robotization, which made its first commercial inroads in the early 1960s, is qualitatively superior to mere automation. There are no universally binding definitions of these processes, but the most productive way to understand their development is to accept evolutionary continuum from simple mechanization to basic automation to advanced robotization.

By the beginning of the 20th century, mechanization of particular tasks and processes produced some amazingly ingenious machines capable of fully automatic operation. Among my favorites are the first fully automatic bottle-making machines that were designed by the Ohio glassblower Michael Joseph Owens (1859–1923). With no formal education and lacking the skills to build the machines himself, he described and sketched his ideas so that his engineering friends could convert them into pioneering machines (Owens 1904). The first model, offered in 1905, could make 17,280 bottles a day at 10 cents per gross, compared to 2,880 bottles made in a shop employing six workers at $1.80 per gross (ASME 1983). An entirely new design introduced in 1912 increased the capacity to an average of 50,400 bottles a day, and it could make them in sizes ranging from prescription ware to gallon containers (figure 4.15). By the year 2000 Owens-Illinois and its affiliates shipped some 100 million bottles every day.

But complete automation, the ultimate stage of mechanization, must go beyond an ingenious machine: it implies controlled deployment of many mechanical devices in order to perform manufacturing tasks in timed sequence without (or with minimal) human intervention. Its success rests not only on integrated deployment of machines but also on rationalizing complete production sequences, and its prerequisites include optimized space allocation and coordinated and streamlined production flows. Not surprisingly, the automo-

M. J. OWENS.
GLASS SHAPING MACHINE.
APPLICATION FILED APR. 13, 1903.

NO MODEL.   10 SHEETS—SHEET 1.

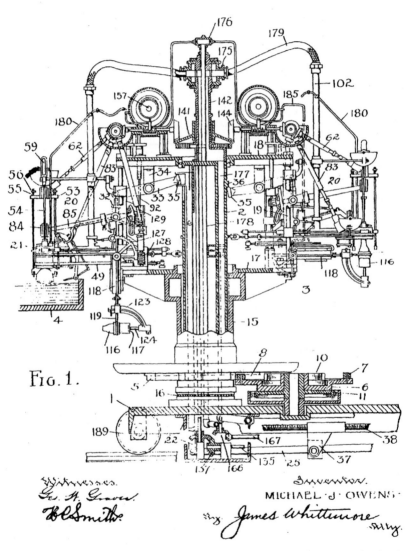

FIG. 1.

FIGURE 4.15. Drawing from U.S. Patent 766,768 of the first fully automatic glass bottle machine designed by Michael J. Owens in 1903. Available from the U.S. Patent Office.

bile industry, the most complex manufacturing activity before WWII, was the birthplace of many key procedures. But the most important post-1945 advances came in response to the unprecedented requirements of military aircraft construction.

Machining large series of complex surfaces of wings for fighter planes or rotors for helicopters and doing so within extremely narrow tolerances could not be done in traditional ways by highly skilled operators using accurate jigs and templates. Electromechanical tracer machines, introduced in the early 1920s in order to duplicate carefully made models, were an unacceptable solution: too many models were needed, and copied surfaces deteriorated with time. By 1947—when Ford set up a new automation department that was to explore electromechanical, hydraulic, and pneumatic techniques of automation—it became clear that a very different approach relying on numerically controlled (NC) machine tools held the best promise. But NC tools became a commercial reality only after more than a decade of complex, and complicated, development (Noble 1984). In 1947 John T. Parsons, the president of a company making helicopter rotor blades, and Frank L. Stulen, one of his engineers, conceived the first design of a milling machine whose automatic contour cutting was to be controlled by using IBM punched cards (figure 4.16). In June 1949 Parsons signed a contract with the U.S. Air Force to develop a prototype for machining wing surfaces.

No commercial model resulted from this effort. In 1985, when Parsons received a National Medal of Technology, he remarked that "the impact of this invention is little understood, yet its applications range from computer chips to jet aircraft machine tools, even to the production of clothing" (White House Millenium Council 2000). Parsons' initial concept of a relatively simple electromechanical machine was transformed once MIT's Servomechanisms Laboratory was brought into the Air Force project: it was turned into a much more complex electronic design that was not easy to produce.

The first NC machine was publicly displayed in September 1952, but the early models were clumsy (250 electronic tubes, and 175 relays) and for many years their economics remained questionable. The prospects improved with MIT's development of the Automatically Programmed Tools (APT) computer language and, in the spring of 1957, with the establishment of a consortium of aircraft companies dedicated to the advancement of NC machining (Ross 1982). By the early 1960s computer-assisted manufacturing (CAM) was reality, and it received an enormous boost from integrated circuits and from increases in computing power. Eventually the assembly of a large number of identical products became completely automated by single-purpose NC machines (Reintjes 1991).

While the early NC machines were recognizable by bulky control boxes and panels, with instructions stored on cards, tapes, or magnetic drums, post-1980 machines were run by progressively smaller microcomputers. The prin-

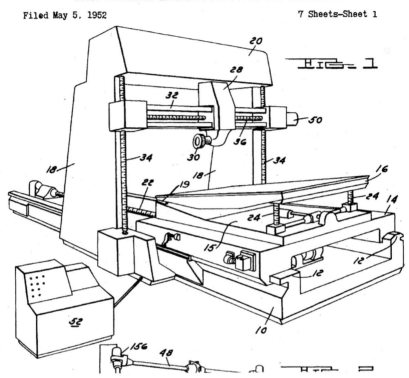

Jan. 14, 1958   J. T. PARSONS ET AL   2,820,187

MOTOR CONTROLLED APPARATUS FOR POSITIONING MACHINE TOOL

Filed May 5, 1952   7 Sheets-Sheet 1

FIGURE 4.16. Parsons and Stulen's pioneering patent for a "motor controlled apparatus for positioning machine tool." The drawing, from U.S. Patent 2,820,187, shows a perspective view of a bridge-type planer mill. A traveling table (*14*) supports a tiltable sine plate (*16*), the cutter head (*30*) moves horizontally by means of a crosshead (*32*) that can also move vertically (*34*), and the control device (*52*) delivers commands to various electric motors (e.g., *28* and *50*). Available from the U.S. Patent Office.

cipal disadvantage of fixed tooling was a lack of flexibility, a drawback that was effectively addressed by the development of programmable industrial robots. Much as with NC tools, their success was a direct function of improved computing capabilities. A small factual correction first: countless recountings of robot history credit Karel Čapek (1890–1938), a Czech writer whose plays, novels, and short stories were known worldwide during the 1920s and 1930s, with the invention of the name for an obedient mechanical automaton. The noun is derived from *robota*, the Czech word for forced labor, and it was used for the first time in 1921 in Čapek's play *R.U.R.: Rossum's Universal Robots*, his "collective drama" about artificial people (Čapek 1921). But it was actually

Karel's brother Josef, painter and also a playwright, who suggested the term (Klíma 2001).

And the concept itself was clearly formulated by the Čapek brothers more than a decade before *R.U.R.* in their story "The System," which was published for the first time in 1908 (see this chapter's epigraph). For decades the heirs of Čapek's literary creation could come alive only in other works of fiction, but I am not interested in the history of such famous fictional robots as *tetsuwan atomu* (aka Astroboy, introduced in 1952), Japan's first sci-fi robot that remains a popular *manga* character, or Arthur C. Clarke's Hal 9000 and Star Wars' R2-D2, the two best-known Hollywood robots. Nor will I pay any attention to the machines designed to mimic animals and people whose late 20th-century development culminated in Sony's Aibo dog, introduced in 1999, and Honda's Asimo walking humanoid that became available for corporate rent a year later. These were merely attention-grabbing toys or expensive advertising gimmicks. Another category of robots that made no practical difference before the century's end included the long-promised household robots for vacuuming and lawn mowing.

Accuracy, repeatability, speed, and quality are the most obvious advantages of industrial robots. Accuracy begins with precise positioning, and robots with only Cartesian or cylindrical configuration have limited flexibility. In order to perform such common tasks as spot welding a car body, a robot must have three degrees of freedom in its arm, to position the welding gun close to the spot to be welded, and three degrees of freedom for its wrist movement to make the weld. With these six degrees of freedom, a robotic arm can work with an error of less than 1 mm to make thousands spot welds on a car body much faster than people ever could. And no group of skilled workers could perform around 4,000 spot welds per car and go for more than 60,000 hours (about 7 years) between failures.

Economic benefits of robotization also include major improvements in worker safety and flexibility that far surpass those of any previous industrial tools. Gains in occupational safety are due to the elimination of such tiresome, unpleasant, or outright risky tasks as welding, spray painting, and manipulation of hazardous materials. Flexibility came to mean not just machines that could be easily reprogrammed to take on a different set of tasks but also systems that could be preprogrammed for a wide array of missions. All of this took place within less than two generations: industrial robots could be deployed only after 1960, when there was a sufficient control capacity to program them and to operate them.

Their development is inextricably bound with the advances in computer science and engineering. Intellectual milestones along this difficult path included George C. Devol's patent for controlling machines by magnetically stored instructions, Alan Turing's paper on computable numbers (Turing 1936), and Norbert Wiener's pioneering writings on cybernetics (Wiener 1948). But

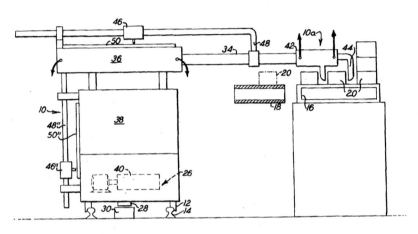

Fig.1

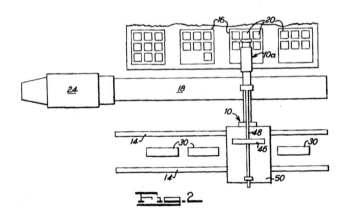

Fig.2

FIGURE 4.17. The first two drawings of George Devol's patent (U.S. Patent 2,988,237 granted in 1961, filed in 1954) for programmed article transfer, the automatic operation of machinery for materials handling. Control unit (*26*) contains the program drum (*40*) to direct the transfer apparatus (*10*), whose head (*10a*) contains a hydraulic actuator (*42*) and a jaw (*44*) to handle articles (*20*) on pallets (*16*). Available from the U.S. Patent Office.

the real intellectual breakthrough came only in 1954 when George Devol designed the first machine for "programmed article transfer" in December of that year (figure 4.17). His patent application spelled out both the novelty of the invention and the critical difference between automation and robotization:

> The present innovation makes available for the first time a more or less general purpose machine that has universal application to a vast diversity of applications where cyclic control is to be desired; and in this aspect, the invention accomplishes many important results. It eliminates the high cost of specially designed cam controlled machines; it makes an automatically operating machine available where previously it may not have been economical to make such a machine with cam-controlled, specially designed parts; it makes possible the volume manufacture of universal automatic machines that are readily adaptable to a wide range of diversified applications; it makes possible the quick change-over of a machine adapted to any particular assignment so that it will perform new assignments, as required from time to time. (Devol 1961:1)

By the time the patent was granted, in June 1961, the invention moved from a concept to a working machine. In 1956 Devol met at a party Joseph F. Engelberger, an aerospace engineer, and they decided to set up the world's first robot company, Unimation (contracted from universal automation). They built the first prototype transfer machine in 1958, and in 1961 their first industrial robot was sent from their Danbury, Connecticut, factory to a GM plant in Trenton, New Jersey, to be used for lifting and stacking hot metal parts made by a die-casting machine. Commands for the operation of its 1.8 t motorized arm were stored on a magnetic drum. Unimation did not make any profit until 1975, but both men continued to advance the process of industrial automation: Devol by working on machine vision (including the now ubiquitous bar coding) and Engelberger by designing automatic assembly systems and promoting robots for service tasks (Engelberger 1989).

While the first Unimation robot was readied for industrial deployment, the American Machine and Foundry offered its first Versatran, a cylindrical robot designed by Harry Johnson and Veljko Milenkovic, in 1960. In 1969 the Stanford Arm, designed by Victor Scheinman, was the first computer-controlled and electrically powered kinematic configuration. In 1973 Cincinnati's Milacron offered the world's first minicomputer-operated industrial robot designed by Richard Hohn (Scott 1984). In May of 1978 Unimation brought out its PUMA (Programmable Universal Machine for Assembly) designed to duplicate the functions of the human arm and hand. But despite these American advances, Japan companies became the world's leaders in robotics. In 1967 the first Versatran was imported to Japan, and a year later Kawasaki Heavy Industries began to produce licensed Unimation machines. Subsequent progress was very rapid. By 1980 Japan had 47,000 robots, compared to fewer than 6,000 in Germany and 3,200 in the United States.

But there is an important caveat: Japanese statistics also include data on simple manipulators that are controlled by mechanical stops, and these machines would not pass a stricter definition of industrial robots used in the United States and the European Union. Comparison of more narrowly defined robots shows 3,000 units in Japan in 1980, compared to 2,145 in the United States (Engelberger 1980). Even so, there is little doubt that Japan's industries were able to introduce robots at a much faster rate, and after they gained the global primacy during the late 1970s they held it for the rest of the century. By the year 2000 the country had 389,400 robots, one third more than the combined total in the United States and the European Union (UNECE 2001). The country's many makers of robots include such leading producers as FANUC, Fujitsu, Kawasaki, Mitsubishi, Muratec, Panasonic, and Yaskawa (Motoman). American car makers embraced robotization only after the post-1974 success of Japanese cars, but the extent of U.S. robotization remained far behind the Japanese level, and in relative terms this was also true for Germany and Italy (see fig. 4-18 for numbers of industrial robots in use 1960–2000).

During the 1990s the price of industrial robots in the United States fell by 63% per unit, and by 82% when adjusted for quality changes (UNECE 2001). Improvements included increased speed and reach (both on the average by

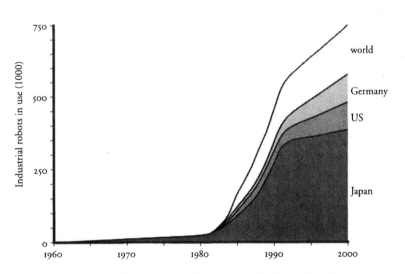

FIGURE 4.18. Industrial robots in use, 1960–2000, worldwide and in Germany, Japan (using a broader definition), and the United States.

nearly 40%) and more than doubling of the mean time between failures. As the number of product variants quadrupled, the worldwide count of industrial robots reached, assuming 12 years of the average service, at least 750,000. But a recent survey showed that the actual length of service may be as high as 15 years, and the total would then be 975,000 robots. Japan had 52% of the world's total (but keep in mind the definitional disparity), followed by Germany and the United States (each about 12%). Japan also led in terms of robots per 10,000 manufacturing workers (nearly 300); South Korean and German rates surpassed 100, Italy was close behind, the United States was just short of 50. High German and Italian rates are due to their robotized car industry: more than 800 per 10,000 production workers, compared to fewer than 600 in the United States.

Besides the well-established tasks that marked the beginning of their use in the 1960s and 1970s—loading and unloading, spot and arc welding, and paint spraying—industrial robots are now widely used for such diverse operations as palletized handling in warehouses and high-speed precision machining. During the 1990s robots were also increasingly used for laser cutting of precision shapes in metal, composites, plastics, and cloth, application of adhesives and sealants (to glass, furniture, vehicles), precision wire cutting (needed to make electronic devices), plastic injection molding, and failure-proof quality control (inspecting with visible, ultraviolet, and infrared light or with x-rays or lasers). Multipurpose robots can also use sensors to locate, distinguish, select, and grasp parts of many sizes (their sensors detect the requisite force to grasp and carry) and perform increasingly complicated assembly tasks (see the bottom image of this chapter's frontispiece).

Engelberger's (1989) vision of household service robots helping the elderly and infirm did not become a reality during the 1990s, but many hospitals came to rely not just on trackless couriers but also on robotic operating systems. Autonomous robotic couriers can transport supplies, meals, medical records, laboratory specimens, or drugs around a hospital, getting on and off elevators without any assistance and navigating through cluttered hospital corridors with interruptions only to recharge their batteries (Pyxis 2004). Development of surgical robots began during the late 1980s; the first robot that helped to perform an operation on a human was a Robodoc machine that assisted in a hip replacement surgery in November 1992, and the first robotic knee replacement was done in February 2000 (Integrated Surgical Systems 2004).

Since 1995 Intuitive Surgical, set up by Fred Moll, Rob Younge, and John Freud, has led in the design and marketing of machines that integrate surgical skills with the ability to operate through tiny ports (Intuitive Surgical 2004). By the late 1990s computerized machines also provided many highly visible, as well as largely unseen, tasks in information, communication, and transportation sectors, which are the topic of chapter 5. But before turning to those advances I should describe the key features of the most innovative late 20th-century factories.

Flexibility and Variety

No other two nouns sum up better the goal of advanced manufacturing: large volumes of production coming from flexible setups capable of delivering unprecedented choice of products. This approach is completely antithetical to the Ford-Taylor pattern that was created at the century's beginning. Instead of mass production of identical items made by single-purpose machines, there is programmable, flexible machining and assembly capable of rapid switches and adjustments and that can yield a mix of low-volume products at competitive costs (Ayres and Haywood 1991). This transformation came about as the markets in high-income countries became saturated with many consumer goods, be it refrigerators (see figure 2.6) or TVs. Greater rewards were clearly waiting in numerous specialized markets where smaller lots could be profitably sold to different age, education, life-style, and income groups.

The last quarter of the 20th century saw a retreat of classical mass consumption that forced the transformation of established mass production. Many companies responded by "paying as little regard as possible to the question of whether anyone else wants it and whether the firm has ever made it before. Mass production in lots of one: that is the aim" (Morton 1994:4). This innovation also provided effective solutions to the productivity paradox, also known as Abernathy's dilemma: increasing standardization and product specialization drives down unit costs but the growing investment in inflexible automation discourages product innovation (Abernathy 1978). But the shift from mass to batch production (there is no binding definition of the divide, but 50 units may do) and eventually even to a single bespoke product could begin in earnest only when the increasing computing capabilities opened several new paths to more flexible manufacturing and when digital controls became indispensable for all major industrial activities (Oullette et al. 1983; Noble 1984; Cortada 2004).

NC machines introduced the age of digital automation. Their diffusion, led by the aircraft industry, was slow as they accounted for less than 5% of all U.S. manufacturing machines in 1964 and for about 15% by 1969 (Cortada 2004). The rise of microprocessors did away with punched media and led to direct computer numerical control (CNC) that allowed for easy modifications of stored programs and for making a range of products with a single tool. One of the most remarkable examples of the CNC machine innovations introduced during the 1990s is Ingersoll's Octahedral Hexapod, a flexible platform that is five times as stiff as conventional machining centers while having only a fifth of their mass (Lindem and Charles 1995). The machine's framework of eight triangular faces joined at six corner junctions is self-contained and hence it needs no foundation for stability. Its cutting edge can be positioned anywhere within the struts' reach and pointed in any direction (figure 4.19). This makes the hexapod an ideal choice for multiple-axis contour precision-machining (with tolerances less than 1 μm) of such large and heavy objects as turbine blades, stamping dies or compressor bodies.

Automation was also extended to any imaginable control function. Monitoring of production processes began commonplace as computers were installed to maintain optimal conditions (temperature, pressure, flow rates, concentrations) in chemical syntheses, crude oil refining, metallurgy, glass, pulp and paper, pharmaceutical, and food and beverage industries. The product directory of Rockwell Automation, one of the leaders in this field, conveys the enormous variety of control circuits, drives, encoders, interfaces, motor controls, programmable controllers, relays, sensors, switches, timers, and wiring systems devoted to these now so ubiquitous functions (Rockwell Automation 2004).

Diffusion of CNC machines paralleled and stimulated the development of computer-assisted design (CAD) and the closely allied computer-assisted manufacturing (CAM). CAD applications, beginning with two-dimensional designs and progressing to complex three-dimensional capabilities, spread much faster than CAM. Military projects came first, but GM began its CAD development during the late 1950s, and commercial aircraft makers joined during the 1960s. CAD did away with slanted drafting boards that used to fill large rooms and with masses of drawings that were needed for major engineering products. Bulky blueprints stored in steel cabinets were replaced by electronic graphics and magnetic storage, and painstaking redrafting gave way to a few additional mouse clicks.

This substitution made the greatest difference in aerospace designs: a WWII bomber required 8,000 drawings, but the Boeing 747 needed about 75,000. That is why during the 1970s the company developed a mainframe-based CAD system that eventually contained more than one million drawings and that was replaced, after more than 25 years of service, by a server-based Sun Solaris operating system (Nielsen 2003). During the 1990s such airplanes as the Boeing 777 and Airbus 340 became the most impressive materialization of pure CAD. Even the earliest CAD systems often halved the time spent on a particular task, and later advances reduced labor requirements to between 10% and 20% of the original need. CAD also allows one to try out a large number of variants and adjustments: the software follows the changes through the entire design and amends everything.

And CAD made it possible, for the first time in history, to dispense with building expensive models, mockups, and prototypes to be subjected to actual physical testing and substitute them with exhaustive virtual reality tests. With

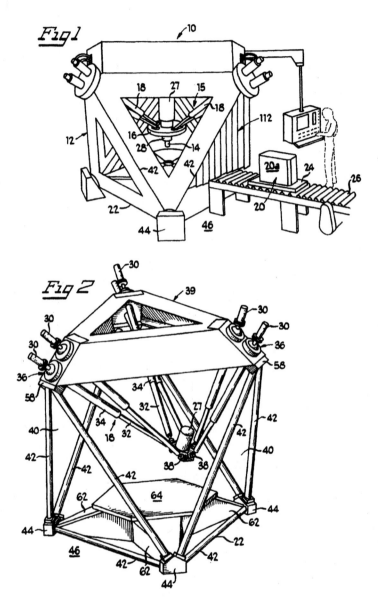

FIGURE 4.19. Two perspective views of Ingersoll's Octahedral Hexapod® CNC machining platform (US patent 5,401,128). Its cutting tool (14) is carried by a servostrut support (15) mounted on extendable and retractable struts (18). The tool engages a workpiece (20) mounted on a table (64). The hexapod can be used either as horizontal or vertical machining center or as a vertical turret lathe.

rising computing power, even such complex phenomena as turbulent airflow or flight emergencies could be simulated with a high degree of accuracy. This led to much shortened lead times from product to market, and this time was further compressed by directly linking CAD with CAM. CAD/CAM combinations pioneered by aerospace industry spread rapidly to semiconductor fabrication, thus lowering the cost and potentiating the overall impact of microprocessors. Once the design is finalized, it can be transmitted from an office into CNC machines in the same building or across an ocean. CAD/CAM also benefited producers of smaller items who may need to judge an object's appearance during the development stage.

CAD can feed alternative forms directly into rapid prototyping machines that can build three-dimensional objects. This can be done either by subtractive or by additive autofabrication (Burns 1993). Subtractive prototyping is just a special application of the just-described CNC tools whose deployment became common by the late 1980s: the final shape will emerge from unattended shaping through cutting, drilling, milling, and polishing or, when working with such hard materials as specialty steels and ceramics, by electrical spark erosion. In contrast, additive fabrication, an innovation of the early 1990s, forms the products by aggrading thin cross sections that are outlined by lasers and built with powder (sintered after a layer is deposited) or photosensitive polymers (hardened by exposure).

CAD/CAM became the foundation of flexible manufacturing system (FMS) whereby CNC machines are linked together to form even more productive and versatile production sequences. By the mid-1980s FMS could be found in companies ranging from aerospace (General Dynamics) to farm machinery (John Deere), and during the 1990s these systems made major inroads particularly in Europe where producers facing extraordinarily high labor costs used them to remain competitive (figure 4.20). The ultimate goal of digitally controlled industrial automation is computer-integrated manufacturing (CIM) that is capable of an almost infinite flexibility at a highly competitive cost: producing small batches tailored to specific consumer demands and tastes at prices that beat the formerly limited choice of mass-produced objects (Ayres and Butcher 1993). CIM goes beyond production to embrace the entire information system (ordering, accounting, billing, payroll, employee records) needed to guide the development of new products and to market them in the most profitable manner.

Cost of many products eventually plummeted even as their quality and reliability improved. Studies showed an average 500% gain in a draftsman's output with CAD, and 44–77% reductions of average unit labor costs with FMS (Ayres and Haywood 1991). But the most obvious consequence of automation was the multiplication of product variety, as retailers began to offer an unprecedented choice with new models introduced at what just two decades ago would seem to be impossibly short intervals (Patterson 1993). Stalk and

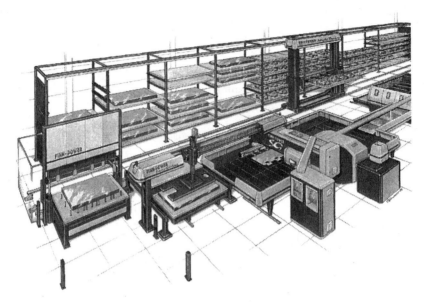

FIGURE 4.20. Night Train, designed by Finn-Power, is a leading flexible manufacturing system with automatic loading and unloading of shelved sheet metal. Digital image courtesy of Finn-Power.

Hout (1990) concluded that reducing time elapsed between an idea and a product determined the success in the late 20th-century markets. They believe that it was a stubborn refusal of many American companies to face the problem of long product development cycles that was mainly responsible for the decline of the country's competitive advantage. During the 1990s we became surrounded by countless manifestations of this competition against time in modern manufacturing: its products were everywhere, ranging from expensive cars to give-away cellular telephones.

Gerber Scientific's (2003) surveys found that since the late 1980s the number of automobile models increased from 140 to 260. The real choice was much wider, as most models came in several configurations: during the late 1990s even the lowly Honda Civic was available in three sedan trims (DX, EX, LX), three coupe (DX, EX, HX) and two hatchback (CX, DX) versions, and as a high-power Si coupe. Moreover, some models allowed for further in-plant customization before the car's shipment to a dealer, and the work shops doing postpurchase alterations and additions were doing record business. The total passenger car choice of the late 1990s approached 1,000 more or less distinct vehicles.

As the choice of car models increased, the size of the production series dropped even in this formerly quintessential mass market. In 1979 GM offered

28 models in its five divisions, with the annual output averaging almost exactly one million vehicles per division; 20 years later the company was selling 36 models in seven divisions, averaging fewer than 400,000 vehicles per division (Ward's Communications 2000). And while during the 1970s it took more than five years of design and development to introduce a new car model, lean production techniques reduced the lead time by more than a third (Cusumano and Nobeoka 1999). And before getting into their cars for their daily commute, U.S. customers can choose from 340 kinds of breakfast cereals and from 70 styles of Levi jeans. And while driving, too many of them will talk on their cell phones, devices that offer one of the best illustrations of a transformed mass market.

The basic hardwired black Bakelite telephone was a perfect expression of long-reigning mass-production based monopolies: the first one-piece set incorporating transmitter and receiver in the same unit (see figure 3.16) was introduced during the late 1920s, and it endured until the 1960s when pushbutton dialing (first in 1963) began to take over and the devices started to change color and shape. But only the conversion to electronic telephony that started in the late 1970s, and the breakup of telephone monopolies during the 1980s ushered in the age of unbridled design that only intensified with the mass diffusion of cellular phones. By the late 1990s choices were running into hundreds as new models were being introduced with lead times of as little as a few weeks.

5

Transportation, Communication, Information: Mass and Speed

> "Oh, I don't know that. The world is big enough."
> "It was once," said Phileas Fogg, in a low tone.
>
> Jules Verne, *Around the World in Eighty Days* (1873)

Many images could exemplify the theme of this chapter, and the gravity-challenging mass of shipping steel containers loaded on a large cargo ship on a long intercontinental voyage is both an impressive and an unexpected choice—but one that is easily justifiable. Just about every consumer item (or at least some of its parts) that was purchased during the last decade of the late 20th century spent some time in a freight container—and it did so most often by traveling via a combination of two or three transport modes, including

FRONTISPIECE 5. Two images, only apparently unconnected, exemplify the late 20th-century innovations in transportation, information, and communication. The top photograph shows the container ship *Cornelius Maersk* (347 m long vessel with bow width of almost 43 m and able to carry 6,600 standard 20-ft containers in its cellularized hold and in up to seven layers on its deck) in the Strait of Malacca. The bottom image depicts the layout of Intel 4004, the world's first microprocessor. Like most modern industrial and service activities, container shipping, now the dominant worldwide means of cargo transport, could not be efficiently managed and continuously monitored without microprocessors in computers, machines, and devices. *Cornelius Maersk* photograph is available from the Maersk corporation, and the microprocessor is available from Intel.

trucks, railroad flat cars, fast ships, and, increasingly, even cargo holds of big jetliners. Some of these containers came just from neighboring states or provinces, others had traveled across a continent, and tens of millions of them arrived from overseas, with increasing numbers coming from Asia in general and China in particular.

And shipping containers are also virtually perfect embodiments of this book's key message about transformative technical advances: their deployment and widespread use required some ingenious design and called for nimble organizational changes—but there was no need to invent any new materials, prime movers, or unheard-of machines. Containers are just big steel boxes with reinforced edges, trucks and railway cars take them to ports, large cranes handle them, and diesel engines propel the fast ships. The enormous transformation of freight transport that began during the late 1950s was thus achieved with techniques that originated before WWI and whose genesis and rapid evolution are traced in *CTTC*. What you see is simple and rudimentarily mechanical: a steel crate, a truck, a flat railway car, and a ship with its stacked cargo.

But the full scale and the pervasive impact of this global transformation would have been impossible without combining these techniques with advances in solid-state electronics. Post-WWII inventions and rapid commercialization of transistors, integrated circuits, and microchips led to entirely new categories of information processing and communication devices, ranging from portable microcomputers and electronic scanners to cellular phones and global positioning systems. What underpins the entire system of global cargo movement are the unseen complex electronic networks that allow a container to arrive just when it is needed after being carried half around the world by a succession of transport modes and that make it possible to check its status at any point of this long journey. Microprocessors are at the heart of these electronic networks; Intel's pioneering model 4004, released in 1971, is shown in the lower part of the frontispiece to this chapter.

And containerized shipping also offers perfect illustrations of this chapter's subtitle and common denominator, the twin advances of mass and speed. At the beginning of the 20th century, break-bulk (general purpose cargo) ships powered by steam engines had typical capacities of 5,000–6,000 dwt, and they traveled at about 15 km/h. After WWII the surplus military ships of the Liberty class became the dominant carriers: their capacity was 10,500 dwt, and they sustained nearly 20 km/h. In 2000 the *Cornelius Maersk* (launched by Lindø Shipyard and shown in the frontispiece) belonged to the largest class of container vessels whose capacity of slightly more than 100,000 dwt allowed them to carry 6,600 standard steel containers and whose 55 MW diesel engine propelled them at up to 46 km/h. And the 20 times larger ship actually took much less time to load and unload!

But before dealing with cargo, I look at advances in transporting people, focusing first on what began as an exciting novelty of an enormous promise and what eventually became one of the key technical markers of the 20th century, the most cherished tool of personal mobility as well a source of many intractable problems: the private automobile. Until the 1950s only the United States and Canada had high rates of car ownership, but then the rising affluence in Europe and Japan brought their automobilization to the North American level. And since the 1970s owning a vehicle had become a reality for tens of millions of more affluent people in low-income countries. Yet despite this powerful preference for cars, and with more than half a billion of them on the roads, railway transport persists. I describe how in some countries this venerable mode of travel was transformed by the introduction of high-speed trains. Then I trace the rapid evolution of air travel from a rare experience to just another way of mundane mass transport. A look at the history of containerized cargo shipments closes the first segment of this chapter.

The second part of this chapter follows the greatest technical transformation of the last two generations of the 20th century, the rise and rapid advances of solid-state electronics. I concentrate on the invention and evolution of its key components, transistors, integrated circuits, and microprocessors, which had transformed computers from expensive, bulky, and relatively low-performance rarities to affordable, portable devices whose gains in processing power spanned many orders of magnitude. After 1970 microprocessors began to move beyond computers, and they gradually penetrated just about every niche of modern life. They are at the heart of cellular phones and programmable thermostats, and they guarantee perfectly cooked rice as well ultra low emissions in car engines. They made it possible to be surrounded by devices that are capable of responding to specific orders and performing, accurately and repeatedly, a range of desirable service—hence broadly fitting the definition of robots. The closing sections of this chapter deal with this pervasive presence, particularly with the role of microelectronics in transforming mass media.

But why not an entire chapter on microelectronics? Because of temporal and functional proportionality. The first commercial computers became available only in 1951; during the 1960s they were widely used only by some industries and services, and they were not widely embraced and hence did not become a critical force even in affluent economies until integrated circuits made them affordable starting in the early 1970s. They reached global ubiquity only during the 1990s. And we should also not forget that, notwithstanding the amazing technical feats of microelectronics, the industry could not exist without the first-order innovations whose origins in the two pre-WWI generations I examined in *CTTC*.

Transport on Mass Scales

Speed of the journeys in pre-industrial societies, no matter if they were made for the sake of trade, religious devotion, or better pastures, was inherently limited by metabolic capacities of human and animal bodies or by inefficient, and often frustrating, conversion of wind into sailing motion. After 1830—once the steam engine, the first fuel-powered prime mover suitable for transportation, was put on rails and ocean-going vessels—these fundamental limits were removed, and trains and ships could accommodate increasing numbers of travelers at higher speeds and lower cost. Rapid extension of rail lines and massive European steamer-borne emigration were the two most remarkable consequences during the latter half of the 19th century.

But the 20th century was fundamentally different because of the unprecedented combination of the total number of people that were taking both relatively short everyday trips as well as journeys not just to distant cities but to other continents, and doing so not only in the quest for livelihood but increasingly as a pastime. Speed and cost of new modes of travel made this both convenient (or at least bearable) and widely affordable. The new reality of travel as a ubiquitous personal choice, often a matter of whim, was expressed most obviously by the rising ownership of passenger cars that often took on unmistakable forms of unmistakable infatuation. Technical prerequisites of this trend and its worldwide manifestations are reviewed first.

In many countries passenger railways became neglected and robbed of their former preeminence, but Japan and France demonstrated the possibilities of modern train travel as they reinvented wheeled machines on steel rails in the form of high-speed trains. But while many more people were boarding passenger ships during the late 1990s than they did a generation earlier, nearly all of them were tourists as cruise industry created demand for going nowhere in particular, on food-laden and alcohol- and gambling-soaked floating cities (figure 5.1). Ships as the means of mass intercontinental travel did not make it beyond the 1960s (as jetliners took over), while ocean-going cargo ships were transformed into a key component of the world's integrated global shipping system. I look at the technical innovations behind this accomplishment after first recounting the evolution of air transport.

The Automobile Century

Because the car's allure was always a critical factor for the machine's acceptance and diffusion, I deal with some of these emotions and aspirations in *CTTC* (chapter 3), and in chapter 6 of this book I look, counterintuitively, at the car as an antithesis of mobility and choice. This leaves me to review here the basic

FIGURE 5.1. Bow and stern views of *Crystal Harmony*, the highest ranked cruise ship in medium size category (49,400 t, 940 passengers), exemplifies the 1990s vogue of luxury cruising with overfurnished staterooms, private verandahs, pools, whirlpools, gyms, saunas, courts, movie theaters, shopping centers, casinos, and restaurants. The cruising industry offered everything from short-budget runs leaving from Miami to months long circumnavigations of the world. Photographs courtesy of John Patrick.

technical and organizational innovations that helped to turn automobiles from rare and expensive possessions at the century's beginning to the most mass-produced complex machines that were regularly used by some two billion people at its end. I concentrate on key long-term trends that reveal much about car's ascent, promise, and troubles.

First, a paragraph about an option that failed to make it. In 1900 the Electric Vehicle Company (EVC) was the largest car maker and the largest owner and operator of motor vehicles in the United States (Kirsch 2000), and many people, including Thomas Edison, believed that electric traction would prevail. But by December 1907 EVC went bankrupt, a year later came Ford's Model T, and then more than six decades of inexpensive crude oil confined electric cars to a historic curiosity. Finally, during the 1990s it appeared that this machine would make its long-promised comeback—but soon all intended adoption goals were abandoned and internal combustion engines remained the unchallenged prime movers of mass-produced passenger cars throughout the entire century.

Rapid pre-1914 maturation of the Otto cycle internal combustion engine (see chapter 3 of *CTTC*) left little room for any fundamental changes in the machine's overall design, but incremental improvements of every one of its parts added up—as illustrated by contrasting Mercedes 35 from 1901 with Mercedes S500 from 2000 in the first chapter's frontispiece—to major performance gains. Intervening improvements that allowed this huge gain in performance included much higher compression ratios (commonly 8–10), lean combustion (excess air:fuel ratio of around 22, well above the stoichiometric ratio of 15), electronic fuel injection, better (higher octane) fuel, and turbocharging.

Turbocharging involves the insertion of a small gas turbine in the car's exhaust stream in order to power a compressor that delivers more air into the engine. Turbocharging was first commercialized before WWII in aeroengines and in large truck engines, and its first, but short-lived, use in serially produced cars came in 1962 and 1963 with Oldsmobile's F-85 Jetfire Sport Coupe and Chevrolet's Corvair Monza. More turbocharged models followed after the technique became standard in racing, but its commercial success in passenger cars began only with the introduction of turbocharged diesels, the Mercedes Benz 300 SD in 1978 and the Volkswagon Golf in 1981. Incremental improvements of other car components were augmented by a stream of major innovations (Flink 1988; McShane 1997; Constable and Somerville 2003).

Abernathy, Clark, and Kantrow (1984) identified slightly more than 600 innovations in the U.S. automobile industry between 1900 and 1981, with only two WWII years (1943 and 1944) without any contributions. During the 1920s open car bodies were replaced by closed structures and wood frames by sheet steel; solid metal wheels, four-wheel brakes, and balloon tires became standard, and new lacquers brought a choice of body colors (Model T came famously only in black). The 1930s saw independent front-wheel suspension for a smoother ride (Mercedes in 1931), power brakes, front-wheel drive (Cord in 1930), more efficient transmissions, and air conditioning (Packard in 1938). Radial tires were introduced in 1948, and automatic transmission using a fluid torque converter came with the 1949 Buick. Power steering, patented by Francis Wright Davis in 1926, became common only during the 1950s. And in 1954 Mercedes-Benz introduced the first passenger car with fuel injection, which was previously used only on racing cars. Transistorized electronic ignition appeared in 1963, the collapsible steering column in 1967, and energy-absorbing bumpers a year later.

Ever since Ford's Model T, automakers tried to come up with basic, affordable cars for the first-time buyers of limited means. Many of these attempts became rapidly forgotten; some of them, because of their innovative design or funky appeal, became classics (Siuru 1989). No such vehicle emerged in the United States after the Model T, and so in terms of the aggregate production, size and longevity (albeit with updates), no car comes close to the one that Adolf Hitler decreed as the most suitable for his people (Nelson 1998; Patton 2003). In autumn 1933 Hitler set down the car's specifications—top speed of 100 km/h, 7 L/km, two adults, three children, air cooling, and the cost below 1,000 reichsmarks—and Ferdinand Porsche (1875–1951) had it ready for production (rather ugly and looking, at Hitler's insistence, like a beetle) in 1938 (figure 5.2). Its serial assembly began only in 1945 under the British Army command. During the early 1960s Volkswagen became the most popular im-

FIGURE 5.2. Front views of the latest incarnations of two small passenger cars whose mass production changed the modern automotive history: the New Beetle, redesigned by J Mays and Freeman Thomas in California and produced since 1998, and the Honda Civic, first introduced in 1972. Photographs courtesy of Douglas Fast.

ported car in the United States. Production in Germany stopped in 1977, but it continued in Brazil until 1996 and in Puebla, Mexico, until 2003: the last car produced at the Puebla plant was number 21,529,464.

France's answer to the Beetle was the Renault 4CV, secretly designed during WWII, with more than one million units made between 1945 and 1961. But the country's most famous basic car was the Citroen 2CV, nicknamed Deux Cheveaux: the numeral stood just for cylinders, the 0.6 L engine actually rated 29 hp, and the car could reach about 65 km/h. Many scorned it, and Siuru (1989:45) found it "hard to believe that people would ever have bought such an unattractive car." Others made it a cult object, and its production continued until 1988. Italy's most famous basic car—Fiat's little mouse, Topolino, a two-seater with a wheelbase just short of 2 m and an engine of 0.569 L—was made between 1936 and 1955. British contributions included the Austin Seven, produced for 16 years during the 1920s and 1930s, and the Morris Minor, whose total production between 1948 and 1971 was about two million units. Morris had a conventional design, but the British Motor Company's Mini introduced in 1959 was more than a cute small vehicle. Its transverse-mounted four-cylinder engine (initially just 0.91 L) driving the front wheels was a layout that was subsequently much copied.

The interwar years also saw an inevitable consolidation in the industry (in the United States there were more than 40 automakers in 1925) and the demise of such once famous marques as Marmon, Nash, Pierce-Arrow, Stutz, and Willys. Yet technical innovations and business consolidations did not result in better mass-produced American cars. Automatic transmissions, power steering, power brakes, air conditioning, and other add-ons needed more powerful engines, and the typical mass and power of bestselling vehicles increased to more than 1.5 t and 110 kWh by the late 1960s. Despite the introduction of compacts—offered for the first time in the 1960 model year in order to compete with European imports—the average performance of new American passenger cars, which was about 15 L/100 km (16 mpg) during the early 1930s, kept slowly deteriorating, with the worst rate at 17.7 L/100 km (13.4 mpg) in 1973 (EIA 2004).

Moreover, frivolous styling was considered more important than safety and reliability. By the mid-1960s "overpowered, undertired, and underbraked cars were traveling at faster speeds on the highways" (Flink 1985:158). And also overadvertized and defective. The average American car was sold with 24 defects, and, as Ralph Nader so memorably documented, these vehicles were unsafe at almost any speed (Nader 1965). The history of the first post-WWII generation of U.S. car making was little more than a quest for quantity and profit that was sustained by low-quality manufacturing and built-in obsolescence. In the absence of any rational attempts at optimizing the use of materials, and given the complete neglect of fuel economy, it also resulted in enormous waste of energy and generated high levels of urban air pollution. This was mass manufacturing reduced to its basest denominator of inelegant quantity bought not only at the cost of user's recurrent frustration but also at considerable risk.

I still vividly recall this engineering ineptitude. After coming to the United States in 1969, we lived without a car in a small university town; after moving to Canada in 1972 we bought one of GM's new models, an experience that led me to foreswear any Detroit designs. At the time I bought that poorly engineered car, the world's automobile industry was just about to undergo three profound transformations that were driven by photochemical smog, rising exports of Japanese cars, and large increases in the price of crude oil. This was, indeed, one of those great "what if" divides that recur in history: how long would have this inefficient, dangerous shoddiness of American car making continued if it were not for smog, Honda, and OPEC?

As the number of American vehicles rose and their fuel efficiency deteriorated, photochemical smog—first noted in Los Angeles of the 1940s and traced by Arie Haagen-Smit (1900–1977) primarily to automotive emissions—began to affect other large metropolitan regions (Colbeck and MacKenzie 1994). Finally, in 1970 the U.S. Clean Air Act called for major reduction of automotive emissions. The more desirable technical fix was to prevent or at least to lower the formation of undesirable gases; the other way was to take care of them just before they were emitted to the atmosphere. The second option became the North American norm in 1974 with the introduction of catalytic converters. This had to be preceded (in 1971) by the formulation of unleaded gas in order to avoid the poisoning of the platinum catalyst. Improved versions of these devices made an enormous difference: compared with the precontrol rates, emissions of hydrocarbons were eventually reduced by 96%, those of carbon monoxide also by 96% and those of nitrogen oxides by 90%.

The first path was followed most innovatively by Honda Motor, the company established by Soichirō Honda (1906–1991) in 1946 to make light motorcycles (Sakiya 1982). In February 1971, Honda revealed its Compound Vortex Controlled Combustion (CVCC, and hence Civic) engine. This involved a small auxiliary combustion chamber that was supplied through a separate carburetor with a rich air:fuel mixture (ratio no higher than 5:1) and that was attached to the main chamber supplied with a lean mixture (18:1 or 20:1). This arrangement kept the temperature in the main combustion chamber to about 1,000°C, low enough to reduce the formation of nitrogen oxides as well as the emissions of carbon monoxide. Honda also took care of hydrocarbon emissions through oxidation within an improved manifold system. In 1972 Honda's CVCC engines were thus the first design in the world to meet the U.S. Clean Air Act standard prescribed for 1975, and did so without resorting to heavy metal catalysts.

The most remarkable transformative factor in the history of post-WWII car making was the surprising rise of the Japanese auto industry that combined rapid growth with unprecedented efficiency of production and, for many years, with unmatched quality. The country's annual motor vehicle production rose from slightly more than 30,000 units made in 1950 strictly for domestic sales to nearly half a million a decade later. By 1970, with the first timid exports to North America under way, the output of 5.3 million vehicles made the country the world's second largest car maker, well ahead of Germany; in 1980 Japan's production surpassed the U.S. total for the first time, and by the century's end Japanese companies at home and abroad were making nearly 30% of the world's passenger and commercial vehicles. This expansion was accompanied by impressive innovations throughout the entire manufacturing process and by relentless improvements in quality (see chapter 4).

The first popular postwar models, such as Toyopet Crown and Datsun 110 (both introduced in 1955), reflected their respective American and English pedigrees. But soon afterward came new designs that were clearly unlike either the American or the European models: they had a much lower number of defects and functioned more reliably, yet making them required less time than in North America and much less time than in Europe (Womack, Jones, and Roos 1991). European import barriers kept them away from the continent, but they began to appear in the United States. Honda Motor Company was an unlikely pioneer of aggressive exports: it made its first car, a small sporty S500, in 1963; its first export to the United States, a tiny two-door sedan N600 in March 1970, was followed in 1972 by the Civic, an entry-level car that combined economy and innovative engineering thanks to its overhead-cam 1.2-L CVVC engine and four-wheel independent suspension; four years later came the first Honda Accord (figure 5.2).

During the early 1970s nobody—and certainly least of all the (at that time) four large American automakers, which looked at these upstarts with condescension—could imagine that by the century's end the car model made in the greatest quantity in North America would be the Honda Civic, followed by the Ford Taurus, followed by the Honda Accord (Ward's Communications 2000). Soon after their introduction, both the Civic and Accord were recognized by automotive experts as the benchmark cars in their class, and Honda kept improving their reliability, performance, and fuel economy through subsequent redesigns. By the end of the 20th century both the Civic and the Accord were in their sixth generation, and the cumulative production of Hondas reached nearly 43 million units.

After the surge of exports during the 1970s came North American–based Japanese manufacturing. Honda was again the pioneer with its Accord plant in Marysville, Ohio, in 1982, and once again, it was an unqualified success: by the century's end Japanese car makers made about 30% of all cars produced in the United States and Canada, and three of the five bestselling models were Japanese (Toyota Camry, Honda Accord, and Honda Civic). The surge of Japanese imports and the setting up of Japanese factories in the United States and Canada were unfolding against the background of dramatically changing crude oil prices: they quintupled between October 1973 and May 1974, and then they rose 2.6 times between January 1979 and January 1981. Smaller Japanese and European models were always more fuel efficient, and the U.S. car makers were forced to approach their performance by complying with Corporate Average Fuel Economy (CAFE) standards and double the fleet's performance to 27.5 mpg (8.6 L/100 km) between 1973 and 1987 (EIA 2004).

These gains were achieved by engine and transmission improvements, lighter bodies, and reduced aerodynamic drag. Material substitutions (high-strength steel for ordinary steel, aluminum and plastics for steel) helped to reduce the mass of average American car by nearly 30% between 1975 and 1985. The subsequent fall in crude oil prices removed the immediate incentive to continue along this highly desirable trajectory, which would have put the average performance at about 40 mpg by the year 2000. Instead, and despite major post-1985 oil price fluctuations, the U.S. market regressed in a way that would have been entirely unpredictable at the beginning of the 1980s.

Pickup trucks and vans always had substantial market niches in North America, but during the late 1980s these vehicles began to be increasingly purchased in order to fill traditional car roles in commuting, shopping, and recreational use. Moreover, they were joined by a new category of oversize and ridiculously named sport utility vehicles (SUVs). By 1999 SUVs, pickup trucks, and vans had gained almost exactly half of new U.S. vehicle sales (Ward's Communications 2000; Bradsher 2002). Few things can illustrate better the U.S. SUV mania than the fact that it became quite normal to use machines with power in excess of 100 kW and with the mass approaching four tonnes (Chevrolet Suburban weighs 3.9 t) to carry a single person in order to buy a small carton of milk from a nearby convenience store.

The often-cited defense of the decision to drive these ridiculously oversized vehicles is that they provide greater safety, but that myth was shattered by the National Highway Traffic Safety Administration study that analyzed the U.S. automotive fatalities between 1995 and 2000 and found that their high center of gravity makes midsize SUVs nine times more likely to be involved in fatal rollover crashes than are passenger cars (NHTSA 2003). Because they are classified as light trucks, these vehicles were exempt from CAFE standards, and fuel efficiency of many models was well below 20 mpg, with the worst ones rating less than 15 mpg. But these incongruous and wasteful machines would have had an even more devastating impact without the benefits of electronic controls that began to appear for the first time during the early 1960s. For example, 1964 was the last year that Ford's cars were made without any electronic components (Horton and Compton 1984).

Microprocessor applications increased steadily in order to control not just panel displays and audio systems but also such key operations as air:fuel ratio, spark timing, recirculation of exhaust gases, and antilock braking (to prevent an uncontrolled slide), which appeared for the first time during the 1980s. By the late 1990s passenger cars contained commonly between 50 and 80 microprocessors: cars thus became very complex machines combining innovative mechanics with advanced electronics. And they also became safer to drive thanks to stronger structural materials, safety glass, better brakes, and greater reliability and durability of principal parts. But, incredibly, the first mandatory seatbelt laws came into effect in Europe only during the 1960s, and in the United States (New York State) in 1984.

The three-point automotive seat belt (combining a lap belt running across the pelvis and a diagonal belt running across the rib cage; figure 5.3) was designed only in 1959 by Nils Ivar Bohlin for Volvo (Bohlin 1962). Ironically, Ohlin's last project at Saab, before moving to Volvo in 1958, was developing the ejector seat for the supersonic fighter J35 Draken. In 1985 the German Patent Office ranked the seat belt among the eight most important innovations of the preceding 100 years, and there is no doubt that during the past two generations it has saved the lives of several hundreds of thousands of people and prevented serious injuries for millions

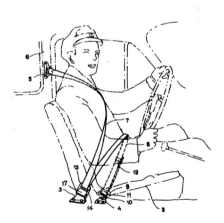

FIGURE 5.3. The first figure in Bohlin's patent (U.S. Patent 3,043,625) for the three-point safety belt, one of the most beneficial inventions of the 20th century. Available from the U.S. Patent Office.

of drivers and passengers. Few innovations can compete with its cost:benefit ratio, as it can save a life with an investment amounting to just several hundred dollars. Airbags, first just on the driver's side, came during the late 1980s.

The greatest accomplishment of 20th-century car making was the transformation from artisanal manufacture of small series of relatively simple but expensive machines to the world's leading industrial enterprise that turned out annually more than 50 million increasingly complex mechatronic vehicles in highly automated plants at rates of hundreds of thousands of units per year, and sold most of them at prices that were well within the reach of hundreds of millions of people. The car's 20th-century history is thus a conjoined sequence of transformations from simplicity to complexity, from expensive oddity to affordable ubiquity. Centennial statistics span differences across orders of magnitude. At the century's beginning artisanal producers were putting annually fewer than 2,000 cars on the market; since 1996 that rate, including both passenger cars and commercial vehicles, has been above 50 million units.

In 1900 the world's passenger car inventory was less than 10,000 vehicles, and most of them were actually electric or steam powered. But the count surpassed one million before WWI, 10 million in 1920, 100 million in 1960, and by the century's end it passed half a billion, with the addition of commercial vehicles raising the total to nearly 700 million (figure 5.4). In terms of people per passenger car, the global ratio dropped to below 50 by 1950 and to 12 by 1999, but these numbers obviously hide very large regional and national disparities. By the late 1990s Africa's mean was about 110; Western European, 2.2. The United States had the lowest ratio for more than seven decades after Ford's Model T went on sale in 1908: down to 3.3 already by 1950 and 2.1 in 1999. European pre-WWII progress was slow, but the post-1960 spurt brought many national ratios to the U.S. level, or even marginally lower, by 1999 (Germany at 2.0, Italy at 2.1, France at 2.2), while Japan's ratio fell to 2.5.

New High-Speed Trains

Steam-driven railways were technically mature well before 1900, and the speed of a mile a minute (96 km/h) was first reached on a scheduled English run already by 1847 (O'Brien 1983). By the beginning of the 20th century record speeds on many sections in Europe and United States exceeded 100 km/h, and during the 1930s engineers designed some very powerful and highly streamlined steam locomotives. In 1934 a Union Pacific train averaged nearly 150 km/h between North Platte and Alda, Nebraska, with a brief maximum of 180 km/h, and in 1936 the German *Borsig* reached the world record speed of 200.4 km/h (Ellis 1977). After WWII many engineers favored gas turbines, and in 1971

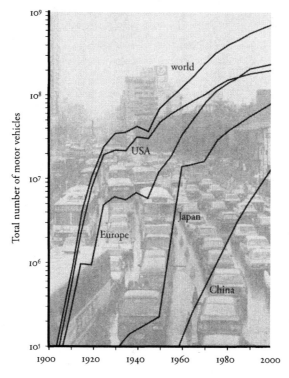

FIGURE 5.4. Motor vehicle numbers and the rate of automobilization, 1900–2000. Based on Fig. 5.19 in Smil (1994) and on data in Ward's Communications (2000).

France's first experimental turbotrain, TGV 001 powered by Sud Aviation's Super Frelon helicopter turbines, was tested at speeds exceeding 300 km/h.

But that route was abandoned after 1974, when OPEC quintupled crude oil prices, and the French efforts turned, following the Japanese example, toward electric traction. Slow, DC-driven trains had been commercialized already during the 1890s, but the tests of single-phase AC traction began only in 1936 in Germany and were eventually abandoned (Bouley 1994). After WWII three international conferences examined this technique, and the last one, in Lille in 1955, was attended by a Japanese delegation. Within months after its conclusion, four major Japanese companies, Hitachi, Toshiba, Fuji, and Mitsubishi Electric, produced suitable AC-commutator motors and rectifier-type locomotives (Sone 2001). But instead of using locomotives, Hideo Shima (1901–1998), at that time the Vice President for Engineering of Japanese National Railways (JNR), advocated the use of multiple electric motors in individual carriages as the best way to limit axle loads, to reduce stress on tracks and structures, and to use the motors for regenerative braking (Shima 1994).

Japan's pioneering role in rapid rail transport is remarkable for several reasons. First is its boldness of vision, as the development of *shinkansen* (new trunk line, to distinguish it from the old narrow gauge) began when the country barely emerged from the enormous destruction of WWII. In May 1956, when JNR launched its feasibility study it was just two years after the country's gross national product finally surpassed its pre-WWII (1939) peak level, and when the average disposable income was only a small fraction of the U.S. rate. Financing the project was a challenge. The World Bank's loan of $80 million was less than 15% of the original budget that JNR set on the low side, at ¥194.8 billion (or US$541 billion in 1958 monies), in order to ensure the government's funding approval. As the cost overruns continued (the final total was ¥380 billion), Shinji Sogo (1884–1981), the president of JNR who promoted the project and insisted on its standard gauge, took responsibility for the rise and resigned in 1963. Shima, whom Sogo personally chose for the vice president job, joined him (Suga 1998).

Second, the commitment to fast trains ran against the prevailing consensus that saw the newly ascendant turbojet-powered flight as the unbeatable choice for rapid travel. Third, although the project's initial phase, the *Tōkaidō shinkansen* between Tōkyō and Ōsaka, had to solve a number of unprecedented technical problems, it was completed successfully on time (just in time for the Olympics), 5 years and 5 months after its construction began in April 1959. Scheduled service was launched on October 1, 1964, and it was improved and expanded with new lines, new trains, and gradual increases in top operating speeds and train frequency (figure 5.5). By 1974 the *Sanyō* line running to the west of Ōsaka was extended to Hakata in northern Kyūshū. The *Tōhoku* line to Morioka in northwestern Honshū, and the *Jōetsu* line to Niigata on the Sea of Japan began service in 1982. *Tōkaidō* trains ran at 210 km/h (for faster *hikari*) until November 1986 when their speed was increased to 220 km/h.

FIGURE 5.5. *Shinkansen Hikari* 100 series (left; now retired) at Kyōto station and 500 series *Nozomi* (right), the last new type of train introduced before the year 2000. Photographs from author's collection.

In 1987 JNR, deeply in debt, was privatized and divided into six regional companies. In 1990 Japan's bubble economy burst, and by the end of the century the Nikkei index stood at less than a third of its December 1989 record—but *shinkansen*'s high standards were maintained, and its progress continued (Fossett 2004). In March 1992 the new 300 series *Nozomi* trains reached speeds of 270 km/h. But since March 1997 the record belongs to the *Sanyō* line, where the 500 series *Nozomi*, easily distinguished by their 15-m-long aerodynamic nose and wing-shaped pantograph, run at up to 300 km/h (figure 5.5). In October 1997 the *Hokuriku* line connected Nagano in the Japanese Alps for the 1998 winter Olympics, and by the year 2000 extensions were under way in Kyūshū and in northernmost Honshū. The frequency of trains on the *Tōkaidō* line was increased from 60 trains in 1964 to 285 by the year 2000, and during the busiest period of the day they follow in intervals of just 3.5 min with average annual delay of astonishing 24 s (JR Central 2004).

The *Tōkaidō* line alone carries annually about 132 million people, slightly more than Japan's total population, and all lines are boarded by nearly 300 million people a year. Perhaps most remarkable, none of the *shinkansen* trains had derailed or collided, so by the end of the year 2000 the system carried 4.5 billion people without a single accidental fatality. All *shinkansen* lines have standard gauge (1,435 mm), continuously welded rails (60 kg/m), and prestressed concrete sleepers, but the use of ballasted track gradually gave way to reinforced concrete slab tracks (Miura et al. 1998). Electricity is supplied by catenary wires (copper or copper-clad steel) with spans of 50 m as 25 kV AC at 60 Hz. Sixteen-car trains, seating up to 1,323 people and lasting for 15–20 years, became soon standard; the latest 700 series has 64 AC motors of 275 kW each for the total of 13.2 MW. This makes frequent accelerations and decelerations, needed for relatively short interstation runs, easier, and the motors also function as dynamic brakes once they become generators driven by the wheels and exert drag on the train. Pneumatic brakes are used for speeds below 30 km/h and as a backup.

Original track specifications were for the minimum of 2.5 km for the radius of curves and the steepest gradient of 2%; maxima for faster trains are 4 km and 1.67%. There are no level crossings, and the probability of mishaps is minimized by advanced safety features, including multipurpose inspection trains that run between midnight and 6 A.M., automatic train control (ATC), the centralized traffic control (CTC), and Urgent Earthquake Detection and Alarm System. ATC keeps proper distance between trains and automatically engages brakes if the speed exceeds the indicated maximum. The CTC carries out route control, train scheduling, and management of trains and crews. The earthquake detection system picks up the very first seismic waves reaching the Earth's surface, uses this information to determine risk levels, and can halt trains, or at least slow them down, before the main shock arrives (Noguchi and Fujii 2000).

France's state railway corporation (SNCF) began testing its experimental high-speed electric locomotive, *Zébulon*, in 1974, and the country's first high-speed service, *train à grand vitesse* (*TGV*) between Paris and Lyon, began in September 1981 (Soulié and Tricoire 2002). After *TGV Sud-Est* came *TGV Atlantique* (western branch to Brittany in 1989, southwest line to Bordeaux a year later), *TGV Nord* (to Calais in 1993, connected to the Channel Tunnel in 1994), the second international link with Belgium (1997), and the first exported *TGV* to Spain for the Madrid and Seville (AVE) line in 1991. The more powerful *TGV Atlantique* (8.8 MW compared to 6.45 MW for the *Sud-Est*) was the first train to travel at up to 300 km/h in regular commercial service, and in May 1990 the world speed record of 515.3 km/h was set on this line (figure 5.6). In order to accommodate the growing demand on the Paris–Lyon line, two trains were coupled together, and then a double-decker *TGV* was introduced in 1996.

TGV status as an object of pride and envy came at a high price: during the late 1990s SNCF—despite the transfer of its huge debts to *Réseau Ferré de France*, the company that owns the track and signals—continued to operate with large annual losses. *TGV*, unlike *shinkansen*, has two locomotives in every trains, each weighing 68 t and capable of 4.4 MW (TGVweb 2000). Electric supply and subsequent conversions are similar to the Japanese practice: the pantograph picks up AC at 25 kV and 50 Hz, the rectifier converts it to 1,500 V DC, and traction inverters convert DC to variable frequency AC that is fed to synchronous motors that are also used for dynamic braking at high speeds.

By the year 2000 the Sanyo *Nozomi* between Hiroshima and Kokura and *TGV Sud-Est* between Valence and Avignon had almost identical speeds as the world's two fastest scheduled trains at, respectively, 261.8 and 259.4 km/h (Tay-

FIGURE 5.6. *TGV Sud-Est* (left)—200 m long, 2.81 m tall, powered by motors capable of 6.45 MW—carries 414 passengers at speeds of up to 300 km/h, and isolines (right) indicating travel time from Paris to cities with high-speed train service. Photograph courtesy of SNCF. Isolines based on a detailed map from Railfan Europe.

lor 2001). Besides the *TGV* exported to Spain, several European countries gradually acquired their own high-speed trains (European Commission 1995). Germany's InterCity Express, launched in 1991, had its fastest scheduled run at about 190 km/h; Italy's ETR500, about 165 km/h; and the fastest British and Swedish trains, 200 km/h. In contrast, all but one of more than a dozen North American high-speed rail projects remained on paper (GAO 1993). In 1976 Amtrak's upgrade of the New York–Washington DC *Metroliner*, capable of up to 200 km/h, cut the travel time between the two cities by an hour, but the Boston–Washington D.C. *Acela*, the first true high-speed train with the peak speed of 257 km/h and the average of 165 km/h in its fastest section, began to operate only in December 2000.

But the Northeast corridor is a singularity: while the country's population expanded by nearly 90% between 1950 and 2000, the total railway passenger-kilometers declined by more than 60%. And although Canada was the world's leading producer of hydroelectricity and Montreal's Bombardier Inc. was building high-speed trains for export (together with French ALSTOM, they built *Acela*), the country's rail travel fell by more than 70% between 1950 and 2000. North America's low population density and highly competitive road and air links were at least as important a reason for this decline as was its infatuation with cars (Thompson 1994). In contrast, railway travel in Japan more than tripled and in France more than doubled during those 50 years. Rapid trains transformed Japan's long-distance travel, but it must be noted that their success is a matter not only of admirable technical advances but also of unusually high usage intensity.

Daily passenger density per kilometer of rail route is nearly six times higher in Japan than it is in France, and in the region served by *Tōkaidō shinkansen* it is about five times Japan's national mean, and not too far below the density experienced by Tōkyō's subways (Smith 2001). In Europe the impact of high-speed railways was by far the greatest in France. High infrastructural cost (commonly on the order of $20–30 million/km) is the key explanation for the slow progress. New trains also demonstrate the limits of wheeled transportation. Indisputable advantage of energy efficiency—per passenger-kilometer, fast trains use 20–25% of the energy needed by airplanes, and only about half as much as cars—began to erode with high speeds (Thompson 1986). Higher speeds yield diminishing returns in time saved per unit of distance, centrifugal forces that people can comfortably tolerate limit the radius of curves, permissible height discrepancies between the levels of the rails decline, and energy consumption rises exponentially (figure 5.7).

These problems have only partial technical solutions. Time savings can be maximized by traveling at maximum speeds over longer distances without frequent stops—but this may greatly limit the overall usage. Tilting trains, whose development was pioneered in Italy beginning in the late 1960s, allow for higher speeds in sharper curves, and massive concrete beds can provide desir-

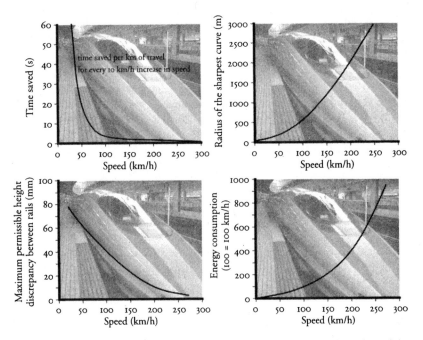

FIGURE 5.7. Relationships between train speed and time saved (top left), radius of the sharpest curve (top right), maximum height discrepancy between rails (bottom left), and relative energy consumption (bottom right). Based on data from Thompson (1986).

able rail-level tolerances—but both cost more. And while aerodynamic design can reduce high-speed drag, the problems of noise and vibration are much more intractable: noise energy becomes much more difficult to control at more than 300 km/h as it goes up in proportion to the 6th power of the speed. And in Japan, where residential and commercial areas amount to 86% of the 513 km between Tōkyō and Ōsaka, the noise must be limited below 70–75 dB, and hence the *shinkansen* trains must slow down far below their capability. But environmental benefits of high-speed trains are clear: *shinkansen* generates less than 20% of the carbon dioxide per passenger-kilometer compared with cars (Okada 1994).

Commercial Aviation

Flying during the prejet era was a rare, expensive, and trying experience. The best planes were well appointed—in 1939 Boeing's 314 trans-Pacific Clipper had a stateroom, dressing rooms, and a dining room, and its seats could convert into bunks (Bauer 2000)—but there was no escape from inadequately pressurized cabins, propeller noise, vibration induced by powerful reciprocating engines, and frequent turbulence encountered at cruising altitudes that put the aircraft in the midst of tropospheric flows, not to mention the tedium of long hours in the air. The first airplane to make commercial aviation profitable— the famous DC-3 by Douglas, originally a sleeper with 14 berths for transcontinental flights of American Airlines—had a maximum cruising speed of 274 km/h, just above the landing speed of modern jetliners (Davies, Thompson, and Veronica 1995).

A few more comparisons highlight the advances achieved by the end of the 20th century. Maximum cruising speeds on long-distance flights tripled: in 1938 Boeing's 314 Clipper could reach 320 km/h; 20 years later the Boeing 707 could go 920 km/h. Before WWII New York to Los Angeles flight took, with the three necessary stops, 15.5 h; two decades later it lasted just 6 h. During the propeller age the flying time from London to Tōkyō was 85 h; the Comet 1 cut it to 36 h, and nonstop flights of the 1990s made it in 11 h. Passenger capacities increased from the maximum of 74 people in the pre-WII Boeing 314 Clipper to 120–160 for short-hauled flights with such planes as the Boeing 737 or Airbus 320, and to 300–500 in various versions of the Boeing 747. And, of course, jetliners cruising near the upper edge of the troposphere avoid all but a small fraction of the atmospheric turbulence.

Gas turbines were just one key component behind the success of the late 20th-century commercial flying. New materials—aluminum alloys, titanium, plastics, and composite materials—were indispensable in order to remove the previous constraints on what kind of engines, fuselages, and wings were structurally possible. Advances in microelectronics brought unprecedented levels of automation both to in-flight monitoring and control and to ground operations (from reservations and ticketing to baggage tagging and flight and crew scheduling). But arguably the most important technical innovation that transformed commercial aviation was the rapid development of radar: without it there could be no accurate aircraft traffic control and no all-weather flying.

Standard accounts of the history of radar (abbreviated from radio detection and ranging, the name chosen by the U.S. Navy) begin with the British concern about the country's vulnerability to German bomber attack and the Air Ministry's call for effective defensive measures. A memorandum by Robert Watson-Watt (1892–1973) of the Radio Research Station at Slough refuted the possibility of incapacitating a pilot of the approaching aircraft by using powerful radio waves but held out, based on calculations done by Arnold F. Wilkins, the possibility of using the reflected waves for long-distance aircraft detection (Watson-Watt 1957; Rowe 1948). But detection of vessels with continuous-wave shipborne broadcasts had already been demonstrated by Christian Hülsmeyer in 1904, and by the time the British scientists began to investigate the technique, its rudimentary demonstrations had taken place in Germany, the USSR, Italy, and France. In December 1934 Albert H. Taylor and Leo C. Young of the U.S. Naval Research Laboratory used pulsed signals to detect a small airplane flying above the Potomac (Buderi 1996; Brown 1999; Seitz and Einspruch 1998).

The first British demonstration was on February 26, 1935, when continuous waves from the BBC's 10 kW Daventry transmitter were bounced off a Royal Air Force (RAF) bomber and received from a distance of more than 10 km. What set the subsequent British developments apart is that they proceeded without delay to improve the technique (by shortening the wavelength to avoid interference with commercial radio signals and designing better metal trans- mitters and wooden receivers) to such an extent that at the outset of WWII the country had a chain of 19 radar stations along its southern and eastern coasts from Portsmouth to the Orkneys. They also succeeded in shrinking the massive ground unit into the first airborne radar and, late in 1939, developing the first IFF (identification friend or foe) transponder, without which it would be impossible to control an aerial battlefield. Radar's first remarkably successful use came during the Battle of Britain, and most fortuitously, in 1940 two Birmingham University physicists, Harry A. Boot and John T. Randall, built a cavity magnetron that made it possible to deploy high-power microwaves, starting with a 9-cm device in 1941.

If modern air warfare is unimaginable without radar, the case is even stronger for commercial aviation: how else could we coordinate and control some 17 million take-offs that were made every year during the late 1990s, and keep track of more than 16,000 airplanes that spent nearly 100,000 h airborne every day (figure 5.8)? Modern air traffic control began in the United States in 1936 when the Bureau of Air Commerce took over the first three centers set up a year earlier and began a steady countrywide expansion (Gilbert 1973). After WWII controls changed radically, with constant and multilayered radar detection—operating near the bottom of the ultrahigh -frequency range, be- tween 1 m and 10 cm (300 MHz to 3 GHz)—and they were further improved during the 1960s with the introduction of computers. Incredibly, many of these early machines remained in service for more than 25 years and became puny relics—by 1990 a 256 kB computer could not even run a popular flight sim- ulator game—as they served alongside an airplane tracking system that used flight-progress paper strips, a manual technique that originated in the 1950s (Stix 1994).

Primary radars receive echoes from all aircraft flying within the control area, while secondary radars interrogate aircraft transponders in order to identify a particular flight, its altitude, and call sign. Increasingly more sophisticated soft- ware came into use to warn about possible conflicting flight paths, insufficient altitude, or intrusion into a restricted air space; elaborate queuing and sched- uling programs sequence the flights with minimum delays in the regions of high air traffic frequency and hand them rapidly over to a neighboring flight control center. Improvements in radar join more reliable jet engines as one of

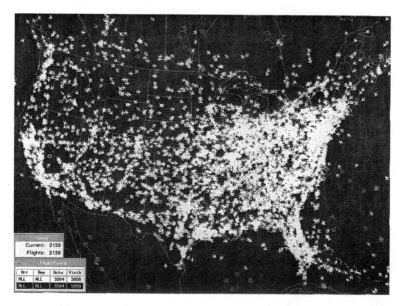

Current: 2159
Flights: 2159

FIGURE 5.8. This image of the master screen of the U.S. Air Traffic Control System Command Center shows more than 5,000 active flights above the United States and in the nearby airspace. The Northeast, Midwest, Florida, Texas, and California have the highest density of flights. Available from the U.S. Federal Aviation Administration.

the key reasons behind the extraordinary safety of modern aviation. As noted in chapter 2, worldwide accidents per million departures declined by more than 96% between 1960 and 2000, and analysis shows that human error was the primary factor in 67% of all cases (Boeing 2003b). Airplane problems caused only 12% of all accidents, and the latest generation of jets has a safety record about 18 times better than the first one.

Flying with certified air carriers remains the safest mode of transportation in terms of the risk of fatality per person per hour of exposure: during the late 1990s the risk was about 10^{-7}, an order of magnitude lower than the risk of dying of disease and about 20 times safer than driving a car. While the risk of driving depends clearly on the distance traveled, the risk of flying is primarily affected by the number of takeoffs (including climbs to cruising altitude) and landings (including descent), the two operations that put the greatest demand on engines and stress on wings and fuselage, but U.S. statistics show that flying is the safest mode of transportation for any distance for which using a scheduled airline is an option (Sivak and Flannagan 2003). And when accidents happen, flight recorders (two black boxes for cockpit voice and flight data), first introduced during the late 1950s, make it much easier to find their cause.

Size and organization of airports had to change in order to cope with the growing traffic (Horonjeff and McKelvey 1983). Many major airports rank among the largest civil engineering projects of the post-WWII era. Notable jet-age expansions took place at the world's two busiest airports, Chicago's O'Hare and Atlanta's Hartsfield, the largest regional hubs in the world's largest commercial aviation market. During the late 1990s each handled annually more than 70 million passengers. On its busiest day ever, after Thanksgiving in 1998, O'Hare handled 252,000 passengers as nearly 3,000 aircraft took off and landed. Major expansions done mostly in order to take care of growing intercontinental traffic also occurred at Los Angeles International Airport and London's Heathrow, the world's third and fourth busiest airports.

New large airports completed during the last quarter of the 20th century included three international hubs in East Asia (Endres 1996). Tōkyō's Narita opened after six years of construction, beset by often violent protests by local farmers, in 1978. Kansai International Airport on an artificial island off Ōsaka opened in September 1994 (18 months behind schedule and 50% over budget) as Japan's only round-the-clock airport. And Hong Kong's Chek Lap Kok was completed in 1998 at the site of a small island off Lantau that was leveled and expanded to house two runways and the world's largest passenger and cargo terminals; the cost of more than $20 billion made it the world's most expensive airport (Thomson and 1998; Airport Technology 2004).

Aprons, approaches, and runways of modern airports have to be built on excellent foundations in order to avoid any shifting or waterlogging of the ground. Reinforced concrete used for these surfaces is up to 1.5 m thick; it must be able to support planes whose mass ranges mostly between 150 t (Boeing 737) and almost 400 t (fully loaded Boeing 747), and on the runways it has to take the impact of planes landing at very short intervals. Large airports also need multiple runways, and in order to accommodate the largest widebodied jets, their length must be at least 3,000 m. Actual lengths are often considerably greater; for example, Los Angeles airport has two parallel runways of 3,630 m, and Narita's principal runway measures 4,000 m.

Organization and management of airline industry had to undergo many adjustments as the total number of people who take flying for granted grew rapidly from thousands to hundreds of millions in less than two generations. U.S. airlines were in the forefront of this expansion ever since the beginnings of the industry during the 1920s, when flying was not just an uncommon experience but an outright adventure (Solberg 1979; Heppenheimer 1995). They carried three million people in 1940, more than 50 million in 1955, and 665 million (i.e., roughly 2.4 flights a year for every inhabitant) in the year 2000. Another indicator of U.S. dominance is the fact that by the century's end the country had 14 of the world's 20 busiest airports, or that Dallas–Forth Worth (America's fourth busiest) handles more traffic than does Frankfurt or Roissy-Charles de Gaulle, continental Europe's two busiest airports.

Increased traffic would have been also impossible without the extension and modification of international rules and institutional commitments (ranging from strict engine licensing to cooperative aircraft control) in order to achieve high levels of reliability and safety. And booking of hundreds of millions of flights a year, many including multiple connections, would be a logistic challenge without computerized reservation systems. By the end of the 1990s there were four such global systems—Amadeus, Galileo, Sabre, and Worldspan—and all of them were rushing to protect their markets by providing services to new Internet-booking sites. Computerized tagging of luggage cut the number of lost or misrouted checked-in items. And without the competition among engine and aircraft makers and among airlines, there would have been much less need to come up with technical solutions that reduced failures, accidents, and costs and lowered environmental impacts of flying.

This competition resulted in the demise of some pioneering companies—most notably of PanAm, the bold pioneer of intercontinental flight and the jumbo jet, in 1991—and in changing balance between the two remaining major aircraft producers. Until the 1970s large jetliner industry was dominated by three U.S. companies that were established during the early years of aircraft production (Pattillo 1998). Allan and Malcolm Lougheed opened their San Francisco seaplane factory already in 1912, and Lockheed Company (spelled the way Allan pronounced his name) began in 1926. William Boeing (1881–1956) set up his Seattle company in 1916, and Donald Douglas (1892–1981) began his four years later in California (figure 5.9). Lockheed's last jetliner (between 1968 and 1984) was Tristar; afterward, the company (since 1995 Lockheed Martin) concentrated only on military and aerospace designs. McDonnell

FIGURE 5.9. William Boeing (left) and Donald Douglas (right), two leading pioneers of innovative aircraft design and construction. From Aiolos Production.

Douglas—maker of the DC-3, the most durable propeller aircraft in history—merged with Boeing in 1997.

And during the 1990s Boeing itself began to lose its global market share to Airbus. This European consortium was set up with French and German participation in 1970, and Spanish and British aircraft makers joined later. Its first plane, the wide-bodied twinjet A300 designed for 226 people, flew in 1974. Afterward the company introduced a range of planes designed to compete with every one of Boeing's offerings. In the year 2000 Airbus sold for the first time more planes than Boeing (300 vs. 285), and in December 2000 it announced that it will proceed with building a double-decker super-jumbo A380 to carry 555 passengers between large international hubs (Airbus 2004).

Competition among airlines, particularly after their deregulation (in the United States starting in 1978, in the European Union since 1997), increased the number of flights and destinations and lowered the average cost of travel: by the year 2000 it was down by more than two thirds in inflation-adjusted terms compared to the late 1970s. As revenues per seat kept declining, and as the industry remained vulnerable to the effects of economic cycles and to fluctuations in fuel prices, the world's carriers found it impossible to remain profitable. As a group they posted annual net operating loss only four times during the third quarter of the 20th century, but between 1975 and 1999 they had, despite direct and indirect subsidies by many governments, 11 loss years. Many airlines tried to deal with these losses by forming business alliances: the three leading groupings formed around United Airlines (Star Alliance), American Airlines (OneWorld), and Air France (SkyTeam). Nevertheless, some major companies continued to lose money even during the strong recovery of the late 1990s, when they were flying record numbers of people.

Moving Freight

Many technical advances that made it possible to move unprecedented numbers of people faster and cheaper across increasing distances had an analogical effect on the movement of goods. Trucking and railroads benefited from better materials and more efficient engines, and jetliners made air transport into an important means of long-distance delivery of more valuable items. And all of forms of freight movement gained from computerization that improved the speed of cargo handling, helped to optimize scheduling and routing, and kept track of inventories and shipments en route. Before WWII railroads dominated long-distance transport of goods not only in Europe but also in North America. The earliest comparative U.S. statistics are available for 1939 when (leaving oil pipelines aside) railways accounted for slightly more than 70% of total freight movements measured by tonne-kilometers; waterborne transport was second with almost 20%, and trucking came third with 10% (USBC 1975).

These shares began to shift immediately after WWII, and by the early 1970s the railways' share fell just below 50%. And there it stayed for the remainder of the century: in 1999 nearly 49% of all U.S. freight tonne-kilometers were on rails, 35% on roads, and a mere 0.5% went by domestic airlines (USCB 2004). Railroads retained their freight traffic share because they aggressively participated in the single most important advance in the 20th-century transportation, in the adoption of standard reusable intermodal containers. These containers can be carried by various means from the place of a product's origins all the way to a retail store, a storage depot, or a construction site. History of technical advances is replete with simple eurekas that had profound economic effects, but it is hard to think about a simpler idea with a greater global impact.

Intermodal containers are just big boxes, rectangular steel prisms with reinforced edges and corners. Their most common dimensions are 20 or 30 ft long, 8 ft wide, and 8.5–9.5 ft high. Only the width remains fixed (to fit on trucks); depending on the construction and size, the container weight ranges between 1.8 and 4.2 t, and they carry between 15 and 30 t of payload (figure 5.10). By the late 1990s they stood next to thousands of factories in cities and towns of China's coastal provinces, waiting to be filled with cellular phones, ceramics, and corduroy pants. They were being loaded on ships in the world's leading export harbors, in Hong Kong, Singapore, and Ōsaka. They were traversing every sea and ocean, following tight crossing schedules and being sometimes so overloaded that in heavy seas waves broke over their decks. They were being unloaded and stacked in the largest receiver ports, in Los Angeles, Rotterdam, and New Jersey, waiting for endless arrivals of trucks or railway cars to take them to their final destinations.

FIGURE 5.10. A Maersk Sealand container being unloaded by a large gantry crane that can lift one 45 t unit or two 30 t units. The image is available from the A.P. Moller-Maersk Group.

Small containers of various sizes had already been used irregularly by some traditional break bulk shippers at the beginning of the 20th century, but standardized commercial containerization began only during WWII. Thoburn C. Brown, who used aluminum boxes for shipping during the 1930s, designed sturdier small (8 ft) containers for the U.S. Army. Containerization on industrial scale began only during the late 1950s with two innovators on America's opposite coasts. Malcolm Purcell McLean (1914–2001), a North Carolina trucker, must be credited with the most radical transformation of global freight delivery. He had to wait nearly two decades between his eureka moment and his first steps toward commercializing an entirely new mode of cargo shipments.

As he later recalled in an interview, the idea came naturally one day in 1937 as a result of frustration with the traditional freight-handling practices:

> I had to wait most of the day to deliver the bales, sitting there in my truck, watching stevedores load other cargo. It struck me that I was looking at a lot of wasted time and money . . . The thought occurred to me, as I waited around that day, that it would be easier to lift my trailer up and, without any of its contents being touched, put it on the ship. (quoted in *The Economist* 1991, p. 91)

Only in 1955 he was ready to act: he sold his share in the family's trucking business, and because designing and building specialized vessels would have been too expensive, he bought seven ships of the Pan-Atlantic Steamship Corporation that operated small tankers between the U.S. Northeast and the Gulf of Mexico (Kendall and Buckley 2001). The next step was a new truck trailer that was reinforced vertically for stacking and horizontally for lifting and crane loading. Then a steel skeleton deck built above the main tanker deck was equipped with sockets to accept stubby container feet for fastening. On April 26, 1956, the first adapted WWII-era T-2 tanker, *Ideal X*, set out from Port Newark, New Jersey, to Houston carrying 58 large (35-ft) containers (altogether about 1,000 t) on its strengthened deck. With the concept successfully proven, McLean converted other ships, and on October 4, 1957, *Gateway City*, a C-2 freighter fitted with cellular compartments and able to transport of up to 226 large containers stacked within a steel framework erected in the hold, became the first true container ship to operate between New York and Texas. With this came also the necessary improvements to secure and to handle the cargo. These included twist-locks to fasten the containers into huge blocks, and spreader machines that could lift the containers by using hooks inserted into corner holes. In 1960 McLean renamed the company Sea-Land.

In 1956, just as McLean began his East Coast operations, the Matson Navigation Company, which had served Hawaii from its California ports since 1882, began a study aimed at optimizing its shipping, and it opted for containerization (Matson Lines 2004). In August 1958, the *Hawaiian Merchant*, a converted freighter, shipped 20 containers on its deck from Los Angeles, and in April 1960 the *Hawaiian Citizen* became the company's first all-container vessel carrying 436 24-ft units.

In 1962 container operations began at the port of Oakland and at the Port Elizabeth Marine Terminal in Newark. Shipments to Europe started in April 1966 when the SS *Fairland* carried 226 containers to Rotterdam. Then the containerization received a major boost because of the Vietnam War: by 1968 the U.S. Department of Defense used more than 100,000 containers to speed up the delivery of military supplies. In that year McLean also launched the first fully containerized service to Japan. A year later, when he sold Sea-Land to R.J. Reynolds, the company had 27,000 containers. During the 1970s schedules and routes were optimized, and by 1980 there were for the first time more fully cellular ships than semicontainerized vessels (Pearson and Fossey 1983). In 1986 Sea-Land was sold to CSX, and in 1999 it was bought by the Danish Maersk to form Maersk Sealand, the world's largest container shipper (Maersk Sealand 2004).

By the late 1960s there was no doubt about the eventual outcome: it was only a matter of time before all standard break-bulk shipments were put into cargo containers, and railroad companies had to face yet another change in their freight operations. In 1952 the Canadian Pacific Railways was the first company in North America to use flat cars for intermodal, piggyback, shipments of truck trailers, the rectangular boxes with permanently attached wheels. Before the end of the 1960s this became a common practice with increasingly longer flatcars (up to 25 m). But just a decade later the railroad companies, which invested heavily into TOFC (trailer on flat car) shipping, had to start thinking about COFC (container on flat car). U.S. statistics show the rapid switch between the two modes: in 1985 nearly 80% of all intermodal moves on railways involved trailers; by the year 2000 75% of all carried units were containers (IANA 2004).

Southern Pacific designed the first double-stack car in 1977, APL Stacktrain pioneered the new practice with large 48-ft containers in 1986, and the doubled configuration came to dominate modern railroad freight transport. Stacktrains have to minimize longitudinal and lateral movements through special connections and reduce vertical motion by setting wheel assemblies closer than in other trains. As you watch these long (at least 50–60 cars) trains roll by you notice a variety of container sizes. Initially Sealand used 35-ft (10.5-m) containers, Matson preferred a smaller (24 ft, 7.2 m) size, and subsequently different international shippers introduced sizes ranging from 20 to 48 ft (6–14.5 m). But there are also smaller containers (10 ft, primarily used in Europe), and in 1989 Stacktrain introduced 53-ft units. During the 1990s marine transport was dominated by two common ISO sizes, 20 and 40 ft, which accounted, respectively, for nearly 60% and 40% of all shipborne units.

In 1969, faced with this lack of standardization when compiling international vessel statistics, the British journalist Richard F. Gibney chose the TEU (twenty-foot equivalent unit) as the common denominator, and the acronym became a standard term in the industry. The first container ships of the late 1950s carried fewer than 300 TEU, a decade later up to 1,300 TEU, and during the 1970s as many as 3,000 TEU. The largest ships able to pass through the Panama Canal carried 4,500 TEU—and in 1996 *Regina Maersk* was the first ship with 6,000 TEU. By the late 1990s Maersk Sealand had S-class ships that carried 6,600 TEU. All other major shipping lines (Hanjin, MSC, P&ONL) had vessels approaching or exceeding the 6,000 TEU mark that can travel at up to about 45 km/h. These ships, double-hulled and double-bottomed, have typically eight layers of containers stacked below the deck line (they have actually no closed deck) and up to seven above it (see the top image of this chapter's frontispiece).

By the late 1990s nearly 60% of the total value of international trade moved in containers. Leaving aside raw materials and commodities that are obviously shipped better in bulk—items that can be pumped on board (crude oil, refined products, many liquid chemicals) or dumped into a hold (metallic ores, coal, grains)—the dominance of containerized transport was nearly complete. And containers carry not only more manufactured goods but also more perishable food in refrigerated units. Worldwide there were about 6.7 million TEU in use by the year 2000, and their total throughput amounted to about 200 million units. This means that, on the average, every unit was handled nearly 30 times a year. This surprisingly large number includes the repositioning of empty containers and trans-shipments using smaller feeder vessels (Hong Kong harbor teems with them). Empty containers handled at ports reached 41 million TEU by 1999, and because of the large trade imbalance between North America and East Asia, the problem is particularly acute in Hong Kong and Malaysia, where about 20% of the throughput in the year 2000 were empties (ESCAP 2000).

On the high seas these containers were carried by more than 7,000 vessels, but the traffic was dominated by roughly 3,000 fully cellular ships that plied regularly the busiest fixed routes between East Asia and North America, with two-way shipments of almost 13 million TEU in 2000, and Asia and Europe with almost 7 million TEU (ESCAP 2000). Hong Kong's huge container port retained its long-held global primacy as it handled slightly more than 18 million TEU, just ahead of Singapore. Busan in South Korea and Taiwan's Kaohsiung were the next two largest ports of origin, while Rotterdam, Los Angeles, Long Beach, and Hamburg were the busiest receiver ports. With larger and faster ships, the speed of offloading and loading became the key bottleneck.

Early gantry cranes could not handle more than 20 containers per hour, and by the 1980s the rate was up to 30 (Gubbins 1986). Two cranes could thus unload a 3,000-TEU ship in two days. By the late 1990s a single yard crane spreader could lift two 20-ft containers at one time (see figure 5.10), and cranes offloading and loading a ship could clear 75–100 TEUs per hour. Designs were under way to raise this productivity to 200 moves so that even the largest container vessels could be turned around in a single day. Every container is identified by the Bureau des Containers code, a combination of four letters (for the operator) and seven digits (inscribed on both outer and inner walls) that is used for computerized routing and tracking. Because of their relatively high speed, container ships are at a greater risk of grounding and collision, and they are also vulnerable to rolling in heavy seas that can cause loss of containers carried on deck. Manual unfastening and fastening of twist-locks of deck-borne containers is the most dangerous part of the port-handling operation. Steps have to be also taken to prevent onboard fire.

Benefits of containerization are obvious. The technique created the first truly global, unbroken chain of freight delivery. Cargoes in sealed containers are protected against easy pilfering and shipping damage, and hence they are eligible for reduced insurance rates. Mechanized handling reduced the time needed to load and unload the containers close to the physical minimum dictated by the power of the dedicated machines and safety of operations. While traditional break-bulk loading or unloading of a 10,000-t ship would take 7–10 days, the same mass of containerized cargo can be handled in a day. When comparing the entire shipping sequence from producer to buyer, the delivery time of many cargoes had been cut by more than 95%.

There were other important innovations that made mass-scale long-distance trade faster and cheaper. Crude oil tankers (see chapter 2) were joined by liquefied natural gas (LNG) vessels that carry methane at −162°C inside five or four insulated spherical containers; the cargo is regasified at the destination. They made it possible to sell this commodity, expensively but profitably, overseas. They were used for the first time in 1958 to ship Algerian gas to the United Kingdom (*Methane Pioneer*) and France and in 1960 (*Bridgestone Maru*) to take Indonesian gas to Japan (Corkhill 1975). By the late 1990s more than 100 LNG vessels, most with capacities in excess of 100,000 m3, carried about a quarter of global natural gas exports, with shipments from Indonesia, Algeria, Brunei, and Malaysia to Japan, South Korea, and the United States dominating the trade.

Roll-on/roll-off (RO/RO) ships to transport passenger cars and trucks were designed for easy ferry operations and in order to ship millions of vehicles across the oceans, above all from Japan to North America and Europe. Before the port of Dover introduced its first two drive-on berths in 1953, it handled only 10,000 cars loaded laboriously by cranes; by the late 1990s the total number of vehicles driving on RO/RO ferries was approaching five million. By that time the worldwide total of RO/RO ships was close to 5,000, with Europe having their largest concentration. None of the specialized bulk carriers transporting coal, ores, other minerals, fertilizers, and chemicals grew as large as oil tankers, but by the 1990s typical capacities of these vessels were an order of magnitude larger than those of their predecessors around 1900.

And as airplanes increased their payloads they began carrying more than just mail, their original cargo assignment dating back to the late 1910s and the early 1920s. Air transport was developed for the first time on a mass scale during WWII when more than 9,500 C-47 Skytrains, a version of the DC-3, were produced for the Allied forces. Worldwide air cargo services amounted to just 200 million t-km in 1950, but then they grew faster than passenger traffic: they were 10 times higher by 1960 and ended the century with about 108 billion t-km, of which 85% were logged on international routes (ICAO 2001). Intensifying integration of global economy in general, and East Asia's economic rise in particular, have been the principal reasons for the more than 500-fold rise of freight tonne-kilometers between 1950 and 1999.

Every passenger jet also carries plenty of goods in its hold as billions of dollars of electronic goods, machine parts, flowers, clothes, or toys share the ride with people. Wide-bodied airplanes on intercontinental routes carry 10–20 t of palletted or containerized cargo; in the United States slightly more than 20% of all air cargo is moved on passenger planes, earning the airlines 10–15% of total revenues. And a frequent flyer could not miss an increasing number of dedicated cargo airplanes. Most large jetliners have been available in cargo versions that carry 50–100 t and that operate on regular daily schedules (e.g., the fleets of FedEx or UPS planes) or are chartered as needed.

During the late 1990s cargo Boeing 747s accounted for half of the world's international air freight: the plane's latest version, the 747-400, had cargo capacity of 105 t loaded on pallets up to 6 m long. But they were not the largest cargo carriers: that primacy belonged to the originally Soviet-designed (in service since 1986) and then Ukrainian-produced Antonov AN-124 (*Ruslan*), whose capacity far surpassed that of the previous record holder, the U.S. military transport C-5 Galaxy that can carry almost 120 t. The AN-124 can load up to 150 t, and their worldwide heavy-lift services provided much needed foreign earnings for the Ukraine during the 1990s (figure 5.11).

Computing Revolutions

Electronic computing, a new way of information handling—the term understood here in the broadest sense of ordering, processing, and transferring any data, text, or images—was invented during the 1940s. During the first two decades after its commercialization these new powers were used mostly for expanding the range of true computing, with numerical tasks ranging from complex scientific and engineering calculations and statistical evaluations to basic business inventory and payroll operations. The invention of integrated circuits and fabrication of increasingly more powerful microprocessors made it

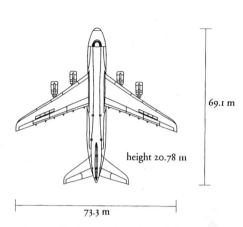

69.1 m

height 20.78 m

73.3 m

FIGURE 5.11. A nose view (left; from author's collection) and a plan of the Antonov AN-124 (right; from Aerospace.org) convey the enormous size of the world's largest commercial cargo airplane.

possible to write detailed instructions in order to computerize almost any conceivable scientific, industrial, or managerial task—and many creative and leisure processes as well. By the century's end there were programs with 10^7 lines of code; microprocessors inside massively parallel supercomputers could do virtual tests of thermonuclear weapons, inside fabrication units they could run complex machining processes (see chapter 4), and inside personal microcomputers they could be used to draw psychedelic images or compose 12-tone music.

There was no such thing as the first computer, when the term is used in the modern sense of a fully electronic machine capable of rapid binary-based operations that use stored instructions (Rojas and Hashagen 2000). Instead, between the late 1930s and the mid-1940s, and in parallel with the introduction of the most advanced electromechanical devices, increasing electronization and greater design complexity led to the first electronically controlled externally programmed computing machines. Their history is a classic case of independent multiple inventions and incremental improvements contributed by individuals and corporate research establishments in several countries. British contributions were particularly important: until the early 1950s British scientists and engineers were ahead in several important respects of what soon became the dominant U.S. computer establishment.

Consequently, there were many firsts and no Edisonian figure to pull all the known strands together and to invent whatever else was needed in order to launch a new fully operational and commercially viable system (Moreau

1984; Campbell-Kelly and Aspray 2004). What is most remarkable about the short history of electronic computing is its rapid sequence of transformations that magnified the performance of dominant designs to the extent that, even remotely, has no match in any other human endeavor. In 1951 UNIVAC, America's first commercial mainframe, cost $930,000, could execute about 60,000 instructions per second, and needed 160 kW of electricity; in 2000 Intel's Pentium III processor, used in personal computers and servers, cost $990 (in large lots), could handle one billion instructions per second, and in the maximum performance mode drew 20.5 W (figure 5.12).

Computing revolutions of the second half of the 20th century thus raised the calculating speed (even when leaving supercomputers aside) by four orders of magnitude, while the relative cost of computing (in constant monies) and its relative energy requirements both fell by eight orders of magnitude. If a passenger car of the early 1950s would have undergone similar transformations, then the late 1990s models would cruise at speeds about 40 times higher than the velocity needed to escape Earth's gravity, one liter of gasoline would be enough to go 20,000 times around the equator, and even the smallest parking fine would be orders of magnitude larger than the car's utterly negligible cost.

The First Electronic Computers

Theoretical foundations came from two brilliant mathematicians, Alan Turing (1912–1954) at Cambridge and Claude Shannon (1916–2001). Shannon was the

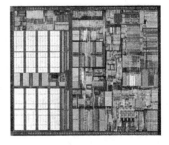

FIGURE 5.12. The room-size UNIVAC 1, the first U.S. commercial computer, offered by *Remington Rand* in 1951 (left; from the National Energy Research Scientific Computing Center), weighed more than 13 t, but its computing power was only 0.006% of the Pentium III microprocessor (with 9.5 million transistors) released by Intel in 1999 (right; from Intel), designed to enhance Internet browsing and download high-quality video.

first mathematician to use, in his MIT master's thesis in 1937, Boolean algebra for a working model of digital circuits, and a decade later he presented the fundamental mathematical theory of communication (Shannon 1948). Turing (1936) introduced the concept of a universal computing machine that could be programmed to do any calculation a human is capable of as long as it receives clear instructions. The most advanced mechanical precursor of electronic computers (tracing its pedigree to Babbage and Scheutzes: see chapter 5 of *CTTC*) was Vannevar Bush's 1932 differential analyzer, an analog mechanical device that did calculus by rotating gears and shafts.

The first electromechanical machines, whose relays represented digits in the binary system with their on and off positions, were built by Georg Stibitz (1904–1995) at Bell Laboratories in 1936 and Konrad Zuse (1910–1995) in Germany between 1936 and 1941, while Howard Aiken's (1900–1973) massive Harvard Mark I (about 5 t, 760,000 parts but no vacuum tubs) used decimal numbers (Cohen 1999). The first small electronic computer that combined digital arithmetic with vacuum tubes was conceived by John Atanasoff (1903–1995) of Iowa State College, at the end of a long random drive that took him across the state border to Illinois late in 1937 (Burks and Burks 1988).

Atanasoff's great pioneering departures were to design a parallel machine (capable of up to 30 simultaneous operations) that was fully electronic in its calculation and data storage, used dynamically refreshed memory capacitors to store binary numbers, and separated memory from processing (Gustafson 2000). Electronic switching and the use of capacitors (now a part of microprocessors) remain among the critical ingredients of every modern computer, as does the separation of memory from processing. The first prototype was built, with the assistance of Atanasoff's graduate student, Clifford Berry (1918–1963), by October 1939, and a larger machine designed to solve simultaneous linear equations was completed by 1942 (figure 5.13). Before war commitments interrupted further development of the machine, Atanasoff showed it to, and discussed it in detail with, John Mauchly (1907–1980), who visited him in Iowa in June 1941.

Between July 1943 and November 1945, Mauchly and John Presper Eckert (1919–1995) built the Electronic Numerical Integrator and Computer (ENIAC) at the University of Pennsylvania, and this decimal device, programmed by manually interconnecting its units with tangles of wires and patented in 1947, was generally recognized as the first American electronic computer. But Mauchly's 1941 Iowa visit played a key role in the decision of Judge Earl R. Larson of the U.S. District Court in Minneapolis in October 1973 when he assigned, as a part of the lawsuit between Sperry Rand (owners of the ENIAC patent) and Honeywell, the invention priority to Atanasoff, who never patented his design (Burks 2002).

The first operational externally programmable vacuum-tube logic calculator was the British Colossus built in 1943 by Tommy Flowers (1905–1998) at the

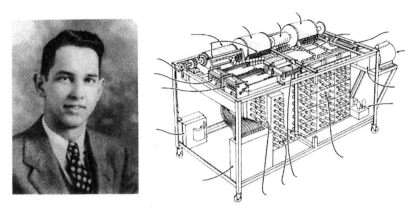

FIGURE 5.13. John Atanasoff in 1938 when he and Clifford Berry were building the first prototype of their electronic computer; major components of a larger machine, completed in 1942, are shown in the drawing. From the Iowa State University Department of Computer Science.

Post Office Research Laboratories in London. Bletchley Research Establishment eventually deployed 10 of them in order to decipher the German code generated by the Lorenz SZ42 cipher machines (Hinsley and Stripp 1993; Sale 2000). The existence of Colossus was officially kept secret until 1974, opening the way for ENIAC's priority claim. In 1945 John von Neumann (1903–1957) outlined the principles of a stored program, and its first installation, at the University of Manchester between 1948 and 1951, was based on F.C. Williams's observation of the stored patterns of electrostatic charge inside a cathode-ray tube (Lavington 2001). The first program run by the university's Small Scale Experimental Machine (SSEM) on June 21, 1948, was written by Tom Kilburn (1921–2001) to find the highest factor of x.

The SSEM served as the prototype of the world's first commercially available electronic computer, the Ferranti Mark I, delivered in February 1951, four months ahead of Eckert and Mauchly's ENIAC-based UNIVAC (Universal Automatic Computer), the first device with magnetic tape storage rather than with punched cards: its first owner was the U.S. Bureau of Census (see figure 5.12). And the British also had the first business computer: in November 1951 LEO (Lyons Electronic Office), a copy of the EDSAC (the first stored-program computer in regular service completed at Cambridge University in 1949) was delivered to J. Lyons & Company, which operated a chain of British teashops. The machine was used to calculate overnight production requirements and later also to keep payroll and inventory. In 1954 J. Lyons actually began building and selling its more advanced versions, with deliveries ending in 1966 when the business was bought by English Electric (Ferry 2003).

Between 1951 and 1958 came the first generation of commercial computers, still fairly massive constructs of limited capacity whose high capital cost greatly restricted their sales. Between 1959 and 1964 came new models equipped with inherently superior transistors, but their high cost (in 1962 the IBM 7090 sold for US$15 million) began to decline only with the introduction of the third generation of machines based on integrated circuits. This trend was carried to its logical conclusions with the emergence of microprocessors that combined all functions in a single microchip. Development of the fourth generation of computers proceeded along two paths: the first one producing smaller but more powerful mainframes, the other one leading to personal computers. Yet another fundamental shift came during the 1990s when much of the mass-produced hardware assumed first portable (laptops) and then entirely mobile (handheld) forms and data input and output devices.

A software-guided classification, focusing on the way computers are instructed to perform their operations, with time periods based on the nature of the interface between machines and users, is much simpler, falling into just three longer categories: until 1957, 1957–1977, and after 1977. During the first post-WWII decade the only way to instruct computers was in cumbersome, tediously produced numerical machine code. Finally, in 1957 IBM released FORTRAN (FORmula TRANslation) developed by a group of nine experts led by John Backus. FORTRAN was the first programming language that made it possible to instruct machines in terms akin to simple mathematical formulas that were translated by a compiler into machine code. ALGOL and business-oriented COBOL followed shortly afterward, and in 1964 came the easier-to-use BASIC (Beginners All-Purpose Symbolic Instruction Code) designed by John Kemeny (1926–1992) and Thomas Kurtz at Dartmouth University.

Development of the most popular programming language of the last three decades of the 20th century began at Bell Labs in 1971, when Dennis Ritchie began to write C, based on Ken Thompson's B (Kernighan and Ritchie 1978). Ritchie and Thompson used the language for the UNIX operating system that eventually spread to operate millions of laptops as well as some of the most complex mainframe systems, including airline reservations. Until the late 1970s the only way to interact with a computer was to learn one of the programming languages. The great divide was the introduction of personal desktop computers—above all, the Apple II in 1977 (the first machine with color graphics) and IBM's PC in 1981 (and its many clones)—which could be used by anybody able to peck at a keyboard and to master a modicum of instructions.

Soon even instructions were not necessary as anybody could just click away by using the improved versions of Engelbart's mouse (see chapter 1). One could also choose time periods based on prevailing input and output modes—punched cards or magnetic tape versus typed instructions versus mouse clicks, low-resolution printers versus high-resolution images produced by ingenious laser and inexpensive jet ink printers—or just cleave the time spent looking at monitors into the cathode ray tube (CRT) display and flat screen (liquid crystal display) eras. All of these choices convey multifaceted progress that transformed every attribute of computing. And all of these advances had one common denominator in the relentless miniaturization of parts and connectors.

Transistors and Integrated Circuits

The miniaturization trend began with the invention of transistors (devices transferring current across a resistor) in 1947 and 1948, but until the late 1950s electronic switching in all computers depended on vacuum tubes. These were either advanced versions of two pre-WWI devices, Fleming's diode and De Forest's triode (see chapter 5 of *CTTC*) or their subsequent elaborations (tetrodes, pentodes). These devices control the flow of electrons in a vacuum and can amplify the current and switch it on and off rapidly, but they were inherently bulky, failure-prone, and inefficient. When deployed in large numbers, they added up to sizable masses of hot glass: a single tube weighed mostly between 50, and 100 g and so even in a smaller computer with just 5,000 tubes they alone would have added up to close half a tonne. Their lifetime was critically dependent on the operating temperature: overheating shortened their durability, which extended anyway to just 50–100 h for some models.

ENIAC parameters illustrate these challenges (Kempf 1961; Van der Spiegel et al. 2000). The machine had 17,648 vacuum tubes of 16 different kinds, as well as 70,000 resistors, 10,000 capacitors, 6,000 manual switches, and 1,500 relays; its 30 separate units occupied about 80 m³, covered an area of 167 m² (roughly the size of two badminton courts), and, including its power supply and forced air cooling, weighed about 30 t. Although it ran at a mere 100 kHz and its random access memory (RAM) was only about 1 kB, it meant that every second there were about 1.7 billion chances of a tube failing. About 90% of all interruptions were due to tube failures, and the need for constant maintenance and tube replacement was very time consuming: the checking routine alone took about 8 h. And although the computer needed 174 kW to operate (a bit more than the power of a 1965 Fastback Mustang), air conditioning installed to take care of large heat dissipation load proved inadequate, and high temperature increased the frequency of failures.

Half a century after the machine's completion, a team at the University of Pennsylvania reconstructed ENIAC on a microchip, on a 7.4 × 5.3 mm sliver of silicon that contained 174,569 transistors (Van der Spiegel et al. 2000). An order of magnitude difference between the number of vacuum tubes and transistors was due to the fact that transistors also replaced all resistors, capacitors, and switches. Differences between ENIAC and ENIAC-on-a-Chip are staggering: the original machine was more than five million times heavier, required

78 different DC voltage levels (compared to just one 5-V input), and consumed about 40,000 times more electricity, yet its speed was at best 0.002% that of the reconstructed processor (100 kHz vs. at least 50 MHz): it needed 24 h of operations to do what the chip does in less than 3 min. This astonishing advance had its origins in the discovery of semiconductivity in germanium and silicon that are insulators when extremely pure but conductors when contaminated ("doped") with minuscule quantities of other atoms (see chapter 3).

The first rectifier using metallurgical-grade crystalline silicon for reception had already been patented (U.S. Patent 836,531) in 1906 by Greenleaf W. Pickard (1877–1956). That was the silicon point-contact diode—commonly known as cat's whisker or the crystal detector—that was used to receive radio signals before it was displaced by Forest's triode. By the 1930s silicon–tungsten whisker diodes were already being used as crystal detectors in the microwave range (Seitz and Einspruch 1998), and after he became the head of Bell Laboratories in 1936, Mervin Kelly (1894–1971), impressed by the simplicity, reliability, and low cost of copper-oxide rectifiers that were used to convert low-frequency AC to DC, initiated a research program to develop a similar semiconductor triode. This work began in earnest only after WWII, and the first success came from a collaboration between Walter Brattain (1902–1987) and John Bardeen (1908–1991), who tried to understand the reasons for failure of the experiments done by their group leader, William Shockley (1910–1989), as he tried to make what later became known as a field-effect transistor (Riordan and Hoddeson 1997).

Shockley's group attributed the failure to surface trapping of electrons, and by further experiments they found that when injecting a current to flow between two close point-contact electrodes, they could amplify power and, by December 16, 1947, both power and voltage, and do so at audio frequencies. Their bipolar point-contact transistor (figure 5.14) was demonstrated to the management on December 23, 1947, and publicly unveiled at a press conference on January 27, 1947. The discovery led to a split between the two inventors and their group leader, who tried to take credit for their invention. But eventually Brattain and Bardeen's names were the only ones on the patent for a "three-electrode circuit element utilizing semiconductive materials" (Bardeen and Brattain 1950). Shockley intensified his efforts to come up with a better, more practical solution. The path to it opened once John Shive discovered that, contrary to Bardeen's conclusion, electron flow is not confined to the surface and can travel through the body of material.

By January 23, 1948, Shockley proposed a major modification of Brattain–Bardeen design. Rather than using point contacts to inject positive charges, he used larger junctions and higher currents. Shockley's three-layer p-n-p design—known as the bipolar junction transistor (with the two outer layers doped to supply electrons and the middle layer to create "holes")—thus functions much like a triode with the n-layer analogical to a vacuum tube grid (Shockley 1964). A small current in the center (base) region controls a larger current between

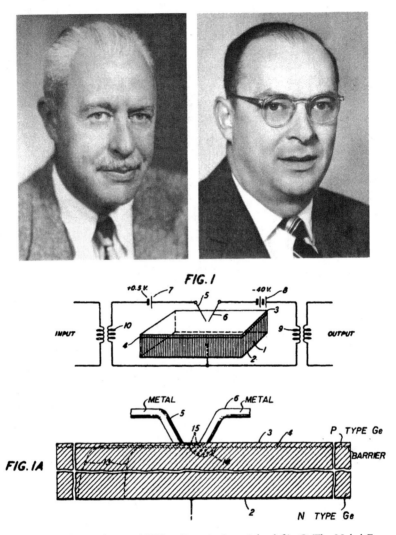

FIGURE 5.14. John Bardeen and Walter Brattain (top right, left); © The Nobel Foundation) and their point-contact transistor (bottom; U.S. Patent 2,524,035; from Bardeen and Brattain 1950).

the emitter and collector and amplifies that flow (figure 5.15). The three physicists were awarded a joint Nobel Prize in 1956, and soon afterward, with the advent of integrated circuits, the importance of their inventions became universally obvious: progressively smaller metal-oxide-silicon field-effect transistors (MOSFET) carried microelectronic circuitry to astonishing densities and amazingly low costs.

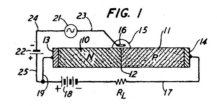

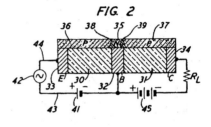

FIGURE 5.15. William Shockley (right; © The Nobel Foundation) and his field-effect transistor (left; U.S. Patent 2,569,347).

Advantages of transistors were obvious even with the earliest designs: the first prototype occupied only 1/200th of the space of an equally effective vacuum tube while its solid state assured higher reliability and lower energy use without any need for any warmup time. Bell Labs began licensing transistor production in 1951 (for a $25,000 fee), but as long as these devices were made from germanium, their applications remained limited: hearing aids were among the first transistorized devices, and the first mass-produced consumer item was a transistor radio in 1954. The first use of transistors in computers came only in 1956, and in 1959 IBM's Stretch and Sperry Rand's LARC were the first large transistorized machines. Wider use of transistors came only when improved silicon fabrication methods (see chapter 4) replaced germanium with a cheaper material.

The conversion was further speeded up by another important discovery made at Bell Labs. In 1955 Carl Frosch and Link Derick found that heating a silicon wafer to about 1,200°C in the presence of water or oxygen creates a thin SiO_2 film on its surface. Selective etching of this film can be used to make p-n junctions with doped silicon. In an all-diffused silicon transistor, impurities permeate the entire wafer while the active parts are protected by the oxide layer. But even this switch would not have made semiconductors as inexpensive as the next radical innovation that led to their miniaturization and mass production. This step was imperative in order to produce more complex circuits. But the traditional fabrication of miniaturized circuit components (resistors, capacitors, transistors) required a variety of substrates, materials, heat treatments, and protection measures, and some of these steps were incompatible.

Making the components separately can cause damage to sensitive parts during the assembly: all of them must have individual terminations and hand-soldered connections between them must be faultless or the circuit fails; moreover, in very complex computing circuits where speed matters, long connections would necessarily slow down the signals. A complex, highly miniaturized circuit would be thus extremely difficult to build. The ingenious solution, the monolithic idea, was first proposed in July 1958 by Jack S. Kilby, who came to Texas Instruments (TI) from a Milwaukee-based electronics company in May of that year. Kilby proposed to use only one material for all circuit elements and a limited number of compatible process steps in order to produce

> a novel miniaturized electronic circuit fabricated from a body of semi-conductor material containing a diffused p-n junction wherein all components of the electronic circuit are completely integrated into the body of semiconductor material. (Kilby 1964:1)

Transistors and diodes, of course, had already been made of semiconducting materials, but to make resistors and capacitors from expensive silicon wafers seemed counterproductive—but it could be done. Kilby detailed two such possibilities in his patent application but noted that "there is no limit upon the complexity or configuration of circuits which can be made in this manner" (Kilby 1964:7). Simple integrated circuits demonstrating the principle were completed early in 1959. By the time the company's lawyers were rushing to patent the invention, the only model they could depict was Kilby's simple demonstration chip with gold wires arching above the chip's surface (figure 5.16). Kilby knew that such a design was antithetical to the idea of an integrated circuit, but as he did not have a better solution ready, he only added a paragraph to the application (submitted on February 6, 1959) noting that the connections may be provided in other ways and gave an example of gold deposited on silicon oxide. An effective solution was proposed, unknown to Kilby, just before he filed his patent application.

In late January 1959, in yet another case of parallel invention, Robert Noyce (1927–1990), director of research at Fairchild Semiconductors (FS), wrote in his lab notebook (cited in Reid 2001:13) that

> it would be desirable to make multiple devices on a single piece of silicon, in order to be able to make interconnections between devices as part of the manufacturing process, and thus reduce size, weight, etc. as well as cost per active element.

FIGURE 5.16. Inventors of integrated circuit—Jack Kilby (left; reproduced courtesy of Texas Instruments) and Robert Noyce (right; reproduced courtesy of Intel)—and key figures from their patents (U.S. Patent 3,138,743, from Kilby 1964 and U.S. Patent 2,981,877; Noyce 1961.). Kilby's figure shows the impractical flying wire connections; Noyce's cross section clearly outlines neighboring n-p-n junctions on a single silicon wafer.

The key idea was identical to Kilby's proposal, but Noyce's design of a planar transistor also solved the problem of miniaturized connections by taking advantage of the SiO_2 layer that Jean Horni (1924–1997) at FS proposed in 1958 to place on top of the n-p-n sandwich in order to protect it from contamination.

Noyce's patent application of July 30, 1959, entitled "Semiconductor device-and-lead structure," depicted a design that looked unmistakably like an integrated circuit (figure 5.16) and specified

> dished junctions extending to the surface of a body of extrinsic semiconductor, an insulating surface layer consisting essentially of oxide of the same semiconductor extending across the junctions, and leads in the form of vacuum-deposited or otherwise formed metal strips extending over and adherent to the insulating oxide layer for making electrical connections to and between various regions . . . (Noyce 1961:1)

While Noyce's patent (U.S. Patent 2,981,877) was granted in April 1961, Kilby's application (U.S. Patent 3,138,743) was approved only in July 1964. The ensuing interference proceeding and lengthy litigation and appeals were settled only in 1971 when the Supreme Court granted Noyce, that is, FS, priority in the matter. This made no practical difference: already by the summer of 1966 the two companies granted each other the production licenses and agreed that outside fabricators will have to arrange separate licenses with both of them. As for the inventive priority, there is no doubt that Kilby's and Noyce's fundamental ideas were identical. Both were awarded the National Medal of Science and the induction to Inventor's Hall of Fame, but only Kilby lived long enough to share a Nobel Prize in Physics in the year 2000.

As with the first transistors, there was no rush to commercial applications of these new devices (TI's first advertisements in 1961 called them Micrological Elements). They were expensive and untried, their individual components could not be tested for reliability, and, unlike with circuits designed by a company for its specific use, their design could not be changed by buyers. As a result, major electronics companies were reluctant to make a switch. The prospects changed once the Apollo missions got under way and once the designers of the first U.S. ICBMs decided to control them with integrated circuits. By 1965 integrated circuits were finally embraced by all of the U.S. armed services.

Microprocessors

In 1965, when integrated circuits contained up to 50 elements, Gordon Moore, at that time the director of research at FS, wrote a paper in which he not only unequivocally stated that "the future of integrated electronics is the future of electronics itself," but also predicted that the trend of complexity for minimum cost, which had increased roughly by a factor of two per year since 1959, will continue over the short term and, although he naturally considered a longer term forecast to be more uncertain, put the minimum number of components per integrated circuit at 65,000 by 1975 (Moore 1965). In 1968, when Burroughs released the first computers made with integrated circuits, Moore and Noyce co-founded Intel (Integrated Electronics), and the company set out to fulfill his forecast.

Also in 1968 another fundamental semiconductor discovery was made at Bell Labs by a group led by Alfred Y. Cho that developed the process of molecular beam epitaxy, whereby single-crystal structures are deposited one atomic layer at a time (Cho 1994). This method, unmatchable in its precision, became the mainstay for making microchips. Intel's first profitable product was static random access memory chip, and in 1969 the company took on a new challenge of designing 12 custom large-scale integration (LSI, with more than 1,000 components) chips for a programmable calculator to be made by Busicom, a Japanese company that funded the development. With only two designers available to work on the project, Marcian Hoff opted for a programmed computer solution composed of a single central processing unit (CPU) that retrieved its instructions from a read-only memory (ROM). Hoff and Stanley Mazor made the original proposal for the MCS-4 chip, Federico Faggin did the logic and circuit design, and Mazor wrote the necessary software (Mazor 1995). The resulting four-chip set could be used for many other applications besides running calculators.

Interestingly, as Mazor noted, the Intel patent of the design (U.S. Patent 3,821,715) did not list the single chip processor among its 17 original claims (Hoff, Mazor, and Faggin 1974). Busicom made only a few large calculator models using the MCS-4 chip set before the company went bankrupt; fortuitously, Intel bought back the rights for the processor for $60,000 before that. The world's first universal microprocessor was formally released in November 1971. The $200 chip was a tiny rectangle of 3 × 4 mm, processed four bits of information at a time at the speed of 400 kHz, and, with 60,000 operations per second, was the functional equal of the ENIAC (Intel 2001). Its success was its simplicity: by the early 1970s it was clear that a computer on a chip will be eventually built, but it was difficult to see how it could be done with fewer than 20,000 transistors. The Intel 4004 had only 2,250 metal oxide semiconductor transistors, but it succeeded, as did other early Intel designs, "because they were scaled down computers. Like a golf cart, they were very limited, 'but got across the green' " (Mazor 1995:1068).

One of the first uses of the Intel 4004 was on the Pioneer 10 spacecraft launched on March 2, 1972. But none of the established makers of integrated circuit-based computers rushed to use the processor for designing the first personal microcomputer: that revolution, as is famously known, came from a Cupertino, California, garage where Steven Jobs and Steven Wozniak designed the first Apple machines between 1975 and 1977 (Moritz 1984). And just seven months before Intel released its first microprocessor, in April 1971, TI introduced the first mass-produced consumer item based on integrated circuits: the Pocketronic, the world's first pocket calculator. Its development was launched in 1965 by Patrick Haggerty (1914–1980), the company's CEO, and Kilby was the engineer in charge. The basic architecture of the machine proved very durable. After owning a number of calculators, I bought TI's TI-35 Galaxy Solar when it came out in 1984: for the past two decades nearly all calculations in my books and papers were done with it, and the first patent listed on its back (U.S. Patent 3,819,921) is the original Kilby-led design (Kilby, Merryman, and Van Tassel 1974).

As the 1970s unfolded, Moore's original forecast of the doubling time for transistor density turned out to be too optimistic: in 1974 Intel's 8080 microprocessor had 5,000 transistors; in 1979 the 8088 reached 29,000. But the slower rate of component doubling—18, rather than just 12, months starting with Intel's 4004 in 1971—held for the remainder of the 20th century, defying many predictions of its impending end, and by the year 2000 there were no reasons for its imminent demise (figure 5.17). IBM's choice of the 8088 as the

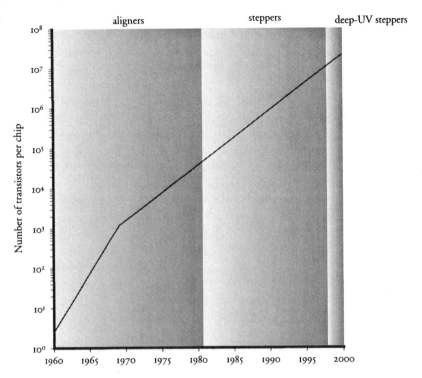

FIGURE 5.17. Moore's law predicts the number of transistors per microchip. Between 1959 (Noyce's first planar transistor) and 1972, the density of components doubled annually. Afterward, with successive Intel microprocessors, it doubled every 18 months. Vertical divides show the time frames for higher-resolution lithography systems. Based on graphs in Moore (1965), Hutcheson and Hutcheson (1996), and Intel (2003).

CPU in its first PC pushed the demand to more than 10 million microprocessors a year. By the year 2000 Intel's Pentium 4 64-bit microprocessor had 42 million transistors, and looking back, Moore, the company's Chairman Emeritus, was

> amazed we can design and manufacture the products in common use today. It is a classic case of lifting ourselves up by our bootstraps—only with today's increasingly powerful computers can we design tomorrow's chips. (Moore 2003:57)

Maintaining the trend required an unending stream of innovations needed to place more circuits on a silicon wafer. After LSI (up to 100,000 transistors on a chip) came very large-scale integration (VLSI, up to 10 million transistors) and ultralarge-scale integration (ULSI). VLSI design, first proposed in 1969, was developed, optimized, and integrated by Carver Mead of Caltech and Lynn Conway of Xerox: thanks to their work, custom design of VLSI circuits became universally possible (Mead and Conway 1980). Density of data stored on high-capacity magnetic hard-drive disks experienced a similar rate of growth: between 1957, when IBM introduced the first commercial disk drive, and the late 1990s the gain was 1.3 million-fold. Rapidly expanding demand for microchips generated a strong positive feedback as increasingly more powerful microprocessors made it possible to make themselves rapidly obsolete while they helped to design even more powerful, as well as more flexible, versions whose sales financed the next round of innovation.

But the fabrication of these microchips also required ever more expensive facilities: by the late 1990s the cost was $3 billion/plant, after doubling every four years (an expensive corollary of Moore's law?). Fabrication requires extraordinarily clean rooms, and it minimizes human handling and exposure to airborne particles of even the smallest size. The process uses chemicals, gases, and light in order to produce complicated sequences of layers on a silicon wafer (Van Zant 2004). A layer of SiO_2 is deposited first, and then it is coated with a light-sensitive material (photoresist). Photolithography is used to project ultraviolet light through a patterned mask (stencil) and a lens onto a coated wafer. After removing the exposed photoresist (unprotected by the mask), the revealed SiO_2 is etched away and the remaining photoresist is removed, leaving behind ridges of the oxide on a wafer. A thinner deposit of SiO_2 is then overlaid by polysilicon and photoresist, and exposed through a second mask. Dissolved photoresist exposes the areas of polysilicon and SiO_2 that are to be etched away.

Repetition of this process produces up to 20 layers in a micro-3D structure with windows for interconnections between the layers. Deposition of a metal layer and another round of masking and etching produce desired connections. The simplest MOSFET based on silicon substrate has just two islands (source and drain) of the element doped with either n-type or p-type channels overlaid with SiO_2 insulator topped with a metal electrode (gate). Their mode of operation could not be simpler: with low-voltage gated electrons cannot flow from source to drain, while a high-voltage gate lowers the energy barrier, sending a signal to the next circuit stage (figure 5.18). By the late 1990s it became possible to fashion gate lengths shorter than 100 nm as photolithography techniques advanced from contact aligners of the early 1970s to deep-ultraviolet steppers after 1998 (figure 5.17). Yet even this incredible feat was still far below the fundamental physical limits. At the same time, the thickness of deposited oxide was just 25 silicon atoms (< 3 nm), and, again, further reductions were under way.

The rising density of microchips had the already-noted obverse trend in

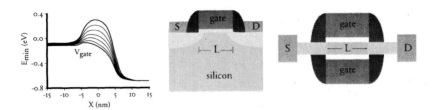

FIGURE 5.18. The principle of MOSFET (metal-oxide field-effect transistor). Minimum electron energy (left) is plotted against position from source to drain (X) under high drain voltage; sections through a planar MOSFET (middle) and a double-gate MOSFET (right) show source (S) and drain (D). L denotes channel length. Based on graphs in Lundstrom (2003).

falling costs. Writing in 1993, Robert W. Keyes highlighted the trend by comparing transistors with staples, the simplest of tiny steel products. He noted that the computer he used to type the article had some 10 million transistors,

> an astounding number of manufactured items for one person to own. Yet they cost less than the hard disk, the keyboard, the display and the cabinet. Ten million staples, in contrast, would cost about as much as the entire computer. (Keyes 1993:70)

Or, as Moore recalled, "initially we looked forward to the time when an individual transistor might sell for a dollar. Today that dollar can buy tens of millions of transistors as a part of a complex circuit" (Moore 2003:57).

In less than two decades microprocessors were transformed from rare, proprietary devices to a mass-produced commodity that was globally traded in bulk. Strong post-1975 expansion of the Japanese semiconductor industry began to erase the pioneering U.S. lead, and by the mid-1980s there were doubts about its very survival. In 1987 a government–industry partnership, SEMA-TECH, headed by Robert Noyce, was set up to help U.S. semiconductor companies. Nevertheless, Intel remained the industry's global leader for the remainder of the century, but by the year 2000 only two other U.S. companies, TI and Motorola, ranked among the world's 10 largest chipmakers. South Korean Samsung and Japan's Hitachi, Mitsubishi, and Toshiba were the Asian leaders.

Electronic Control and Communication

No other fabricated product in history had ever experienced such a cost reduction as did microprocessors, and the combination of cheapness and power made them ubiquitous in an ever-growing array of both highly specialized machines and assemblies, as well as in everyday consumer products; to quote Moore (2003:57) once more, "nearly any application that processes information today can be done most economically electronically." During the last four decades of the 20th century, entire industries, individual processes and products, and everyday actions were sequentially transformed by the introduction of transistors, integrated circuits, and microprocessors: very few complex items now remain outside their orbit. Much of this transformation was visible as inexpensive computers diffused throughout the industrial and service sectors and, after 1980, became common household items in most affluent nations.

But a partially, or entirely, hidden impact of microprocessors was no less important. Outwardly, countless processes and functions—be it drilling for oil, driving a car, or preparing a dinner—remained the same, but many, or most, of their controls were transferred from direct human action to automated guidance through microprocessors (Cortada 2004). Virtually every aspect of scientific instrumentation was transformed by reliance on computers, and many methods, relying on massive data processing, are simply unthinkable without it. Several of these methods, including magnetic resonance imaging (the first U.S. patent by Raymond Damadian filed in 1972), became indispensable diagnostic tools of modern medicine, whose principal mode of intervention has been also greatly aided by computers. Modern drug discovery relies on computer-controlled analytical machinery, clinical trials require complex statistical analyses, and safe dispensation of prescriptions is best monitored by computerized databases.

The combination of inexpensive computing and instant telecommunications transformed nearly every aspect of the energy business. Modern remote sensing depends on advanced electronics to store and process enormous volumes of data acquired by geophysical prospecting. By the mid-1990s traditional two-dimensional seismic data used in oil and gas exploration were almost completely replaced by 3-D images, and the latest 4-D monitoring (time-lapse 3-D) of reservoirs makes it possible to trace and to simulate the actual flow of oil in hydrocarbon-bearing formations and to double the oil recovery rates (Morgan 1995; Lamont Doherty Earth Observatory 2001). Computers also control refinery operations and maintain (still imperfectly, as recurrent blackouts make clear) the stability of high-voltage transmission networks.

In chapter 3 and earlier in this chapter I have already given many examples how modern industrial production and transportation were transformed by microprocessors. In transportation, the global positioning system makes it possible for a company to be instantaneously aware of the exact location of every one of its trucks crisscrossing a continent or every one of its cargo vessels, and optimizing algorithms that receive information about road closures and detours or about extreme weather events (cyclones, fog) can minimize fuel consumption and improve the chance of on-time delivery by rerouting these carriers.

The only major segment of electronic transformations that remains to be re-viewed after recounting the advances in computing includes the innovations that shaped the three modern communication media: radio, movies, and TV.

From Mainframes to the World Wide Web

The shrinking size of dominant machines was the most obvious physical proof of successive computer revolutions, one that even nonexperts could not miss. The earliest room-filling commercial mainframes, vacuum tube computers used by large research organizations and major businesses, weighed in excess of 10 t, but their transistorized progeny dropped below 5 t: UNIVAC I totaled 13.5 t; UNIVAC Solid State 90, released in 1958, had 3.28 t. A decade later the CPU of the IBM 360/67, the machine that claimed a major part of my days after we arrived in the United States in 1969, was 1.26 t, but the entire system, including core and disk storage, control units, punches, and card readers, added up to 12 t. Contrast this with the late 1990s laptops, most of which weighed less than 5 kg (and often no more than twice as much with attached printers), and personal digital assistants brought the weight reduction (albeit with re-duced power) to mere hundreds of grams. But the key objective of computer design was higher speed in order to execute increasingly complicated tasks and to do so in less time.

The fastest supercomputers of the late 1990s were more than 10 trillion times speedier than the best electromechanical calculators. As a result, today's complex global atmospheric circulation models that are used routinely for five-day weather forecasts would have taken at least half a year to process with UNIVAC. At the other end of the celerity spectrum were the increasingly more powerful microcomputers that introduced an entirely new combination of capabilities beginning with basic word processing and simple games and progressing to highly sophisticated processing of text and data and to stunning graphics. Nearly all other key components that ingeniously combined hardware and software and made user-friendly desktop computing possible—stand-alone personal computer, mouse, WYSIWYG editing, graphical user interface (GUI) with icons and pop-up menus, laser printing, spell checkers and thesaurus, the combination of computing, text editing, and graphics, and access to file servers and printers with point-and-click actions—were created during the 1970s by Xerox's Palo Alto Research Center (PARC) that was set up in 1970 (PARC 2003).

A generation later—after Xerox Corporation ignored the invention (Smith and Alexander 1988), nearly disintegrated, and then began to recover—the uninformed majority came to equate the predatory Microsoft with personal computing, and only a small number of technical *cognoscenti* appreciated the enormous role that PARC had in creating the PC era. Without PARC's array of techniques, Apple's Steven Jobs and Steven Wozniak could not have launched the first successful commercial PC, the Apple II with color graphics, in 1977 (Moritz 1984). Apple was also the first company that brought the GUI (graphical user interface) to the mass market with its Macintosh in 1984, and soon afterward Microsoft's PARC-derived Windows 1.0 was released for IBM PCs (Stross 1996). Microsoft's rise to a megacompany status epitomized the emergence of software, an intangible commodity that is easy to steal but whose economic contributions are difficult to quantify, as one of the leading products of the 1990s (Jones 1998).

Early mainframes had software as part of the machine; early programming was done by switches (in 1975 the Altair 8800, the first hobby kit microcomputer, had them), and programming languages, no matter how much closer they were to human language than was machine code, could never enter universal use. Readily available software, for purchase or free to download, virtually eliminated the need for individual programming, and the largest programs adding up to tens of millions of lines of code became indispensable drivers of tasks ranging from word processing to flexible manufacturing, and from mindless and violent games to ingenious virtual reality tests.

But the late 20th-century history of mass-produced software was also littered with overpriced ephemeral products of dubious utility and poor quality. A study by the National Institute of Standards and Technology estimated that software bugs cost the U.S. economy some $60 billion a year. At least one correction in this overblown field took place: market valuations of software megacompanies (with Oracle, CAI, Novell, and SAP ranking behind Microsoft) rose to such unsustainable levels that a brutal correction was inevitable: Microsoft's stock fell from nearly $60 by the end of 1999 to nearly $20 a year later, and many other software companies fared even worse.

The utility of PCs was greatly potentiated by the launching of the World Wide Web in 1990, and its rapid adoption deserves to be singled out as the century's last great transformative computing trend. Internet's origins go to 1962 when Joseph Licklider (1915–1990) became the first director of the Pentagon's Advanced Research Project Agency's (ARPA) Command and Control Research and soon proposed a nationwide "Intergalactic Computer Network" (Waldrop 2001). His successor, Robert W. Taylor, decided to start its construction, and ARPANET began its operation, initially with just four sites at the Stanford Research Institute, UCLA, University of California at Santa Barbara, and the University of Utah, in 1969. By 1971 there were nearly two dozen sites using protocols for remote terminal access (Telnet) and file transfer (ftp). A year later Ray Tomlinson of BBN Technologies designed two programs for sending messages to other computers: "It just seemed like a neat idea. There was no directive to 'go forth and invent e-mail' " (Tomlinson 2002:1). He also picked the "@" sign as the locator symbol for e-mail addresses.

In 1974 Vinton Cerf and Robert Kahn released a protocol that enabled computer communication across a system of networks (TCP/IP). By 1980 AR-PANET connected more than 400 computers that could be accessed by about 10,000 users. By 1983 ARPANET officially converted to TCP/IP, and the Internet was in place with fewer than 600 hosts; six years later, when ARPANET ended its existence, there were more than 100,000 hosts. In 1990 Tim Berners-Lee created the hypertext-based World Wide Web at Geneva's CERN in order to organize on-line scientific information (Abbate 1999). But the WWW would have been restricted to its initially specialized existence without an easy means to move around it. This was first supplied in 1993 by Mosaic, designed by Mark Andreessen and his colleagues at the University of Illinois, and a year later this software morphed into Netscape's Navigator, and the publically accessible electronic superhighway was born.

Microsoft's derivative Explorer 1.0 followed in 1995, but as it was bundled with the Windows, it soon became the dominant choice. Domain surveys regularly undertaken by the Internet Systems Consortium show the host total surpassing five million during the first half of 1995 and 100 million by the end of 2000 (ISC 2004), and worldwide PC sales nearly doubled between 1996 and 2000, to 130 million units a year. Text, still images, video (even movies), sound (including complete recordings) became accessible to anybody able to click and follow simple instructions. By the century's end the highest rate of Internet access was in Scandinavia, North America, and Australia.

The Internet brought a new vocabulary of inevitable acronyms (ftp, http, URL) and new means of looking for information by using browsers and search engines, with Google, somewhat more capable than the rest but still rather nondiscerning, rising to the leading spot. Soon the ease with which new websites could be created led to the emergence of an unprecedented depository of information that spans a complete range from archival repositories of books and scientific periodicals and fascinating real-time, or near-real-time, sites fed by satellites and remote cameras, to a flood of misleading, offensive, and outright deranged and criminal postings. New ways of doing business emerged with on-line retail and company-to-company sales and auctions and were almost immediately followed by new ways of offensive advertising (spam), breaching of privacy, and facilitating criminal activities ranging from credit card and identity theft to mass disruption of traffic by hacker-generated viruses, which led to rising outlays on data security, encryption, firewalls, and virus identification.

Mass Media and Personal Choices

By 1914 mass editions of periodicals and books, illustrated with inexpensively produced half-tone images (see chapter 5 of *CTTC*) were common; movie attendance, the number of annually produced feature films, and their lengths were growing; radio, an uncommon communication device limited to a few specialized tasks, was about to become an eagerly embraced public service; and technical foundations were also almost complete in order to take the first steps toward television. But the pre-WWI advances gave only an inkling of possibilities that were transformed into commercial realities of the 20th century when such disparate information and communication means as publishing, telephony, sound recordings, movies, radio, and television benefited from replacement of mechanical, electromechanical, and vacuum tube devices by solid-state electronics; consequently, their state-of-the-art designs of the 1990s were largely secondary innovations, special applications of microchips.

Typesetting, dominated by linotypes, did not see any fundamental innovations until the 1950s. In September 1946 Louis M. Moyroud and René Alphonse Higonnet revealed their photo composing machine that replaced cast metal with the strobe light projection of characters on a spinning disk onto photographic paper. The machine made "it possible to obtain directly composed text of justified lines" and to change "the length of lines, sizes of characters and fonts . . . by simple means" (Higonnet and Moyroud 1957:1). The Graphic Arts Research Foundation of New York improved the design, and the first book composed by the Photon machine came out in 1953. Eventually all mechanical parts were eliminated as solid-state components took over after 1960.

But linotypes dominated composition well into the 1960s. John Updike's most famous fictional character, Rabbit Armstrong, became one of the late victims of a switch ("So no Linotypers, huh?") in 1969 when his boss tells him about the new technique: "Offset, you operate all from film, bypass hot metal entirely. Go to a cathode ray tube, Christ, it delivers two thousand lines a minute . . ." (Updike 1971:296). During the 1980s microcomputers, inexpensive and easy-to-use typographic software, and laser printers ushered in the era of desktop publishing, and in large commercial establishments direct computer-to-plate techniques did away with resin-coated paper or film.

Unlike typesetting, the classical pre-WWI mode of movies was transformed twice before the middle of the century, by the introduction of color (first Technicolor in 1922, and an improved version during the 1930s) and electronically recorded sound after 1926 (Lloyd 1988; Friedman 1991). But, except for wide screens (Cinerama starting in 1952) and surround sound, there were no fundamental changes to the movie-going experience. The first Kodachrome (color) film was released in 1935, but color film began to be used more widely in cameras only after 1950, when the traditional dominance of German optics began to be challenged by Japan's targeted development of superior photographic hardware. By the early 1970s Japanese cameras—led by Nikon, Pentax, Minolta, and Fujica—dominated the world single-lens reflex market, while Kodak kept a substantial share only in the low-end amateur niche. As in so many other instances, transistors and then microchips changed cameras from mechanical to electronic devices, and the first digital cameras for consumer market were introduced in 1994 and 1995: the end of film was near.

Much like typesetting, telephony remained relatively static until the early 1960s, largely as a result of major monopolies that were not interested in making their huge infrastructural investments obsolete through rapid technical innovation. For decades the telephone ownership was limited to hardwired rotary dialing models (see figure 3.16), long-distance calls remained expensive, and intercontinental traffic was rare: the first trans-Atlantic telephone cable was laid from Scotland to Nova Scotia only in 1956, and it could carry just 36 simultaneous calls. But soon afterward varieties of telephone hardware and available services multiplied as the cost of long-distance calls plummeted and as satellites opened the path toward inexpensive intercontinental calling.

The first overt transformation (in 1963) was to replace the rotary dial with the touch-tone telephone, but beneath the buttons there was still the decades-old electromechanical assembly that included a make-and-break circuit driving a clapper against two bells. Still, touch-tone dialing made possible new telephone services and uses (voice mail, call centers), including the often frustrating automated recordings with numbered menus.

Development of the electronic telephone began during the 1970s (Luff 1978). The bell ringer, the tone oscillator, and the speech network were replaced by integrated circuits, and two dynamic transducers acted as transmitter and receiver. But the most important post-1960 advances were not in the hand-held devices but in techniques not seen by the user that increased the throughput of the system while cutting its cost and improving its quality. Bell Laboratories in Murray Hill, New Jersey, was on the forefront of many of these innovations (Lucent Technologies 2004).

As already noted, the first telecommunication satellite was launched in 1962 (see figure 3.20). In the same year Bell Labs introduced the first digitally multiplexed transmission of signals that created more economical yet more flexible and more robust way for voice traffic and led to services ranging from 911 to 800 calls to call waiting. In 1979 came the first single-chip digital signal processor, the forerunner of cellular phones and modems of the 1990s, and in 1988 the first fiber-optic trans-Atlantic cable could handle 40,000 calls. And even before this innovation wave could largely spend itself, a much larger and much faster, and largely unanticipated, wave of cellular telephony began to roll during the early 1990s. Bell Labs had already made the first demonstration of cellular telephony in 1962, and it introduced digital cellular transmission, with higher channel capacity and lower cost, in 1980. But despite the pioneering work at Bell Labs, the first markets that were nearly saturated with cellular telephones were in Western Europe (the "Nokia effect") and in Japan and Hong Kong.

WWI delayed radio's commercial expansion, and limited ownership of receivers marked radio's first public decade. But by the mid-1930s the medium was well established throughout the Western world. The most important technical innovation of the 1930s was Edwin Armstrong's (1890–1954) development of frequency modulation (FM) broadcasting that eliminated the notorious static interference in AM (amplitude modulation). But the broadcasting industry with its heavy investment in AM resisted the innovation, and FM became common only after 1950. Radio's capability to captivate instantly an unprecedented number of people was famously demonstrated by Orson Welles's 1938 *War of the Worlds* broadcast. Inexpensive transistorized radios introduced during the 1950s had three welcome consequences: they made radios cheaper, shrank the size of home units, and made the device easily portable. The first portable radio went on sale in October 1954: the TR-1 by Regency Electronics had four TI's germanium transistors, was available in six colors, and cost $49.95 (Lane and Lane 1994).

While TI did not pursue the further development of the portable radio, a small Japanese company, Tōkyō Tsushin Kōgyo, set up in 1946 by Akio Morita and Masaru Ibuka and renamed Sony in order to have an internationally pronounceable name, followed its release of the TR-55 radio in August 1955 by the world's first transistor television (in 1960) and compact videotape recorder (in 1963). And although its Betamax video cassette recorder, introduced in May 1975, lost to Matsushita's VHS design, its stereo Walkman (1979), Discman (1984), Watchman (handheld micro-TV, 1988), camcorder (1989), digital camcorder (1995), and Memory Stick Walkman (1999) continued the tradition of small portable solid-state devices that found a ready global market and made the company the world's second largest (after Matsushita) maker of electronic goods (Sony 2004). The century's last major radio innovation was the rapid expansion of World Wide Web stations, with broadcasts sent along telephone lines and listeners using their PCs. In 1995 Radio Hong Kong became the first 24-h Internet-only station. No need for licensing and no scramble for a sliver of valuable spectrum soon led to hundreds of new Web stations.

By the time radio's audience was peaking, television was making rapid inroads. Its commercial beginnings in the United States and United Kingdom during the 1930s were so tentative that the true TV era began only after 1945, and the relatively expensive and bulky black-and-white sets were in the majority of North American households only during the 1950s and in Western Europe and Japan roughly a decade later. As noted in chapter 1, television could have been born before WWI. Its early development is akin to the evolution of movies, as many innovations led to a commercial product. Its American origins center on the patent dispute between Philo T. Farnsworth (1906–1971) and Vladimir K. Zworykin (1889–1982). Farnsworth, a self-educated Mormon, conceived the idea of an all-electronic TV at age 14 and transmitted the first picture (of a piece of glass painted black with a scratched center line) using a CRT camera in 1927 when he patented a complete television system (Godfrey 2001; figure 5.19).

FIGURE 5.19. Philo Farnsworth in 1926 (left), just before he filed his patent for television system, and inspecting (right), with Mable Bernstein, one of the first portable TV cameras built in 1934. From Donald G. Godfrey, Arizona State University.

Zworykin, a Russian engineer who immigrated to the United States in 1919, claimed that he designed a similar CRT camera (iconoscope) in 1923 (Friedman 1991). But he did not build any working device at that time; his first patent for "an apparatus for producing images of objects" was granted only in 1935, and his 1923 application was approved, after an extraordinarily long period of delays and revisions, only in 1938. But in 1935 the U.S. Patent Office ruled that Zworykin's original 1923 design would not work, and awarded the invention priority to Farnsworth. It was RCA, Zworykin's corporate sponsor, whose engineers developed the system for commercial use and began broadcasting in 1939. Meanwhile, in the United Kingdom John L. Baird (188–1952) demonstrated his low-resolution (30 lines per picture) electromechanical design in 1926, and by 1930 he also used it to test color broadcasts. The BBC began regular broadcasts based on Baird's invention in 1932 and replaced them with the world's first high-resolution (405 lines per picture) service in 1936 (Smith and Paterson 1998).

Transistorization and later the use of microchips shrank the size, cut the cost, and boosted the capabilities of the entire TV system. Bulky black-and-white TVs of the late 1940s cost $500, an equivalent of nearly a fifth of an average annual salary; half a century later a standard CRT color TV could be bought for less than a tenth of an average monthly salary. As a result, the global TV count rose from 100 million units in 1960 to 300 million by 1979 and to about 1.2 billion by 2000, with saturation complete in affluent countries and also in many urban areas in low-income nations. Introduction of cable TV (for the first time in the United States in 1948, but widely delivered only since the 1970s) led to the proliferation of channels and to the pervasiveness of the medium that now offers round-the-clock niche broadcasts in a quantity that is predictably correlated with the decline in quality. Finally, before the century's end a superior alternative to bulky and energy-inefficient CRTs became available as liquid crystal display panels allowed perfectly flat and also much wider screens, and high-definition TV (first demonstrated by Phillips in 1988) began its slow commercialization process.

ℰↄ 6

New Realities and Counterintuitive Worlds:
Accomplishments and Concerns

The changes have come so fast that man's customs, mores,
ethics, and religious patterns may not have adapted to them
. . . Man's role in the environment is becoming so enormous
that his energetic capacity to hurt himself by upsetting the
environmental system is increasing . . . We may wonder
whether the individual human being understands the real
source of the bounty to him of the new energy support.

Howard Odum, *Environment, Power, and Society* (1971)

The great technical saltation that took place during the two pre-WWI generations introduced new forms of energy, new prime movers, new materials,
new industrial, agricultural, transportation, and household machines, and new

FRONTISPIECE 6. Two images from 1950 illustrate the progress of the 20th century's
technical transformation. TV's key components (top) were available before WWI, regular broadcasts began before WWII, but rapid diffusion of the medium took place only
after WWII. This console receiver with a 30-cm cathode ray tube screen was made by
the long-defunct Capehart-Farnsworth Corporation (from author's collection). Flying
underwent a fundamental technical transformation (bottom) as gas turbines entered
commercial service after WWII: a young American boy contemplates ("some day") a
trip to far-distant lands by a machine that became a commercial reality eight years later.
Drawing reproduced courtesy of INCO.

253

ways of communication and information processing. Advances of the 20th century improved all of these techniques and brought major innovations in energy conversion, materials, agricultural mechanization, industrial manufacturing, and telecommunication, many of them possible only thanks to solid-state microelectronics that had rapidly penetrated every segment of modern economies. These technical transformations created a civilization that differs in several fundamental ways from all previous societies.

Our lives now depend on using a still growing array of artifacts and on following a still expanding set of procedures that are required in order to accomplish countless productive and leisure tasks. In return for affluence, comfort, convenience, speed, accuracy, and reliability, we must conform to the requirements of these complex systems—and we have no choice to do otherwise. As modern economies became more dependent on concatenated technical advances, they passed the point of no return: this dependence now assures not only our affluence but also our very survival. Inklings of this new reality came in parts of the Western world before WWI, but most pre-1914 societies still had a long way to go before technical transformations made our dependence on complex techniques so pervasive.

Two mid-century images used as this chapter's frontispiece exemplify this process of gradual technical transformation. TV's key components were available before WWI, but practical service was developed only during the 1930s and began to diffuse rapidly only after WWII. Flying underwent a fundamental transformation as gas turbines entered commercial service after WWII. In the United States these new realities were largely in place soon after WWII, in Europe they became common only during the 1960s, and the pervasiveness and complexity of artificial environments reached new heights everywhere with the post-1970 automation and computerization. As if this were not enough, the 1990s brought a new trend that is detaching individuals and societies even further from the physical world and submerging them in virtual reality.

Higher energy use was a key prerequisite of these technical transformations, and its most obvious pay-offs were higher physical quality of life and vastly expanded individual and collective horizons as a surfeit of information, affordable travel, and instant means of communication changed the patterns of work, education, leisure, and social interaction. Displacement of animate energies by fossil fuels and primary electricity, rise of mass production, and new means of control—progressing from ingenious mechanical devices to electromechanical setups to solid-state electronics—transformed the structure, efficiency, and labor intensity of all economic activities. Quest for higher productivity, improved quality, minimized labor force, and perpetual expansion of output resulted in unprecedented rates of economic growth.

Although the world's population nearly quadrupled during the 20th century, both the average per capita economic product and typical disposable income grew much faster. At the same time, a highly skewed distribution of these accomplishments left humanity with greater relative welfare disparities. Highly uneven distribution of natural resources needed to generate these advances, as well as many instances of comparative advantage in producing particular goods or offering specific services, led to unprecedented levels of interdependence. This trend had gone beyond the expansion of international trade as it embraced leisure travel (the world's single largest economic activity), migration, flows of information (patents, international consulting, education, scientific collaboration), and personal styles and tastes. All of these shifts not only were closely connected with urbanization but also were to a large extent its products. At the same time, precipitous urbanization was also a major reason of persistent, even deepening, social and economic inequalities.

Complexities of global interdependence are just one of many new concerns that arose from the success of the 20th century's technical advances. New risks were created by new techniques, and it has not been easy to subject them to dispassionate and convincing cost–benefit assessments. And no century had seen so many deaths in violent conflicts, as aggression was made easier thanks to vastly increased destructiveness of weapons. And while the concerns about the unthinkable, the thermonuclear exchange between the two superpowers, receded with the peaceful disintegration of the USSR in 1991, the 1990s were marked by heightened awareness of a multitude of environmental changes. These ranged from destruction and degradation of ecosystems and biodiversity on local and regional scales to concerns about global effects, above all about the consequences of a rapid climate change whose genesis is directly linked to the key driver of modern civilization, the combustion of fossil fuels.

Gains and Losses

On a personal level, modernity's most obvious manifestation is the increasing accumulation of possessions. On the collective level, more complex and more durable artifacts combine to produce artificial environments of concrete, metals, glass, and asphalt, where trees are planted according to design, beaches are trucked in, streams are trained, air is polluted, and invisible greenhouse gases keep changing the Earth's radiation balance. None of this has diminished the drive to amass material possessions. In some places the first steps toward this new reality began many generations ago. During the 15th and 16th centuries homes of wealthy Dutch merchants displayed paintings, maps, rugs, tea services, musical instruments, and upholstered furniture; soon afterward, incipient mass consumption of "frivolities" spread to population segments with lower incomes as modern materialism was born (Mukherji 1983). Similar acquisition of luxuries was taking place at the same time in Muromachi and Tokugawa Japan and in Ming and early Qing China (Pomeranz 2000).

Industrialization enriched this trend by adding affordable mechanical devices (clocks, watches, sewing machines, cameras), increasingly more complex machines (bicycles, automobiles), and ingenious converters of electricity (lights, motors). The unprecedented technical saltation of the two pre-WWI generations began to extend new infrastructures as households acquired indoor plumbing, electricity, and telephones. Concurrently, new factories, transportation networks, and rapidly expanding industries began to transform previously tightly confined settlements—maximum diameters of pre-industrial walled cities were on the order of 5 km—as they encroached on the surrounding countryside. Eventually this anthropogenic world began

> to impose itself everywhere, to change everything, to take over all social activities and forms, and to become a true environment . . . We can survive neither in natural environment nor in a social environment without our technical instruments. Our gadgets are as necessary to us as food. (Ellul 1989:133)

From the fundamental physical point of view, the most obvious outcome of the 20th century's technical transformation was the creation of high-energy societies where even ordinary citizens could command, affordably and also effortlessly, power that was just a few generations ago beyond anybody's reach (or even imagination). Consequences of this achievement ranged from the most welcome increases in longevity and reductions in morbidity to ostentatious and wasteful overconsumption. Perhaps the most fascinating truth about this situation is that, as discussed further below, no important indicators of a rationally defined quality of life require the tremendous levels of per capita energy use that were taken for granted in the world's most affluent countries during the 1990s. Higher energy use also transformed our lives by expanding both physical and mental horizons thanks to affordable and speedy transportation and communication. But these advances also offer perfect examples of serious, unintended, and often unanticipated side effects and worrisome consequences of technical innovations.

Expanded transportation became a leading contributor to environmental degradation, mainly because of automotive and airplane emissions and the effects of transportation infrastructure on the reordering of inhabited space; it also remained a major cause of accidental death and injuries, and as its intensity grew even its most cherished benefits, speed and saving of time, declined. New means of communication and new ways of disseminating and processing information—from inexpensive printed matter to multifaceted capabilities of computers—can obviously be tools of both formal and informal education and expanded knowledge and more subtle understanding of complex realities. They can be also valuable repositories of historical records, collective memories, and cultural accomplishments, as well as the foundations needed for informed decision making. But during the 20th century these powerful technical means were often used as the tools of propaganda and misinformation, were deployed as agents of deliberate forgetting and mass control, and were found to be ideal choices to debase cultural standards and to weaken social structures.

High-Energy Societies and the Quality of Life

Improved quality of life was bought with higher flows of useful energy. Transformations of pre-WWI prime movers and the post-WWII deployment of gas turbines made it possible to produce, move, process, and convert fossil fuels with throughputs and efficiencies that were unprecedented in history. A new high-energy civilization was born as global consumption of fossil fuels and primary electricity expanded 16-fold between 1900 and 2000 and as the share of biomass energies fell from nearly 50% to just 10% of the total (figure 6.1). This large expansion meant that even with the near-quadrupling of the global population (from 1.6 to 6.1 billion), average annual per capita supply of primary energies still more than quadrupled. The century's global cumulative production of coal and crude oil was roughly equal in energy terms, but oil's post-1960 global dominance makes it a better choice for equivalent measures.

Using kilograms of oil equivalent (kgoe) as the common denominator, average per capita consumption of fossil energies rose from about 300 kgoe in 1900 to more than 1,250 kgoe (or roughly nine barrels, in standard oil industry parlance) by the year 2000 (Smil 1994; UNO 2002; BP 2004). Addition of primary electricity (since the 1880s hydrogeneration, since the mid-1950s also nuclear, and small amounts of geothermal, wind, and solar generation) raises the 1900 total only marginally, but it adds roughly 11% to the 2000 rate. But because of the enormous inequalities of commercial energy use, it is much

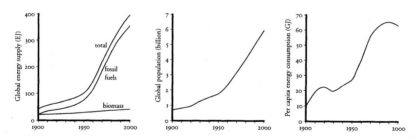

FIGURE 6.1. Global energy supply (left), population (middle), and per capita energy consumption (right), 1900–2000. Although the worldwide biomass consumption doubled during the 20th century, by its end it provided only about 10% of the global primary energy supply dominated by fossil fuels and primary (hydro and nuclear) electricity. Based on figure 5.15 in Smil (1994) and 1.2 and 6.10 in Smil (2003).

more important to know the modal rate and the global range of values. In the year 2000 the modal rate (for more than 50 countries) was below 250 kgoe; the global ranges go, on the national level, from less than 100 kgoe in sub-Saharan Africa to about 8,000 kgoe for the United States and Canada, and from nothing (for the poorest populations relying still solely on biomass fuels) to about 12,000 kgoe for the most affluent populations living in the richest U.S. counties.

In the United States and in many European countries, coal consumption was already high in 1900 and hence the per capita supply of fossil fuels "just" tripled or quadrupled by the year 2000. But Japan's use of fossil fuels grew nearly 30-fold, and because in China or India consumption of fossil fuels in 1900 was limited to small amounts of coal, the centennial multiples were extremely large. But all of these comparisons are flawed because they are based on the gross energy content of fossil fuels and primary electricity and do not reflect higher conversion efficiencies that delivered much more useful energy (heat, motion, light) from the same inputs in the year 2000 than they did in 1900. Space heating illustrates these gains. Wood stoves were usually less than 20% efficient; coal stoves doubled that rate, and fuel oil furnaces brought it to nearly 50%. Natural gas furnaces initially rated up to 65%, but by the 1990s many of them delivered more than 90%. Consequently, every unit of gross heating energy now provides roughly five times more useful service than it did in 1900.

In affluent countries the overall efficiencies of primary energy use at least doubled and even tripled during the 20th century. When coupled with the absolute rise in energy use, this means that these countries had experienced 8- to 12-fold increases in per capita supply of energy services. But even this adjustment fails to capture fully the actual gain because the new converters and new ways of consumption also brought improvements in comfort, safety, and reliability, all of them most welcome but none of them easy (and some impossible) to quantify. Another way to illustrate increased energy use in modern societies is to contrast the flows controlled directly by individuals in the course of their daily activities. Peak unit capacities of prime movers that can deliver sustained power rose about 15 million times in 10,000 years—from 100 W from sustained human labor to 1.5 GW for the largest steam turbogenerators—with more than 99% of the rise taking place during the 20th century (figure 6.2).

Although the citizens of affluent societies take these levels of individually and collectively commanded energies for granted, their magnitudes still astonish (Smil 2003). In 1900 even a prosperous Great Plains farmer controlled no more than 5 kW of sustained animate power as he held the reins of six large horses when plowing his fields—and he had to do so sitting in the open on a steel seat; a century later his great-grandson performed the same task from

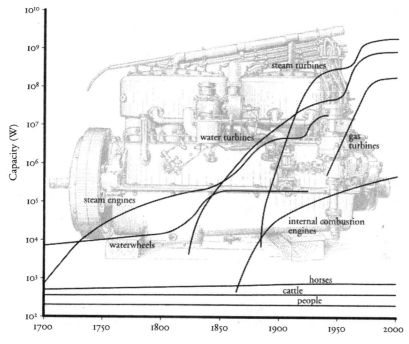

FIGURE 6.2. Maximum capacity of individual animate and inanimate prime movers, 1700–2000. The background shows an internal combustion engine (an early Rolls-Royce model) because no other prime mover has reached such a large aggregate installed capacity: in the year 2000 the engines (mostly in passenger vehicles and trucks) had more than 20 times as much installed power as did all of the world's steam turbogenerators. Based on a graph in Smil (1994).

air-conditioned comfort of an insulated cabin of a huge tractor capable of 300 kW. In 1900 engineers of the most powerful locomotives that could pull transcontinental trains at about 100 km/h commanded about 1 MW of steam power while exposed to blasts of heat and rushing air; in 1999 a captain of Boeing 747-400 could let onboard microprocessors control four jet engines whose aggregate cruise power of some 45 MW could retrace the train's route 11 km above the Earth's surface at an average speed of 900 km/h.

In 1900 even well-off U.S. urban households had only half a dozen low-power lightbulbs and one or two small appliances whose combined power rating was far below 1 kW; during the late 1990s an all-electric, air-conditioned exurban house had more than 80 switches and outlets ready to power lights and appliances that could draw more than 30 kW, and adding the family's three vehicles would raise the total power under the household's control close to 500 kW! In the past this power—although nowhere near a comparable level of convenience, versatility, flexibility, and reliability—could be commanded only by an owner of a Roman *latifundia* with about 6,000 strong slaves, or during the 1890s by a landlord with 3,000 workers and 400 big draft horses.

Fossil fuels and electricity were indispensable in order to increase farm productivity and hence drastically reduce agricultural population, to mechanize industrial production and release the labor force to move into the service sector, to make megacities and conurbations a reality, and to globalize trade and culture. And the energy industries also had to energize themselves as they imposed many structural uniformities onto the diverse world. Fortunately, given the high energy densities (J/g) of fossil fuels and high power densities (W/m²) of their deposits, net energy return in coal and hydrocarbon industries has been very high. This is particularly impressive because these industries require many expensive infrastructures—coal mines, oil and gas fields, pipelines, tankers, refineries, power stations, transformers, high-voltage transmission, and overhead and underground distribution lines—and a great deal of energy to operate them.

While higher energy flows correlate highly with greater economic outputs, all of the quality-of-life variables relate to average per capita energy use in a nonlinear manner, as there are some remarkably uniform saturation levels beyond which further increases of fuel and electricity consumption produce hardly any additional gains. No matter which quality-of-life indicator one graphs against the average per capita energy use (figure 6.3), clear inflections become evident at annual consumption levels of between 1 and 1.6 tonnes of oil equivalent (toe) per capita, with obviously diminishing returns afterward and with basically *no* additional gains accompanying primary energy consumption above 2.6 toe per capita. These realities led me to conclude that a society concerned about equity and willing to channel its resources into the provision of adequate diets, health care, and basic schooling could guarantee decent physical well-being with an annual per capita use of as little as 1–1.2 toe (Smil 2003).

A more desirable performance, with infant mortalities below 20, female life expectancies above 75, and the United Nations Development Programme (UNDP) Human Development Index (HDI) above 0.8, appears to require annually at least 1.4–1.5 toe per capita, while currently the best global rates (infant mortalities below 10, female life expectancies above 80, high rates of house ownership, good access to postsecondary education, HDI above 0.9) need about 2.6 toe per capita. And the level of political freedom has little to do with any increases of energy use above the existential minima (figure 6.3). By the end of the 20th century U.S. per capita energy consumption was more than three times the desirable minimum of 2.6 toe, and almost exactly twice as much as in Japan or the richest countries of the European Union (8 vs. 4 toe/year)—yet it would be ludicrous to suggest that American quality of life was twice as high. In fact, the United States ranked behind Europe and Japan in a number of important indicators because of its higher infant mortality,

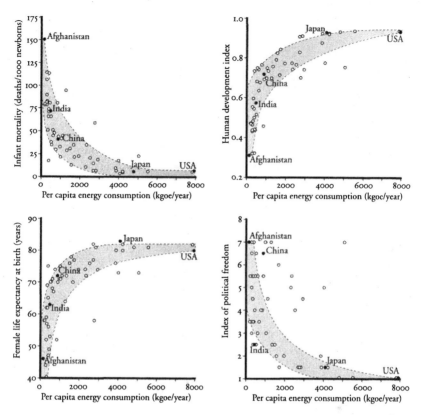

FIGURE 6.3. Improvements in all major quality-of-life indicators show diminishing returns with increasing per capita energy consumption and virtually no gains above the average level of 2.6 toe per capita. Based on graphs in Smil (2003).

more homicides, lower levels of scientific literacy and numeracy, and less leisure time.

Pushing beyond 2.6 toe per capita has brought no fundamental quality-of-life gains, only further environmental degradation. And given still a very large potential for higher energy conversion efficiencies, it is realistic to conclude that lifestyles that were supported by 2.6 toe during the late 1990s could have been achieved by using less than 2 toe per capita, close to the actual average global consumption of about 1.5 toe per capita per year. This fact puts one of the greatest concerns of modern affluent civilization into a different perspective: equitable distribution of available energy supplies and their rational use could have alone guaranteed high worldwide quality of life!

Mobility and Its Price

New means of transportation expanded physical horizons to the extent that is quite magical when seen from the pre-1900 perspective. Coaches, averaging about 10 km/h, were the fastest means of land transport until the 1830s; by 1900 steam-powered trains averaged 60–80 km/h; reciprocating aeroengines pushed cruising speeds above 200 km/h by the early 1930s and to more than 600 km/h by the early 1950s. Then travel speeds rose and leveled off abruptly with the introduction of gas turbines as jetliners began to cruise at the edge of the stratosphere at subsonic speeds of up to about 950 km/h or Mach 0.9 (figure 6.4). In cities the introduction of streetcars and buses, averaging about 20 km/h (but only 10 km/h in congested downtowns), quadrupled the walking speed, and passenger cars (and subways in cities with high train frequency) traveling at 40–50 km/h at least doubled the speed of surface public transport (Ausubel, Marchetti, and Meyer 1998).

Time allocation studies show that people, regardless of the transportation mode, spend about one hour a day traveling; in that time an urban driver, going about eight times faster than a pedestrian, can make return trips inside a roughly 60 times larger area. A driver traveling on an interstate highway at 120 km/h acquires access to an area nearly 580 times larger than available to a pedestrian, and because cars eliminate waiting time for departure and transfers

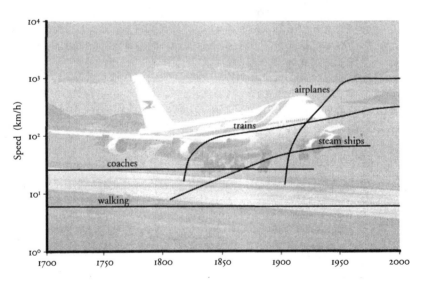

FIGURE 6.4. Maximum speed of commercial travel, 1800–2000. The supersonic Concorde cruised at Mach 2, but it operated only on limited routes between 1976 and 2003, when the fleet was retired, and was an uneconomical oddity. Based on Shevell (1980) and Smil (1994).

(often between two transport modes), they also offer a considerable advantage compared with trains. The price paid for these magically expanded horizons included not only the construction, and maintenance of the requisite infra-structures, inevitable accidents and environmental degradation but also some less noted negatives that include a counterintuitive decline of typical car travel speeds and the geochemical supremacy of automobiles over people.

Road construction was one of the 20th century's most remarkable, most massive, and hence also most destructive enterprises. The U.S. example illus-trates best the magnitude of this transformation: in 1900 there were just a couple hundred kilometers of paved roads; a century later paved roads added up to nearly four million kilometers. Only 256,000 km of these belonged to the National Highway System, but these national roads carried more than 40% of all highway traffic and 75% of heavy truck traffic (Slater 1996). The back-bone of this network is the nearly 75,000 km of the Interstate Highway Sys-tem, whose construction, begun in 1956, amounted to the world's largest public works construction program. But this enviable achievement also poses a for-bidding maintenance challenge: repairing and replacing the enormous mass of emplaced reinforced concrete adds up to expenditures that vastly surpass the original investment.

Absolute death rates in car accidents declined or stabilized in all high-income countries where stricter safety standards, better roads, and better en-forcement of seatbelt legislation not only stopped but actually reversed the fatality trend. The U.S. peak in 1972 was 54,589 deaths, but during the 1990s the annual total never surpassed 44,000 despite the fact that the total distance driven by vehicles grew by almost 25%. But in low-income countries, total death rates continued to rise (WHO 2002). In the year 2000 traffic deaths amounted to 1.26 million people and 25% of all fatal injuries, roughly equal to the combined total of all homicides and suicides and four times as many as casualties of wars—and 90% of these fatalities occurred in low- and middle-income countries.

Among the populous countries the highest road traffic mortality was in China (50 deaths/100,000 people) and India (30 deaths/100,000 people), while the North American and Western European rates were between 10 and 15/100,000. These differences are not surprising given that the total number of traffic deaths increases rapidly during earlier stages of automobilization while the rate of fatalities per 1,000 vehicles declines (Evans 2002; figure 6.5). Because of the disproportionately large share of young victims (particularly males in their late teens and early 20s), every traffic fatality also represented roughly 33 disability-adjusted life years (defined as years of healthy life lost either due to premature death or disability).

Numerous improvements of the car's overall design, better fuel, greatly im-proved driving conditions, and after 1970, the effort to lower its polluting emissions combined to make the passenger automobile a considerably more

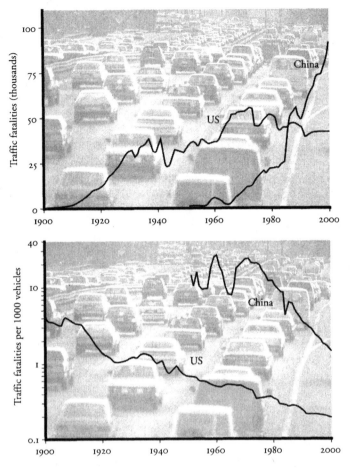

FIGURE 6.5. Traffic fatalities (annual totals, top, and deaths per 1,000 vehicles, bottom) in the United States and China, 1900–2000. Based on graphs in Evans (2002). In spite of the much steeper post-1970 decline of relative fatality rates in China, driving there during the late 1990s was still about 10 times more risky than in the United States.

efficient, more reliable, safer, and less offensive machine. But—notwithstanding the growing sales of "sport" cars, the myth propagated by their makers, and the impression that immature buyers of these vehicles wish to convey—there were no corresponding increases in speed for the majority of car trips, that is, daily commutes and errands. Road congestion that limits average speed has been the norm in every large city, no matter whether its traffic was dominated by horse-drawn vehicles (see figure 1.7 in *CTTC*), low-power automobiles (in the 1920s), or a mix of increasingly more powerful vehicles in the

1990s. But the rate of automobilization presented an unprecedented escalation of transport density.

For example, in 1939 the Paris region had about half a million cars; by 1965 the total was two million, but the street surface in the city had increased by just 10% since 1900 (Ross 1996). Consequently, parking became as much, if not more of, a problem as driving. Many studies demonstrated that new roads brought only temporary time savings before they, too, became clogged or encouraged longer drives for the same pattern of activities. And while the average distance driven per year had stabilized in Europe and Japan, in the United States it began to rise (after 50 years of remarkable constancy at around 15,000 km) during the 1980s, and by the year 2000 it was about 19,000 km/car.

More fundamentally, hundreds of millions of machines that were driven every year during the late 1990s over the cumulative distance in excess of one trillion kilometers became not only the embodiments of speed and providers of choice but also mechanical enslavers and demanding dominators. A succinct counterintuitive perspective on what had since become a global phenomenon was skillfully presented by Ivan Illich (1926–2002), a Catholic priest and an unorthodox thinker. Illich's approach was one of comprehensive accounting, and his effectiveness was in subverting the illusion of ever-speedier travel:

> The model American male devotes more than 1,600 hours a year to his car. He sits in it while it goes and while it stands idling. He parks it and searches for it. He earns the money to put down on it and to meet the monthly installments. He works to pay for gasoline, tolls, insurance, taxes, and tickets. He spends four of his sixteen waking hours on the road or gathering his resources for it. And this figure does not take into account the time consumed by other activities dictated by transport: time spent in hospitals, traffic courts, and garages; time spent watching automobile commercials. . . . The model American puts in 1,600 hours to get 7,500 miles: less than five miles per hour. (Illich 1974:18–19)

By the end of the 20th century, this situation got considerably worse. Increasing cost of cars meant that cash purchases nearly disappeared and interest charges became extended over periods of several years; growing numbers of families with more cars than people meant higher outlays for vehicles that spent all but a few hours a week just standing in garages or driveways; insurance premiums and repair bills of accidentally damaged cars soared; growing traffic congestion reduced the speeds in every major urban area; semipermanent rush hours led to a spreading phenomenon of road rage; car thefts increased the cost of policing and recovery. Illich's estimate of 8 km/h is equivalent to a very fast walk: by the year 2000 the adjusted speed was most likely as low as 5 km/h, a pace that millions of fit retirees could match.

Another surprising perspective comes from my studies of the biosphere's carbon cycle. Imagine an exceedingly sapient civilization that periodically explores our star system for signs of life, which it defines (not quite like we do) as the combination of carbon-based metabolism, large size, and mobility. Its recurrent monitoring of the Earth would have shown slow evolution and diversification of large quadrupeds and then the appearance and relatively rapid diffusion of large-brained bipeds whose numbers would rise to more than one billion by the beginning of what was our 19th century. Then, a century later, composition of the dominant mobile mass began to change with the appearance of four-wheeled organisms that also released carbon dioxide (CO_2) but metabolized carbon in a different way. While the bipeds subsist largely on carbohydrates [approximated as $(CH_2O)_n$] which they converted at ambient temperature, the four-wheeled creatures required large volumes of liquid hydrocarbons [homologs of $C_nH_{(2n+2)}$ series] which they metabolized at high temperatures and elevated pressures.

Just before the end of the 20th century the planet's anthropomass (dry matter of its bipeds) was about 100 Mt, while the mass of four (or more)-wheeled organisms was an order of magnitude larger, in excess of one billion tonnes, and they became metabolically dominant. Every year during the 1990s the bipeds harvested about 1.3 billion tonnes of carbon for their food while they were busily engaged, in servantlike or slavelike capacities, to secure almost one billion tonnes of fossil carbon (coke and hydrocarbon feedstocks) in order to produce the wheeled creatures (initially almost solely with iron, later with increasing use of aluminum, glass, rubber, and plastics) and about 1.5 billion tonnes of gasoline and diesel fuel to energize them. Further studies would show that the wheeled organisms, besides killing annually more than one million bipeds and maiming more than 10 million of them, were also responsible for much of the accelerating increase of atmospheric CO_2, a trend that may bring a very rapid climate change and make life for the bipeds increasingly precarious.

Despite all of this, the bipeds were spending ever more time inside these organisms (in some countries averaging up to 90 min every day), and they actually worshipped the metallic creatures through many peculiar rituals that range from elaborate grooming and safeguarding to fanciful displays and expensive accessories and decorations. Kenneth Boulding's insight explains best this extraordinary human devotion to cars. The car, he concluded,

> turns its driver into a knight with the mobility of the aristocrat. . . . The pedestrian and the person who rides public transportation are, by comparison, peasants looking up with almost inevitable envy at the knights riding by in their mechanical steeds. Once having tasted the delights of a society in which almost everyone can be a knight, it is hard to go back to being peasants. (Boulding 1974:255)

Automobilization is a perfect example of difficulties faced by any attempt at comprehensive cost–benefit analyses of the 20th century's technical advances: it is often impossible to come up even with at a conclusive verdict. Beyond the factors noted in the preceding pages, there are many advantages that modern drivers and passengers do not think about. Cars, besides being efficient killing machines, have been also immensely beneficial tools for saving lives. As Ling (1990:27) concluded, "no amount of nostalgia can obscure the needless suffering and fatalities in rural America prior to the motor car." By the time a horse was harnessed and a victim of a farm accident transported to the nearest town, it was too often too late. And a fast ambulance ride may make the difference between life and death for heart attack victims or, indeed, for people severely injured in traffic accidents.

Cars that isolate drivers in private cocoons have also increased social interactions and personal choices. In rural areas they turned an uncomfortable day-long drive in a horse-pulled buggy to visit friends or relatives to an easy one-hour trip, and opened up the choice of shops and schools and entertainment. Being great social equalizers—the road belongs to everybody, and once cars became broadly affordable, previously hard-to-reach destinations and uncommon experiences were within everybody's reach—cars were the key tool of *embourgeoisement* that had sequentially swept the industrializing countries during the 20th century. They were also the keystone machines of 20th-century modernity, the leading prime movers of modern economies, and critical indicators of their performance. By the mid-1920s, the U.S. car industry led U.S. manufacturing in terms of value, and this accomplishment was later repeated in every nation that concentrated on automobile design and production: after Europe, the last wave of the 20th century was the rise of Japanese and then South Korean car making and their determined pursuit of the global market.

Cars, perhaps more than any other machine in history, also became cultural icons, a phenomenon as obvious in the young and expanding United States as it was in old and introspective France (Ross 1996). Their presence permeates modern literature, popular music, and, to a particularly large extent, movies, where cars play roles in both romance and thrills. Their allure combines industrial design, mechanical ingenuity, and perceptions of control, power, daring, and adventure. But these perceptions may be also seen as immature illusions, even delusions, and their combination with alcohol is repeatedly deadly: although down from a peak of about 60%, some 40% of all U.S. traffic deaths are alcohol related. And road rage had become more than an anecdotal phenomenon.

Cars also became prime, and economically and environmentally very expensive, examples of planned obsolescence, embodiments of an enormous waste of resources, and ephemeral showcases of poor taste and ostentatious display. Average longevity of cars has increased with improved quality: in most Western countries, it was between 10 and 15 years during the 1990s, but cars can be built to last 20 (Swedish Volvos average that much) to 25 years (Nieuwenhuis and Wells 1994). Proper engineering should have also facilitated car dismantling, and sensible regulations should have mandated their complete recycling. Moves in both directions came after 1970, but millions of abandoned cars still litter the environment, many in ugly car cemeteries.

Flying, too, has its many *yin-yang* qualities. No other means of transportation has expanded physical horizons and created previously unthinkable personal experiences and business opportunities on scales ranging all the way to intercontinental and global. The annual total of passenger-kilometers flown globally by scheduled airlines rose from less than 100 million during the late 1920s to nearly 1.5 billion in 1939; it surpassed 40 billion in the early 1950s, and then its doubling time averaged less than six years for roughly a 75-fold increase to nearly 3 trillion passenger-kilometers in the year 2000 (figure 6.6; ICAO 1971, 2001). With the introduction of more affordable European flights, many offered by smaller discount airlines, and with the economic rise of East Asia, the U.S. share of this global aggregate declined from 50% during the late 1960s to about 38% in the year 2000.

Intercontinental flight also became a routine experience with steadily declining real costs, as tens of millions of people traveled every year to family reunions, business meetings, or beaches. Although travel on the first generation of jetliners was relatively expensive, it marginalized ship travel on its most

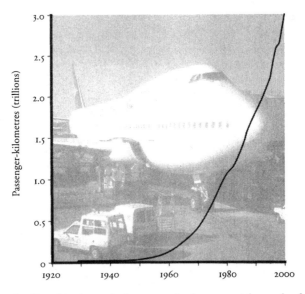

FIGURE 6.6. Semilogarithmic graph shows sustained exponential growth of passenger-kilometers flown worldwide by commercial airlines between 1920 and 2000. Plotted from data in ICAO (2001) and in a number of previous annual ICAO reports.

lucrative crossing in a matter of years: when North Atlantic shipborne passenger traffic peaked in 1957, airlines already carried the same number of people (slightly more than one million), and 10 years later the ratio was better than 10:1 in favor of jet airplanes, about 5.5 million versus 500,000 (ICAO 1971). By the year 2000 discounters offered last-minute trans-Atlantic trips for $100 and trans-Pacific flights from the West Coast for less than $1,000. In contrast, in 1939 one trans-Pacific ticket on the Clipper cost $10,000 (in 2000 US$). As soon as an "exotic" place got a runway that accommodated wide-bodied jets, travel agencies found ways to offer affordable package tours: that is how Bali (Denpasar airport), Mauritius (Seewoosagur Ramgoolam airport), and Fiji (Nadi airport) changed from rarely visited islands to mass tourist destinations.

Negative aspects of this unprecedented mobility include the threat of aircraft hijacking, widespread drug smuggling, and virtually instantaneous diffusion of many infectious diseases. The first two waves of aircraft hijacking were from Castro's Cuba beginning in the early 1960s and the Palestinian attacks of the late 1960s and the early 1970s. Of course, the most deadly of all hijackings—the one that killed nearly 3,000 people, destroyed of New York's World Trade Center, damaged the Pentagon, and caused enormous losses to the U.S. economy—took place on September 11, 2001. By the 1970s airborne drug smuggling evolved into a truly global business, and before the century's end its most profitable routes were Colombian shipments of cocaine and Asian exports of heroine to the two largest markets, the United States and European Union. And rapid airborne diffusion of infectious diseases is particularly worrisome as it reintroduced previously eradicated diseases from the regions where they are still endemic: tuberculosis is the most common example of this risk.

The Electronic World

Four waves of technical innovations that transformed the world of electronics came in progressively shorter intervals: the first wave of electronic devices used vacuum tubes (invented before WWI), and in the United States it crested with mass ownership of radios and with the first generation of television and computers between the late 1930s and the early 1950s. Then, during the mid-1950s, came the first transistorized versions of these devices. During the 1960s the new integrated circuits were not yet used widely in consumer products, but the 1970s saw their widespread diffusion in the form of microprocessors whose cost declined as their increased speeds and lower unit costs allowed for previously unthinkable applications. A multitude of general-purpose as well as dedicated microprocessors had transformed, subtly or radically, nearly every aspect of economic activities and many habits and routines of everyday life.

The pervasive (albeit usually well hidden) presence of microprocessors affected not only every branch of traditional electronics—leading to cheaper, more reliable, and also miniaturized radios, TVs, and recorders as well as to inexpensive long-distance and mobile (cellular) telephony—but also those industrial and transportation techniques and processes that used to be purely mechanical. Microprocessors transformed computers from unwieldy, costly, energy-intensive, and rather inflexible tools of scientific inquiry and business management to common, inexpensive, and continuously evolving personal possessions. During the 1980s their deployment also transformed older electronic designs into affordable, mass-produced personal possessions. These items ranged from PCs to cell phones and from VCRs (Betamax in 1975, VHS in 1976) to CD players and CD-ROMs (both introduced in 1984).

The underlying impulse, the unwavering increase in computing speed, had roughly followed Moore's law, and comparisons are done commonly in terms of flops (floating point operations per second), that is, basic arithmetic procedures done with numbers whose decimal point is not fixed). Depending on the complexity of a task, the head-hand-paper combinations will take mostly between one and a hundred seconds (1–0.01 flop). The best electromechanical machines of the early 1940s could not average more than one flop; a decade later UNIVAC topped 1,000 flops, and by the early 1960s the transistorized LARC reached one megaflop (figure 6.7). Seymour Cray's (1926–1996) first supercomputer, the CRAY-1 completed in 1976, reached 160 megaflops, and three years later the CRAY Y-MP was the first machine to break through one gigaflop. IBM's ASCI Red, the first teraflop (trillion operations per second) supercomputer, was in operation by 1996 at Sandia Laboratory in New Mexico.

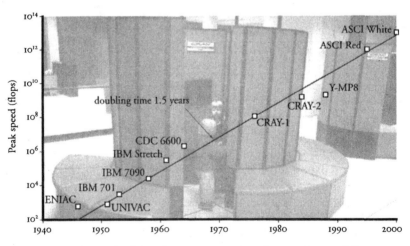

FIGURE 6.7. Peak speed of digital computing increased more than 10 billion times between 1944 and 2000, from less than 1,000 flops for ENIAC to 12 teraflops to IBM's ASCI White. Based on graph in Pulleyblank (2003).

By the century's end the fastest machine, IBM's ASCI White, surpassed 12 teraflops: it was installed at the Lawrence Livermore National Laboratory to do virtual testing of thermonuclear weapons and other complex computations. But at that time much more powerful supercomputers, including Japan's NEC Earth Simulator with 35.86 teraflops completed in 2002, were in design stage, all intended for extremely demanding problems in such fields as hydrodynamics, nuclear fusion, and global atmospheric circulation (Top500 2004). While supercomputers remain reserved for special tasks, inexpensive microprocessors had, as already described, invaded every industrial and commercial niche. Consequences of this transformation were truly magical.

Telephony, the oldest of all personal electrical communication techniques, was made much cheaper and much faster thanks to solid-state electronics. During the late 1990s any one of the world's more than one billion telephones was almost instantly accessible (within seconds and with clarity comparable to face-to-face conversation) from any other machine just after punching about a dozen digits, forming the world's most impressive anthropogenic network (the area code scheme for the entire world was put in place in 1969). Time–space convergence in the electronic universe, the rate at which places approach one another, was complete as there was no significant difference between the time required to get a local connection and to complete the process of automatic switching for a long-distance call—while in 1915 the first U.S. transcontinental call needed five operators and 23 min to arrange.

And although cost–space differentials were not yet eliminated on the global scale, they were gone, or reduced to minima, on many national levels as it was possible to make calls for the same rate regardless of the distance between the parties even within such large countries as United States and Canada. Conversation via Hertzian waves is telephone's dominant role—yet this was not always so as telephones were initially seen only as replacements for telegraph messages, and an analysis of AT&T's advertisements showed that before WWI only a few percent of them featured social uses of the apparatus (Fischer 1997). By the 1930s close to, or more than, half of advertisements promoted sociability; between 1979 and 1984 AT&T's biggest advertising hits were its commercials based on the "Reach out and touch someone" tag line (Massey 2004), and contentless yakking on cell phones was emblematic of the 1990s.

Turning to television, I do not intend to recount the charges against this indubitably addictive medium: "[T]hese spurts of light are drunk in by my brain, which sickens quickly, till it thirst again" (Updike 2003:104). Since the 1950s too much has been already written about biased and manufactured newscasts (who decides what makes news?) and the repeated use of lacerating images and the instantaneous global coverage of violence and catastrophes that creates the impression of unceasing crises. And so perhaps just a single noteworthy addition to that long list of charges: after controlling for other effects, Hu et al. (2003) found that each two-hour increase in daily TV watching was associated with a 23% increase in obesity and a 7% increase in the risk of diabetes.

While TV's cost–benefit appraisals remain highly controversial, there is no doubt that only a few electronic innovations can ever equal the payoff from satellites for communication and Earth observation. Affordable intercontinental calls and (beginning with TIROS 1 in April 1960) more reliable weather forecasting had the most widespread impact, and real-time monitoring of tropical cyclones has prevented many thousands of deaths because early warnings made it possible to safely evacuate low-lying coastal areas subject to sea surges. Satellites also made it possible to monitor the Earth's land-use changes, vegetation, and oceans and to pinpoint locations through the global positioning system (Hofmann-Wellenhof et al. 1997).

During the last two decades of the 20th century, multiple benefits of personal computers have been uncritically extolled by too many irrepressible promoters of high-tech nirvanas and the New Economy. True, by the late 1990s their capabilities were quasi-magical. Any person with a PC (and a credit card) could book a flight without a travel agent's help, send e-mails around the world, read instantly hundreds of newspapers in scores of languages, find air humidity in Tonga and the cost of a ferry from Positano, download one of the classical books from the constantly growing Project Gutenberg, or search databases that contained more than one billion items. Or spend all free time in obscure chatrooms or selecting from hundreds of thousands of books at Amazon.com.

I address the link between computers and economic growth and labor productivity later in this chapter; here I confine myself to a brief annotated listing of things that computers cannot do, and to some undesirable consequences and negative side effects of their use. First, a note about the processing speed: it is obvious that the PCs that were in widespread use during the late 1990s were not 10,000 times faster than the pioneering machines of the late 1970s. Most of the newly available cycles went into delivering lots of features quickly, into integration (universal character sets, drag-and-drop functions, etc.) and compatibility with older hardware and software—and only a factor of 10 went into faster responses (Lampson 2003).

Perhaps the least arguable statement regarding what computers cannot do is that they cannot provide a superior teaching and learning experience (Oppenheimer 1997). This delusion, widely held since the 1980s by many unimaginative experts and by too many American school boards, is just the latest transmutation of the overrated promise of image-driven education: Edison believed that movies would become a superior teaching tool (in 1922 he said that "motion picture is destined to revolutionize our educational system"); during the early 1960s the famous behaviorist B.F. Skinner believed that teaching machines will accelerate learning, and during the 1990s Clinton and Gore believed that computers should be as much a part of every classroom as blackboards. Their goal was largely accomplished—but functional illiteracy and stunning innumeracy in American schools only deepened.

Jumping from K-12 education to graduate studies and scientific research, it might seem gratuitous to stress that while many computer simulations of physical and chemical processes are very faithful replications of complex realities, simulations of social and economic affairs are only as good as their inevitably incomplete and biased inputs. Unfortunately, too many researchers, enamored of their ever more complex models, have been putting too much faith in their creations that will be always subject to the most inexorable of all computer simulation laws (garbage in/garbage out). And when IBM's Deep Blue II beat Garry Kasparov in 1998, many artificial intelligence enthusiasts saw this as a critical milestone in the coming triumph of machines—but as John Casti (2004:680) noted, this "taught us nothing about human thought processes, other than that world-class chess-playing can be done in ways completely alien to the way in which human grandmasters do it."

The environmental impact of computers surpasses that of any manufactured device of comparable mass (Kuehr and Williams 2003). While the production of cars or refrigerators needs fossil fuel that is roughly equal to their mass, a PC needs about 10 times its weight, and also as much as 1.5 t of water. This is not surprising given a large share of such energy-intensive inputs as microchips, rare metals, and plastics. An even greater impact arises from the failure to recycle these machines. Discarded PCs contain relatively large amounts of lead (in cathode ray tubes, circuit-board solder), mercury (in backlighting, boards, switches), beryllium, cadmium (in batteries), hexavalent chromium, and several rare elements (Eu, Nb, Y), and during the late 1990s they were the fastest growing solid waste stream in the United States. This led to their exports to low-income countries and to the first regulations regarding better design, proper disposal, and mandatory recycling.

Finally, a few observations that embrace the entire universe of electronic communication and information. One thing that its expansion did not do (despite repeated predictions of electronic telecommuting) is to make any real dent in the frequency of transportation: in fact, the intensity of travel increased concurrently with the pervasiveness of affordable communication. No less remarkably, the great flood of words and images did not turn out to be a zero-sum affair. In 1950 it would have been logical to expect that radio broadcasters, publishers, and movie producers will struggle as television ownership spreads, and that conclusion would only have been reinforced with the introduction of VCRs, CDs, PCs, and WWW. Yet none of this turned out to be true, at least not in the simplest terms of the overall output. During the 1990s movie attendance increased, newspapers got thicker, and the variety of periodicals and annual totals of new book titles and reprints reached unprecedented numbers.

Unfortunately, as Aldridge (1997:389) noted, this flood led some theorists to leap "from quantitative measurement of the volume of information and the velocity of its circulation to sweeping conclusions about the qualitative changes in culture and society." This is an unfortunate delusion. To begin with, it is unclear how to identify and measure the overall flux of information, and given the quantity of text, data, and images that is now generated, it is unavoidable that the quality and the significance of what is communicated must be rapidly declining. This conclusion is supported by the best available estimates of aggregate global information recordings and flows in 1999–2000 (Lyman and Varian 2003). The grand total of recorded information amounted to at least two exabytes per year, with more than 97% of this put into magnetic storage media: videotapes, digital tapes, computer hard drives, audiotapes, and floppy disks. Most of the rest were photographs and x-rays, while all new printed matter added up to a mere 0.01% (and no more than 0.04%) of the total.

This is not surprising given the high byte density of images—this book's text adds up to about 1.1 MB, which is less than a single high-resolution photograph or 10 s of high-fidelity sound—all it tells us is that we live in a world suffused with images and sound, but even a perfunctory perusal of their bestselling varieties (*National Enquirer*, World Wrestling Federation TV, rap music) makes the inverse relationship between information volume and quality painfully evident. As for the annual information flows, they were at least three times as large as all new information stored on all media, but about 97% of this huge total was due to voice telephone traffic: again, only a delusionary mind could see the largely contentless yammering on cell phones as a sign of enhanced quality.

Person's (1930) observation, made long before it became fashionable to analyze the power of media, provides an apposite ending of these musings. In 1930 he noted that technical advances that "multiplied the number and the variety of stimuli with which the individual may pay" created

> a culture without a unifying dominant interest and without stabilizing patterns of conduct . . . It is causing social forces to become centrifugal instead of centripetal, and the individual's interests and standards of conduct to be conceived in terms of self-satisfaction without a stabilizing sense of group responsibility. (Person 1930:91)

And that was generations before the access to hundreds of cable channels, thousands of rental movies, tens of thousands of chatrooms and blogs, and billions of websites.

Changing Economies

Technical advances have transformed modern economies in many fundamental ways. The three most conspicuous consequences of technical transformations are their indispensable role in raising the quality of life through mass production, their radical restructuring of the labor force, and their critical role in achieving high rates of economic growth. I pay particular attention to several factors that make standard quantifications of such essential concepts as manufacturing, services, gross domestic product, and its growth surprisingly questionable. And I also stress the persistence of major inequalities on both national and global scales: more worrisome than their presence is the fact that in too many cases the gap had actually widened during the 20th century.

And yet there were also matters that were not affected at all by technical advances or that were changed only marginally. Technical transformations did little to eliminate the traditional segregation of occupations by sex: in affluent Western countries, secretarial, nursing, and retail jobs remained overwhelmingly female throughout the century. Nor did they make the fate of businesses less risky and firm management more rational and more predictable, something one might have expected given the vastly increased flow of information and many unprecedented opportunities for its analysis and evaluation. Yet this was not enough to protect even some of the companies that had pioneered entirely new industrial fields or that transformed major segments of modern economies. Unexpected hardships and stunning declines experienced by these firms proved that inventing new keys (or perhaps especially by doing so?) is not enough to open the doors to long-term prosperity.

Mass Production and Innovation

By the century's end we lived in the world that produced annually more than two quintillion bytes of new information and that had more than two billion radios, more than one billion phones, and TVs, more than 700 million motor vehicles and about 500 million personal computers (Lyman and Varian 2003; UNESCO 1999). And also in a world of nearly 30 million kilometers of roads, almost one million kilometers of high-voltage transmission lines, and more than 10,000 jetliners aloft at any given time. Producing these prodigious inventories and emplacing and operating these complex and far-flung infrastructures could not have been done without resorting to mass production, be it of microprocessors or concrete—and the requisite economies of scale would have been impossible without mechanization that culminated in automation and robotization (see chapter 4). Mechanized production clearly favored larger enterprises not only in the manufacturing/fabrication sector but all along the productive chain, starting with agriculture, forestry, and extraction of natural resources and including transportation and distribution of retail items.

Some notable examples of this universal concentration trend are cited throughout this book, so here is just a handful of additional illustrations. A commonly used measure of this process is the four-firm concentration ratio (percentage of the market held by four leading companies), and in the United States of the late 1990s, its highs ranged from 100% for commercial airplanes to about 80% for beef packing and soybean crushing (Heffernan and Hendrickson 2002). Concentration at the global level has been equally high. By the late 1990s a duopoly of Airbus and Boeing made all large jetliners (and another duopoly, Bombardier and Embraer, made all commuter jets) and just three companies (GE, Pratt & Whitney, and Rolls-Royce) supplied all of their engines. Four chipmakers (Intel, Advanced Micro Devices, NEC, and Motorola) made about 95% of all microprocessors, three companies (Bridgestone, Goodyear, and Michelin) sold some 60% of all tires, two producers (Owens-Illinois and Saint Gobain) pressed two thirds of the world's glass bottles, and four carmakers (GM, Ford, Toyota-Daihatsu, and DaimlerChrysler) assembled nearly 50% of the world's automobiles.

This concentration trend did not bypass highly specialized industries or the makers of very small series of products or even unique items, as just one or two, and commonly no more than half a dozen, companies serve the entire global market with their unique assemblies and machines. Japan's Jamco, which dominates the global market for lavatories and custom-built galleys and inserts in commercial jetliners, and the world's largest construction equipment made by Caterpillar (United States), Komatsu (Japan), and Liebherr (Germany) are excellent examples in this category. And the companies that specialized in the worldwide fighting of oil and gas well blowouts (Red Adair of Houston and Safety Boss of Calgary) exemplify the concentration of unusual expertise in the field of uncommon services. Another way to demonstrate high economic concentration is to compare revenues of the world's largest companies with national gross domestic products (GDPs). By the year 2000 GM's annual revenues surpassed $170 billion, and those of GE reached $130 billion: even the lower figure was higher than the aggregate GDP of about 120 of the world's 180 countries!

All innovating industries had to go through distinct stages of market expansion, saturation, maturity, and retreat as their aggregate production rates first tended to rise exponentially and then relatively brief peaks were followed by often rapid declines. These declines were caused by inevitable saturation of respective markets or, even before that could take place, by introduction of new replacement products. The first universal trend can be illustrated by U.S. tractor production, which rose from a few hundred machines a year before 1910 to nearly 600,000 units by 1951 and then declined to fewer than 200,000 since 1969; the second process is exemplified by successive waves of new electronic devices (gramophones, tape decks, CD players) used to play recorded music.

Inevitably, these production waves were reflected in often rapid changes in total employment in the affected manufacturing sectors and in surprisingly high rate of creative destruction: a U.S. study found that between 1987 and

1997, 27% of all plants with more than 10 employees shut down during any five-year period (Bernard and Jensen 2004). Even some of the largest companies found it difficult to maintain their place in the hierarchy of mass production. As noted in chapter 4, the practice of simple mass production of identical copies of items began to unravel more than a generation ago as the overall rise in production volumes had to reckon with the tendency toward shorter product cycles (under the mantra of "new and improved") that affected everything from small household items to expensive electronic devices ("nth generation") and passenger cars (increasingly "loaded"). A single miss of an unpredictable shift in consumer tastes could result in punishing revenue losses—no matter how large or how well established a leading maker may be.

And it is remarkable how many individual inventors or early corporate pioneers that developed major innovations turned to be either outright losers or at best also-runs while nimble marketing made fortunes for latecomers. Lives of quite a few innovators ended in bitter disappointment or marginal existence, some even in suicide. William C. Durant (1861–1947), the founder of GM in 1908, lost, regained, and lost again control of the company and died in 1947 as a manager of a bowling alley in Flint, Michigan. Philo Farnsworth's Radio and Television company could not compete with RCA in developing commercial TV, and after years of patent disputes and business problems, he finally sold out in 1949, depressed, alcoholic, and addicted to painkillers. Edwin H. Armstrong did not get any royalties for his radio FM and ended his impoverished existence in suicide. Many exceptional inventors are remembered only by a small number of experts while their epoch-making ideas served to enrich and aggrandize others.

Nothing illustrates this better than the genesis of DOS, Microsoft's disk operating system. Gary Kildall (1942–1994; figure 6.8) wrote Programming Language/Microprocessor for Intel's 4004, the first microchip released in 1971, and for its successors (8008 and 8080), and in 1973 he and his students at the Navy's Postgraduate School in Monterey, California, created a short Control Program for Microcomputers (CP/M) that made it possible to read and write files from the newly developed eight-inch floppy disk. Later he made it independently installed on the computer hardware by adding a BIOS (Basic Input/Output System) module, and by 1980 more than 600,000 copies of enhanced CP/M were sold by Kildall's Digital Research Inc. (DRI) to operate early PCs by Apple, Commodore, Radio Shack, Sharp, and Zenith.

But Kildall, preoccupied by other projects, was slow in upgrading the system, first for hard disks and then for new 16-bit Intel microprocessors. That is why Tim Paterson of Seattle's Computer Products, a maker of memory cards, decided to write his own CP/M-based operating system for Intel's 16-bit 8086 and spent about two man-months doing so (Conner 1998; Paterson Technology 2004). Paterson's QDOS (Quick and Dirty OS) was released in August 1980, and an enhanced 86-DOS version 1.00 came out in April 1981. Mean-

FIGURE 6.8. Gary Kildall wrote the first control program for microcomputers, and by 1980 its commercial version, CP/M, was the world's most successful operating system. But he did not jump on IBM's offer to supply an operating system for their new PC, a fateful decision that led to Microsoft DOS, its global monopoly, and Gates's wealth. Kildall's photo courtesy of Joe Wein.

while, DRI released its CP/M-86 and IBM began to cooperate with Microsoft on its belated launch of a PC. Microsoft recommended CP/M as the obvious choice, but when IBM approached DRI to get a license, it could not make a quick deal.

As Kildall's former colleague recalls, "Gary was very laid back. He didn't care that much. Dorothy [his former wife] ran the business and he ran the technical side and they did not get on" (Eubanks 2004). Besides, IBM was at that time just one of many companies in the new microcomputer business, and even more important, it was impossible to foresee that it would let its PC design be freely copied, a decision that eventually made the clones, and not the IBM machines, globally dominant. IBM then contracted Microsoft to provide a new operating system, and Microsoft, which never wrote such a software, delivered by simply buying SPC's 86-DOS in July 1981 in exchange for $50,000 and a license, and then renaming it MS-DOS (Paterson Technology 2004). Five years later, after a lawsuit regarding the specifics of that license, Microsoft bought it back for $975,000. The success of IBM's PC and its clones made the upgraded versions of 86-DOS the world's bestselling software, and DRI's last attempt at an operating system comeback, DR-DOS released in 1989, could not survive Microsoft's aggressive marketing.

Paterson eventually rejoined Microsoft as a programmer, but he turned his main attention to off-road racing. His 1997 *Forbes* profile made him sound egomaniacal—"I was 24 when I wrote DOS. It's an accomplishment that probably can't be repeated by anyone ever"—but a year later, talking about the QDOS origins, he was realistic: "I prefer 'original author.' I do not like the word 'inventor' because it implies a certain level of creativity that wasn't really the case" (Conner 1998). Quite: he bought the CP/M manual before he started to write QDOS. Kildall died in 1994, and his former partner's words could be his epitaph: "Gary could have owned this business if he had made the right strategic decisions" (Eubanks 2004). Gates made them instead, and before Microsoft stocks retreated in the 2000, they made him the world's richest man.

No matter that the company's fortune was based on two twice-derived products (what was true about DOS was also true about Windows 1.0, which followed Apple's windows, which were derived from PARC's Star), that its first software, a version of BASIC for Altair in 1976, was itself a derivation of Kemeny-Kurtz innovation, or that its first Internet Explorer was nothing but Spyglass Mosaic (developed at Urbana-Champaign concurrently with Netscape) with some changes. No matter that Microsoft then continued to distinguish itself by a conspicuous lack of originality and by often sloppy software open to hacker attacks. What mattered was that its products were pushed with aggressive alacrity that sprang from arrogance and hostility toward any potential competition and that this predatory monopolistic course was not checked by applying existing laws: yet another victory of adroit marketers over ingenious inventors. And outside of a narrowing circle of people who witnessed or studied the genesis of modern software, nobody now recognizes the name of the man who wrote the first desktop operating system and hence opened the way to the PC era.

Closing decades of the 20th century also had no shortage of failed or struggling corporate innovators and, again, the history of computing offers many examples of the fate common in the early phases of technical revolutions, the demise of pioneers. How many people remember, a generation later, such pioneering microcomputer models as Radio Shack's TRS-80 (with Zilog's Z-80 microprocessor), Sinclair Spectrum, and Commodore PET? More surprising has been the retreat or demise of companies that emerged a long time ago as the winners of innovative contests but, despite their size and experience, could not maintain that leading status. The two most prominent generic examples are the U.S. automobile and aircraft industries. In 1974, when the first oil crisis struck, U.S. automakers had 85% of the North American market. Afterward they could never quite meet the challenge posed by the Japanese companies that mastered and transformed the lessons of U.S. mass production (see chapter 4).

Chrysler survived only thanks to the 1979–1980 federal bailout, and at that time Ford also narrowly escaped bankruptcy. Chrysler was soon again in trouble, and it merged with Daimler-Benz or, more accurately, was taken over by it (Vlasic and Stertz 2000). During the boom years of the 1990s the U.S. car makers came closer to Japan in average productivity and made some big profits on the newly fashionable SUVs, but they continued to lose the market share to Japanese vehicles made in the United States and to Asian imports. The market total for the big three fell from 73% in 1996 to 63% by the year 2000, and the prospects were dim enough to contemplate the end of Detroit (Maynard 2003). As troublesome as this situation was, the U.S. aerospace companies were in even greater disarray. European aircraft makers were the dominant innovators until the early 1930s, but then the U.S. companies took over, first with their iconic commercial designs (exemplified by DC-3) that were exported worldwide and during WWII with their superior fighters and bombers (B-29, B-32).

This strong leadership continued for three decades following WWI, so by the mid-1970s the U.S. aviation industry dominated the global jetliner market, and its military planes were at least a generation ahead of foreign designs (Hallion 2004). But the remainder of the 20th century saw such an appalling decline in the U.S. aerospace industry that a commission convened to deliberate on its future concluded that the country had come dangerously close to squandering the unique advantage bequeathed to it by prior generations (Walker and Peters 2002). By the year 2000 only five major airplane makers remained (from the high of 47 on VJ-Day), the labor force had declined by nearly half during the 1990s, Boeing was steadily yielding to Airbus in the global commercial market, most top-performing military planes (F-16, F/A-18, A-10) had been flying for more than a quarter century, and U.S. rocket engines were outclassed by refurbished Russian designs.

Two high-profile instances that illustrate the impact of rapid technical advances on the fortunes in communication and information business are the cases of AT&T and Xerox. American Telephone & Telegraph was formed in 1885 as a subsidiary of American Bell Telephone in order to develop and operate long-distance telephony, but in 1899 it became the parent of the Bell System (AT&T 2004). An abbreviated list of its remarkable firsts must include transcontinental calls (1915), dial phones (1919), commercial radio station (1922), demonstration of TV (1927), concept of cellular telephony (1947), direct long-distance dialing (1951), trans-Atlantic (1956) and trans-Pacific (1964) telephone cables, communication satellites (1962), the touchtone keypad (1963), electronic call switching (1965), and 911 (1968). Moreover, its famous Bell Labs in Murray Hill, New Jersey, produced seven Nobel Prize winners and a large number of fundamental technical innovations. Without exaggeration, the progress of telephone techniques is the history of AT&T.

The company became a government-sanctioned monopoly in 1913, and it divested itself of all local telephone services only on January 1, 1984, as a result of an antitrust suit launched in 1974. Its post-breakup future seemed assured, and the outlook appeared even better for Lucent Technologies, a spin-off company created in 1996 that included Bell Labs. Values of both companies rose to record highs during the economic bubble years of the late 1990s, to nearly $100/share for AT & T and to more than $60/share for Lucent (which was worth at one time more than a quarter trillion dollars) before their precipitous fall reduced them by, respectively, more than 85% and 95%.

Xerox's prehistory goes back to 1938 when Chester Carlson (1906–1968) began to offer his patented process of xerography to more than 20 companies, including the electronic giants GE, IBM, and RCA: they all turned him down (Alexander and Smith 1988). Finally, in 1944 Batelle Memorial Institute of Columbus, Ohio, agreed to develop the machine, and in 1946 it was joined by Haloid Company from Rochester, New York; the company, renamed Xerox, marketed the first xerographic machine in 1949 but did not produce the first plain-paper copier until 1959. During the 1960s the company's pioneering machines transformed office work and provided a convenient and affordable way for storing and diffusing information. The company's profits allowed it to set up a large research establishment for electronic information and communication techniques: as noted in chapter 5, PARC became a leading innovator in interactive computing, including Robert Metcalfe's design of Ethernet, the first local area network (PARC 2003).

The first system that combined the key components of the modern graphical user interface (GUI)—a mouse, bit-mapped display, and graphical windows—was PARC's Alto completed in April 1973, and the first Alto-based commercial model was the Xerox Star in 1981, which also featured double-clickable icons, overlapping windows, and dialog boxes (figure 6.9). But Xerox did not pursue this innovative advantage, and in 1983, as the late-starting IBM and Apple were claiming the PC business, it diversified instead into financial services (Alexander and Smith 1988). Meanwhile, Japanese copier makers cut its share of the market for its core products, and during the 1990s cheap desktop printers further eroded copier sales. The company's insurance group was finally sold at a huge loss; there were repeated layoffs of thousands of employees, and by the year 2000 the company's stock fell to $7 from the peak of $64 in 1999.

Transformation of Labor

Technical advances of the 20th century brought several universal transformations of labor force: as expected, their onset and rates of change had differed among countries, but no modernizing economy could follow a different path. I illustrate these trends largely with reliable historical U.S. statistics (Fisk 2001). Perhaps the most important change is that child labor, common before WWI, had virtually disappeared in all affluent countries. U.S. federal law prohibits any full-time work for teenagers under the age of 16, whereas in 1900 6% of the labor force, or 1.75 million workers, were children 10–15 years of age (USBC 1975). For example, before Michael Owens invented automatic bottle-making machines (see chapter 4), boys worked commonly in glass-blowing workshop. Owens himself began shoveling coal at age 10, carried the hot glassware at 11, and worked with adult glass blowers since he was 15.

Although he later recalled these early years with fondness, his inventions made such experiences, thankfully, unrepeatable: in 1913 the national Child

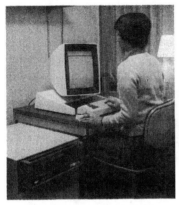

FIGURE 6.9. Alto (left) and Star (right), the two pioneering desktop computers designed by the Xerox PARC in, respectively, 1973 and 1981. Courtesy of Palo Alto Research Center, Palo Alto, California.

Labor Committee credited the machines' rapid commercial acceptance with doing more to eliminate child labor in glass-container plants than it was able to accomplish through legislation (ASME 1983)—and similar effects were seen thanks to mechanization in many other manufacturing industries. While children left the workplaces, women entered the labor market in unprecedented numbers: in the United States only 19% of females of the working age were employed in 1900, compared with 60% in 1999. The dominant nature of their jobs shifted from domestic to public services, and their share in the best-paying professions rose substantially, from 1% to 29% for lawyers and from 6% to 24% for physicians.

As already noted, continuing mechanization and chemicalization of crop farming and animal husbandry kept on releasing the rural labor force until it declined to less than 5% of the total in nearly all Western countries (see chapter 4, and figure 4.1). Shares of workers employed in mining, construction and manufacturing decreased less precipitously, in the United States from the post-WWI peak of about 47% to about 19% in 2000. The manufacturing sector usually gets special attention because it is seen both as a key indicator of a country' technical prowess and as a major source of some of the best-paid blue-collar jobs. Not surprisingly, decline in manufacturing employment is seen to be much more consequential development than job losses in agriculture or transportation. But advancing automation and robotization and the ubiquitous presence of microprocessors in industrial machines transformed the entire manufacturing sector to such an extent that the very term is misleading—many products are not even touched by a human hand before they are shipped to consumers.

More important, if we attribute job losses in manufacturing to automation that is impossible without special microchips and complex software, should not we extend the sector's new definition to embrace custom chip design and code writing? After all, during the last quarter of the 20th century these activities became as indispensable for industrial production as did dexterous manual control of new electricity-driven machines a century ago. Long-term declines in manufacturing employment had differed substantially among the leading economies: the U.S. rate peaked at above 39% right after WWI, its decline was briefly reversed during WWII, and by the century's end the share was just 14%. But in absolute terms U.S. manufacturing employed as many people in the year 2000 as it did in 1965, and more than it did in the early 1940s when 32% of the workforce were in wartime industries.

Moreover, while the annual increase of the overall nonfarm productivity averaged about 2% between 1950 and 2000, manufacturing productivity advanced at 2.9%/year, which means that an hour of factory labor generated about 4.2 times as much value in 2000 as in 1950 (CEA 2000; Cobet and Wilson 2002). This, in turn, increased real wages and improved the country's competitiveness. By these standards even U.S. manufacturing has done rather well, but many people still see the sector's relative decline in employment and the increased manufactured imports as the more important trends. These are emotional matters where economics clashes with national pride and strategy: it is one thing when the world's largest economy loses nearly all of its domestic capacity to make plastic toys or children's shoes, and another thing entirely when it sheds large shares of the labor force in industries that were seen for most of the 20th century as the keystones of economic progress, including steelmaking, automobiles, machine tools, and electronic components.

Technical advances dictated this general outcome: they raised industrial productivity to such an extent that declining employment in manufacturing was inevitable and that increased production (the total value of the U.S. industrial output rose more than 11-fold between 1940 and 2000) could be accommodated without hiring more workers, and higher returns on investment in more capital-intensive sectors mean that affluent countries will inevitably tend to lose many kinds of basic manufacturing to economies at lower levels of overall development. Inexorably, the same trend that worries many people in the United States exacted its toll in Japan, where manufacturing employment was down to about 20% by the year 2000, and in the European Union, where it slipped during the century's last two decades from 37% to less than 25% in Germany and from 27% to less than 14% in the United Kingdom. During the same time, vigorous growth of East Asian exports pushed the manufacturing employment up in China, South Korea, and Malaysia.

With every other sector in decline, services absorbed the growing labor force: in the United States their share rose from 31% in 1900 to slightly more than 80% by 2000, European Union's overall rate in the year 2000 was 68%, and in Japan it was nearly 60%. Expanded governments were an important part of this trend: in the United States their share of the labor force doubled between 1900 and 2000. Service jobs also exemplified the trend toward a more educated labor force and higher investment per worker. In 1900 only one in seven Americans graduated from high school, and only about two out of 100 had postsecondary education; a century later these rates were, respectively, 83% and 25%. Technical transformations also required continuous upgrading of skills and retraining as many job categories were redefined by modern techniques. Drafting and graphic design are excellent examples of this transformation: the work is not done by pencils, pens, and brushes on paper but by mice and electrons on screens. Given such shifts, average capital investment per worker had to rise, and after the 1960s it included not only new hardware but also new versions of the requisite software.

These universal labor transformations brought three fundamental personal benefits to every segment of modern workforce: real wages rose, average work hours declined, and workplace safety improved. In the United States average per capita income (in 1999 US$) was $2,400 in 1900 and $33,700 a century later, and manufacturing wages rose from about $3.50 to $13.90 per hour (Fisk 2001). Pay-offs for higher qualification were substantial: hourly wages of university graduates were 60–65% above those of people with only a high-school diploma. The average workweek in American manufacturing was cut from 53 hours in 1900 to 39–41 hours after WWII, and in retail to only 29 hours (more part-time workers). Declines went even further in Europe: the French working week has been legally limited to 35 hours. Improved workplace safety had already been illustrated by the example of U.S. coal-mining accidents (see figure 4.8), and that improvement is indicative of the general trend toward safer workplaces.

But technical advances did little to eliminate, or even to attenuate, business cycles: in the United States there were 19 of them during the 20th century (USCB 2004). They brought periods of unemployment ranging from very low (between 1900 and 1908 less than 3%, between 1995 and 2000 less than 5%) to very high (in excess of 8% during the recessions that peaked in 1921, 1975, and 1982) and to the record level of about 25% in 1933, the worst year of the Great Depression. What technical advances did—particularly because of inexpensive communication tools that allow instantaneous transfers of complex designs overseas and because of cheap intercontinental transportation—was to extend the potential pool of labor force far beyond the traditional confines. If the conditions are right (above all, political stability and access to containerized shipping), then a multinational corporation can use labor forces in new plants on a different continent more profitably than it has done in its home locations.

Growth, Interdependence, and Inequalities

Desirability of high rates of economic growth became one of the least questioned mantras of good governance. This is not surprising given the nature of compound growth, as even slightly higher average rates make a huge long-term difference: a 2.4% rate will raise total economic product 11-fold in a century; 3% will result in a 20-fold increase. As "healthy" economic growth became one of the best-known indicators of national fortunes, even the otherwise economically illiterate public learned that the GDP measures the aggregate output of goods and services of an economy. Unfortunately, GDP does not make any distinction as to the quality and desirability of its contents.

The aggregate GDP rises as money is invested in more efficient and more profitable ways of industrial fabrication or in measures to reduce soil erosion and hence to improve crop yields or the purity of local water supplies—but it also grows as more asthma inhalers are bought and more emergency hospital visits are made with asthmatic children in cities with high frequencies of photochemical smog, or as more policemen are hired to control violence in ghettoized cities. And, of course, there is no consideration of quality and desirability when quantifying mass production: the GDP grows with goods made by child labor or based on theft of intellectual property rights, with sales of repulsively violent computer games or as psychotic crowds of shoppers fight over a piece of ephemeral junk that somebody declared as the latest must-have gift item.

Despite these shortcomings, long-term GDP trends clearly indicate the overall performance of economies. That is why many economists devoted their time and ingenuity to the reconstructions of past GDPs (or GNPs) for individual nations, why others prepared more or less extensive international comparisons (Bairoch 1976; Summers and Heston 1991; Prados de la Escosura 2000), and why Angus Maddison (1995, 2001) had boldly undertaken the integration of GDP estimates at the global level. These reconstructions (expressed in constant monies) leave no doubt that the 20th century experienced economic growth that was unmatched in history. Maddison's (2001) approximations show the compound growth rates of gross world product (GWP) averaging only about 0.2%/year (0.05% in per capita terms) for the first eight centuries of the second millennium, rising to 0.93% for the 50 years between 1820 and 1870 and to 2.1% between 1870 and 1913. Despite the two world wars and the Great Depression of the 1930s, absolute GWP grew an average of 1.85% between 1913 and 1950, or 0.91% in per capita terms (figure 6.10).

The years between 1950 and 1973 saw unprecedented rates of annual per capita GDP growth on all continents, resulting in a nearly 5% annual rise of the GWP (almost 3% in per capita terms). Rates were generally lower afterward, and average per capita GWP grew by about 1.35% between 1973 and 2000. For the world's largest economies the record during the 20th century

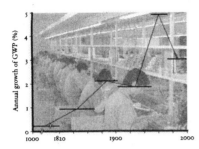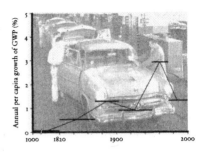

FIGURE 6.10. Average compound rates of growth of world economic product (gross world product, GWP): annual growth (left) and annual per capita growth (right). Plotted from data in Maddison (2001).

was as follows: American per capita GDP increased about eightfold (it doubled between 1966 and 2000), and the average Western European economic product rose about sixfold; Japanese per capita GDP grew about 17 times, with the fastest rate (about 8%) between 1956 (when it surpassed the 1941 peak) and 1973 (when it was checked, as the rest of the world, by OPEC's sudden oil price rise). By far the most impressive achievement during the century's last quarter was post-Mao China's rise, with real per capita GDP quadrupling in a single generation!

But all of these multiples showing the secular rise of per capita GDP or average family income are substantial underestimates of real gains. In 1900 an income eight times larger than the average could not buy the American standard of living in the year 2000 because so many goods and services taken for granted in 2000 did not even exist in 1900. And, as we have already seen with the example of U.S. electricity, its real prices fell by about 98% (factor of 50), but because of huge increases in efficiency, the same monies bought a century later more than 4,000 times more illumination (see chapter 1 and figure 1.5). Even greater multiples would be obtained for electricity that is used to do calculations (large and heavy electromechanical machines of 1900 vs. microprocessors of 2000). Consequently, in many ways the real gains have been practically infinite.

But two serious weaknesses of standard economic accounts make all GDP figures questionable: their exclusion of underground economic activities (which undervalues the actual GDP) and the fact that they ignore cumulative changes in natural assets whose use and environmental services are indispensable for any economy (this omission greatly overvalues the real achievements). While there are serious disagreements about the ways to estimate the size of the black (shadow, underground) economy, there is little disagreement about the fact its share was growing during the last decades of the 20th century (Lippert and Walker 1997). Even conservative estimates put its size at about 15% of officially reported GDP in high-income nations and at one third in low-income countries, with the highest shares in excess of 40% in such countries as Mexico, the Philippines, and Nigeria (Schneider and Ente 2003). The global shadow economy added up to about $9 trillion in 1998 compared to $39 trillion of the world economic product (at purchasing power parity): missing nearly a quarter of all activities, or an output equivalent to another U.S. economy, is hardly trivial!

More fundamentally, standard economic accounts ignore the degradation of the environment caused by human activities and treat the depletion of irreplaceable, or difficult-to-regenerate, natural assets as current income that boosts GDP totals—although it is obvious that no society can keep running down its fundamental natural capital, treat this process as income, and hope to survive for long (Smil 1993). Because macroeconomic growth encroaches on a larger, and obviously limited, whole of the Earth's biosphere, it incurs an opportunity cost that does eventually surpass its marginal benefit (Daly 2001). Daly and Cobb (1989) attempted to capture this reality (ignored by mainstream economics) by calculating a per capita index of sustainable welfare (ISEW) that includes costs of commuting, car accidents, urbanization, water, air and noise pollution, loss of farmland and wetlands, depletion of nonrenewable resources, and an estimate of long-term environmental damages. Their reconstruction showed the U.S. per capita GDP rising slightly more than 20% between 1976 and 1986 but per capita ISEW falling by 10%.

Similarly, a reevaluation of national accounts for Costa Rica found that more than a quarter of the country's economic growth between 1970 and 1989 disappeared when adjustments were made for the depreciation of forests, soils, and fish stocks (Repetto et al. 1991). And my assessment of economic losses attributable to China's environmental degradation showed them to be equal every year to 6–8% of the country's GDP during the early 1990s, or almost as much as the measure's annual growth (Smil 1996). And all of these losses would rise even more by quantifying the value of lost forests as wildlife habitats, tourist attractions, water storages, and repositories of unique biodiversity—and even more so with attempts to quantify the consequence of possibly rapid global warming.

Finding the real rates of growth is thus a surprisingly elusive task. But no matter if GDP growth rates are exaggerated or overcorrected; it is quite clear that a large fraction of the overall increase must be attributed to technical advances. Remarkably, this seemingly obvious conclusion began to be quantified only during the 1950s. Contrary to the common belief that saw the combined input of labor and capital as the key factor in explaining economic growth (Rostow 1990), Abramovitz (1956) demonstrated that since 1870 this combination accounted for just 10% of the growth of per capita output in the U.S. economy. His result for labor productivity growth was similar, with capital per worker-hour explaining just 20% of the total. Technical advances had to be a major part of the residual (known as the total factor productivity), and Solow (1957) came out with a startling attribution: between 1909 and 1949 the U.S. economy doubled its gross output per hour of work, and some 88% of that increase could be attributed to technical changes in the broadest sense, with the higher capital intensity accounting for the small remainder.

The following decades saw many studies elaborating and extending these basic conclusions. Edward Denison published a number of studies designed to identify the components of Solow's broad category. Most important, he found that between 1929 and 1982, 55% of U.S. economic growth was due to advances in knowledge, 16% to improved resource allocation (labor shift from farming to industry), and 18% to economies of scale (Denison 1985). As the last two factors depend on technical advances, Denison's disaggregation implied that at least three-quarters of all growth was attributable to technical innovation. In his Nobel lecture, Solow concluded that "the permanent rate of growth of output per unit of labor input . . . depends entirely on the rate of technological progress in the broadest sense" (Solow 1987:xii). Solow, Denison, and others considered technical change as an exogenous variable: innovators make fundamental discoveries or come up with new ideas that are eventually adopted by enterprises and converted into commercial products or practices.

But such a unidirectional interpretation ignores the learning process and numerous feedbacks that exist in any economy. Arrow (1962) was the first economist to link the learning function with already accumulated knowledge, and during the 1960s others related technical advances to labor resources devoted to R&D. Endogenous models of economic growth, the idea that technical change is induced by previous actions within an economy and not the result of autonomous forces that impinge from outside, became very popular during the 1980s and 1990s (Romer 1990; Grossman and Helpman 1991). These models saw continued increase in the level of resources devoted to innovation as the key factor in continued increase in economic growth.

Solow (2001:14) did not find their key claim—"that the rate of growth of this is a function of the level of that, where 'that' is some fairly simple and accessible variable that can be maneuvered by policy"—persuasive. Others pointed out that the claim is inconsistent with historical evidence. Jones (1995) found that despite a substantial increase in the number of U.S. scientists engaged in R&D, there was no comparable rise in economic growth during the previous 40 years. De Loo and Soete (1999) concluded that the lack of correlation between rising R&D and productivity growth during the post-WWII period was mainly due to the fact that those efforts became increasingly devoted to product differentiation rather than to product or process innovation: this improves the consumer's welfare but has little effect on economic growth. Moreover, R&D expenditures are highly skewed toward a handful of sectors (precision instruments, electrical machinery, pharmaceuticals, chemicals).

David (1990) explained the productivity paradox of the 1980s—the failure of the wave of microprocessor and memory chip innovations to bring about a surge in U.S. productivity—by a historical analogy with the dynamo: electricity generation had little impact on the manufacturing productivity before the early 1920s, four decades after the commissioning of the first power plants. The slowdown in labor productivity growth (to less than 1.5%/year between 1973 and 1995) was eventually reversed, and during the late 1990s it was almost as high (2.5%) as between 1960 and 1973 (USDL 2002). And Landau (2003: 219) turned the basic premise on its head, arguing that "what needs to be explained is not growth but the failure to grow, the failure to engage in the natural process of investment and innovation." I find this search for disaggregating and quantifying the drivers of economic growth and productivity fascinating, but I am not surprised that it has brought so many mixed answers.

Decompositions of the famous Solow residual performed by Denison and others may be inappropriate for drawing any inferences about the underlying causes of economic growth (Grossman and Helpman 1991). Identified factors are not independent entities but rather dynamically linked variables of a complex system, and the exogenous–endogenous dichotomy is to a large extent artificial as both of these impulses are clearly at play. Perhaps the best illustration of these preconditions, interactions, and synergies is the genesis of the proliferating Silicon Valley microelectronic companies that began in September 1957 when eight young scientists and engineers left Shockley Semiconductor (Moore 1994). They pooled $4,000 of their own money, but Sherman Fairchild (1896–1971), inventor of an aerial camera, advanced $1.3 million in order to establish Fairchild Semiconductors (FS). Six months later the new subsidiary made profit by selling custom transistors to IBM; in 1958 came its first planar transistor, and in 1959 Robert Noyce designed the first integrated circuit (see chapter 5).

Key factors that determine the growth of productivity clicked in this case: top education (six of the eight men had a PhD), existence of adequate venture capital and relatively open access to it, innovative drive, willingness to take risks, ability to tap into established commerce and opportunities to create new demand, a legal framework that makes it comparatively easy to set up new ventures, and effective protection of intellectual property. And FS was just the beginning. In 1968 Robert Noyce and Gordon Moore left it to establish Intel Corporation. In 1972 Eugene Kleiner (1923–2003), who helped to arrange the initial FS financing, set up Kleiner Perkins (later Kleiner Perkins Caufield & Byers), the country's leading venture capital firm that helped to create new companies with combined assets in tens of billions of dollars. Eventually at least 200 companies besides Intel (including Advanced Micro Devices and National Semiconductor) were founded by former employees of FS.

Qualitative conclusions regarding the sources of productivity growth thus remain preferable, even more so when one considers the already outlined inherent flaws of aggregate measures of economic performance. Significant shares of modern economic growth must be attributed to narrowly targeted R&D and to endogenous technical innovation in general, and even larger shares are due to broadly conceived technical advances (regardless of their origins) and to such first-order preconditions as the need for a more educated labor force and adequate investment in ancillary techniques (in turn, these factors are stimulated by successful advances). What is much more important is to know if economic growth, regardless of its respective drivers, has done in the long-run what it is expected to do: has it reduced the gap between rich and poor countries, has it helped to eliminate some of the worst income inequalities?

There is no clear-cut answer to these critical questions. Neoclassical growth theory predicts convergence of average per capita incomes around the world, and an unmistakable post-WWII trend toward increasing interdependence of national economies should have accelerated this process. I prefer the term "interdependence" to globalization: not because the latter noun has become so emotionally charged but because interdependence describes more accurately the realities of modern economies that came to rely on more distant and more diverse sources of raw materials, food, and manufactured products and on increasingly universal systems of communication and information processing.

Genesis of this progression in interdependence goes back to the beginning of the early modern world, and the process was accelerated with the expansion and maturation of the British Empire during the 19th century (Cain and Hopkins 2002). During the last generation of the 19th century, food grains (from the United States and Canada) and frozen meat (from the United States, Australia, and Argentina) joined textiles as major consumer items of new intercontinental trade that was made possible by inexpensive steam-driven shipping. By the middle of the 20th century the combination of progressing conversion from coal to liquid fuels and of the highly uneven distribution of crude oil resources elevated tanker shipments to perhaps the most global of all commercial exchanges. But only after 1950 did the trend embrace all economic activities. Inexpensive manufacturing was the first productive segment affected by it, beginning with the stitching of shirts and stuffing of toy animals and culminating, during the century's last quarter, with the assembly of intricate electronic devices.

During the 1990s the level of attendant specialization and product concentration reached unprecedented levels as increasing shares of particular items were originating in highly mechanized assembly plants or in fully automated fabrication facilities located increasingly in just a few countries in East Asia. Microprocessors are the best example of fully automated industrial production, while many electronic products, be they cheap cellular phones or expensive flat computer screens, are among the most prominent illustrations of highly mechanized assembly. And the 1990s was also the first decade when globalization extended into many services. The trend, both extolled and reviled by clashing constituencies of free market promoters and antiglobalization activists, had not run its course. But has it helped to narrow huge income gaps?

Reconstructions of historic data sets and more reliable macroeconomic statistics of the second half of the 20th century made it possible to quantify inequality in global (international) terms, between countries and regions and also within a particular country. Outcomes of these exercises depend on the choice of data and analytical techniques. The simplest approach is to use national averages of GDP or GNP per capita (exchange rated or in terms of purchasing power parity, or PPP) derived from standard national accounts; a more realistic choice is to weigh the national averages by population totals, and theoretically, the most revealing approach is to use average disposable incomes (from household surveys) and their distribution within a country in order to assign a level of income to every person in the world. Comparisons of the best available studies (figure 6.11) show that unadjusted global inequality changed little between 1950 and 1975 but that it subsequently increased, and not only because Africa has been falling behind (Milanovic 2002).

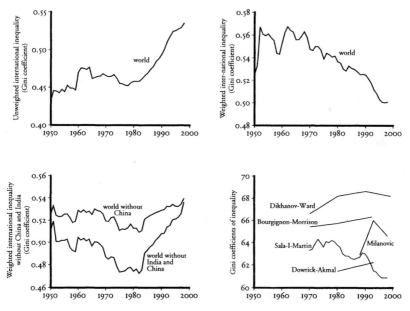

FIGURE 6.11. Four views of global inequality of per capita GDPs and incomes, 1950–2000. Unweighted international inequality (top left) shows considerable divergence; population-weighted assessment (top right) indicates an encouraging convergence, but that trend was almost solely due to China's post-1980 progress (bottom left); and Gini coefficients for evaluations based on income surveys show no clear trend (bottom right). Based on Milanovic (2002).

In contrast, population-weighted calculations show a significant convergence of incomes across countries since the late 1960s—but a closer look reveals that this desirable shift has been entirely due to China's post-1980 gains: weighted analysis for world income without China shows little change between 1950 and 2000. And comparisons of post-1970 studies that use household incomes and within-country distributions indicate only a minor improvement (Sala-i-Martin 2002), slight deterioration, or basically no change (figure 6.11). These disparities are attributable to inaccuracies of different household surveys and to the use of different inequality indexes. Still, a few conclusions are clear. Except for the WWII years, inequality of per capita GDPs among the Western nations has been declining throughout the entire 20th century. As this included the interwar period of reduced internationalization and post-WWII decades of vigorous globalization, the convergence does not appear to be related to openness but rather to rapid application of technical advances that has characterized all Western economies.

As a result, North America and Western Europe have been pulling ahead of the rest of the world. The U.S. GDP per capita was 3.5 times the global mean in 1913, 4.5 times in 1950, and nearly 5 times in the year 2000 (Maddison 2001). Even China's spectacular post-1980 growth did not narrow the income gap with the Western world very much (but China pulled ahead of most of the low-income countries). The obverse of this trend has been the growing number of downwardly mobile countries: in 1960 there were 25 countries whose GDP per capita was less than a third of the poorest Western nation; 40 years later there were nearly 80. Africa's post-1960 economic (and social) decline accounted for most of this negative shift (by the late 1990s more than 80% of the continent's countries were in the poorest category), but, China's and India's progress aside, the Asian situation also deteriorated. Income-based calculations confirm this trend as most global disparities can be accounted for by across-country and not within-country disparities (Sala-i-Martin 2002).

Perhaps the most stunning consequence of these inequalities is "the emptiness in the middle" (Milanovic 2002:92), the emergence of a world without a middle class. By 1998 fewer than 4% of world population lived in countries with GDPs between $(PPP)8,000 and $(PPP)20,000 while 80% were below the threshold. Everything we know about social stability tells us that this is a most undesirable trend. And yet our technical capabilities are more than adequate to secure decent quality of life for the entirety of humanity; our inability to do so is one of the greatest failures of rational governance. In November 1946 George Orwell wondered about this disparity between what was and what could be in one of his incisive "As I Please" *Tribune* essays:

[N]ow we have it in our power to be comfortable, as our ancestors had not . . . And yet exactly at the moment when there is, or could be, plenty of everything for everybody, nearly our whole energies have to be taken up in trying to grab territories, markets and raw materials from one another. (reprinted in Orwell 2002:1137)

There are still many violent (and some seemingly interminable) conflicts in Africa, Asia, Latin America, and even Europe, but during the last half of the 20th century most of our inability to use technical advances for the worldwide provision of decent quality of life had to be ascribed to a multitude of causes. On the one hand are heedlessly wasteful Western lifestyles of excessive consumption; on the other are horrendous corruption and greed of governing elites in most low-income countries and readiness to resort to violence, often ethnically motivated, in many of them. There is also general unwillingness to compromise, cooperate, and (notwithstanding all the talk about sustainability) work within new economic paradigms. But the great and persistent global inequality gap is just one of many risks that modern civilization faces and that raise questions about its longevity.

Levels of Risk

The great pre-WWI technical saltation followed by the advances of the 20th century added entire new categories of risk to the unavoidable threat of natural catastrophes and to historically ever-present dangers of food shortages and famines, tainted water, fatal infectious diseases, and violent conflicts. These new risks included many forms of environmental pollution (ranging from exposures to gases and particulates released by combustion of fossil fuels to contaminated water and long-lasting pesticide residues), the already-described transportation accidents (motor vehicles, airplanes, crude oil tankers), and the chance of major malfunctions of complex technical systems (radioactivity from nuclear electricity-generating plants, failed high-voltage transmission networks instantly depriving tens of millions of people of electricity).

At the same time, the overall level of everyday risks faced by an average citizen of an affluent country had substantially decreased. Famines were eliminated (in fact, overeating became a major risk); safe water became available by turning on a tap (as a result, U.S. cases of typhoid fever fell from nearly 100/100,000 in 1900 to 0.1 in 2000); the incidence of infectious diseases plummeted thanks to the combination of vaccination and antibiotics, better materials, and better emergency responses; and stricter safety rules reduced the frequency and consequences of home and industrial accidents. Yet paradoxically, the emergence of many new risks arising from technical advances and often exaggerated reporting of their possible effects created a widespread impression of having to face a more perilous world. Statistical evidence firmly contradicts this perception. No matter what has been alleged about the perils of persistent pesticides, particulate air pollution, dental amalgam, or low-intensity electromagnetic fields, none of their effects was reflected deleteriously in basic demographic statistics.

Life expectancies at birth kept rising to unprecedented levels (see figure 1.2), overall morbidity rates kept on declining, and when mortalities due to cardiovascular diseases and various forms of cancer are corrected for aging populations, there is no evidence of runaway increases in their frequency, just the opposite: U.S. heart disease mortality was cut in half between 1950 and 2000, and between 1975 and 2000 primary cancers declined in all age groups below 54 years (Ries et al. 2003). Moreover, epidemiological evidence shows that a significant number of these diseases are linked to choice of lifestyle rather than to unavoidable environmental factors caused by technical advances.

Mokdad et al. (2004) estimated that tobacco use, poor diet, inadequate physical activity, and alcohol consumption caused about 900,000 deaths in the United States in the year 2000 compared to 127,000 for all toxic agents, motor vehicle and accidents, and firearm use. Consequently, I do not offer quantifications of major risks arising from technical advances: whatever their undeniable effects may be, they have been more than compensated for by numerous benefits brought by other, or in many cases the very same, modern techniques. I do concentrate on two classes of risks that really matter: violent conflicts and their enormous death toll, and global biospheric change.

Although many accounts must remain imperfect, statistics confirm that in absolute terms the 20th century was by far the deadliest in history, and technical advances greatly contributed to this toll because of the greatly increased destructiveness of weapons used in the two world wars and in hundreds of smaller conflicts. Development of nuclear weapons, enmity between the two superpowers, and tens of thousands of accumulated warheads made the possibility of a massive thermonuclear exchange the most worrisome of all risks the modern world had faced between the late 1950s and the late 1980s. Easing of superpower tensions with Gorbachev's post-1985 reformist policies was followed by the unexpected nonviolent disintegration of the USSR and the end of the Cold War in 1990. But just as the risk of a catastrophic superpower confrontation was receding, new concerns about the global consequences of environmental change began to emerge during the late 1980s.

None of these concerns was as acute as the danger of global thermonuclear war, but all of them could bring unprecedented changes whose eventual consequences were difficult to predict. Resolute attention to one of those changes—loss of stratospheric ozone—and the fortuitous availability of an effective technical solution combined to produce a very rapid response to avert its further destruction by chlorofluorocarbons (CFCs). But this success cannot serve as a model for dealing with an immensely more complex challenge of greenhouse gas emissions whose rising atmospheric concentrations increase the risks of relatively rapid and rather pronounced global warming. There are other major environmental problems—including the loss of biodiversity in general and tropical deforestation in particular, the biosphere's enrichment with reactive nitrogen, and elevated concentrations of tropospheric ozone—but none of them poses as broad and as radical ecosystemic, economic, and social consequences as does the prospect of living on a planet whose average surface temperature could be as much as 5°C warmer in less than 100 years.

Weapons and Conflicts

Explosives of unprecedented power and new weapons to deliver them were first introduced during the two pre-WWI generations (see chapter 4 of *CTTC*). Pursuit of these murderous innovations continued throughout the 20th century when the more advanced designs were augmented by three techniques that further raised the destructiveness of modern warfare: nuclear weapons, and jet and rocket engines (see chapter 2). Consequently, the century saw gains in destructive power even more stunning than the already-cited gains in useful energy controlled by individuals. The kinetic energy of a WWI shrapnel shell was about 50,000 times that of a prehistoric hunter's stone-tipped arrow, but kinetic energy of the largest tested thermonuclear weapon (Soviet 100 Mt bomb in 1961) was 240 billion times that of the gun shrapnel. For the first time in history it became possible to envisage the almost instantaneous death of tens of millions of people. Even a limited thermonuclear exchange (targeting only strategic facilities and no cities) between the two superpowers would have caused at least 27 million and up to 59 million deaths (von Hippel et al. 1988).

This horrifying trend began with Nobel's dynamite and other high-power explosives of the late 19th century. Pre-WWI and WWI innovations included machine guns, tanks, dreadnoughts, submarines, gas warfare, and the first military planes, including light bombers (O'Connell 1989; Waitt 1942). The two interwar decades saw rapid development of weapons that defined WWII: battle tanks, fighter planes, long-range bombers, and aircraft carriers. The war's closing months brought the deployment of two new prime movers (gas turbines and rockets) and the destruction of Hiroshima on August 6, 1945, and of Nagasaki three days later. These horrible innovations were further developed in the context of superpower confrontation. Increased destructiveness of weapons led to much higher combat casualties. When expressed as fatalities per 1,000 men fielded at the start of a conflict, these were below 200 during the Crimean War (1853–1856) and the Franco-Prussian War (1870–1871), but they surpassed 2,000 for both the United Kingdom and Germany during WWI, and during WWII they were about 3,500 for Germany and almost 4,000 for Russia (Richardson 1960).

Civilian casualties grew even faster, and during WWII they reached at least 30 million people or 60% of the 50 million total (White 2003). The most devastating prenuclear techniques of mass destruction could kill as many people as the first atomic bombs (1963). Allied bombing of Germany killed nearly 600,000, and about 100,000 people were killed by nighttime raids by large fleets of B-29 bombers as incendiary bombs were used to level about 83 km2 of Japan's four principal cities between March 10 and 20, 1945 (Odgers 1957). Five months later, two nuclear bombs killed close to 200,000 people in Hiroshima and Nagasaki. Modern wars also caused an enormous economic drain on the warring parties (Smil 2004b).

Total U.S. expenditures (all in 2000 US$) were about $250 billion for WWI, $2.75 trillion for WWII, and $450 billion for the Vietnam War (1964–1972). Peak WWII spending, expressed as a share of national economic product, ranged from 54% in the United States in 1944 to 76% in the USSR in 1942 and in Germany in 1943 (Harrison 1988). And wartime economic losses took a long time to repair; for example, Japan's per capita GDP surpassed its pre-WWII peak only in 1956. Peacetime expenditures on military were also large. The highly militarized Soviet economy was spending for decades on the order of 15% of its GDP on the development of weapons and on its large standing army, border guard, and paramilitary forces. In contrast, the U.S. defense spending reached nearly 10% of GDP during the peak year of the Vietnam War (Smil 2003).

The two world wars stand out because of their combat casualties (nearly 9 and 20 million) and total deaths (approximately 15 and 50 million) and because they involved all major military and economic powers in conflicts whose outcomes shaped so much in modern history—but the century's most regrettable statistic is the never-ending list of other armed conflicts. Detailed compilations show that interstate and civil conflicts that caused the death of more than about 30 people had roughly the same frequency (20–40 per decade) during the first half of the 20th century and that the frequency of interstate conflicts fell to about 10 per decade by the 1990s while the civil conflicts peaked at nearly 80 during the 1960s and then leveled off at about 50 per decade (Brecke 1999). The duration of major conflicts ranged from days (Arab-Israeli Six Day War of June 1967) to decades (Sudan's civil war started in 1955 and was not over by 2000), and the deadliest of them claimed millions of lives: Vietnam (Second Indochina War, 1964–1973) about 3.5 million, and Korea (1950–1953) about 2.8 million (White 2003).

Technical advances also made it much easier, and very affordable, to use small arms—assault rifles (Russian AK-47, U.S. M-16, Israeli Uzi), hand grenades, mortars, and land mines—in order to wage new total wars where gratuitously destruction, looting, burning, absence of any sanctuaries, and indiscriminate killings are the norm (figure 6.12). During the 1990s nearly 100 countries were producing small arms, and the decade saw more than 100 largely small-weapons conflicts. Their extraordinary brutality was shown with the

FIGURE 6.12. These mass-produced assault rifles—Russian AK-47 (top), U.S. M-16 (middle), and Israeli Uzi (bottom)—became the weapons of choice in scores of the conflicts during the last quarter of the 20th century, when they killed more people than did the two nuclear bombs dropped in Japan in August 1945. Reproduced from weapon catalogues.

most devastating effects in Afghanistan, Angola, Bosnia, Chechnya, Colombia, Congos, Eritrea, Ethiopia, Haiti, Liberia, Rwanda, Sierra Leone, Sudan, and Uganda (Boutwell and Klare 2000).

And even after the killing sprees are over, more than tens of millions of mines that are in place in some 40 countries, many of them hard-to-detect plastic varieties made in colors and shapes that help them to blend with the background, continue killing and maiming: at a worldwide rate of more than 15,000 a year during the late 1990s (Strada 1996). And technical advances also made it much more deadly, and much easier, for terrorists to strike at their targets. A suicide bomber whose belt contains a few kilograms of high explosives (RDX, often spiked with metal bits) unleashes about 50 times more explosive energy than a TNT-filled grenade thrown into a crowd. And car bombs can be 10–20 times more devastating than a suicide bomber. These devices—able to destroy massive buildings and kill hundreds of people (as they did at the U.S. Marine base in Lebanon in October 1983 or at the Murrah federal building in Oklahoma in May 1996)—are made from the mixture of ammonium nitrate, a commonly solid fertilizer that can be purchased, or stolen, at thousands of locations around the world, and fuel oil that is even more widely available.

Technical advances thus clearly provided new, more affordable, and readily accessible weapons with which to carry on old dreams of aggression, revenge, or aimless brutality. At the same time, nuclear weapons clearly acted as an effective war deterrent, and a major, but hardly noticed, landmark was passed in 1984 as the major powers of the affluent world had managed to remain at peace with each other for the longest continuous stretch since the emergence of nation states in Europe more than a millennium ago (Mueller 1989). And by the century's end, the probability of a major war between any two (or more) leading economic powers—United States, European Union, Japan, China, and Russia—became comfortably negligible. While smaller (and often extremely violent) conflicts continued to erupt, affluent countries became more concerned about very different risks that could undermine their future, about the changing biosphere.

Global Environmental Change

Human actions were shaping the Earth's envelope of life long before the beginning of recorded history, and centuries of pre-industrial agriculture, slow urban expansion, expanding metallurgy, shipbuilding, and artisanal manufactures had left many locales and even extensive regions scarred with excessive soil erosion, deforestation, landscape degradation, and air and water pollution (Krech, McNeill, and Merchant 2004). The great technical saltation of the two pre-WWI generations began to change the magnitude of these impacts as the total number of localities that were seriously affected by some kind of environmental degradation multiplied rapidly, and as previously localized impacts began to spread to entire urban and industrial areas.

Two key contrasts illustrate this quantitative jump. In 1860 global coal extraction reached about 100 Mt; by 1913 it surpassed 1 Gt. In 1860 the most intensive point users of coal were the largest blast furnaces that consumed less than 200 t of coke a day; by 1913 a large electricity-generating plant was burning daily more than 1,000 t of coal in its boilers. But, as detailed in chapters 2 and 3, these were just the beginnings: technical transformations of the 20th century increased such performances commonly by more than order of magnitude. More worrisome has been the emergence of two kinds of global environmental changes. The first category includes problems that affect nearly every major region of the inhabited world and have many ecosystemic and socioeconomic impacts—but whose progression in one region has little or no direct impact on a situation elsewhere: excessive soil erosion, depletion of aquifers, deforestation, and irrigation-induced salinization are among old environmental problems that were elevated by technical advances into this new category.

The worldwide presence of countless bits of degradation-resistant fragmented plastic found in the oceans and marine sediments (Thompson et al.

2004) and contamination of biota with leaded gasoline exemplify new 20th-century additions. As noted in chapter 4, in 1921 Thomas Midgley (see figure 4.12) solved the problem of knocking in internal combustion engines by adding tetraethyl lead to gasoline, and fuel with this additive went on sale in 1923. By the early 1970s every large urban area with high vehicular traffic had elevated lead levels as well as recurrent periods of photochemical smog, high levels of sulfur dioxide, acid precipitation, and most likely also inadequately treated (or untreated) waste water and problems with the disposal of solid waste that included higher shares of plastics.

Many of these global problems were effectively eliminated or reduced to tolerable levels by technical fixes. In the United States the phasing out of leaded gasoline began in 1975; catalytic converters cut dramatically the precursor emissions of photochemical smog; the switch to low-sulfur fuels and flue gas desulfurization of large power plants cut sulfur dioxide levels and began to lower the precipitation acidity; better water treatment techniques and recycling of many solid waste products became compulsory in many places. Similarly, a mixture of unchecked impacts and effective local and regional improvements marked such nonurban problems as soil erosion and deforestation. But the closing decades of the 20th century brought the second category of global environmental problems, whereby anybody's actions anywhere are eventually translated into biospherewide impacts that could alter the fundamental biophysical parameters within which any civilization has to operate.

By far the most worrisome challenges in this new category are the destruction of stratospheric ozone and human interference in global cycles of carbon and nitrogen (Smil 2002). The ozone saga begins again, incredibly, with Thomas Midgley. Unlike the choice of a lead compound for gasoline (its toxicity was well known, and Midgley himself had lead poisoning in 1923), Midgley's selection of CFCs as perfect refrigerants made impeccable sense (Midgley and Heene 1930). These compounds were not only inexpensive to synthesize but also, unlike previously used gases that included ammonia and carbon dioxide, completely inert, noncorrosive, nonflammable, and nontoxic (figure 6.13). This combination made them a perfect choice for household refrigerators and air conditioners, and later also for aerosol propellants, as foam-blowing agents, and for cleaning electronic circuits and extracting plant oils (Cagin and Dray 1993).

What was totally unsuspected for some four decades after their introduction is that, once these gases reach the stratosphere (they are much heavier than air, but turbulent mixing will eventually transport them in small concentrations higher than 15 km above the ground), they can be dissociated there by light wavelengths (between 290 and 320 nm, the ultraviolet B [UVB] part of the spectrum) that are entirely screened from the troposphere by the stratospheric ozone. This breakdown releases free chlorine atoms, which then break down ozone (O_3) molecules and form chlorine oxide (ClO); in turn, ClO reacts with

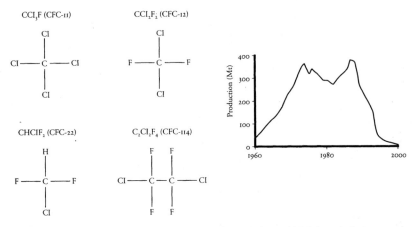

FIGURE 6.13. The four most common chlorofluorocarbons (CFCs) and their annual global production, 1960–2000. Annual production is plotted from data from the Alternative Fluorocarbons Environmental Acceptibility Study.

oxygen to produce O_2 and frees the chlorine atom. Before its eventual removal, a single chlorine atom can destroy on the order of 10^5 O_3 molecules. This destructive sequence was outlined for the first time by Molina and Rowland (1974), but its confirmation came only in 1985 from the British Antarctic Survey base at Halley Bay, Antarctica, where measurements showed that the lowest spring (October) O_3 levels had declined by about a third (Farman, Gardiner, and Shanklin 1985).

The continuing decline of stratospheric ozone and its possible extension beyond Antarctica posed some very serious concerns. Complex terrestrial life developed only after the oxygenated atmosphere gave rise to a sufficient concentration of stratospheric ozone that prevented all but a tiny fraction of UVB radiation from reaching the biosphere. Without this molecular shield, productivity of phytoplankton, the base of complex marine food webs, would decline, crop yields would be reduced, and both humans and animals would experience higher incidences of basal and squamous cell carcinomas, eye cataracts, conjunctivitis, photokeratitis of the cornea, and blepharospasm as well as effects of the immune system (Tevini 1993). That is why the annual, and more pronounced, recurrence of what became known as the Antarctic ozone hole led to rapidly concluded treaties aimed at cutting and then eliminating all CFC emissions (figure 6.13) and replacing them by less dangerous hydrochlorofluorocarbons (UNEP 1995).

Because of their long atmospheric lifetimes, CFCs' stratospheric effects will be felt for decades to come, but atmospheric concentrations of these compounds have been falling since 1994, and the stratosphere may return to its pre-CFC composition before 2050. Just as this concern eased, a relatively rapid anthropogenic change of the Earth's radiation balance caused by rising concentrations of anthropogenic greenhouse gases began to be widely recognized as perhaps by far the most worrisome environmental challenge in history. The greenhouse effect is indispensable for life: if several atmospheric gases (mainly water vapor, CO_2, and CH_4) were not selectively absorbing some of the outgoing radiation (before reradiating it both down- and upward), the Earth's surface temperature would be 33°C colder, and there could be no liquid water.

Yet water vapor, the most important greenhouse gas, cannot act as the temperature regulator because its changing concentrations amplify any departures from long-term equilibrium: water evaporation declines with cooling and rises with warming. Moreover, changes in soil moisture have little effect on chemical weathering. Only long-term feedback between CO_2 levels, surface temperature, and the weathering of silicate minerals explains a relative stability of tropospheric temperatures (Berner 1998). Atmospheric CO_2 levels are now known accurately for the past 740,000 years thanks to the analyses of air bubbles from ice cores retrieved in Antarctica (Petit et al. 1999; EPICA 2004). This record shows that during all of recorded history, before the beginning of fossil-fueled era, CO_2 levels had fluctuated within a very narrow range of 250–290 ppm (figure 6.14).

Accelerating combustion of fossil fuels pushed the concentration to about 320 ppm by 1958, the year when continuous CO_2 measurements began in Hawaii and at the South Pole (Keeling 1998). Such monitoring was later extended to other locations and other gases, including methane, nitrogen dioxide, and CFCs. By the year 2000 Mauna Loa's mean CO_2 levels surpassed 370 ppm, a more than 30% increase in 150 years (figure 6.14). The combined effect of all anthropogenic greenhouse gases had already burdened the troposphere with an additional 2.8 W/m^2 by the late 1990s (Hansen et al. 2000). This is equivalent to little more than 1% of solar radiation reaching the ground. Fur-

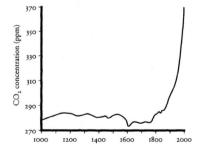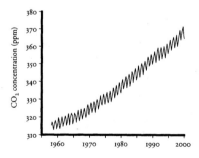

FIGURE 6.14. Atmospheric CO_2 levels derived from air bubbles in the Antarctic ice (1000–1958), and concentrations of the gas from continuous monitoring at Mauna Loa (1958–2000). Plotted from data from the Carbon Dioxide Information Analysis Center at Oak Ridge National Laboratory.

ther increases would eventually double the pre-industrial greenhouse gas levels and raise the average tropospheric temperatures by 1.4–5.8°C above the 2000 mean.

Much remains uncertain, many outcomes are disputed, and key points of broad scientific consensus on all of these matters are best summarized in the latest report by the Intergovernmental Panel on Climatic Change (Houghton et al. 2001). The warming would be more pronounced on land and during nights, with winter increases about two to three times the global mean in higher latitudes than in the tropics, and greater in the Arctic than in the Antarctic. Its major impacts would include intensification of the global water cycle, changed precipitation, higher circumpolar runoffs, later snowfalls and earlier snowmelts, thermal expansion of seawater and gradual melting of mountain glaciers leading to appreciable (up to 1 m) sea-level rise, changed photosynthesis and shifts of ecosystemic boundaries, and poleward extension of some tropical diseases.

These possible threats generated an enormous amount of research and a great deal of policy debates, but the challenge cannot be tackled without limiting, and eventually replacing, the energetic foundation of modern civilization. Because of the rising combustion of fossil fuels, annual CO_2 emissions rose from less than half a gigatonne of carbon (0.5 Gt C) in 1900 to 1.5 Gt C in 1950, and by the year 2000 it surpassed 6.5 Gt C, with about 35% originating from coal and 60% from hydrocarbons (Marland et al. 2000). There was also a net release of 1–2 Gt C from the conversion of natural ecosystems, mainly from tropical deforestation. In addition, methane levels have roughly doubled since 1860. The main anthropogenic sources of methane are anaerobic fermentation in landfills and rice paddies, ruminant livestock, and direct emissions from coal mines, natural gas wells, and pipelines (Warneck 2000).

Human interference is relatively much more intensive in the global nitrogen cycle than in carbon's flows. During the 1990s losses of nitrogen from synthetic fertilizers and manures, nitrogen added through biofixation by leguminous crops, and nitrogen oxides released from combustion of fossil fuels added up to about as much reactive nitrogen as the element's total mass fixed by terrestrial and marine ecosystems and by lighting (Smil 2002). In contrast, carbon from fossil-fuel combustion and land-use changes is equal to less than 10% of the element's annual photosynthetic fixation. But various impacts of this interference—nitrogen enrichment of aquatic and terrestrial ecosystems, water pollution, contributions to photochemical smog and acid precipitation—do not pose such a large array of risks as does relatively rapid planetwide climate change.

〜 7

A New Era or an Ephemeral Phenomenon?
Outlook for Technical Civilization

> "Where are you riding to, master?" "I don't know," I said, "only away from here, away from here. Always away from here, only by doing so can I reach my destination." "And so you know your destination?" he asked. "Yes," I answered, "didn't I says so? Away-From-Here, that is my destination."
>
> Franz Kafka, "Das Ziel" (1922)

Unavoidable natural catastrophes—whose ever-present risk I noted at the beginning of this book and whose consequences could imperil, or even destroy, any civilization—are not, fortunately, all that common. Although there is nothing regular about those phenomena, their recurrence is on the order of once every ten thousand to one million years, compared to less than the 10,000 years that have elapsed since the beginning of settled human cultures. Consequently, there is a very high probability that we could double, triple, or even

FRONTISPIECE 7. We have no clearer idea of the world in the year 2100 than we had of the world of the year 2000 in 1913, when *Scientific American* (in its July 26 issue) published this cover illustration of elevated sidewalks that "will solve city transportation problems" as each kind of transport "will be then free to develop itself along its own lines." But during the course of the 20th century, rather than elevating sidewalks, we had elevated highways, and railways and in many cities the situation is exactly the *reverse* of this image.

quadruple the span of the recorded history without encountering any extraordinary volcanic eruptions or asteroid impacts. Yet this is not as comfortable as it might seem, as there are other perils that pose increasing risks to long-term survival of a civilization that is based on high energy flows and mass consumption. As explained chapter 6, we were able to identify and rapidly reduce one of those dangers (reduction of stratospheric ozone by CFCs), but so far, we have no clear global strategy to deal with the potentially enormously disruptive risk of rapid global warming.

There are many nonenvironmental concerns besides Islamic terrorism and running out of cheap crude oil, the two challenges that preoccupied the affluent world during the first years of the 21st century. Persistence, and indeed an increase, of economic inequality (see chapter 6) is a major cause of political instability, and if it were to intensify it could become a growing source of violence, anarchy, and new failed states. New infectious diseases and the virtual inexorability of the reprise of such pandemics as the great influenza of 1918 (Collier 1996) obviously pose greater dangers in the world of more than six billion people, mass intercontinental travel, and containerized transport than they did on a less populous and much less interconnected planet. And during the 21st century we will have to rely more on solar energies that have much lower power densities than do fossil fuels and are produced with much lower net energy returns (Smil 2003). This inevitably protracted and complex transition will affect every infrastructure, process, and habit that was created by the enormous fossil-fuel flows of the 20th century.

Concatenations of these and other worries make for very scary, yet not implausible, scenarios. Think, for example, of increases of terror attacks, crude oil prices, pandemic viruses, nuclear proliferation, and global surface temperatures taking place alongside steep declines of net energy ratios of energy production and global biodiversity and accompanied by climate change whose progress would be faster than at any time in history. Consequently, one of the most fascinating questions to be asked about humanity's prospect is simply this: have the last six generations of great technical innovations and transformations been merely the beginning of a new extended era of unprecedented accomplishments and spreading and sustained affluence—or have they been a historically ephemeral aberration that does not have any realistic chance of continuing along the same, or a similar trajectory, for much longer?

Contrasting Views

Some techno-optimists have no doubt about prospects for the future: "We are convinced that the progress of the 20th century is not a mere historical blip but rather the start of a long-term trend of improved life on earth" (Moore and Simon 1999:7). Several facts bolster their case. To begin with, correction or elimination of enormous inefficiencies and irrational policies could extend benefits of technical advances to billions of people without any new, untried techniques. More important is the well-documented recurrent and profound underestimation of human inventiveness and, even more so, of our adaptability. New anthropological evidence indicates that, in contrast to all other organisms, including our much less encephalized hominin ancestors, humans have evolved not to adapt to specific conditions but to cope with change (Potts 2001).

In contrast to optimistic views of a future that is elevated by technical advances, there is a long, and continuously flourishing, tradition of highlighting the negatives and unforeseen consequences of technical change, which is never seen as real progress. These writings range from Jacques Ellul's eloquent condemnations of *la technique* (Ellul 1964, 1990) and enumerations of deleterious side effects and costly surprises (Tenner 1996) to arguments about the limits of technical efficiency and diminishing returns of technical innovation (Giarini and Loubergé 1978). In Ellul's bleak view, technical advances bring consequences that are independent of our desires, leaving no room for moral considerations, no choice but "all or nothing": "If we make use of technique, we must accept the specificity and autonomy of its ends, the totality of its rules. Our own desires and aspirations can change nothing" (Ellul 1964:141).

And environmental costs of creating fabulous new opportunities and rising incomes have been high not only in the case of classical heavy industries but also with the latest high-tech endeavors. No other place exemplifies this better than Santa Clara County, south of San Francisco. Until the early 1950s this was one of the country's richest agricultural areas, with highly fertile alluvial soil and climate ideal for fruit: it produced nearly half of the world's prunes, apricots, and cherries, and people came to admire some eight million blooming trees in the world's largest near-continuous orchard spread over more than 50,000 ha (Sachs 1999). This Valley of the Heart's Delight was transformed into Silicon Valley, the paragon of the late 20th century's technical progress and an area with one of the highest per capita incomes in the world. But the price of this achievement was destroyed orchards, the densest concentration of hazardous waste dumps in the United States, polluted aquifers, shellfish contaminated by heavy metals, near-continuous ugliness of thousands of nondescript buildings housing electronics companies, exorbitantly priced inadequate housing, and chronic traffic congestion.

As different as they are, these opposite reactions to technical advances share two traits with the tenets of bizarre Pacific cargo cults that expect goods to descend from heavens and to change everything. Both of these beliefs—in autonomous technical advances that exert either uplifting (*pace* Simon) or downgrading (*pace* Ellul) powers—err by exaggerating the impacts of technical innovations. Techno-optimists and techno-utopians see them as solutions for even the most intractable problems (Simon and Kahn 1984; Segal 1985; Bradley

2000). The latest manifestation of this delusion involved the Internet: previously both telegraph and radio were initially expected to reduce or eliminate conflicts as they promoted better communication, and Michael Dertouzos (1997) of MIT succumbed to a similar wishful thinking when he saw the Internet as a tool that may bring "computer-aided peace." At the same time, critics see technical advances as a source of unpredictable problems, as destroyers of the best human qualities and despoilers of natural environments (Braun 1984; McKibben 2003; Lightman, Sarewitz, and Desser 2003).

Realities are much more complex. Many innovations arise organically, and seemingly inevitably, from previous accomplishments, but generally there is nothing automatic about the process, and there are many examples of unfulfilled expectations and failed cargo deliveries. After half a century of promises, we are still waiting for true artificial intelligence, for nuclear electricity that is too cheap to meter, for energy from fusion, and for victory over viruses and cures for common cancers. On the other hand, there have been many technical advances whose truly miraculous nature, from the late 19th century point of view, has vastly outweighed any undesirable side effects. Electricity did not do away with economic cycles, and electronic communication did not eliminate conflicts, but how many of us—even when mindful of air pollutants from fuel combustion, electromagnetic fields along high-voltage transmission lines, or risks of electrocutions—would volunteer for a nonelectric economy and pre-electronic society?

And as much as I like some of Ellul's penetrating criticisms of *la technique*, I think he is wrong when he concludes that human desires and aspirations are powerless against the inexorable, self-augmenting progression of technical advances. Sensible public policies (still too rare, admittedly) have stopped several advances that 20–30 years ago were seen by many experts as near-certainties by the century's end and that received temporarily large government funding; the most prominent items on this list are intensive manned exploration of Mars, large-scale supersonic air travel (the Concorde remained an expensive oddity with a limited service), mass extraction of crude oil from shales, and accelerated development of nuclear breeder reactors (Smil 2003).

And even the most destructive technical advances were not responsible for the worst death tolls of the 20th century. Horrific as their contribution was, technical innovations were not the leading cause of what Rhodes (1988) labeled "public man-made death" and what he called perhaps the most overlooked cause of 20th century mortality. Most of the 160–180 million people who died were not killed by nuclear bombs, napalm, or air raids but by ageless disdain for life, hatred, cold, disease, or lack of food or medical care. History's largest famine caused by Mao's economic delusions killed at least 30 million Chinese between 1959 and 1961 (Smil 1999); Stalin's long reign of terror (1924–1953) cost at least 20 million but possibly as many as 40 or even 60 million lives (Solzhenitsyn 1973–1975; Medvedev 1972).

During the late 1970s some 20% of Cambodia's people (about 1.7 million) died because of Pol Pot's creation of a new society; between 1915 and 1923 some 1.5 million Armenians died in Turkey just because they were Armenians, and for the same reason 1.2 million Tutsis and Hutus were hacked to death or shot in Rwanda and Burundi between 1959 and 1995 (White 2003). And Mesquida and Wiener (1999) demonstrated that a key human factor that is responsible for violence and that is highly correlated with a society's chance to be involved in a conflict is simply the ratio of young (15–29) men in a country's population. Evolutionary psychology thus provides a better explanation for the genesis of killings than does the availability of weapons: as the share of young men in a population declines, the weapons of any kind stay unused.

Human evolution has been always contingent on complex unfolding and synergy of many factors, and although technical evolution undeniably has its special dynamism, it is not exempt from this general rule. Twenty years ago, when I was writing a book on complex interplays of modern realities, myths, and options, I chose to end it by a backcasting exercise, by describing the world of the early 1980s through the eyes of the early 1930s. I concluded that "there is no reason to believe that the next fifty years will see changes less profound and less far-reaching," that we cannot foresee the totality of these changes, that the effects of the unpredictable will remain strong, and that "this uncertainty cannot be shed: it is the quintessence of the human condition" (Smil 1987:348).

These lasting realities mean that tomorrow's technical advances may lead us into a civilizational *cul-de-sac*, or, after a period of stagnation, their new wave can be generated by a non-Western society. Jacob Bronowski (1973:437) closed his sweeping examination of human history by concluding that humanity's ascent will continue:

> But do not assume that it will go on carried by Western civilisation as we know it. We are being weighed in the balance at this moment. If we give up, the next step will be taken—but not by us. We have not been given any guarantee that Assyria and Egypt and Rome were not given. We are waiting to be somebody's past too, and not necessarily that of our future.

Siding with Bronowski, I would just note that six generations is not enough time to embed any long-lasting automatism that will self-perpetuate for centuries. The era of astonishing technical innovations energized by fossil fuels and electricity has been a very short one when compared to tens of thousands of years that our species had spent in paleolithic foraging (circumscribed by the deployment of nothing but somatic energy and fire for warmth and primitive cooking), or the thousands of years it lived in traditional societies based on biomass fuels, animate energies, and a limited array of simple mechanical devices. The era's brevity is even greater when one dates it not from its genesis during the two pre-WWI generations but from the time when the great innovations had spread sufficiently in order to benefit majorities of industries and households in the innovating nations.

Many statistics illuminate the recent nature of affluent societies that were created by technical advances. For example, in 1900 only 8% of American households were connected to electricity or telephone networks, fewer than 15% had a bathtub and indoor toilet, but 40% of them had incomes below the poverty line (USBC 1975; USCB 2004). The European situation was in some ways distinctly premodern even after WWII. In 1954 a French census showed only a quarter of homes with an indoor toilet and just 10% with a bathtub, shower, or central heating (Prost 1991). At that time even a lengthy interruption of electricity supply in most European cities would have made no impact on cooking or heating (done by coal, or wood stoves), access to money or shopping (all transactions were in cash, and there were no electronic registers).

As for transportation, the entirely car-dependent structure of U.S. cities is largely a post-1960 phenomenon, while in most European countries more distance was covered by bicycles than by cars until the 1950s; for example, the break-even point in the Netherlands was reached only in 1962 (Ploeger 1994). In the same year still fewer than 10% of French homes had a telephone (and new subscribers had to wait one and a half years to get it), and on July 10, 1962, the first intercontinental TV transmission took place: *Telstar I* sent a black-and-white picture of the U.S. flag flapping in a Maine breeze; two weeks later it carried the first live images (including the Statue of Liberty and the Sistine Chapel) between the United States and Europe. And, of course, the world of complicated electronics could come about only after transistors were miniaturized and crowded as microprocessors onto slivers of silicon, that is, after the early 1970s.

Consequently, even in the world's most affluent countries, most people have enjoyed a large range of these advances, now taken so much for granted, only for two generations, a historically ephemeral span. And if we were to specify the beginning of technically advanced civilization only from the time when its benefits embraced more than half of the humanity, then—even if our criteria include just such basic quality-of-life indicators as average longevity in excess of 60 years, adequate food supply in excess of 2,600 kcal/day, and basic schooling—the new age would have begun, largely thanks to China's accomplishments, only during the 1990s. And if we assume that the era begins only once an attenuated replication of Western means reaches at least half of the world's population, then its onset may be still more than half a century away.

Given these realities, any forecasts of the long-term course of high-energy mechatronic civilization might be as informed, and as reliable, as projections about the long-term prospects of steam engines made during the 1830s, six generations after Newcomen's first clumsy designs and just as the machine began to conquer both land and waterborne transportation. You know the outcome: during the following six generations even the most advanced steam engines became rare museum pieces. The same may happen within a century to our microprocessors or gasoline-fueled vehicles. But, unless one believes that technical progress is an inexorably autonomous process, this ignorance cuts also the other way: we may, as Bronowski put it, give up and find ourselves on a regressive course. What would matter most then would be the rate of decline, but chances are that it would not be a slow unraveling akin to the centuries-long demise of the Western Roman Empire.

Magnum mysterium of unknown tomorrows remains as deep as ever: despite our armies of scientists and engineers, our observational and analytical capabilities, complex computer models, think tanks, and expert meetings, we have no clearer idea of the world at the end of the 21st century than we had of the world of the 1990s in 1900. We can only ask all those fascinating questions. Has the era of ingenious machines, ever more accomplished techniques, and complex interconnections been nothing but a historically ephemeral phenomenon—or have we lived in a mere prelude to even more impressive accomplishments? Did its genesis during the two pre-1914 generations see the peak of hopes that were subsequently crushed by world wars and then, after a short post-WWII interlude, darkened by the growing realization of the possibly irreparable harm that technical advances inflict on the biosphere? Will this complex, high-energy, machine-dependent civilization survive the 21st century?

We cannot know. What we do know is that the past six generations have amounted to the most rapid and the most profound change our species has experienced in its 5,000 years of recorded history. During the two pre-1914 generations we laid the foundations for an expansive civilization based on synergy of fossil fuels, science, and technical innovation. The 20th century had followed along the same path—and hence the profound indebtedness and the inevitable continuities. But we had traveled along that path at a very different pace—and hence many deep disparities and many more disquieting thoughts accompany the process of technical transformation. There is much in the record to be proud of, and much that is disappointing and abhorrent. And the record contains the promise both of yet greater ascent and of unprecedented failure. Neither of these courses is preordained, and one thing that no technical transformation could have done is to eliminate the unpredictable: the future is as open as ever—and as uncertain.

References

AA (The Aluminum Association). 2003. *The Industry*. Washington, DC: AA.

Abbate, Janet. 1999. *Inventing the Internet*. Cambridge, MA: MIT Press.

Abernathy, William J. 1978. *The Productivity Dilemma*. Baltimore, MD: Johns Hopkins University Press.

Abernathy, William J., Kim B. Clark, and Alan M. Kantrow. 1984. *Industrial Renaissance: Producing a Competitive Future for America*. New York: Basic Books.

Abramovitz, Moses. 1956. Resource and output trends in the United States since 1870. *American Economics Review* **46**:5–23.

Adams, Walter, and Joel B. Dirlam. 1966. Big steel, invention, and innovation. *Quarterly Journal of Economics* **80**:167–189.

AGOC (Alexander's Gas & Oil Connections). 1998. Drilling went beyond 10 km in UK's Wytch Farm. *Alexander's Gas & Oil Connections* **3**(8):1.

Airbus. 2005. Air 380 Navigator. Toulouse: Airbus. http://events.airbus.com/A380/default1.aspx

Airport Technology. 2004. *Hong Kong International Airport Construction, Chek Lap Kok, Hong Kong*. London: SPG Media PLC. http://www.airport-technology.com/projects/cheklapkok_new/

AISI (American Iron and Steel Institute). 1998. *Hot Oxygen Injection into the Blast Furnace*. Washington, DC: AISI.

AISI. 2002. *Perspective: American Steel & Domestic Manufacturing*. Washington, DC: AISI.

Albrecht, Donald, ed. 1995. *World War II and the American Dream*. Cambridge, MA: MIT Press.

Aldridge, A. 1997. Engaging with promotional culture. *Sociology* **37**(3):389–408.

Alexander, Robert C., and Douglas K. Smith. 1988. *Fumbling the Future—How Xerox Invented, Then Ignored, the First Personal Computer*. New York: William Morrow & Company.

Allardice, Corbin, and Edward R. Trapnell. 1946. *The First Reactor*. Oak Ridge, TN: U.S. Army Environmental Center.

Allaud, Louis, and Maurice Martin. 1976. *Schlumberger: Histoire d'une Technique*. Paris: Berger-Levrault.

Allen, Roy. 2000. *The Pan Am Clipper: The History of Pan American's Flying Boats 1931 to 1946*. New York: Barnes & Noble.

Almqvist, Ebbe. 2003. *History of Industrial Gases*. New York: Kluwer Academic.

Ambrose, S.H. 1998. Late Pleistocene population bottlenecks, volcanic winter, and differentiation of modern humans. *Journal of Human Evolution* **34**:623–651.

Anderson, George B. 1980. *One Hundred Booming Years: A History of Bucyrus-Erie Company, 1880–1980.* South Milwaukee, WI: Bucyrus-Erie.

Anderson, Sara H., John T. Kopfle, Gary E. Metius, and Masahiro Shimizu. 2001. Green steelmaking with the MIDREXR and FASTMETR processes. *Direct from MIDREX.* No. 33:3–5.

APC (American Plastics Council). 2003. About Plastics. Arlington, VA: APC. http://www.americanplasticscouncil.org/s_apc/sec.asp?CID=290&DID=886

Apelt, Brian. 2001. *The Corporation: A Centennial Biography of United States Steel Corporation, 1901–2001.* Pittsburgh, PA: Cathedral Publishing.

Arrow, Kenneth. 1962. The economic implications of learning by doing. *Review of Economic Studies* **29**:155–173.

ASME (American Society of Mechanical Engineers). 1983. *Owens "AR" Bottle Machine (1912).* New York: ASME. http://www.asme.org/history/roster/H086.html

ASME. 1985. *Oxygen Process Steel-Making Vessel.* New York: ASME. http://www.asme.org/history/brochures/h104.pdf

ASME. 1988. *The World's First Industrial Gas Turbine Set at Neuchâtel (1939).* New York: ASME. http://www.asme.org/history/brochures/h135.pdf

ASN (Aviation Safety Network). 2003. *De Havilland DH-106 Comet.* [Amsterdam, The Netherlands]: ASN. http://aviation-safety.net/database/type/190/shtml

AT&T. 2004. *Milestones in AT&T History.* [n.p.]: AT&T. http://www.att.com/history/milestones.html

Ausubel, Jesse H. 2003. *Decarbonization: The Next 100 Years.* New York: Rockefeller University. http://phe.rockefeller.edu/AustinDecarbonization

Ausubel, Jesse H., and Cesare Marchetti. 1996. *Elektron*: electrical systems in retrospect and prospect. *Daedalus* **125**:139–169.

Ausubel, Jesse H., Cesare Marchetti, and Perrin S. Meyer. 1998. Toward green mobility: the evolution of transport. *European Review* **6**:137–156.

Avalon Project. 2003. *The Atomic Bombings of Hiroshima and Nagasaki.* New Haven, CT: Yale Law School. http://www.yale.edu/lawweb/avalon/abomb/mp10.htm

Aylen, Jonathan. 2002. *The Continuing Story of Continuous Casting.* Keynote address to 4th European Continuous Casting Conference, Birmingham, 14–16 October 2002. London: IOM Communications.

Ayres, Robert U., and Duane C. Butcher. 1993. The flexible factory revisited. *American Scientist* **81**:448–459.

Ayres, Robert U., and William Haywood. 1991. *The Diffusion of Computer Integrated Manufacturing Technologies: Models, Case Studies and Forecasts.* New York: Chapman & Hall.

Baekeland, Leo H. 1909. *Condensation Product and Method of Making Same.* Specification of Letters Patent 942,809, December 7, 1909. Washington, DC: USPTO. http://www.uspto.gov

Bagsarian, Tom. 1998. Unveiling Project M. *Iron Age New Steel* **14**(12):56–58. http://www.newsteel.com/features/NS9812f3.htm

Bagsarian, Tom. 2000. Strip casting getting serious. *Iron Age New Steel* **16**(12):18–22. http://www.newsteel.com/2000/NS0012fl.htm

Bagsarian, Tom. 2001. Blast furnaces' next frontier: 20-year campaigns. *Iron Age New Steel.* http://www.newsteel.com/articles/2001/July/nsx0107f2blast.htm

Bairoch, Paul. 1976. Europe's Gross National Product: 1800–1975. *Journal of European Economic History* **5**:273–340.

Barczak, T.M. 1992. *The History and Future of Longwall Mining in the United States.* Washington, DC: U.S. Bureau of Mines.

Bardeen, John, and Walter H. Brattain. 1950. *Three-Electron Circuit Element Utilizing Semiconductive Materials.* U.S. Patent 2,524,035, October 3, 1950. Washington, DC: USPTO. http://www.uspto.gov

Barker, K.J., et al. 1998. Oxygen steelmaking furnace mechanical description and maintenance considerations. In: Richard Fruehan, ed., *The Making, Shaping and Treating of Steel, Steelmaking and Refining Volume*, Pittsburgh, PA: AISE Steel Foundation, pp. 431–474.

Barnett, F.D., and R.W. Crandall. 1986. *Up from Ashes: The Rise of the Steel Minimill in the United States.* Washington, DC: Brookings Institution.

Bathie, William W. 1996. *Fundamentals of Gas Turbines.* New York: John Wiley.

Bauer, Eugene E. 2000. *Boeing: The First Century.* Enumclaw, WA: TABA Publishers.

Beck, P.W. 1999. Nuclear energy in the twenty-first century: examination of a contentious subject. *Annual Review of Energy and the Environment* **24**:113–137.

Bernard, Andrew B., and J. Bradford Jensen. 2004. *The Deaths of Manufacturing Plants.* Cambridge, MA: National Bureau of Economic Research.

Berner, Robert A. 1998. The carbon cycle and CO_2 over Phanerozoic time: the role of land plants. *Philosophical Transaction of the Royal Society London B* **353**:75–82.

Bernstein, Jeremy. 1993. Revelations from Farm Hall. *Science* **259**:1923–1926.

Berry, Bryan, Adama Ritt, and Michael Greissel. 1999. A retrospective of twentieth-century steel. *Iron Age New Steel.* http://www.newsteel.com/features/NS9911f2.htm

Bertin, Leonard. 1957. *Atom Harvest: A British View of Atomic Energy.* San Francisco: W.H. Freeman.

Bessemer, Henry. 1891. On the manufacture of continuous sheets of malleable iron and steel, direct from the fluid metal. *Journal of the Iron and Steel Institute* **6**(10): 23–41.

Bethe, Hans. 1993. Bethe on the German bomb program. *Bulletin of the Atomic Scientists* **49**(1):53–54.

Bijker, Wiebe E. 1995. *Of Bicycles, Bakelites, and Bulbs: Toward a Theory of Sociotechnical Change.* Cambridge, MA: MIT Press.

Bilstein, Roger. 1996. *Stages to Saturn: A Technological History of the Apollo/Saturn Launch Vehicles.* Washington, DC: NASA. http://history.nasa.gov/SP-4206/sp4206 .htm

Boeing. 2001. *The 767 Is the Atlantic Airplane.* Seattle, WA: Boeing. http://www .boeing.com/commercial/767family/pdf/etops.pdf

Boeing. 2003a. *Boeing 777-300ER Completes Extended Operations Flight Testing.* Seattle. WA: Boeing. http://www.boeing.com/news/releases/2003/q4/nr_031222g.html

Boeing. 2003b. *Statistical Summary of Commercial Jet Airplane Accidents.* Seattle, WA: Boeing.

Bohlin, Nils I. 1962. *Safety Belt.* U.S. Patent 3,043,625, July 10, 1962. Washington, DC: USPTO. http://www.uspto.gov

Bohr, Niels. 1913. On the constitution of atoms and molecules. *Philosophical Magazine* Series 6 **26**:1–25.

Bolton, William. 1989. *Engineering Materials.* Boca Raton, FL: CRC Press.

Boulding, K.E. 1973. The social system and the energy crisis. *Science* **184**:255–257.

Bouley, Jean. 1994. A short history of "high-speed" railway in France before the TGV. *Japan Railway & Transport Review* 3:49–51.

Boutwell, Jeffrey, and Michael T. Klare. 2000. A scourge of small arms. *Scientific American* **282**(6):48–53.

BP. 2004. *BP Statistical Review of World Energy 2004.* London: BP.

Bradley, Robert L. 2000. *Julian Simon and the Triumph of Energy Sustainability.* Washington, DC: American Legislative Exchange Council.

Bradsher, Keith. 2002. *High and Mighty SUVs: The World's Most Dangerous Vehicles and How They Got That Way.* New York: Public Affairs.

Brantly, J.E. 1971. *History of Oil Well Drilling.* Houston, TX: Gulf Publishing.

Braun, Ernst. 1984. *Wayward Technology.* Westport, CT: Greenwood Press.

Breck, Donald D. 1974. *Zeolite Molecular Sieves: Structure, Chemistry and Use.* New York: John Wiley & Sons.

Brecke, Peter. 1999. *Violent Conflicts 1400 A.D. to the Present in Different Regions of the World.* Atlanta, GA: Sam Nunn School of International Affairs. http://www.inta.gatech.edu/peter/taxonomy.html

Bronowski, Jacob. 1973. *The Ascent of Man.* Boston: Little, Brown & Company.

Brookman, Robert S. 1998, Vinyl usage in medical plastics: new technologies. In: *Medical Plastics and Biomaterials.* Los Angeles: Cannon Communications LLC. http://www.devicelink.com/mpb/archive/98/07/003.html

Brown, Louis. 1999. *A Radar History of World War II: Technical and Military Imperatives.* Bristol, UK: Institute of Physics Publishing.

Brydson, J.A. 1975. *Plastic Materials.* London: Newnes-Butterworth.

Buck, John L. 1937. *Land Utilization in China.* Nanjing: Nanjing University Press.

Buderi, Robert. 1996. *The Invention That Changed the World: How a Small Group of Radar Pioneers Won the Second World War and Launched a Technical Revolution.* New York: Simon & Schuster.

Buehler, Ernest, and Gordon K. Teal. 1956. *Process for Producing Semiconductive Crystals of Uniform Resistivity.* U.S. Patent 2,768,914, October 30, 1956. Washington, DC: USPTO. http://www.uspto.gov

Burks, Alice R. 2002. *Who Invented the Computer? The Legal Battle That Changed Computing History.* New York: Prometheus Books.

Burks, Alice R., and Arthur W. Burks. 1988. *The First Electronic Computer: The Atanasoff Story.* Ann Arbor, MI: University of Michigan Press.

Burns, Marshall. 1993. *Automated Fabrication: Improving Productivity in Manufacturing.* Engelwood Cliffs, NJ: PTR Prentice-Hall.

Burton, William M. 1913. *Manufacture of Gasolene.* US. Patent 1,049,667, January 7, 1913. Washington, DC: USPTO. http://www.uspto.gov

Burwell, Calvin C. 1990. High-temperature electroprocessing: steel and glass. In: Sam H. Schurr, et al., eds. *Electricity in the American Economy,* New York: Greenwood Press, pp. 109–129.

Burwell, Calvin C., and Blair G. Swezey. 1990. The home: evolving technologies for satisfying human wants. In: Sam H. Schurr, et al., eds. *Electricity in the American Economy,* New York: Greenwood Press, pp. 249–275.

Cagin, S., and P. Dray. 1993. *Between Earth and Sky: How CFCs Changed Our World and Endangered the Ozone Layer.* New York: Pantheon.

Cain, P.J., and A.G. Hopkins. 2002. *British Imperialism 1688–2000.* Harlow: Longman.

Campbell, Donald L., et al. 1948. *Method of and Apparatus for Contacting Solids and Gases.* US. Patent 2,451,804, October 19, 1948. Washington, DC: USPTO. http://www.uspto.gov

Campbell-Kelly, Martin, and William Aspray. 2004. *Computer: A History of the Information Machine.* Boulder, CO: Westview Press.

Čapek, Karel. 1921. *R.U.R.: Rossum's Universal Robots,* Prague: Aventinum.

Carothers, Wallace H. 1937. *Linear Condensation Polymers.* US. Patent 2,071,250, February 16, 1937. Washington, DC: USPTO. http://www.uspto.gov

Casti, John L. 2004. Synthetic thought. *Nature* 427:680.

CEA (Council of Economic Advisors). 2000. *Economic Report to the President, 2000.* Washington, DC: U.S. Government Printing Office.

Chadwick, James. 1932. Possible existence of a neutron. *Nature* **129**:312.

Chapin, Douglas M., et al. 2002. Nuclear power plants and their fuel as terrorist targets. *Science* **297**:1997–1999.

Cho, Alfred, ed. 1994. *Molecular Beam Epitaxy.* Woodbury, NY: American Institute of Physics.

CJD Surveillance Unit. 2004. *CJD Statistics.* Edinburgh: Creutzfeldt-Jakob Surveillance Unit. http://www.cjd.ed.ac.uk/

Coalson, Michale. 2003. Jets fans. *Mechanical Engineering,* Suppl., *100 Years of Flight,* 125(12):16–17, 38.

Cobet, Aaron E., and Gregory A. Wilson. 2002. Comparing 50 years of labor productivity in U.S., and foreign manufacturing. *Monthly Labor Review,* June, 51–65.

Cohen, Bernard. 1999. *Howard Aiken: Portrait of a Computer Pioneer.* Cambridge, MA: MIT Press.

Colbeck, Ian, and A.R. MacKenzie. 1994. *Air Pollution by Photochemical Oxidants.* Amsterdam: Elsevier.

Collier, Richard. 1996. *The Plague of the Spanish Lady: The Influenza Pandemic of 1918–1919.* London: Allison & Busby.

Committee for the Compilation of Materials on Damage Caused by the Atomic Bombs in Hiroshima and Nagasaki. 1981. *Hiroshima and Nagasaki: The Physical, Medical, and Social Effects of the Atomic Bombings.* New York: Basic Books.

Compton, Arthur H. 1956. *Atomic Quest.* New York: Oxford University Press.

Conner, Doug. 1998. Father of DOS having fun at Microsoft. *MicroNews.* Issaquah, WA: Paterson Technology. http://www.patersontech.com/Dos/Miconews/paterson 004_10_98.htm

Conner, Margaret. 2001. *Hans von Ohain: Elegance in Flight.* Washington, DC: American Institute of Aeronautics and Astronautics.

Constable, George, and Bob Somerville. 2003. *A Century of Innovation: Twenty Engineering Achievements That Transformed Our Lives.* Washington, DC: Joseph Henry Press.

Constant, E.W. 1981. *The Origins of Turbojet Revolution.* Baltimore, MD: Johns Hopkins University Press.

Cooper, G.A. 1994. Directional drilling. *Scientific American* **270**(5):82–87.

Copley, Frank B. 1923. *Frederick W. Taylor: Father of Scientific Management.* New York: Harper & Brothers.

Corkhill, Michael. 1975. *LNG Carriers: The Ships and Their Market.* London: Fairplay Publications.

Cortada, James W. 2004. *The Digital Hand: How Computers Changed the Work of American Manufacturing, Transportation, and Retail Industries.* New York: Oxford University Press.

Cousins, Norman 1972. *The Improbable Triumvirate: John F. Kennedy, Pope John, Nikita Khrushchev.* New York: W.W. Norton.

Cowan, Robin. 1990. Nuclear power reactors: a study in technological lock-in. *Journal of Economic History* 50:541–567.

Cowell, Graham. 1976. *D.H. Comet: The World's First Jet Airliner.* Hounslow, UK: Airline Publications and Sales.

Crowley, Kevin D., and John F. Ahearne. 2002. Managing the environmental legacy of U.S. nuclear-weapons production. *American Scientist* 90:514–523.

Cusumano, Michael M., and Kentaro Nobeoka. 1999. *Thinking Beyond Lean: How Multi-project Management Is Transforming Product Development at Toyota and Other Companies.* New York: Free Press.

Czochralski, Jan. 1918. Ein neues Verfahren zur Messung des Kristallisationsgeschwindigkeit der Metalle. *Zeitschrift der Physikalische Chemie* 92:219–221.

Daly, Herman. 2001. Beyond growth: avoiding uneconomic growth. In: Mohan Munasinghe, Osvaldo Sunkel, and Carlos de Miguel, eds., *The Sustainability of Long-Term Growth: Socioeconomic and Ecological Perspectives.* Cheltenham, UK: Edward Elgar, pp. 153–161.

Daly, H.E., and J.B. Cobb, Jr. 1989. *For the Common Good.* Boston: Beacon Press.

Darmstadter, J. 1997. *Productivity Change in U.S. Coal Mining.* Washington, DC: Resources for the Future.

David, Paul A. 1990. The dynamo and the computer: an historical perspective on the modern productivity paradox. *American Economic Review* 80:355–361.

Davies, R.E.G. 1987. *Pan Am: An Airline and Its Aircraft.* New York: Orion Books.

Davies, Ed, and Nicholas A. Veronico, Scott A. Thompson. 1995. *Douglas DC-3: 60 Years and Counting.* Elk Grove, CA: Aero Vintage Books.

Davis, C.G., et al. 1982. Direct-reduction technology and economics. *Ironmaking and Steelmaking* 9(3):93–129.

De Beer, Jeroen, Ernst Worrell, and Kornelis Blok. 1998. Future technologies for energy-efficient iron and steel making. *Annual Review of Energy and the Environment* 23:123–205.

De Loo, Ivo, and Luc Soete. 1999. *The Impact of Technology on Economic Growth: Some New Ideas and Empirical Considerations.* Maastricht, The Netherlands: Maastricht Economic Research Institute on Innovation and Technology.

De Mestral, George. 1961. *Separable Fastening Device.* U.S. Patent 3,009,235, November 21, 1961. Washington, DC: USPTO.

Denison, Edward F. 1985. *Trends in American Economic Growth, 1929–1982.* Washington, DC: Brookings Institution.

Denning, R.S. 1985. The Three Mile Island unit's core: a post-mortem examination. *Annual Review of Energy* 10:35–52.

Dertouzos, Michael L. 1997. *What Will Be: How the New World of Information Will Change Our Lives.* San Francisco: HarperEdge.

Devereux, Steve. 1999. *Drilling Technology in Nontechnical Language.* Tulsa, OK: PennWell Publications.

Devol, George C. 1961. *Programmed Article Transfer.* U.S. Patent 2,988,237, June 13, 1961. Washington, DC: USPTO. http://www.uspto.gov

Diebold, John. 1952. *Automation: The Advent of the Automatic Factory.* New York: Van Nostrand.

Dieffenbach, E.M., and R.B. Gray. 1960. The development of the tractor. In: *Power to Produce: 1960 Yearbook of Agriculture.* Washington, DC: US Department of Agriculture, pp. 24–45.

Drnevich, R.F., C.J. Messina, and R.J. Selines. 1998. Production and use of industrial gases for iron and steelmaking. In: Richard Fruehan, ed., *The Making, Shaping and Treating of Steel, Steelmaking and Refining Volume,* Pittsburgh, PA: AISE Steel Foundation, pp. 291–310.

DuPont. 2003. *Teflon.* Wilmington, DE: DuPont. http://www.teflon.com

Durant, Frederick C. 1974. Robert H. Goddard and the Smithsonian Institution. In: Frederick C. Durant and George S. James, eds., *First Steps toward Space,* Washington, DC: Smithsonian Institution, pp. 57–69.

Durant, Frederick C., and George S. James, eds. 1974. *First Steps toward Space.* Washington, DC: Smithsonian Institution.

Durrer, Robert. 1948. Sauerstoff-Frischen in Gerlafingen. *Von Roll Werkzeitung* **19**(5): 73–74.

Dutilh, Chris E., and Anita R. Linnemann. 2004. Modern agriculture, energy use in. In: Cutler J. Cleveland, ed., *Encyclopedia of Energy,* Vol. 2, Amsterdam: Elsevier, pp. 719–726.

The Economist. 2001. Obituary: Malcolm McLean. *The Economist,* 2 June 2001, p. 91.

EF (Engineering Fundamentals). 2003. *Polymer Material Pro*perties. Sunnyvale, CA: Engineering Fundamentals. http://www.efunda.com/materials/polymers/properties

EIA (Energy Information Administration). 1999. *A Look at Residential Energy Consumption in 1997.* Washington, DC: EIA.

EIA. 2003. *Annual Coal Report 2002.* Washington, DC: EIA.

EIA. 2004. *Historical Data.* Washington, DC: EIA. http://www.eia.doe.gov/neic/historic/historic.htm

Einstein, Albert. 1907. Über das Relativitätsprinzip und die aus demselben gezogenen Folgerungen. *Jahrbuch der Radioaktivität und Elektronik* **4**:411–462.

Ellers, Fred S. 1982. Advanced offshore oil platforms. *Scientific American* **246**(4):39–49.

Ellis, C. Hamilton. 1977. *The Lore of the Train.* New York: Crescent Books.

Ellul, Jacques. 1964. *The Technological Society.* New York: A.A. Knopf.

Ellul, Jacques. 1989. *What I Believe.* Grand Rapids, MI: W.B. Eerdmans.

Ellul, Jacques. 1990. *The Technological Bluff.* Grand Rapids, MI: W.B. Eerdmans.

Emerick, H.B. 1954. European oxygen steelmaking is of far-reaching significance. *Journal of Metals* **6**(7):803–805.

Endres, Günter G. 1996. *Global Airport Expansion Programmes.* Alexandria, VA: Jane's Information Group.

Energomash. 2003. *NPO Energomash Engines History.* Moscow: Energomash. http://www.aerospace.ru/English/partners/energomash/engines.htm

Engelbart, Douglas C. 1970. *X-Y Position Indicator for a Display System.* U.S. Patent 3,541,541, November 17, 1970. Washington, DC: USPTO. http://www.uspto.gov

Engelberger, Joseph F. 1980. *Robotics in Practice: Management and Applications of Industrial Robots.* New York: AMACOM.

Engelberger, Joseph F. 1989. *Robotics in Service.* Cambridge, MA: MIT Press.

EPICA (European Project for Ice Coring in Antarctica). 2004. Eight glacial cycles from an Antarctic ice core. *Nature* **429**:623–628.

Erasmus, Friedrich C. 1975. Die Entwicklung des Steinkohlenbergbaus im Ruhrrevier in den siebziger Jahren. *Glückauf* **11**:311–318.

ESCAP (Economic and Social Commission for Asia and the Pacific). 2000. *Major Issues in Transport, Communications, Tourism and Infrastructure Development: Regional Shipping and Port Development Strategies under a Changing Maritime Environment.* Bangkok: ESCAP.

Eubanks, Gordon. 2004. *Recollections of Gary Kildall.* http://www.maxframe.com/ EUBANKS.HTM

European Commission. 1995. *L'Europe à Grande Vitesse.* Luxembourg: European Commission.

Evans, Leonard. 2002. Traffic crashes. *American Scientist* **90**:244–253.

Fairlie, Ian, and Marvin Resnikoff. 1997. No dose too low. *Bulletin of Atomic Scientists* **53**(6):52–56.

FAO (Food and Agriculture Administration of the United Nations). 2000. *The Energy and Agriculture Nexus.* Rome: FAO.

FAO. 2002. *The State of World Fisheries and Acquaculture.* Rome: FAO.

FAO. 2004. *FAOSTAT Statistics Database.* Rome: FAO. http://apps.fao.org

Farber, Darryl, and Jennifer Weeks. 2001. A graceful exit? Decommissioning nuclear power reactors. *Environment* **43**(6):8–21.

Farman J.C., B.G. Gardiner, and J.D. Shanklin. 1985. Large losses of total ozone in Antarctica reveal seasonal ClOx/NOx interaction. *Nature* **315**:207–210.

Farnsworth, Philo T. 1930. *Television System.* U.S. Patent 1,773,980, August 26, 1930. Washington, DC: USPTO. http://www.uspto.gov

Feinman, J. 1999. Direct reduction and smelting processes. In: David H. Wakelin, ed., *The Making, Shaping and Treating of Steel, Ironmaking Volume,* Pittsburgh, PA: AISE Steel Foundation, pp. 763–795.

Fenichell, Stephen. 1996. *Plastic: The Making of a Synthetic Century.* New York: HarperBusiness.

Fermi, Enrico, and Leo Szilard. 1955. *Neutronic Reactor.* U.S. Patent 2,708,656, May 17, 1955. Washington, DC: USPTO. http://www.uspto.gov

Ferry, Georgina. 2003. *A Computer Called Leo: Lyons Teashops and the World's First Office Computer.* London: Fourth Estate.

Fischer, Claude S. 1997. "Touch someone": the telephone industry discovers sociability. In: Stephen H. Cutcliffe and Terry S. Reynolds, eds., *Technology and American History,* Chicago: University of Chicago Press, pp. 271–300.

Fisk, Donald M. 2001. American labor in the 20th century. *Compensation and Working Conditions,* Fall, 3–8. http://www.bls.gov/opub/cwc/cm20030124ar02p1.htm

Flink, James J. 1985. Innovation in automotive technology. *American Scientist* **73**:151–161.

Flink, James J. 1988. *The Automobile Age.* Cambridge, MA: MIT Press.

Fluck, Richard C., ed. 1992. *Energy in Farm Production.* Amsterdam: Elsevier.

Föll, Helmut. 2000. *Electronic Materials.* Kiel: University of Kiel.

Fossett, David A.J. 2004. *Byun2 Shinkansen.* Tōkyō: David A.J. Fossett. http://www .h2.dion.ne.jp/dajf/byunbyun/

Franz, John E. 1974. *N-Phosphonomethyl-glycine Phytotoxicant Compositions.* U.S. Patent 3,799,758, March 26, 1974. Washington, DC: USPTO. http://www.uspto.gov

Freedonia Group. 2002. *World Industrial Gases.* Cleveland, OH: Freedonia Group.

Fridley, David, ed. 2001. *China Energy Databook*. Berkeley, CA: Lawrence Berkeley Laboratory.

Friedman, Jeffrey, ed. 1991. *Milestones in Motion Picture and Television Technology: The SMPTE 75th Anniversary Collection*. White Plains, NY: Society of Motion Picture and Television Engineers.

Fruehan, Richard, ed. 1998. The Making, Shaping and Treating of Steel Steelmaking and Refining Volume. Pittsburgh, PA: The AISE Steel Foundation.

Fujimoto, Takahiro. 1999. *The Evolution of a Manufacturing System at Toyota*. New York: Oxford University Press.

Fulton, Kenneth. 1996. Frank Whittle (1907–96). *Nature* **383**:27.

Furniss, Tim. 2001. *The History of Space Vehicles*. San Diego, CA: Thunder Bay Press.

GAO (General Accounting Office). 1993. *High-Speed Ground Transportation*. Washington, DC: GAO.

GAO. 1995. *Nuclear Safety: Concerns with Nuclear Facilities and Other Sources of Radiation in the Former Soviet Union*. Washington, DC: GAO.

GE. 2004. *LM6000 Sprint Aeroderivative Gas Turbine*. New York: GE. http://www.gepower.com/prod_serv/products/aero_turbines/en/lm6000_sprint.htm

GEAE (General Electric Aircraft Engines). 2002. *GEAE History*. Cincinnati, OH: GEAE. http://www.geae.com/aboutgeae/history.html

GEAE. 2003. *The GE90 Engine Family*. Cincinnati, OH: GEAE. http://www.geae.com/engines/commercial/ge90/index.html

GEPS (General Electric Power Systems). 2003. *Gas Turbine and Combined Cycle Products*. Atlanta, GA: GEPS.

Gerber Scientific. 2003. *What Is Mass Customization?* South Windsor, CT: Gerber Scientific. http://www.mass-customization.com/

Giampietro, Mario. 2002 Fossil energy in world agriculture. In: *Nature-Encyclopedia of Life Sciences*. London: Nature. http://www.els.net

Giarini, O., and H. Loubergé. 1978. *The Diminishing Returns of Technology*. Oxford: Pergamon.

Gilbert, Glen A. 1973. *Air Traffic Control: The Uncrowded Sky*. Washington, DC: Smithsonian Institution Press.

Glover, T.O., et al. 1970. *Unit Train Transportation of Coal: Technology and Description of Nine Representative Operations*. Washington, DC: U.S. Bureau of Mines.

Goddard, Robert H. 1926. Goddard to Abbot, 29 June 1926. In: Esther C. Goddard and G. Edward Pendray, eds., *The Papers of Robert H. Goddard*, Vol. 2, New York: McGraw-Hill, pp. 587–590, 1970.

Godfrey, Donald G. 2001. *Philo T. Farnsworth: The Inventor of Television*. Salt Lake City, UT: University of Utah Press.

Gold, Bela, et al. 1984. *Technological Progress and Industrial Leadership: The Growth of the U.S. Steel Industry, 1900–1970*. Lexington, MA: Lexington Books.

Goldberg, Stanley. 1992. Groves takes the reins. *Bulletin of the Atomic Scientists* **48**(10): 32–39.

Golley, John, and Frank Whittle. 1987. *Whittle, the True Story*. Washington, DC: Smithsonian Institution Press.

Goodman, Sidney H. 1999. *Handbook of Thermoset Plastics*. Norwich, NY: Noyes Publications.

Görlitz, Walter. 1953. *History of the German General Staff*. New York: Praeger.

Greenpeace. 2003. *Polyvinyl Chloride.* [Amsterdam, The Netherlands]: Greenpeace.
http://www.greenpeace.org/international/campaigns/toxics/polyvinyl-chloride
Greissel, Michael. 2000. The power of oxygen. *Iron Age New Steel* **16**(4):24–30. http://
/www.newsteel.com/2000/NS0004f2.htm
Grossman, Gene M., and Elhanan Helpman. 1991. *Innovation and Growth in the Global
Economy.* Cambridge, MA: MIT Press.
Groueff, Stephane. 1967. *Manhattan Project.* Boston, MA: Little, Brown and Company.
Groves, Leslie R. 1962. *Now It Can Be Told: The Story of the Manhattan Project.* New
York: Harper.
Gubbins, Edmund J. 1986. *The Shipping Industry: The Technology and Economics of
Specialisation.* New York: Gordon & Breach.
Gunston, Bill. 1995. *The Encyclopedia of Russian Aircraft, 1875–1995.* Osceola, WI: Mo-
torbooks International.
Gunston, Bill. 1997. *The Development of Jet and Turbine Aero Engines.* Sparkford, UK:
Patrick Stephens.
Gunston, Bill. 2002. *Aviation: The First 100 Years.* Hauppauge, NY: Barron's.
Gustafson, John. 2000. Reconstruction of the Atanasoff-Berry computer. In: Raúl Rojas
and Ulf Hashagen, eds., *The First Computers—History and Architectures,* Cambridge,
MA: MIT Press, pp. 91–105.
Hahn, Otto. 1946. *From the Natural Transmutations of Uranium to Its Artificial Fission.*
Nobel Lecture, December 13, 1946. Stockholm: Nobel Foundation. http://www
.nobel.se/chemistry/laureates/1944/
Hahn, Otto. 1968. *Mein Leben.* Munich: Verag F. Bruckmann KG.
Hahn, Otto, and Fritz Strassman. 1939a. Nachweis der Entstehung activer Bariumiso-
tope aus Uran und Thorium durch Neutronenbestrahlung. *Naturwissenschaften* **27**:
89–95.
Hahn, Otto, and Fritz Strassman. 1939b. Über den Nachweis und das Verhalten der
bei der Bestrahlung des Urans mittles Neutronen entstehenden Erdalkalimetalle.
Naturwissenschaften 27:11–15.
Haley, J. Evetts. 1959. *Erle P. Halliburton, Genius with Cement.* Duncan, OK: Halli-
burton Oil Well Cementing Company.
Hall, Christopher G.L. 1997. *Steel Phoenix: The Fall and Rise of the U.S. Steel Industry.*
New York: St. Martin's Press.
Hallion, Richard P. 2004. Remembering the legacy: highlights of the first 100 years of
aviation. *The Bridge* **34**:5–11. http://www.nae.edu/NAE/naehome.nsf/weblinks/
MKEZ-5X5NAK?OpenDocument
Halweil, Brian. 2002. *Home Grown.* Washington, DC: Worldwatch Institute.
Hansel, James G. 1996. Oxygen. In: *Kirk-Othmer Encyclopedia of Chemical Technology,*
Vol. 17, New York: Wiley, pp. 919–940.
Hansen, J., et al. 2000. Global warming in the twenty-first century: an alternative
scenario. *Proceedings of the National Academy of Sciences of the USA* **97**:9875–9880.
Hansen, Teresa, and, Robert Smock. 1996. Gas turbines aim at world power market
dominance. *Power Engineering* **100**(6):23–32.
Harrison, M. 1988. Resource mobilization for World War II: The U.S.A., U.K.,
U.S.S.R., and Germany, 1938–1945. *Economic History Review* **41**:171–192.
Hawkins, David, Edith C. Truslow, and Ralph C. Smith 1961. *Manhattan District
History: Project Y, the Los Alamos Project.* Los Alamos, NM: Los Alamos Scientific
Laboratory.

Heffernan, William D., and Mary K. Hendrickson, 2002. *Multi-national Concentrated Food Processing and Marketing Systems and the Farm Crisis.* Paper presented at Science and Sustainability, a AAAS Symposium, Boston, MA, February 14–19, 2002.

Heilbroner, Robert L. 1967. Do machines make history? *Technology & Culture* **8**:335–345.

Helsel, Zane R. 1992. Energy and alternatives for fertilizer and pesticide use. In: Richard C. Fluck, ed., *Energy in Farm Production,* Amsterdam: Elsevier, pp. 177–201.

Heppenheimer, T.A. 1995. *Turbulent Skies: The History of Commercial Aviation.* New York: John Wiley.

Heppenheimer, T.A. 1997. *Countdown: A History of Space Flight.* New York: John Wiley & Sons.

Hermes, Matthew E. 1996. *Enough for One Lifetime: Wallace Carothers, Inventor of Nylon.* Washington, DC: American Chemical Society and Chemical Heritage Foundation.

Hess, G.W. 1989. Is the blast furnace in its twilight? *Iron Age* **5**(11):16–26.

HFMGV (Henry Ford Museum and Greenfield Village). 2004. *The Great American Production.* Greenfield, MI: HFMGV.

Hicks. J., and G. Allen. 1999. *A Century of Change: Trends in UK Statistics since 1900.* London: House of Commons Library. http://www.parliement.uk/commons/lib/research/rp99/rp99-111.pdf

Higonnet, René, and Louis Moyroud. 1957. *Photo Composing Machine.* U.S. Patent 2,790,362, April 30, 1957. Washington, DC: USPTO. http://www.uspto.gov

Hinsley, F. Harry, and Alan Stripp, eds. 1993. *Codebreakers: The Inside Story of Bletchley Park.* Oxford: Oxford University Press.

Hoff, Marcian E., Stanley Mazor, and Federico Faggin. 1974. *Memory System for a Multi-chip Digital Computer.* U.S. Patent 3,821,715, June 28, 1974. Washington, DC: USPTO. http://www.uspto.gov

Hofmann-Wellenhof, B., et al. 1997. *Global Positioning System: Theory and Practice.* New York: Springer-Verlag.

Hogan, William T. 1971. *Economic History of the Iron and Steel Industry in the United States.* Lexington, MA: Lexington Books.

Hohenemser, Christopher. 1988. The accident at Chernobyl: health and environmental consequences and the implications form risk management. *Annual Review of Energy* **13**:383–428.

Holbrook, Stewart H. 1976. *Machines of Plenty: Chronicle of an Innovator in Construction and Agricultural Equipment.* New York: Macmillan.

Hollingsworth, John A. 1966. *History of Development of Strip Mining Machines.* Milwaukee, WI: Bucyrus-Erie Company.

Holley, I.B. 1964. *Buying Aircraft: Material Procurement for the Army Air Forces.* Washington, DC: Department of the Army.

Holmes, Peter. 2001. *WP 6—RTD Strategy.* Plenary address presented at the CAME—GT Workshop, October 2001. Brussells: Thematic Network for Cleaner and More Efficient Gas Turbines. http://www.came-gt.com/second-workshop/2wStrategy.pdf

Hong, B.D., and E.R. Slatick, 1994. Carbon emission factors for coal. *Quarterly Coal Report* **1994**(1):1–8.

Horlock, J.H. 2002. *Combined Power Plants Including Combined Cycle Gas Turbine Plants.* Malabar, FL: Krieger Publishers.

Horonjeff, Robert, and Francis McKelvey. 1983. *Planning and Design of Airports.* New York: McGraw-Hill.

Horton, Emmett J., and W. Dale Compton. 1984. Technological trends in automobiles. *Science* **225**:587–592.

Houdry, Eugène. 1931. *Process for the Manufacture of Liquid Fuels.* U.S. Patent 1,837,963, December 22, 1931. Washington, DC: USPTO. http://www.uspto.gov

Houghton, John T., et al., eds. 2001. *Climate Change 2001: The Scientific Basis.* New York: Cambridge University Press.

Hu, Frank, et al. 2003. Television watching and other sedentary behaviors in relation to risk of obesity. *JAMA* **289**:1785–1791.

Hughes, Howard R. 1909. *Drill.* U.S. Patent 930,759, August 10, 1909. Washington, DC: USPTO. http://www.uspto.gov

Hunley, J.D. 1999. *The History of Solid-Propellant Rocketry: What We Do and Do Not Know.* Paper presented at American Institute of Aeronautics and Astronautics/ ASME/SAE/ASEE (American Society of Mechanical Engineers/Society of Automotive Engineers/Society for Engineering Education) Joint Propulsion Conference and Exhibit, Los Angeles, CA, June 20–24, 1999. http://www.dfrc.nasa.gov/DTRS/ 1999/PDF/H-2330.pdf

Hutcheson, G. Dan, and Jerry D. Hutcheson. 1996. Technology and economics in the semiconductor industry. *Scientific American* **274**(1):54–62.

Huzel, Dieter K., and David H. Huang. 1992. *Modern Engineering for Design of Liquid-Propellant Rocket Engines.* Washington, DC: American Institute of Aeronautics and Astronautics.

IAEA (International Atomic Energy Agency). 2001. *Status of Nuclear Power Plants Worldwide in 2000.* Vienna: IAEA. http://www.iaea.org/cgi-bin/db.page.pl/pris .main.htm

IANA (Intermodal Association of North America). 2004. *Industry Statistics.* http:// www.intermodal.org/fact.html

ICAO (International Civil Aviation Organization). 1971. *The ICAO Annual Report.* Montreal: ICAO.

ICAO. 2001. *The ICAO Annual Report.* Montreal: ICAO.

IFA (International Fertilizer Industry Association). 2001. *World Nitrogen Fertilizer Consumption.* Paris: IFA. http://www.fertilizer.org

IISI (International Iron and Stee Institute). 2002. *World Steel in Figures.* Brussels: IISI. http://www.worldsteel.org

Illich, Ivan D. 1974. *Energy and Equity.* New York: Harper & Row.

Integrated Surgical Systems. 2004. *Redefining Surgery . . . around the World.* Davis, CA: Integrated Surgical Systems. http://www.robodoc.com/eng/

Intel. 2001. *The History of Intel, 30 Years of Innovation.* Santa Clara, CA: Intel. http:// www.intel.com

Intel. 2003. *Moore's Law.* Santa Clara, CA: Intel. http://www.intel.com/research/ silicon/mooreslaw.htm

Intuitive Surgical. 2004. *Da Vinci Surgical System.* Sunnyvale, CA: Intuitive Surgical. http://www.intuitivesurgical.com

IPCC (Intergovernmental Panel for Climatic Change). 1996. *Revised 1996 IPCC Guidelines for National Greenhouse Gas Inventories.* Geneva: IPCC.

Irving, Robert R. 1979. World's largest platform drills the Gulf for oil. *Iron Age* **222**(13): 68–69.

ISC (Internet Systems Consortium). 2004. *ISC Domain Survey.* Redwood City, CA: ISC (Internet Systems Consortium). http://www.isc.org/ops/ds/host-count-history .php

Islas, Jorge. 1999. The gas turbine: a new technological paradigm in electricity generation. *Technological Forecasting and Social Change* 60:129–148.

Jackson, Kenneth A., ed. 1996. *Materials Science and Technology: A Comprehensive Treatment.* New York: Wiley.

Jansen, Marius B. 2000. *The Making of Modern Japan.* Cambridge, MA: Belknap Press.

Jay, Kenneth E.B. 1956. *Calder Hall: The Story of Britain's First Atomic Power Station.* London: Methuen.

JISF (Japan Iron and Steel Federation). 2003. *Energy Consumption by the Steel Industry at 2,013 PJ.* Tokyo: JISF. http://www.jisf.or.jp/sji/energy.html

JNCDI (Japan Nuclear Cycle Development Institute). 2000. *The Monju Sodium Leak.* Tokyo: JNCDI. http://www.jnc.go.jp/zmonju/mjweb/NaL.htm

Jones, Capers. 1998. Sizing up software. *Scientific American* 279(6):104–109.

Jones, C.I. 1995. R&D-based models of economic growth. *Journal of Political Economy* 103:759–784.

Jones, Glyn. 1989. *The Jet Pioneers.* London: Methuen.

Jones, Jeremy A.T. 2003. *Electric Arc Furnace Steelmaking.* Pittsburgh, PA: AISI. http://www.steel.org/learning/howmade/eaf.htm

Jones, Jeremy A.T., B. Bowman, and P.A. Lefrank. 1998. Electric furnace steelmaking. In: Richard Fruehan, ed., *The Making, Shaping and Treating of Steel, Steelmaking and Refining Volume,* Pittsburgh, PA: AISE Steel Foundation, pp. 525–660.

Joy Mining Machinery. 2004. *Joseph Francis Joy: Character, Inventor, Reformer.* Warrendale, PA: Joy Mining Machinery. http://www.joy.com/company_overview/history .htm

JR Central 2004. *Welcome to the Tokaido Shinkansen.* Tokyo: JR Central. http://jr -central.co.jp/english.nsf/index

Kakela, Peter J. 1981. Iron ore: from depletion to abundance. *Science* 212:132–136.

Kanigel, Robert. 1997. *The One Best Way: Frederick Winslow Taylor and the Enigma of Efficiency.* New York: Viking.

Kawamoto, Kaoru, et al. 2000. *Electricity Used by Office Equipment and Network Equipment in the U.S.* Berkeley, CA: Lawrence Berkeley National Laboratory.

Keeling CD. 1998. Reward and penalties of monitoring the Earth. *Annual Review of Energy and the Environment* 23:25–82.

Kelly, Thomas D., and Michael D. Fenton. 2004. *Iron and Steel Statistics.* Washington, DC: U.S. Geological Survey. http://minerals.usgs.gov/minerals/pubs/of01–006/ ironandsteel.html

Kempf, Karl. 1961. *Electronic Computers within the Ordnance Corps.* Aberdeen Proving Ground, MD: U.S. Army Ordnance Corps.

Kendall, Lane C., and James J. Buckley. 2001. *The Business of Shipping.* Centreville, MD: Cornell Maritime Press.

Kernighan, Brian, and Dennis Ritchie. 1978. *The C Programming Language.* Englewood Cliffs, NJ: Prentice-Hall.

Kerr, George T. 1989. Synthetic zeolites. *Scientific American* 261(1):100–105.

Keyes, Robert W. 1993. The future of the transistor. *Scientific American* 268(6):70–78.

Khariton, Yuli, and Yuri Smirnov. 1993. The Khariton version. *Bulletin of the Atomic Scientists* 49(3):20–31.

Kilby, Jack S. 1964. *Miniaturized Electronic Circuits.* U.S. Patent 3,138,743, June 23, 1964. Washington, DC: USPTO.

Kilby, Jack S., Jerry D. Merryman, and James H. Van Tassel. 1974. *Miniature Electronic Calculator.* U.S. Patent 3,819,921, June 25, 1974. Washington, DC: USPTO. http://www.uspto.gov

King, C.D. 1948. *Seventy-five Years of Progress in Iron and Steel.* New York: American Institute of Mining and Metallurgical Engineers.

Kirsch, David A. 2000. *The Electric Vehicle and the Burden of History.* New Brunswick, NJ: Rutgers University Press.

Klíma, Ivan. 2001. *Karel Čapek: Life and Work.* North Haven, CT: Catbird Press.

Kloss, E. 1963. *Luftkrieg über Deutschland, 1939–1945.* Munich: Deutscher Taschenbuch Verlag.

Krech, Shepard, John R. McNeill, and Carolyn Merchant, eds. 2004. *Encyclopedia of Environmental History.* New York: Routledge.

Krimigis, S.M., et al. 2003. Voyager 1 exited the solar wind at a distance of 85 AU from the sun. *Nature* **426**:45–48.

Kuehr, Ruediger, and Eric Williams, eds. 2003. *Computers and the Environment: Understanding and Managing Their Impacts.* Dordrecht: Kluwer Academic.

Kumar, Shashi N. 2004. Tanker transportation. In: Cutler J. Cleveland, ed., *Encyclopedia of Energy,* Vol. 6, Amsterdam: Elsevier, pp. 1–12.

Lamont, Lansing. 1965. *Day of Trinity.* New York: Atheneum.

Lamont Doherty Earth Observatory. 2001. *Lamont 4D Technology.* New York: Lamont Doherty Earth Observatory. http://www.ldeo.columbia.edu/4d4/

Lampson, Butler. 2003. Computing meets the physical world. *The Bridge,* Spring, 1–7.

Landau, Daniel. 2003. A simple theory of economic growth. *Economic Development and Cultural Change* **52**:217–235.

Lane, David R., and Robert A. Lane, 1994. *Transistor Radios: A Collector's Encyclopedia and Price Guide.* Radnor, PA.: Wallace-Homestead Books.

Langston, Lee S., and George Opdyke. 1997. *Introduction to Gas Turbines for Nonengineers.* Atlanta, GA: ASME International Gas Turbine Institute. http://www.asme.org/igti/resources/articles/intro2gta.html

Lanouette, William. 1992. *Genius in Shadows: A Biography of Leo Szilard.* New York: Charles Scribner's Sons.

Lavington, Simon. 2001. Tom Kilburn (1921–2001). *Nature* **409**:996.

Leach, Barry. 1973. *German General Staff.* New York: Ballantine Books.

Leckie, A.H., A. Millar, and J.E. Medley. 1982. Short- and long-term prospects for energy economy in steelmaking. *Ironmaking and Steelmaking* **9**:222–235.

Lee, Jasper S., and Michael E. Newman. 1997. *Aquaculture: An Introduction.* Danville, IL: Interstate Publishers.

Levy, Jonathan I., James K. Hammitt, and John D. Spengler. 2000. Estimating the mortality impacts of particulate matter: what can be learned from between-study variability? *Environmental Health Perspectives* **108**:109–117.

Lewchuk, Wayne. 1989. Fordism and the moving assembly line: the British and American experience, 1895–1930. In: Nelson Lichtenstein and Stephen Meyer, eds., *On the Line: Essays in the History of Auto Work,* Urbana, IL: University of Illinois Press, pp. 17–41.

Lightman, Alan, Daniel Sarewitz, and Christina Desser, eds. 2003. *Living with the*

Genie: Essays on Technology and the Quest for Human Mastery. Washington, DC: Island Press.

Linde, Carl P. 1916. *Aus meinem Leben und von meiner Arbeit.* München: R. Oldenbourg.

Linde AG. 2003. *Linde and the History of Air Separation.* Höllriegelskreuth, Germany: Linde AG. http://www.linde-process-engineering.com

Lindem, Thomas J., and Paul A.S. Charles. 1995. *Octahedral Machine with a Hexapodal Triangular Servostrut Section.* U.S. Patent 5,401,128, March 28, 1995. Washington, DC: USPTO. http://www.uspto.gov

Ling, Peter J. 1990. *America and the Automobile: Technology, Reform and Social Change.* Manchester: Manchester University Press.

Lippert, Owen, and Michael Walker. 1997. *The Underground Economy: Global Evidence of Its Size and Impact.* Vancouver, BC: Fraser Institute.

Lloyd, Ann, ed. 1988. *History of the Movies.* London: Macdonald Orbis.

Loftin, Laurence K. 1985. *Quest for Performance: The Evolution of Modern Aircraft.* Washington, DC: NASA.

Lombardi, Michael. 2003. *Century of Technology.* Seattle, WA: Boeing. http://www.boeing.com/news/frontiers/cover1.html

Lourie, Richard. 2002. *Sakharov: A Biography.* Waltham, MA: Brandeis University Press.

Lucent Technologies. 2004. *10 Bell Labs Innovations That Changed the World.* Murray Hill, NJ: Lucent Technologies. http://www.bell-labs.com/about/history/changed world.html

Luff, Peter. 1978. The electronic telephone. *Scientific American* **238**(3):58–64.

Luiten, Ester E.M. 2001. *Beyond Energy Efficiency: Actors, Networks and Government Intervention in the Development of Industrial Process Technologies.* Utrecht: Universiteit Utrecht.

Lundstrom, Mark. 2003. Moore's law forever? *Science* **299**:210–211.

Lyman, Peter, and Hal R. Varian. 2003. *How Much Information?* Berkeley, CA: University of California. http://www.sims.berkeley.edu/how-much-info-2003

Maddison, Angus. 1995. *Monitoring the World Economy 1820–1992.* Paris: Organization for Economic Cooperation and Development.

Maddison, Angus. 2001. *The World Economy: Millennial Perspective.* Paris: Organization for Economic Cooperation and Development.

Maersk Sealand. 2004. *A New Dimension in Shipping.* Copenhagen, Denmark: Maersk Sealand. http://www.maersksealand.com/

Manhattan Project Heritage Preservation Association. 2004. *Manhattan Project History.* Mountour Fall, NY: MPHPA. http://www.childrenofthemanhattanproject.org

Marchelli, Renzo. 1996. *The Civilization of Plastics: Evolution of an Industry Which Has Changed the World.* Pont Canavese, Italy: Sandretto Museum.

Marland, G., et al. 2000. *Global, Regional, and National CO_2 Emission Estimates for Fossil Fuel Burning, Cement Production and Gas Flaring.* Oak Ridge, TN: Oak Ridge National Laboratory. http://cdiac.esd.ornl.gov

Martin, D.H. 1998. *Federal Nuclear Subsidies: Time to Call a Halt.* Ottawa, ON: Campaign for Nuclear Phaseout. http://www.cnp.ca/issues/nuclear-subsidies.html

Massey, David. 2004. *Bell System Memorial.* [No city]: David Massey. http://www.bellsystemmemorial.com/

Matos, Grecia. 2003. *Materials 2000.* Microsoft Excel File. Washington, DC: U.S. Geological Survey.

Matos, Grecia, and Lorie Wagner. 1998. Consumption of materials in the United States, 1900–1995. *Annual Review of Energy and the Environment* **23**:107–122.

Matson Lines. 2004. *History*. Oakland, CA: Matson Lines. http://www.matson.com/corporate/about_us/history.html

Maycock, P.D. 1999. *PV Technology, Performance, Cost: 1975–2010*. Warrenton, VA: Photovoltaic Energy Systems.

Maynard, Micheline. 2003. *The End of Detroit: How the Big Three Lost Their Grip on the American Car Market*. New York: Doubleday/Currency.

Mazor, Stanley. 1995. The history of microcomputer—invention and evolution. *Proceedings of the IEEE* **83**:1600–1608.

McGraw, Michael G. 1982. Plant-site coal handling. *Electrical World* **196**(7):63–93.

McKibben, Bill. 2003. *Enough: Staying Human in an Engineered Age*. New York: Times Books.

McKinzie, Matthew G., et al. 2001. *The U.S. Nuclear War Plan: A Time for Change*. Washington, DC: Natural Resources Defence Council.

McManus, George J. 1981. Inland's No. 7 start-up more than pushing the right buttons. *Iron Age* **224**(7):MP-7–MP-16.

McManus, George J. 1988. Blast furnaces: more heat from the hot end. *Iron Age* **4**(8):15–20.

McManus, George J. 1989. Coal gets a new shot. *Iron Age* **5**(1):31–34.

McManus, George J. 1993. The direct approach to making iron. *Iron Age* **9**(7):20–24.

McShane, Clay. 1997. *The Automobile: A Chronology*. New York: Greenwood Press.

Mead, Carver, and Lynn Conway. 1980. *Introduction to VLSI systems*. Reading, MA: Addison-Wesley.

Medvedev, Roy A. 1972. *Let History Judge: The Origins and Consequences of Stalinism*. London: Macmillan.

Meher-Homji, Cyrus B. 1997. Anselm Franz and the Jumo 004. *Mechanical Engineering* **119**(9):88–91.

Meier, A., and W. Huber. 1997. *Results from the Investigations of Leaking Electricity in the USA*. Berkeley, CA: Lawrence Berkeley Laboratory. http://EandE.lbl.gov/EAP/BEA/Projects/Leaking/Results

Meikle, Jeffrey L. 1995. *American Plastic: A Cultural History*. New Brunswick, NJ: Rutgers University Press.

Meitner, Lise, and Otto R. Frisch. 1939. Disintegration of uranium by neutrons: a new type of nuclear reaction. *Nature* **143**:239–240.

Mellanby, Kenneth. 1992. *The DDT Story*. Farnham, UK: British Crop Protection Council.

Mellberg, William F. 2003. Transportation revolution. *Mechanical Engineering*, Suppl., *100 Years of Flight*, **125**(12):22–25.

Mesquida, Christian G., and Neil I. Wiener. 1999. Male age composition and severity of conflicts. *Politics and the Life Sciences* **18**:181–189.

Messer, Robert L. 1985. New evidence on Truman's decision. *Bulletin of the Atomic Scientists* **41**(4):50–56.

Midgley, Thomas, and Albert L. Heene. 1930. Organic fluorides as refrigerants. *Industrial and Engineering Chemistry* **22**:542–545.

MIDREX. 2000. *2000 World Direct Reduction Statistics*. Charlotte, NC: Midrex Technologies.

Milanovic, Branko. 2002. *Worlds Apart: Inter-national and World Inequality, 1950–2000.* Washington, DC: World Bank.

Miller, J.R. 1976. The direct reduction of iron ore. *Scientific American* **235**(1):68–80.

Mitchell, Brian R., ed. 2003. *International Historical Statistics.* London: Palgrave.

Mitchell, Walter, and Stanley E. Turner. 1971. *Breeder Reactors.* Washington, DC: U.S. Atomic Energy Commission.

Miura, Shigeru, et al. 1998. The mechanism of railway tracks. *Japan Railway & Transport Review* **15**:38–45.

Mokdad, Ali H., et al. 2004. Actual causes of death in the United States, 2000 *Journal of American Medical Association* **291**:1238–1245.

Mokyr, Joel. 2002. *The Gifts of Athena: Historical Origins of the Knowledge Economy.* Princeton, NJ: Princeton University Press.

Molander, Roger C., and Robbie Nichols. 1985. *Who Will Stop the Bomb? A Primer on Nuclear Proliferation.* New York: Facts on File.

Molina, Mario J., and Rowland, F. Sherwood. 1974. Stratospheric sink for chlorofluoromethanes: chlorine atom catalyzed destruction of ozone. *Nature* **249**:810–812.

Moore, Gordon. 1965. Cramming more components onto integrated circuits. *Electronics* **38**(8):114–117.

Moore, Gordon. 1994. The accidental entrepreneur. *Engineering & Science* **57**(4). http://nobelprize.org/physics/articles/moore/

Moore, Gordon. 2003. *No Exponential Is Forever . . . But We Can Delay Forever.* Paper presented at International Solid State Circuits Conference, February 10, 2003. Santa Clara, CA: Intel. http://www.intel.com/research/silicon/mooreslaw.htm

Moore, Stephen, and Julian L. Simon. 1999. *The Greatest Century That Ever Was: 25 Miraculous Trends of the Past 100 Years.* Washington, DC: Cato Institute.

Moreau, R. 1984. *The Computer Comes of Age: The People, the Hardware, and the Software.* Cambridge, MA: MIT Press.

Morgan, N. 1995. 3D popularity leads to 4D vision. *Petroleum Economist* **62**(2):8–9.

Morita, Zen-ichiro, and Toshihiko Emi, eds. 2003. *An Introduction to Iron and Steel Processing.* Tokyo: Kawasaki Steel 21st Century Foundation. http://www.jfe-21st-cf.or.jp

Moritz, Michael. 1984. *The Little Kingdom: The Private Story of Apple Computer.* New York: W. Morrow.

Morrison, Philip. 1945. *Observations of the Trinity Shot, July 16, 1945.* Record Group 227, OSRD-S1 Committee, Box 82 folder 6, "Trinity." Washington, DC: National Archives. http://www.nuclearfiles.org/redocuments/1945/450716-morrison.html

Morrison, Philip. 1995. Recollections of a nuclear war. *Scientific American* **273**(2):42–46.

Morton, Oliver. 1994. *Between Two Worlds. The Economist*Survey, March 5, 1994.

Mossman, Susan, ed. 1997. *Early Plastics: Perspectives, 1850–1950.* London: Science Museum.

MSHA (Mining Safety and Health Administration). 2004. *Coal Fatalities by State.* Washington, DC: MSHA. http://www.msha.gov/stats/charts/coalbystate.asp

Mueller, John. 1989. *Retreat from Doomsday: The Obsolescence of Major War.* New York: Basic Books.

Mukherji, Chandra. 1983. *From Graven Images: Patterns of Modern Materialism.* New York: Columbia University Press.

Müller, Paul H. 1948. *Dichloro-diphenyl-trichloroethane and Newer Insecticides.* Nobel Lecture, December 11, 1948. Stockholm, Sweden: The Nobel Foundation. http://www.nobel.se/medicine/laureates/1948/muller-lecture.pdf

Murphy, P.M. 1974. *Incentives for the Development of the Fast Breeder Reactor.* Stamford, CT: General Electric.

Nader, Ralph. 1965. *Unsafe at Any Speed: The Designed-in Dangers of the American Automobile.* New York: Grossman.

NAE (National Academy of Engineering). 2000. *Greatest Engineering Achievements of the 20th Century.* Washington, DC: NAE. http://www.greatachievements.org/

Nagengast, Bernard. 2000. It's a cool story. *Mechanical Engineering* **122**(5):56–63.

NEA (Nuclear Energy Agency). 2002. *Chernobyl: Assessment of Radiological and Health Impacts.* Paris: NEA.

Neal, Valerie, Cathleen S. Lewis, and Frank H. Winter. 1995. *Spaceflight: A Smithsonian Guide.* New York: Macmillan USA.

Nehring, Richard. 1978. *Giant Oil Fields and World Oil Resources.* Santa Monica, CA: Rand Corporation.

Nelson, Walter H. 1998. *Small Wonder: The Amazing Story of the Volkswagen Beetle.* Cambridge, MA: Robert Bentley, Publishers.

New Steam Age. 1942. First practical gas turbines. *New Steam Age* **1**(1):9–10, 20.

NHTSA (National Highway Transportation Safety Administration). 2003. *Rollover.* Washington, DC: NHSTA. http://www.nhtsa.dot.gov/cars/problems/Rollover/index.htm

Nielsen, Stephanie. 2003. Boeing turns to Russian programming talent in massive database project. *Serverworld* **2003**(1):1–4.

Nieuwenhuis, Paul, and Peter Wells, eds. 1994. *Motor Vehicles in the Environment: Principles and Practice.* Chichester: John Wiley.

NIRS (Nuclear Information and Resource Service). 1999. *Background on Nuclear Power and Kyoto Protocol.* Washington, DC: NIRS. http://www.nirs.org/globalization/CDM-Nukesnirsbackground.htm

NKK (Nippon Kokan Kabushiki). 2001. *Development and Application of Technology to Utilize Used Plastics for Blast Furnace.* NKK: Tokyo. http://www.eccj.or.jp/succase/eng/00a/nkk.html

Noble, David F. 1984. *Forces of Production: A Social History of Industrial Automation.* New York: A.A. Knopf.

Noguchi, Tatsuo, and Toshishige Fujii. 2000. Minimizing the effect of natural disasters. *Japan Railway & Transport Review* **23**:52–59.

Norris, Robert S., and William M. Arkin. 1994. Estimated U.S., and Soviet/Russian nuclear stockpiles, 1945–94. *Bulletin of the Atomic Scientists* **50**(6):58–60.

Northeast-Midwest Institute. 2000. *Overcoming Barriers to the Deployment of Combined Heat and Power.* Washington, DC: Northeast-Midwest Institute. http://www.nemw.org/energy_linx.htm

Noyce, Robert N. 1961. *Semiconductor Device-and-Lead Structure.* U.S. Patent 2,981,877, April 25, 1961. Washington, DC: USPTO. http://www.uspto.gov

NRDC (Natural Resources Defence Council). 2002. *U.S., and Russian Strategic Nuclear Forces.* Washington, DC: NRDC. http://www.nrdc.org/nuclear/nudb/datainx.asp

NRDC. 2004. *Table of Known Nuclear Test Worldwide: 1945–1996.* Washington, DC: NRDC. http://www.nrdc.org/nuclear/nudb/datab15.asp

NWA (Nuclear Weapons Archive). 1999. *A Guide to Nuclear Weapons.* [No city]: NWA. http://nuclearweaponarchive.org/

O'Brien, P., ed. 1983. *Railways and the Economic Development of Western Europe, 1830–1914.* New York: St. Martin's Press.

O'Connell, Frobert L. 1989. *Of Arms and Men: A History of War, Weapons, and Aggression.* New York: Oxford University Press.

Odgers, George. 1957. *Air War Against Japan, 1943–1945.* Canberra: Australian War Memorial.

Odum, Howard T. 1971. *Environment and Power.* New York: Wiley-Interscience.

Ogura, Takekazu, ed. 1963. *Agricultural Development in Modern Japan.* Tokyo: Japan FAO Association.

Ohashi, Nobuo. 1992. Modern steelmaking. *American Scientists* **80**:540–555.

Okada, Hiroshi. 1994. Features and economic and social effects of the shinkansen. *Japan Railway & Transport Review* **3**:9–16.

Okumura, Hirohiko. 1994. Recent trends and future prospects of continuous casting technology. *Nippon Steel Technical Report* **61**:9–14.

Olmstead, Alan L., and Paul Rhode. 1988. An overview of California agricultural mechanization, 1870–1930. *Agricultural History* **62**:86–112.

OneSteel. 2005. *Interim Report.* Whyalla, South Australia, Australia: OneSteel. http://www.onesteel.com/images/db_images/presentations/2005%20hy%20results%20incl%20price%20increase%20update%20april%202005.pdf.

Ōno, Taiichi. 1988. *Toyota Production System: Beyond Large-scale Production.* Cambridge, MA: Productivity Press.

Oppenheimer, Todd. 1997. The computer delusion. *Atlantic Monthly* **280**(1):45–62.

Orwell, George. 2002. *Essays.* New York: A.A. Knopf.

Ouelette, Robert P., et al. 1983. *Automation Impacts on Industry.* Ann Arbor, MI: Ann Arbor Science.

Owens, Michael J. 1904. *Glass-Shaping Machine.* U.S. Patent 766,768, August 2, 1904. Washington, DC: USPTO. http://www.uspto.gov

PARC (Palo Alto Research Center). 2004. *PARC History.* Palo Alto, CA: PARC. http://www.parc.xerox.com/about/history/default.html

Parsons, John T., and Frank L. Stulen. 1958. *Motor Controlled Apparatus for Positioning Machine Tool.* U.S. Patent 2,820,187, January 14, 1958. Washington, DC: USPTO. http://www.uspto.gov

Paterson Technology. 2004. *DOS.* Issaquah, WA: Paterson Technology. http://www.patersontech.com/DOS/Encyclo.aspx

Patterson, Marvin L. 1993. *Accelerating Innovation: Improving the Process of Product Development.* New York: Van Nostrand Reinhold.

Pattillo, Donald M. 1998. *Pushing the Envelope: The American Aircraft Industry.* Ann Arbor, MI: University of Michigan Press.

Patton, Phil. 2003. *Bug: The Strange Mutations of the World's Most Famous Automobile.* New York: Simon & Schuster.

Peacey, J.G., and W.G. Davenport. 1979. *The Iron Blast Furnace.* Oxford: Pergamon Press.

Pearson, Roy, and John Fossey. 1983. *World Deep-Sea Container Shipping.* Aldershot, UK: Gower Publishing.

Person, H.S. 1930. Man and the machine: the engineer's point of view. *Annals of the American Academy of Political and Social Science* **149**:88–93.

Petit, J.R., et al. 1999. Climate and atmospheric history of the past 420,000 years from the Vostok ice core, Antarctica. *Nature* **399**:429–426.

PHS (Plastics Historical Society). 2003. *The Plastics Museum.* London: PHS. http://www.plastiquarian.com/museum/index.htm

Piszkiewicz, Dennis. 1995. *The Nazi Rocketeers: Dreams of Space and Crimes of War.* Westport, CT: Praeger.

Plank, Charles J., and Edward J. Rosinski. 1964. *Catalytic Cracking of Hydrocarbons with a Crystalline Zeolite Catalyst Composite.* U.S. Patent 3,140,249, July 7, 1964. Washington, DC: USPTO. http://www.uspto.gov

Ploeger, Jan. 1994. The bicycle as part of a green integrated traffic system. In: Paul Nieuwenhuis and Peter Wells, eds., *Motor Vehicles in the Environment: Principles and Practice,* Chichester: John Wiley, pp. 47–62.

Pomeranz, Kenneth. 2000. *The Great Divergence: China, Europe, and the Making of the Modern World.* Cambridge: Cambridge University Press.

Potts, R. 2001. *Complexity and Adaptability in Human Evolution.* Paper presented at Development of the Human Species and Its Adaptation to the Environment, a AAAS conference. Cambridge, Massachusetts, 7–8 July 2001. http://www.uchicago .edu/aff/mwc-amacad/biocomplexity/conference_papers/PottsComplexity.pdf

Prados de la Escosura, L. 2000. International comparisons of real product, 1820–1890: an alternative data set. *Explorations in Economic History* **37**:1–41.

Pratt & Whitney. 1999. *JT9D Engine.* East Hartford, CT: Pratt & Whitney. http://www.pratt-whitney.com/engines/gallery/bak/jt9d.html

Pratt & Whitney. 2004. *Pratt & Whitney Power Systems—Advanced Aeroderivative Gas Turbines.* East Hartford, CT: Pratt & Whitney. http://www.power-technology .com/contractors/powerplantequip/pratt/

Prost, Antoine. 1991. Public and private spheres in France. In: Antoine Prost and Gérard Vincent, eds., *A History of Private Life,* Vol. 5, Cambridge, MA: Belknap Press, pp. 1–103.

Pulleyblank, William R. 2003. *Application Driven Supercomputing: An IBM Perspective.* Yorktown Heights, NY: IBM. http://www.spscicomp.org/ScicomP9/Presentations/ Pulleyblank_CINECA.pdf

Pyxis. 2004. *Pyxis HelpMate®, the Trackless Robotic Courier.* San Diego, CA: Cardinal Health.

Rampino, M.R., and S. Self. 1992. Volcanic winter and accelerated glaciation following the Toba super-eruption. *Nature* **359**:50–52.

Ratcliffe, K. 1985, August. *Liquid Gold Ships: History of the Tanker (1859–1984).* London: Lloyds.

Reich, Robert. 2003. The future of ETOPS. *Air Line Pilot*:22. http://www.alpa.org/ alpa/DesktopModules/ViewDocument.aspx?DocumentID=4431

Reid, T.R. 2001. *The Chip: How Two Americans Invented the Microchip and Launched a Revolution.* New York: Simon & Schuster.

Reintjes, J. Francis. 1991. *Numerical Control: Making a New Technology.* New York: Oxford University Press.

Repetto, Richard, et al. 1991. *Accounts Overdue: Natural Resource Depletion in Costa Rica.* Washington, DC: World Resources Institute.

Rhodes, Richard. 1986. *The Making of the Atomic Bomb.* New York: Simon & Schuster.

Rhodes, Richard. 1988. Man-made death: a neglected mortality. *JAMA* **260**:686–687.

Richardson, Lewis F. 1960. *Statistics of Deadly Quarrels*. Pacific Grove, CA: Boxwood Press.

Ries, L.A.G., et al., eds. 2003. *SEER Cancer Statistics Review, 1975–2000*. Bethesda, MD: National Cancer Institute. http://seer.cancer.gov/csr/1975_2000/

Rife, Patricia. 1999. *Lise Meitner and Dawn of the Nuclear Age*. Boston: Birkhäuser.

Riordan, Michael, and Lillian Hoddeson. 1997. *Crystal Fire: The Birth of the Information Age*. New York: Norton.

Ritt, Adam. 2000, November. Endless casting and rolling of bar. *Iron Age New Steel*: (n.p.). http://www.newsteel.com/2000/NS0011f4.htm

Roberts, John. 1981. *The Circulation of D.D.T. Throughout the World Biosphere*. Newcastle, NSW: University of Newcastle.

Rockwell, Theodore. 1992. *The Rickover Effect: How One Man Made a Difference*. Annapolis, MD: Naval Institute Press.

Rockwell Automation. 2004. *Product Directory*. Milwaukee: Rockwell Automation. http://www.rockwell.com

Rojas, Raúl, and Ulf Hashagen, eds. 2000. *The First Computers—History and Architectures*. Cambridge, MA: MIT Press.

Rolls-Royce. 2004. *History*. London: Rolls-Royce. http://www.rolls-royce.com/history/default.jsp

Rolt, L.T.C. 1965. *Tools for the Job: Short History of Machine Tools*. London: B.T. Batsford.

Romer, Paul. 1990. Endogenous technological change. *Journal of Political Economy* **98**: 71–102.

Ross, Douglas T. 1982. *Origins of the APT Language for Automatically Programmed Tools*. New York: ACM Press.

Ross, Kristin. 1996. *Fast Cars, Clean Bodies: Decolonization and the Reordering of French Culture*. Cambridge, MA: MIT Press.

Rostow, W.W. 1990. *Theories of Economic Growth from David Hume to the Present*. New York: Oxford University Press.

Rowe, Albert P. 1948. *One Story of Radar*. Cambridge: Cambridge University Press.

Ruse, Michael, and David Castle, eds. 2002. *Genetically Modified Foods: Debating Biotechnology*. Amherst, NY: Prometheus Books.

Rutherford, Ernest. 1911. The scattering of α and β particles by matter and the structure of the atom. *Philosophical Magazine*, Series 6, **21**:669–688.

Ruthven, Douglas M., S. Farooq, and K.S. Knaebel. 1993. *Pressure Swing Adsorption*. New York: John Wiley.

Sachs, Aaron. 1999. Virtual ecology: a brief environmental history of Silicon Valley. *WorldWatch*, January/February, 12–21.

Sakiya, Tetsuo. 1982. *Honda Motor: The Men, the Management, the Machines*. New York: Kodansha International.

Sala-i-Martin, Xavier. 2002. *The Disturbing "Rise" of Global Income Inequality*. Cambridge, MA: National Bureau of Economic Research.

Sale, Anthony E. 2000. The colossus of Bletchley Park—the German cipher system. In: Raúl Rojas and Ulf Hashagen, eds., *The First Computers—History and Architectures*, Cambridge, MA: MIT Press, pp. 351–364.

Sample, Frank R., and Maurice E. Shank. 1985. Aircraft turbofans: new economic and environmental benefits. *Mechanical Engineering* **107**(9):47–53.

Saravanamuttoo, H.I.H., G.F.C. Rogers, and H. Cohen. 2001. *Gas Turbine Theory.* New York: Prentice Hall.

Schneider, Friedrich, and Domink H. Ente. 2003. *The Shadow Economy: An International Survey.* Cambridge: Cambridge University Press.

Schrewe, H.F. 1991. *Continuous Casting of Steel: Fundamental Principles and Practice.* Düsseldorf: Stahl und Eisen.

Schumacher, M.M., ed. 1978. *Enhanced Oil Recovery: Secondary and Tertiary Methods.* Park Ridge, NJ: Noyes Data.

Schurr, Sam H., and Bruce C. Netschert. 1960. *Energy in the American Economy 1850–1975.* Baltimore, MD: Johns Hopkins University Press.

Scott, Peter B. 1984. *The Robotics Revolution.* Oxford: Basil Blackwell.

Scott, Walter G. 1997. Micro-size gas turbines create market opportunities. *Power Engineering* **101**(9):46–50.

Segal, Howard P. 1985. *Technological Utopianism in American Culture.* Chicago: University of Chicago Press.

Seitz, Frederick, and Norman G. Einspruch. 1998. *Electronic Genie: The Tangled History of Silicon.* Urbana, IL: University of Illinois Press.

Semon, Waldo L. 1933. *Synthetic Rubber-like Composition and Method of Making Same.* US. Patent 1,929,453, October 10, 1933. Washington, DC: USPTO. http://www.uspto.gov

SEPCo (Shell Exploration and Production Company). 2004. *Shell in the Gulf of Mexico.* Robert, LA: SEPCo. http://www.shellus.com/sepco/where/offshore_shell/deepwater_general.htm

Seymour, Raymond B., ed. 1989. *Pioneers in Polymer Science.* Boston: Kluwer Academic Publishers.

Shah, A., et al. 1999. Photovoltaic technology: the case for thin-film solar cells. *Science* **285**:692–698.

Shannon, C.E. 1948. A mathematical theory of communication. *Bell System Technical Journal* **27**:379–423, 623–656. http://cm.bell-labs.com/cm/ms/what/shannonday/paper.html.

Shell Poll. 1998. The millennium. *Shell Poll* **1**(2). http://www.shellus.com/products/poll/poll_millen_fs.html b

Sherwin, Martin. 1985. How well they meant. *Bulletin of the Atomic Scientists* **41**(7): 9–15.

Shevell, R.S. 1980. Technological development of transport aircraft—past and future. *Journal of Aircraft* **17**:67–80.

Shima, Hideo. 1994. Birth of the Shinkansen—a memoir. *Japan Railway & Transport Review* **3**:45–48.

Shockley, William. 1964. Transistor technology evokes new physics. In: *Nobel Lectures: Physics 1942–1962,* Amsterdam: Elsevier, pp. 344–374.

Sime, Ruth Lewin. 1996. *Lise Meitner: A Life in Physics.* Berkeley, CA: University of California Press.

Simon, Julian L. amd Herman Kahn. 1984. *The Resourceful Earth.* Oxford: Basil Blackwell.

Simpson, James R., et al. 1999. *Pig, Broiler and Laying Hen Structure in China, 1996.* Davis, CA: International Agricultural Trade Research Consortium.

Singerman, Philip. 1991. *An American Hero: the Red Adair Story.* Thorndike, ME: Thorndike Press.

Siuru, B. 1989. Horsepower to the people. *Mechanical Engineering* 111(2):42–46.

Sivak, Michael, and Michael J. Flannagan. 2003. Flying and driving after the September 11 attacks. *American Scientist* 91:6–8.

Slater, Rodney E. 1996. The National Highway System: a commitment to America's future. *Public Roads* 59(4):1–3.

Smil, Vaclav. 1976. *China's Energy.* New York: Praeger.

Smil, Vaclav. 1983. *Biomass Energies.* New York: Plenum.

Smil, Vaclav. 1987. *Energy Food Environment: Realities, Myths, Options.* Oxford: Oxford University Press.

Smil, Vaclav. 1988. *Energy in China's Modernization.* Armonk, NY: M.E. Sharpe.

Smil, Vaclav. 1991. *General Energetics.* New York: John Wiley.

Smil, Vaclav. 1992. Agricultural energy cost: national analysis. In: Richard C. Fluck, ed., *Energy in Farm Production,* Amsterdam: Elsevier, pp. 85–100.

Smil, Vaclav. 1993. *Global Ecology.* London: Routledge.

Smil, Vaclav. 1994. *Energy in World History.* Boulder, CO: Westview.

Smil, Vaclav. 1996. *Environmental Problems in China: Estimates of Economic Costs.* Honolulu, HI: East-West Center.

Smil, Vaclav. 1999. China's great famine: 40 years later. *British Medical Journal* 7225: 1619–1621.

Smil, Vaclav. 2000a. *Feeding the World.* Cambridge, MA: MIT Press.

Smil, Vaclav. 2000b. Jumbo. *Nature* 406:239.

Smil, Vaclav. 2001. *Enriching the Earth: Fritz Haber, Carl Bosch, and the Transformation of World Food Production.* Cambridge, MA: MIT Press.

Smil, Vaclav. 2002a. *The Earth's Biosphere: Evolution, Dynamics, and Change.* Cambridge, MA: MIT Press.

Smil, Vaclav. 2002b. Eating meat: evolution, patterns, and consequences. *Population and Development Review* 28:599–639.

Smil, Vaclav. 2003. *Energy at the Crossroads: Global Perspectives and Uncertainties.* Cambridge, MA: MIT Press.

Smil, Vaclav. 2004a. *China's Past, China's Future.* London: Routledge.

Smil, Vaclav. 2004b. War and energy. In: Cutler J. Cleveland, ed., *Encyclopedia of Energy,* Vol. 6, Amsterdam: Elsevier, pp. 363–371.

Smil, Vaclav, Paul Nachman, and Thomas V. Long, II. 1983. *Energy Analysis in Agriculture: An Application to U.S. Corn Production.* Boulder, CO: Westview.

Smith, Anthony, and Richard Paterson. 1998. *Television: An International History.* Oxford: Oxford University Press.

Smith, Douglas K., and Robert C. Alexander. 1988. *Fumbling the Future: How Xerox Invented, Then Ignored, the First Personal Computer.* New York: W. Morrow.

Smith, Roderick A. 2001. Railway technology—the last 50 years and future prospects. *Japan Railway & Transport Review* 27:16–24.

Smock, Robert. 1991. Gas turbine, combined cycle orders continue. *Power Engineering* 95(5):17–22.

Society of Petroleum Engineers. 1991. *Horizontal Drilling.* Richardson, TX: Society of Petroleum Engineers.

Solberg, Carl. 1979. *Conquest of the Skies: A History of Commercial Aviation in America.* Boston: Little, Brown.

Solow, Robert M. 1957. Technical change and the aggregate production function. *Review of Economics and Statistics* 39:312–320.

Solow, Robert M. 1987. Nobel Prize Lecture. In: Robert M. Solow, *Growth Theory: An Exposition*, New York: Oxford University Press, pp. ix–xxvi.

Solow, Robert M. 2001. *Addendum, August 2001*. Stockholm: Nobel e-museum. http://www.nobel.se/economics/laureates/1987/solow-lecture.html

Solzhenitsyn, Aleksandr. 1973–1975. *Arkhipelag Gulag, 1918–1956*. Paris: YMCA Press.

Sone, Satoru. 2001. Japan's rail technology development from 1945 to the future. *Japan Railway & Transport Review* **27**:4–15.

Sony. 2004. *History: Products and Technology Milestones*. Tokyo: Sony. http://www.sony.net

Soulié, Claude, and Jean Tricoire 2002. *Le grand livre du TGV*. Paris: Vie du rail.

Spada, Alfred T. 2003. *In Search of Light-Weight Components: Automotive's Cast Aluminum Conversion*. Schaumburg, IL: American Foundry Society. http://www.moderncasting.com

Spillman, William J. 1903. Systems of farm management in the United States. In: *Yearbook of the United States Department of Agriculture*, Washington, DC: U.S. Government Printing Office, pp. 343–364.

Splinter, W.E. 1976. Centre-pivot irrigation. *Scientific American* **234**(6):90–99.

Stalk, George, and Thomas M. Hout. 1990. *Competing against Time: How Time-based Competition Is Reshaping Global Markets*. New York: Free Press.

Starratt, F. Weston. 1960. LD . . . in the beginning. *Journal of Metals* **12**(7):528–529.

Steinhart, John S., and Carol E. Steinhart. 1974. Energy use in the U.S. food system. *Science* **184**:307–316.

Stellman, Jeanne M., et al. 2003. The extent and patterns of usage of Agent Orange and other herbicides in Vietnam. *Nature* **422**:681–687.

Stix, Gary.. 1994. Aging airways. *Scientific American* **270**(5):96–104.

Stoltzenberg, Dietrich. 2004. *Fritz Haber: Chemist, Nobel Laureate, German, Jew*. Philadelphia: Chemical Heritage Press.

Stone, Richard. 1999. Nuclear strongholds in peril. *Science* **283**:158–164.

Stout, B.A., J.L. Butler, and E.E. Garett. 1984. Energy use and management in U.S. agriculture. In: George Stanhill, ed., *Energy Use and Agriculture*, New York: Springer-Verlag, pp. 175–176.

Strada, Gino. 1996. The horror of land mines. *Scientific American* **274**(5):40–45.

Stross, Randall E. 1996. *The Microsoft Way: The Real Story of How the Company Outsmarts Its Competition*. Reading, MA: Addison-Wesley.

Suga, T. 1998. Mr. Hideo Shima (1901–1998). *Japan Railway & Transport Review* **16**:59.

Sugawara, T., et al. 1986. Construction and operation of no. 5 blast furnace, Fukuyama Works, Nippon Kokan KK. *Ironmaking and Steelmaking* **3**(5):241–251.

Summers, Lawrence, and Alan Heston. 1991. The Penn World Table (Mark 5): an expanded set of international comparisons, 1950–1988. *Quarterly Journal of Economics* **106**:327–368.

Sutton, Ernest P. 1999. *From Polymers to Propellants to Rockets: A History of Thiokol*. Paper presented at 35th Joint Propulsion Conference, Los Angeles, 20–24 June, 1999. Edina, MN: ATK. http://www.thiokol.com/assets/history/aiaa_sutton/aiaa_index.htm

Sutton, George P. 1992. *Rocket Propulsion Elements: An Introduction to the Engineering of Rockets*. New York: John Wiley & Sons.

Sutton, George P., and Oscar Biblarz. 2001. *Rocket Propulsion Elements*. New York: John Wiley & Sons.

Szekely, Julian. 1987. Can advanced technology save the U.S. steel industry? *Scientific American* **257**(1):34–41.

Takahashi, Makoto, Akira Hongu, and Michiyasu Honda. 1994. Recent advances in electric arc furnaces for steelmaking. *Nippon Steel Technical Report* **61**:58–64.

Takeuchi, Hidemaro, et al. 1994. Production of stainless steel strip by twin-drum strip casting process. *Nippon Steel Technical Report* **61**:46–51.

Tanner, A. Heinrich. 1998. *Continuous Casting: A Revolution in Steel.* Fort Lauderdale, FL: Write Stuff Enterprises.

Taylor, Colin. 2001. World rail speed survey 2001. *Railway Gazette International.* Surrey, UK: Railway Gazette. http://www.railwaygazette.com/1999/1999speedsurvey.asp

Taylor, Frederick W. 1907. On the art of cutting metals. *Transactions of ASME* **28**:31–350.

Taylor, Frederick W. 1911. *Principles of Scientific Management.* New York: Harper & Brothers.

Tegler, Jan. 2000. *B-47 Stratojet: Boeing's Brilliant Bomber.* New York: McGraw Hill.

Tennekes, Henk. 1997. *The Simple Science of Flight.* Cambridge, MA: MIT Press.

Tenner, Edward. 1996. *Why Things Bite Back: Technology and the Revenge of Unintended Consequences.* New York: A.A. Knopf.

Tennies, W.L., et al. 1991. MIDREX ironmaking technology. *Direct from MIDREX* **16**(3):4–7.

Tevini M, ed. 1993. *UV-B Radiation and Ozone Depletion: Effects on Humans, Animals, Plants, Microorganisms, and Materials.* Boca Raton, FL: Lewis Publishers.

TGVweb. 2000. *Under the Hood of a TGV.* Pisa, Italy: Railfan Europe. http://mercurio.iet.unipi.it/tgv/motrice.html

Thompson, Louis S. 1986. High-speed rail. *Technology Review* **89**(3):33–41, 70.

Thompson, Louis S. 1994. High-speed rail (HSR) in the United States—why isn't there more? *Japan Railway & Transport Review* **3**:32–39.

Thompson, Richard C., et al. 2004. Lost at sea: where is all the plastic? *Science* **304**: 838.

Thyssen Krupp Stahl. 2003. *Western World's Largest BF Celebrates 30 Years.* Duisburg, Germany: Thyssen Krupp Stahl. http://www.manufacturingtalk.com/news/thy/thy112.html

The Times. 1915. *History of the War,* Vol. 5. London: *The Times.*

Tomlinson, Ray. 2002. The invention of e-mail just seemed like a neat idea. *SAP INFO.* Mannheim, Germany: SAP AG. http://www.sap.info

Top500. 2004. *Top 500 Supercomputer Sites.* Mannheim: University of Mannheim. http://www.top500.org

Toyota Motor Company. 2004. *Smoothing the Flow.* Toyota City, Japan: Toyota Motor Company. http://www.toyota.co.jp/Irweb/corp_info/Virtual_Factory/sf/sf.html

Transocean. 2003. *Facts and Firsts.* Houston, TX: Transocean. http://www.deepwater.com/FactsandFirsts.cfm

Troyer, James R. 2001. In the beginning: the multiple discovery of the first hormone herbicides. *Weed Science* **49**:290–297.

Turing, Alan. 1936. On computable numbers, with an application to the Entscheidungsproblem. *Proceedings of the London Mathematical Society,* Ser. 2, **42**:230–265.

UIG (Universal Industrial Gases). 2003. *Overview of Cryogenic Air Separation.* Easton, PA: UIG. http://www.uigi.com/cryodist.html

UNECE (United Nations Economic Commission for Europe). 2001. *World Robotics 2001: Statistics, Market Analysis, Forecasts, Case Studies and Profitability of Robot Investment.* Geneva: UNECE.

UNEP (United Nations Environmental Programme). 1995. *Montreal Protocol on Substances That Deplete the Ozone Layer.* Nairobi: UNEP.

UNESCO (United Nations Educational and Scientific Organization). 1999. *World Communication and Information Report.* Paris: UNESCO.

UNO (United Nations Organization). 1956. World energy requirements in 1975 and 2000. In: *Proceedings of the International Conference on the Peaceful Uses of Atomic Energy,* Vol. 1., New York: UNO, pp. 3–33.

UNO. 2002. *Energy Statistics Yearbook.* New York: UNO.

Updike, John. 1971. *Rabbit Redux.* New York: Knopf.

Updike, John. 2003. TV. *Atlantic Monthly* **292**(2):104.

USBC (U.S. Bureau of Census). 1975. *Historical Statistics of the United States.* Washington, DC: U.S. Department of Commerce.

USCB (U.S. Census Bureau). 2004. *Mini Historical Statistics.* Washington, DC: USCB. http://www.census.gov/statab/www/minihs.html

USDA (U.S. Department of Agriculture). 1980. *Energy and U.S. Agriculture: 1974 and 1978.* Washington, DC: USDA.

USDA. 2003. *Agricultural Statistics 2003.* Washington, DC: USDA. http://www.usda.gov/nass/pubs/agr03/acro03.htm

USDL (U.S. Department of Labor). 2002. *Trends in Labor Productivity.* Washington, DC: USDL. http://www.dol.gov/21cw/aei-conference.htm

USDOE. 2000. *Energy Use: Steel Industry Analysis Brief.* Washington, DC: USDOE. http://www.eia.doe.gov/emeu/mecs/iab/steel/

USDOE. 2001. *Price-Anderson Act.* Washington, DC: USDOE. http://www.gc.doe.gov/Price-Anderson/default.html

USEPA (Environmental Protection Agency). 1972. *DDT Ban Takes Effect.* Washington, DC: USEPA. http://www.epa.gov/history/topics/ddt/01.htm

USFPC (Federal Power Commission). 1965. *Northeast Power Failure: November 9 and 10, 1965.* Washington, DC: USFPC.

USGS (U.S. Geological Survey). 1999. *Natural Aggregates—Foundation of America's Future.* Washington, DC: USGS.

Valenti, Michael. 1991. Combined-cycle plants: burning cleaner and saving fuel. *Mechanical Engineering* **113**(9):46–50.

Valenti, Michael. 1993. Propelling jet turbines to new uses. *Mechanical Engineering* **115**(3):68–72.

Van der Spiegel, Jan, et al. 2000. The ENIAC: history, operation and reconstruction in VLSI. In: Raúl Rojas and Ulf Hashagen, eds., *The First Computers—History and Architectures,* Cambridge, MA: MIT Press, pp. 121–178.

Van Dyke, Kate. 2000. *Drilling Fluids.* Austin, TX: Petroleum Extension Service.

Van Middelkoop, J.H. 1996. *High-Density Broiler Production—the European Way.* Edmonton, AB: Agricultural Food and Rural Development.

Van Zant, Peter. 2004. *Microchip Fabrication.* New York: McGraw-Hill.

Vendryes, Georges A. 1977. Superphénix: a full-scale breeder reactor. *Scientific American* **236**(3):26–35.

Vinylfacts. 2003. *Vinyl.* Arlington, VA: The Vinyl Institute. http://www.vinylfacts.com

Vlasic, Bill, and Bradley A. Stertz. 2000. *Taken for a Ride: How Daimler-Benz Drove Off with Chrysler.* New York: W. Morrow.

VÖEST (Vereinigte Österreichische Eisen- und Stahlwerke). 2003. *Das LD-Verfahren.* Linz, Austria: VÖEST. http://www.ooezeitgeschichte.at/Ld.htm

Vogel, H.U. 1993. The great well of China. *Scientific American* **268**(6):116–121.

von Braun, Wernher, and F.I. Ordway. 1975. *History of Rocketry and Space Travel.* New York: Thomas Y. Crowell.

von Hippel, Frank, and Suzanne Jones. 1997. The slow death of the fast breeder. *Bulletin of the Atomic Scientists* **53**(5):46–51.

von Hippel, Frank, et al. 1988. Civilian casualties from counterforce attacks. *Scientific American* **259**(3):36–42.

Voss, C.A., ed. 1987. *Just-in-Time Manufacture.* Berlin: Springer-Verlag.

Wade, Louise Carroll. 1987. *Chicago's Pride: The Stockyards, Packingtown, and Environs in the Nineteenth Century.* Urbana, IL: University of Illinois Press.

Wagner, Wolfgang. 1998. *The History of German Aviation: The First Jet Aircraft.* Atglen, PA: Schiffer Publishing.

Waitt, Alden H. 1942. *Gas Warfare: The Chemical Weapon, Its Use, and Protection against It.* New York: Duell, Sloan and Pearce.

Wakelin, David H., ed. 1999. *The Making, Shaping and Treating of Steel, Ironmaking Volume.* Pittsburgh, PA: AISE Steel Foundation.

Waldrop, M. Mitchell. 2001. *The Dream Machine: J.C.R. Licklider and the Revolution That Made Computing Personal.* New York: Viking.

Walker, Bryce. 1983. *Fighting Jets.* New York: Time-Life Books.

Walker, R.D. 1985. *Modern Ironmaking Methods.* Brookfield, VT: Gower Publishing.

Walker, Robert, and F. Whitten Peters. 2002. *The Commission on the Future of the U.S. Aerospace Industry.* Washington, DC: U.S. Federal Government. http://www.aerospacecommission.gov

Ward, Colin. 1984. *Coal Geology and Coal Technology.* Oxford: Blackwell Scientific.

Ward, Steven, and Simon Day. 2001. Cumbre Vieja volcano—potential collapse and tsunami at La Palma, Canary Islands. *Geophysical Research Letters* **28**:3397–3400.

Ward's Communications. 2000. *Ward's Motor Vehicle Facts & Figures 2000.* Southfield, MI: Ward's Communications.

Warneck, Peter. 2000. *Chemistry of the Natural Atmosphere.* San Diego: Academic Press.

Watson-Watt, R.A. 1957. *Three Steps to Victory: A Personal Account by Radar's Greatest Pioneer.* London: Odhams Press.

Wattenberg, Albert. 1992. A lovely experiment. *Bulletin of the Atomic Scientists* **48**(10): 41–43.

WCI (World Coal Institute). 2001. *Coal Facts.* London: WCI. http://www.wci-coal.com/facts.coal99.htm

Weinberg, Alvin M. 1972. Social institutions and nuclear energy. *Science* **177**:27–34.

Weinberg, Alvin M. 1973. Long-range approaches for resolving the energy crisis. *Mechanical Engineering* **95**(6):14–18.

Weinberg, Alvin. 1994. *The First Nuclear Era.* Washington, DC: American Institute of Physics.

Wescott, N.P. 1936. *Origins and Early History of the Tetraethyl Lead Business.* Wilmington, DE: Du Pont Corporation.

White, Matthew. 2003. *Historical Atlas of the Twentieth Century.* [No city]: Matthew White. http://users.erols.com/mwhite28/20centry.htm

White House Millennium Council. 2000. National Medal Winner. Washington, DC: The White House. http://clinton4.nara.gov/Initiatives/Millennium/capsule/parsons .html

WHO (World Health organization). 2002. *The Injury Chart Book.* Geneva: WHO.

Wiener, Norbert. 1948. *Cybernetics.* New York: John Wiley.

Wilesmith, John W. 1998. *Manual on Bovine Spongiform Encephalopathy.* Rome: FAO.

Williams, Eric. 2003. Forecasting material and economic flows in the global production chain for silicon. *Technological Forecasting & Social Change* **70**:341–357.

Williams, Robert H., and Eric D. Larson. 1988. Aeroderivative turbines for stationary power. *Annual Review of Energy* **13**:429–489.

Williams, Thomas, et al. 2001. *Sound Coil-Tubing Drilling Practices.* Washington, DC: USDOE.

Williams, Trevor I. 1987. *The History of Invention.* New York: Facts on File.

WNA (World Nuclear Association). 2001. *Chernobyl.* London: WNA. http://www .world-nuclear.org/

Womack, James P., Daniel T. Jones, and Daniel Roos. 1991. *The Machine That Changed the World: The Story of Lean Production.* New York: Harper Perennial.

Wood, Gaby. 2002. *Edison's Eve: A Magical History of the Quest for Mechanical Life.* New York: Knopf.

World Oil. 2000. Marine drilling rigs 2000/2001. Houston, TX: Gulf Publishing.

Younossi, Obaid, et al. 2002. *Military Jet Engine Acquisition: Technology Basics and Cost-Estimating Methodology.* Santa Monica, CA: Rand Corporation.

Ziegler, Karl. 1963. Consequences and development of an invention. Nobel Lecture, December 12, 1963. In: *The Nobel Prize in Chemistry 1963,* Stockholm: Nobel e-Museum. http://www.nobel.se/chemistry/laureates/1963/press.html

Zulehner, Werner. 2003. Historical overview of silicon crystal pulling development. *Materials Science and Engineering B* **73**:7–15.

Name Index

Corporate Index

Air
  Liquide, 119
  Products, 119
Airbus, 73–74, 77, 191, 215, 220, 276, 280
Alleghany Ludlum Steel, 102
Advanced Micro Devices, 276, 289
Alpine Montan, 98
ALSTOM, 213
American
  Airlines, 215
  Bell Telephone, 280
  Machine and Foundry, 187
  Telephone & Telegraph (AT&T), 11, 280,
    271
Apple, 231, 239, 245, 277
Armco, 95
Atlantic Research Corporation, 84

Badische
  Anilin- & Soda-Fabrik (BASF), 9, 119–
    120
  Stahlwerke, 101
Batelle Memorial Institute, 281
BBN Technologies, 245
Bell
  Laboratories, 133, 135, 229, 231, 233, 235,
    238, 248, 280
  System, 11
Bethlehem Steel, 99, 112–113, 173, 176
B.F. Goodrich, 131
Boeing, 69, 70–75, 77, 83, 191, 215, 218, 220,
  276
Bombardier, 213, 276
Bridgestone, 276
British
  Broadcasting Corporation (BBC), 250
  Motor Company, 203
  Oxygen Company (BOC), 119
  Petroleum Solarex, 136
  Thomson-Houston, 67

Broken Hill Proprietary (BHP), 105
Brown Boveri, 75
Bucyrus-Erie, 160–161
Bühler Versatile, 145
Burroughs, 238
Busicom, 238–239

Canadian Pacific Railway, 223
Capehart-Farnsworth, 252–253
Caterpillar, 276
Chrysler, 279
Cincinnati Milling Machine Company, 174
Citroen, 203
Commodore, 277
Concast AG, 87, 103
Continuous Metalcast Corporation, 103

Daimler
  Benz, 279
  Chrysler, 3, 276, 279
Digital Research Inc. (DRI), 277–278
Disney, 112
Dow Chemical, 126
DuPont, 125–128

Electric Vehicle Company (EVC), 201
Electricité de France (EdF), 6
Embraer, 276
Energomash, 82
English Electric, 230

Fairchild Semiconductors (FS), 236, 238, 289
FANUC, 138–139, 188
FedEx, 226
FIAT, 177, 203
Finn-Power, 194
Ford Motor Company, 175–178, 183, 276
Fuji, 210
Fujica, 247
Fujitsu, 188

Subject Index